The Montessori Way

The Montessori Foundation Press

Tim Seldin
Paul Epstein, Ph.D.

Acknowledgments

October, 2003

Ever since we first established The Montessori Foundation, we have said to one another that one day we would write a book that introduced Montessori as clearly as the articles in our magazine, *Tomorrow's Child*.

Thanks to an extraordinarily generous contribution by **Tony Low-Beer**, a wonderful man who has become very supportive of our work at the Foundation, this book has been made possible. The authors wish to express their deepest appreciation to Mr. Low-Beer and his family. We also wish to extend our commitment to the role that The Montessori Foundation continues to play around the world in helping to spread the insights and approach to educating the world's children that was developed by Dr. Maria Montessori.

The authors have contributed all rights to this book to The Montessori Foundation. We hope that, in addition to helping to spread the word of the Montessori approach to parents and educators around the world, the proceeds from the sales of *The Montessori Way* will help to ensure the Foundation's future.

In addition, we would like to express our deep appreciation to everyone who helped to bring this book to life. This loyal band of colleagues and friends includes: **Dr. Ann Epstein** for her excellent chapter on *Children with Exceptionalities*; **David Kahn** of the North American Montessori Teachers Association (NAMTA) for his description of the Hershey Montessori Farm School and his essay on the role of imagination in Montessori Elementary education; **Marta Donahoe** of the Clark Montessori High School for contributing descriptions of their Secondary Programs; **Susan Tracy** for her assistance in preparing the chapter on Infants and Toddlers; **Melody Mosby** of the Athens Montessori School for her description of their Montessori Middle School; and **Eileen Roper Ast** of the American Montessori Society for her help proofreading this publication.

We also want to thank the teachers and children of **A Love of Learning Montessori School** (Columbia, MD); **Athens Montessori School** (Athens, GA); **Montessori School of Anderson** (Anderson, SC); **Lake Norman Country Day School** (Huntersville, NC); **Oneness Family School** (Chevy Chase, MD); **Chiaravalle Montessori School** (Evanston, IL); **Henson Valley Montessori School** (Camp Springs, MD); **Montessori School of Raleigh** (Raleigh, NC); **New Gate School** (Sarasota, FL); **Montessori Children's Center at Burke** (White Plains, NY); **Mater Amoris School** (Ashton, MD); **Montessori Educational Center** (Alexandria, LA); **Raritan Valley Montessori School** (Bridgewater, NJ); **Montessori Children's House** (Dunedin, New Zealand); **Westwood Montessori Schools** (Dallas, TX); **Washington Montessori Charter Public Schools** (Washington, NC); **Century House Montessori School** (Tortola, BVI); and **Renaissance School** (Oakland, CA) for allowing us to capture the magic of their classrooms on film.

We owe special thanks to **Larry Canner** for his excellent photography and to **Margot Garfield-Anderson**, **Joanna Voultsides**, and **Chelsea Howe**, staff members of The Montessori Foundation, for their tireless work every step of the way. In addition, many thanks to **Rodney Lackey,** who gave us shelter from the storm when Hurricane Isabelle took down power lines at the worst possible moment! And finally, we want to thank Tim's lovely and multi-talented wife, **Joyce St. Giermaine**, Executive Director of The Montessori Foundation, who, as editor and designer, brought *The Montessori Way* to life.

Paul Epstein	**Tim Seldin**
Evanston, IL	Sarasota, FL

Dedication

My involvement with The Montessori Foundation and *The Montessori Way* project stems from two sources. Looking back, it is clear that my children, Susanna and Nick A., could have benefited greatly from a Montessori education; because of my ignorance and stubbornness when they were young, I regretfully did not provide them with the opportunity. It took my wonderful friend and business partner, Dominique Lahaussois, and her son, Pierre Alexander, as well as two other dear friends, Peter Cherneff and Rachel Lorentzen, to open my eyes. It is to these four people I love so dearly, that this book is dedicated.

— Tony Low-Beer

Foreword

What is education for? How we answer this question is critical for the future of our children, our nation, and our world. Yet all too often it gets lost in debates about standards, testing, and other procedural reforms that treat education as something to be *done* to children rather than *for* and *with* them.

The Montessori Way shows that we can, and must, go back to basics – to the real purpose of education as drawing forth from each one of us our full human potential. It is a highly practical book. But it is much more than that. It describes a way of life – a way of thinking about the nature of intelligence, talent, and the potential for goodness and greatness among all people, a way to nurture and inspire the creativity, curiosity, leadership, love, and imagination that lies within us all. It reminds us that the child is the mother/father of the woman/man she or he will one day become, and that the most important human task is to nurture and educate children.

Based on the pioneering work of Maria Montessori, as well as more recent knowledge about how children develop, learn, and access their full humanity, *The Montessori Way* embodies what I call partnership education. It is designed not only to help young people better navigate through our difficult times, but also to help them create a more peaceful, equitable, and sustainable future.

Rather than relying on a paradigm of domination and submission, of winning and losing, of external rewards and punishments, of top-down rankings, fear, manipulation, indoctrination, and pressure to conform, *The Montessori Way* presents an education that focuses on partnership, independence, mutual trust, and respect, on both individual achievement and collaboration, while developing our minds and hearts.

Explicitly or implicitly, education gives young people a mental map of what it means to be human. Much of what young people worldwide learn through both their formal and informal education holds up a distorted mirror of themselves. When their vision of the future comes out of this limited world view, they cannot develop their full humanity or meet the unprecedented challenges they face.

In *The Montessori Way*, Tim Seldin and Paul Epstein offer sound guidelines, practical tools, and inspiring real-life stories of how, working together teachers, children, parents, and others can create learning communities where everyone can feel safe and seen for who we truly are, where our essential humanity and that of others shines through, lifting our hearts and spirits, empowering us to realize our highest intellectual, emotional, and spiritual potentials.

In her unshakable faith in the human spirit and her fearless challenge to traditions of domination, Maria Montessori is one of my role models. Her legacy, as expanded and enriched by countless others, is the gift of this wonderful book.

— **Riane Eisler** is author of *Tomorrow's Children: A Blueprint for Partnership Education in the 21st Century, The Power of Partnership,* and *The Chalice and The Blade.*

CONTENTS

SECTION
1

THE MONTESSORI WAY

Introduction 8
A Typical Montessori Day   11
The Montessori Way   16

History of the Montessori Movement 18
The San Lorenzo Discoveries   21
Montessori's Legacy   25

Montessori's Philosophy 30
Core Values   30
Intrinsic Motivation   31
Independence and Movement:
Acquiring Self-Discipline   31
Respectful Communities of
Mixed-Age Groups   32
The Prepared Environment   33
The Control of Error   36
The Three-Period Lesson   36

Certified Montessori Teachers 38

SECTION 2

MONTESSORI PROGRAMS

The Planes of Development 42

Sensitive Periods 46

The Method of Observation 51

The Normalized Child 53

A Guided Tour of the
Montessori Classrooms 55

Montessori for the
Kindergarten Year 109

Elementary Programs 115

Secondary Programs 147

Infant-Toddler Programs 175

Montessori in the Home for
Young Children 191

Montessori for Learners with
Exceptionalities 199

SECTION 3

CLOSING THOUGHTS

Preparing Children for the
Real World: Reflections on a Montessori
Education 213

The *Montessori Way* 221

SECTION 4

APPENDIXES

Brief Answers to Questions
Parents Often Ask 228

Finding the Right School 237

Standards 243

Bibliography 260

Resources 266

Index 270

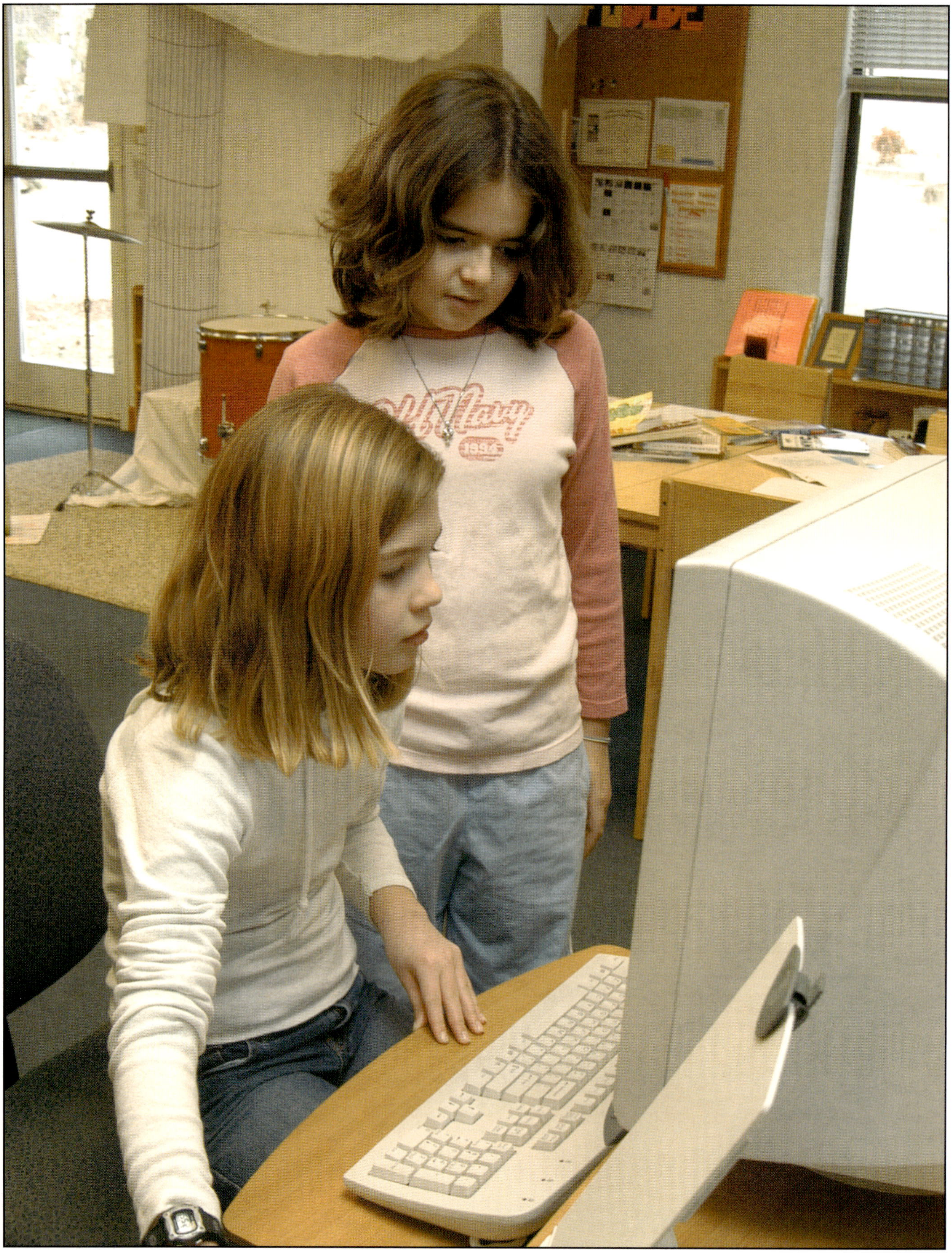

SECTION 1

THE MONTESSORI WAY

INTRODUCTION

HISTORY OF THE MONTESSORI MOVEMENT

MONTESSORI'S PHILOSOPHY

CERTIFIED MONTESSORI TEACHERS

Introduction

In 1907, an Italian physician was invited to open a child-care facility for fifty preschool-aged children in a section of Rome that was avoided and neglected because of its oppressive poverty and crime. The children's parents worked sixteen or more hours a day. In the absence of adult supervision, these children were vandalizing recently renovated housing. Years later, Dr. Maria Montessori recalled her experience of personal transformation in which she discovered something previously unknown about children:[*]

(Above) Dr. Maria Montessori, c. 1934.

"What happened will always remain a mystery to me. I have tried since then to understand what took place in those children. Certainly there was nothing of what is to be found now in any House of Children. There were only rough large tables.

I brought them some of the materials which had been used for our work in experimental psychology, the items which we use today as sensorial material and materials for the exercises of practical life. I merely wanted to study the children's reactions. I asked the woman in charge not to interfere with them in any way, as otherwise I would not be able to observe them. Someone brought them paper and colored pencils, but, in itself, this was not the explanation of the further events. There was no one who loved them. I myself only visited them once a week, and during the day, the children had no communication with their parents.

The children were quiet; they had no interference either from the teacher or from the parents, but their environment contrasted vividly from that which they had been used to; compared to that of their previous life, it seemed fantastically beautiful. The walls were white, there was a green plot of grass outside, though no one had yet thought to plant flowers in it, but most beautiful of all was the fact that they had interesting occupations in which no one, no one at all, interfered. They were left alone, and little by little, the children began to work with concentration, and the transformation they underwent was noticeable. From timid and wild as they were before, the children became sociable and communicative. They showed a different relationship with each other, of which I have written in my books. Their personalities grew and, strange though it may seem, they showed extraordinary understanding, activity, vivacity and confidence. They were happy and joyous.

This fact was noticed after a while by the mothers who came to tell us about it. As the children had had no one to teach them or interfere with their actions, they acted spontaneously; their manners were natural.

But the most outstanding thing about these strange children of the St. Lorenz Quarter was their obvious gratitude. I was as much surprised by this as everyone else. When I entered the room, all the children sprang to greet me and cried their welcome. Nobody had taught them any manner of good behavior. And the strangest thing of all was that although nobody had cared for them

---

[*] Maria Montessori (1942), *How It All Happened;* http://www.montessori-ami.org/ami.htm (January 4, 2003)

physically, they flourished in health, as if they had been secretly fed on some nourishing food. And so they had, but in their spirit. These children began to notice things in their homes: a spot of dirt on their mother's dress, untidiness in the room. They told their mothers not to hang the washing in the windows but to put flowers there instead. Their influence spread into the homes, so that after a while these also became transformed.

Six months after the inauguration of the House of Children, some of the mothers came to me and pleaded that as I had already done so much for their children and they themselves could do nothing about it because they were illiterate, would I not teach their children to read and write?

At first I did not want to, being as prejudiced as everyone else that the children were far too young for it. But I gave them the alphabet in the way I have told you. As then it was something new for me also. I analyzed the words for them and showed that each sound of the words had a symbol by which it could be materialized. It was then that the explosion into writing occurred.

The news spread, and the whole world became interested in this phenomenal activity of the writing of these children who were so young and whom nobody had taught. The people realized that they were confronted by a phenomenon that could not be explained. For besides writing, these children worked all the time without being forced by anyone to do so.

This was a great revelation, but it was not the only contribution of the children. It was also they who created the lesson of silence. They seemed to be a new type of children. Their fame spread and, in consequence, all kinds of people visited the House of Children, including state ministers and their wives, with whom the children behaved graciously and beautifully, without anyone urging them. Even the newspapers in Italy and abroad became excited. So the news spread, until finally also the Queen became interested. She came to that Quarter, so ill famed that it was considered hell's doors, to see for herself the children about whom she had heard wonders.

What was the wonder due to? No one could state it clearly. But it conquered me forever, because it penetrated my heart as a new light. One day I looked at them with eyes which saw them differently, and I asked myself: 'Who are you? Are you the same children you were before?' And I said within myself: 'Perhaps you are those children of whom it was said that they would come to save humanity. If so, I shall follow you.' Since then, I am she who tries to grasp their message to follow them.

And in order to follow them, I changed my whole life. I was nearly forty. I had in front of me a doctor's career and a professorship at the University. But I left it all, because I felt compelled to follow them and to find others who could follow them, for I saw that in them lay the secret of the soul.

You must realize that what happened was something so great and so stirring that its importance could never be sufficiently recognized. That it will never be sufficiently studied is certain, for it is the secret of life itself. We cannot fully know its causes. It is not possible that it came because of my method, for at the time my method did not yet exist. This is the clearest proof that it was a revelation that emanated from the children themselves.

(Below) A meal at the Montessori School in the Convent of the Franciscan Nuns, Rome, c. 1912.

My educational method has grown from these, as well as from many other revelations, given by the children. You know, from what I have told you, that all the details included in the method have come from the efforts to follow the child. The new path has been shown us. No one knows exactly how it arose; it just came into being and showed us the new way.

It has nothing to do with any educational method of the past nor with any educational method of the future. It stands alone as the contribution of the child himself. Perhaps it is the first of its kind, which has been built by him, step by step.

It cannot have come from an adult person; the thought, the very principle that the adult should stand aside to make room for the child, could never have come from the adult.

Anyone who wants to follow my method must understand that he should not honor me, but follow the child as his leader."

Maria Montessori discovered that when young children concentrate and investigate a set of purposefully designed activities, they tend to develop self-control; their movements become ordered, and they appear peaceful. Their demeanor towards others becomes kind and gentle.

These characteristics and other discoveries made with the children of San Lorenzo in 1907 were quickly replicated, as new Montessori schools opened throughout Europe and around the world. Children in Elementary and Secondary Montessori schools displayed tremendous enthusiasm as they explored and studied topics in great detail. Their learning achievements were profound. The overall Montessori experience, however, is deeper than an academic course of study. Because the Montessori process fully engages children's natural learning potentials, Montessori students learn about themselves, develop self-confidence, communicate effectively, and work well in groups.

Today's Montessori schools incorporate the discoveries of Maria Montessori as well as recent understandings of how learning and development take place. Montessori schools are now found in private, public, and home-school settings in the United States and abroad. The educational programs located in these schools range from infant care to high school students.

Many of these schools are affiliates of, or are accredited by, one of a dozen national and/or international Montessori organizations. Teachers receive Montessori teacher certification after completing rigorous courses of study. Many teachers describe their own experiences of personal transformation as they, too, witness in children astounding capabilities. From a family's perspective, becoming part of a Montessori school could be thought of as adopting a natural lifestyle we call *The Montessori Way*.

(Below) Students at the Montessori School in the Convent of the Franciscan Nuns, Rome, c. 1912.

A Typical Montessori Day

It is dark at 7:45 A.M. on this mid-winter's morning when Jeanne Saunders pulls up to the drop-off circle at the Montessori school her three children have attended since they were two years old.

Jeanne has made this trip so often over the years that the school feels like her second home. Jeanne works in town and typically cannot leave work until after 5:00 P.M. Her husband, Bill, teaches in the local public school and is off much earlier. He will pick up the children from the after-school program at 4:30 P.M., but if he's late, he knows that they'll be fine until he arrives. The school prides itself on being "family friendly." Working families appreciate its extended-day and summer-camp programs.

Imani, Justin, and Madison definitely think of their Montessori school as their second family. Madison is one of those children who, after eleven years in Montessori, speaks about the school with affection and conviction. Visitors often find her coming up without a moment's hesitation to greet them and offer them a cup of coffee before they start the campus tour. When people ask if she likes it in Montessori, she smiles and says, "Sure! How could anyone not love it here? Your teachers are your best friends, the work is really interesting, and the other kids are my friends, too. You feel really close to everyone."

THE MONTESSORI WAY

(Above) Montessori empowers children to take care of their basic needs.

Madison walks her five-year-old sister, Imani, to her morning supervision room. Seven-year-old Justin goes ahead on his own. After dropping off Imani, Madison walks into the middle school wing, where she is a seventh grader. She joins two of her friends in the Commons, and they sit and talk quietly, waiting for class to start at 8:30 A.M.

Imani's morning supervision takes place in her regular classroom. After hanging up her coat, she walks over to Judy, the staff member in charge of her room, and asks if she can help. Judy asks Imani to look over the breakfast table and provide any missing napkins and spoons. Imani does this, and when the table is finally ready, she makes herself a bowl of cereal. Imani adds milk and walks to a breakfast table to eat. Children and their parents drift into the room every so often; gradually the number of children in the early-morning program grows to about fifteen.

After eating her breakfast, Imani brings her bowl and spoon to a dishwashing table. Bowls and spoons are stacked in a bin. Later in the morning, several children will choose the dish-washing activity. All items will be completely cleaned and sterilized afterwards by the dishwasher located in the classroom.

Next, Imani walks to the easel and begins to paint with Teresa, a little girl of just three, who has only joined the class over the last few weeks. They paint quietly, talking back and forth about nothing in particular.

Eventually, Imani tires of painting and cleans up. For a moment, she is tempted to walk away and leave the easel messy; instead, she carefully cleans up and puts the materials away, as she has learned from more than two years in Montessori.

At 8:30 A.M., Imani's full-day teacher and her assistant arrive, along with several more children. Other children follow over the next few minutes until all twenty-four students and the two adults quietly move about the room. During the next several hours, Imani and her classmates will choose learning activities and will involve themselves individually, as well as in small groups. They will have a variety of lessons from their teachers. Some are demonstrations, during which their teachers show them how to use the learn-

(Right) Most Montessori schools have art materials in the classroom for use throughout the day. Some schools have art specialists who instruct the children as part of their weekly curriculum or extended-day program.

ing materials. Other lessons are in the form of direct instruction on, for example, the phonetic sounds of letters or on names for numerals, geometric shapes, and geographic terms for landforms, continents, and nations.

In another part of the school, Justin and his classmates begin their lower-elementary day (for children between the ages of six and nine) with a writing prompt: *"Wisdom is ..."* As each child completes the writing prompt, the teachers meet with students to review the progress of their work plans. This morning, Justin will join a small group for an introductory lesson on how to use the science discovery boxes. The focus of the lesson will involve asking investigative questions.

The middle school students start their day with "sharing," one of several components of their morning meeting. By speaking about something that has taken place during the past twenty-four hours, students come to know one another better and build trust.

Afterwards, they will break into math groups. Madison, along with two of her classmates, will present a lesson demonstrating the predictive power of a linear equation. Following math, the students will regroup into smaller teams. Each team is completing research for multimedia presentations based on several topics from their global studies.

Imani, with one of her friends, is also working to construct and solve a mathematical problem: 2,346 + 1,421. This activity reflects their learning accomplishments during the past two years. Each child has used other materials to build an understanding of number and place value. Today, they use a set of numeral cards to make the first addend: 2,346. The cards showing the "units" 1 to 9 are printed in green. The cards showing the "tens" numerals from 10 to 90 are printed in blue. The "hundreds" from 100 to 900 are printed in red, and the cards showing 1,000 to 9,000 are printed in green again, because they represent units of thousands.

Imani and her friend look through the cards and find a green 6, a blue 40, a red 300, and a green 2,000. They place these numeral cards across the top of a wooden tray and carry it to the "bank," a central collection of golden bead materials. They place their tray on the floor, and they gather 6 "unit" beads.

Next, they count out 4 bars of "ten" beads, which will represent 40. This process is repeated until their tray is filled with the correct number of "hundred" squares, and "thousand" cubes. They walk back to their work space and unroll a rug on the floor. The two girls then place their numeral cards across the top of the rug. They place the "unit" beads under the green 6 card; 4 bars of "ten" beads each under the blue 40 card; 3 squares of "hundred" beads each under the red 300 card; and 2 cubes of "thousand" beads each under the green 2,000 card. The girls now fill their empty tray with cards to form the numeral 1,421. Walking to the "bank," they again select the correct quantity of bead materials and return to their work rug. They build 1,421 under the 2,346.

The two addends are combined in an addition process: the "unit" beads are combined and placed in the lower-right corner of the rug. The bars of "ten" are combined and placed to the left of the "units." This process continues for the "hundred" squares and "thousand" cubes. Their movements mimic the pencil and paper process. Beginning with the "units," the children count the combined quantities to determine the result of adding the two together. In this example, the result is 7 "unit" beads. They find a green 7 card to represent this partial sum. If their addition resulted in a quantity of ten beads or more, the children would stop at the count of 10 and carry the 10 "unit" beads to the "bank," where they would exchange the 10 "unit" beads for 1 "ten" bar: 10 "units" equals 1 unit of "ten." This process of counting and labeling quantities is repeated for the "tens," "hundreds," and "thousands."

To complete this activity, Imani and her friend collect pieces of math paper, and green, blue, and red pencils. They copy their problem on their papers: 2,346 + 1,421 = 3,767. They put their papers in their cubbies and they return the pencils, numeral cards, bead materials, and tray to their proper places. Finally, they roll up their work rug and

(Above) The Stamp Game

*The **Stamp Game** is not really a game at all — it is a set of concrete materials that allows young children to solve four-digit math problems; it is a next step on the road to abstraction in the Montessori Math curriculum.*

return it to the rug holder. This is, as the children proudly say, a "big work."

It is now almost 10:00 A.M. and Imani is hungry. She moves to the snack table and prepares several pieces of celery stuffed with peanut butter. She pours a cup of apple juice, using a little pitcher that is just the right size for her hands. When she is finished, Imani takes the cup to the dish-washing table and wipes the place mat. As with the breakfast dishes, dish washing is a real-life activity; the children will wash their own dishes and learn to take care of their own needs. (Dishes and utensils will go through the dishwasher before the next morning.)

Montessori children are usually energized by "big work." Cleaning up from her snack has put Imani in the mood to *really* clean something. Younger children will direct their energies into a table-washing activity.

Five-year-old Imani has another plan. She finds her friend Chelsea, and the two girls begin talking about a puppy named Sam. They begin to laugh as their story becomes increasingly elaborate. Their teacher, Ann, acknowledges their creativity and suggests they write a story. This lesson involves a work rug, a box of wooden letters called the *Moveable Alphabet,* pencils, paper, and writing tables. Like the earlier math work, it reflects enormous achievements in language learning. They have already learned the phonetic sounds of letters and how to blend sounds together to write and read words. This activity also reflects enormous achievements in developing focus or concentration and self-discipline. Imani and Chelsea use the alphabet to compose a story about a dog named Sam.

Throughout the morning, Imani's classmates have completed learning activities involving sorting and sequencing objects, identifying names for nations, arranging geometric shapes, and exploring scientific properties.

In a very real sense, Imani and her classmates are responsible for the care of this child-sized environment. Older children show younger children how to use the materials. When the children are hungry, they prepare their own snacks by cutting raw fruits and vegetables. They go to the bathroom without assistance. When something spills, they help each other clean up. They also enjoy sweeping, dusting, and washing windows. They set tables, tie their own shoes, polish silver, and steadily grow in their self-confidence and independence. Noticing that the plants need water, Imani carries the watering can from plant to plant, barely spilling a drop.

A Typical Montessori Day

Children move freely around the class, selecting activities that capture their interests. Imani and her classmates have demonstrated self-sufficiency. They are developing an inner sense of order, a greater sense of independence, and a higher ability to concentrate and follow a complex sequence of steps.

Imani's day continues and she eats her lunch with the class at 11:45 A.M., after which she goes outside with her friends to play. After lunch, the Spanish teacher comes into the room and begins to work with small groups of students.

Throughout their day, Imani and her classmates make responsible choices regarding which learning activities to do next. Each activity engages the children in a number of movement patterns that form a foundation for neurological development. The hands-on learning materials are also concrete models for thinking processes and abstract concepts.

Young children are also comparative thinkers. They learn things are *big* when something else is *small*; things are *loud* when something else is *soft*. Young children are problem solvers. They can group objects together that are congruent; other objects are arranged sequentially by one or more properties of size and color. Repeated use of the materials allow young students to build a clear inner image of, for example, place value: *How big is a thousand as compared with hundreds, tens, and units?*

The design of the learning materials – their sizes, shapes, colors, textures, and weights – holds the interest and attention of Imani and her classmates for long periods of time. Concentration is normal; these young children explore and discover differences and similarities between the objects.

As these children engage in long periods of concentration with the learning materials, they also develop and display self-discipline. Their movements are orderly. Children act with grace and courtesy; they are considerate and respectful towards one another. At the same time, children are energized by their discoveries and investigations. Self-discipline involves learning to channel their energies by choosing new activities.

During the afternoon Imani becomes occupied with an art activity, listens to selections from a recording of the *Nutcracker* ballet, writes the names of shapes taken from the geometric cabinet, and completes a puzzle map of the United States.

When the day is over, Imani will have completed ten to fifteen different activities, most representing curriculum content quite advanced for someone who, after all, just turned five two months ago. But when her dad picks her up at 4:50 P.M., her response to the usual question of, "What did you do in school today?" is no different from many children: "Stuff. I did a map and, oh, I don't know." Madison and Justin will furnish similar responses, focusing instead on what might happen during the evening at home.

The design of the learning materials — their sizes, shapes, colors, textures, and weights — holds the interest and attention of Montessori students. Above is a set of the **Metal Insets**, one of the materials children use to develop eye-hand coordination.

The Saunders explain a typical school day in this way: "Our children are very happy in Montessori. They are excited about coming, and they can't wait to get here. Their teachers genuinely care for our children; more than that, they *know* our kids. When we describe what our kids are learning, our friends and family are amazed. Our neighbors tell us their children are not learning anything like what our kids do here."

The Montessori Way

Children experience a school day like Imani's in one of the more than four thousand Montessori schools found throughout the United States. Montessori schools are also found in North and South American nations, throughout Europe, Africa, Asia, Australia, and New Zealand. Some schools only offer early childhood programs; others offer early childhood through elementary or secondary. Most are private or independent schools, founded either by an individual teacher or a parent board. There are a growing number of public school programs, and many home schools implement aspects of the Montessori approach.

Each Montessori school is built upon the educational legacy of Dr. Maria Montessori and her influential work, which began nearly one hundred years ago. Since 1907, the year of her first school, children and adults have engaged in an approach to learning that addresses all aspects of growth: cognitive, physical, social, emotional, and spiritual. In Montessori schools throughout the world, children develop the habits and skills of lifelong learning. Guided by teachers trained to observe and identify children's unique learning capabilities, children learn in educational partnership with their teachers. Because children's interests are heard and honored, Montessori students develop confidence and become self-directed. A powerful learning formula emerges as a result of this self-directed, self-initiated orientation to learning. When interested, a child becomes self-motivated. Self-motivation leads to becoming self-disciplined. When self-disciplined, a child engages in a process of mastery learning and fully develops his or her potential.

Dr. Maria Montessori called this a "normal" approach to education. We call this *The Montessori Way*. *The Montessori Way* refers to: the knowledge of how children naturally learn;

Two of the many faces of Montessori ...

(Above) Montessori in the Gardens, a small school for children aged eighteen months through six years located in Dunedin, New Zealand. (Below) The Chiaravalle Montessori School in Evanston, Illinois, has an enrollment of approximately 370 students, serving some of Montessori's youngest students (aged twelve months) through the eighth grade.

a curriculum based on that knowledge designed for the developmental needs of infants, toddlers, three-to-six-year-olds, elementary, middle, and secondary students; a method of instruction involving learning how to observe and how to develop learning environments in which teachers challenge each child to extend fully his or her unique style of learning; a profession; a school characterized by calm, orderly, focused, and respectful learning behaviors; and, a person named Maria Montessori.

In 1907, Dr. Maria Montessori discerned a fundamental premise about children and humanity in general: *All children are uniquely intelligent.* This premise challenged long-held beliefs about intelligence and the inherent nature of mankind as violent and competitive. Whereas Montessori wrote about unique, individual potential, it is more fashionable today to discuss each person's "multiple intelligences."

This is the belief that intelligence is not fixed at birth and that the human potential is without limit. The validity of this belief has been confirmed by the research of Piaget, Gardner, Goleman, and many others. Accordingly, then, the practice of highly selective educational institutions requires further examination: Does the design and conduct of schools, including the forms of testing they use, privilege some forms of intelligence while ignoring others?

We know that each child is a full and complete individual in her own right. Even when very small, she deserves to be treated with the full and sincere respect that would be extended to her parents. Respect breeds respect and creates an atmosphere within which learning is tremendously facilitated.

Montessori educators work with infants, toddlers, young children, and adolescents. In each age, we see an inherent tendency towards discovery, cooperation, kindness, and nonviolence. These observations challenge ideas about life and human motives in the social order, including subjecting millions of children to impoverished learning conditions.

Each day, children exhibit the vast wonder of the human spirit, the endless faces of intelligence, creativity, and inventiveness in Montessori schools throughout the world. This suggests a far richer and more pleasant, productive, and peaceful world than most of us have ever known or imagined.

The Montessori Way stands in sharp contrast to the current fervor to use children as measures of adults' performances: Test scores, not complete potential; prescribed standards and objectives, not self-empowerment.

Parents are required to accept a political definition of teacher effectiveness. Teaching "to" the test and rehearsed test taking may result in schools with test scores that reward adults with jobs and funding. But what is the cost to children? Why are too many children under this regime now denied music, art, physical education, recess — and, in some schools, science and history?

What is a child's daily experience of sitting in classrooms led by anxious or even frightened teachers waiting to be graded by these scores? Current brain research urges adults to establish learning environments that are stimulating and relaxed; intriguing and safe for exploration. Thinking, problem solving, and forming trusting relationships are all possible once a child is freed from stress.

> *"When interested, a child becomes self-motivated. Self-motivation leads to becoming self-disciplined. When self-disciplined, a child engages in a process of mastery learning and develops his or her potential."*

SHARING A COMMON PHILOSOPHY AND APPROACH ...

Although Montessori schools may appear different, they all share a common philosophy and basic approach. The Montessori approach has four great qualities: this educational model is replicable; it can be adapted successfully to new situations; it can include educational innovations based on recent understandings of learning; and, it is sustainable, operating in many schools continuously for fifty years or longer.

The History of the Montessori Movement

Maria Montessori was nominated for the Nobel Peace Prize for her work with children and education. She summarized her work towards the end of her life:

"To aid life, leaving it free, however, to unfold itself, that is the basic task of the educator.

Ours was a House for children rather than a real school. We had prepared a place for children, where a diffused culture could be assimilated, without any need for direct instruction...Yet these children learned to read and write before they were five, and no one had given them any lessons. At that time, it seemed miraculous that children of four and one-half should be able to write and that they should have learned without the feeling of having been taught.

We puzzled over it for a long time. Only after repeated experiments did we conclude with certainty that all children are endowed with this capacity to 'absorb' culture. If this be true, we then argued, if culture can be acquired without effort, let us provide the children with other elements of culture. And then we saw them 'absorb' far more than reading and writing: botany, zoology, mathematics, geography, and all with the same ease, spontaneously and without getting tired.

And so we discovered that education is not something which the teacher does, but that it is a natural process which develops spontaneously in the human being. It is not acquired by listening to words but in virtue of experiences in which the child acts in his environment. The teacher's task is not to talk but to prepare and arrange a series of motives for cultural activity in a special environment made for the child.

My experiments, conducted in many different countries, have been going on for forty years (ed. now ninety-seven years), *and as the children grew up, parents kept asking me to extend my methods to the later ages. We then found that individual activity is the one factor that stimulates and produces development, and that this is not more true for the little ones of preschool age than it is for the junior, middle, and upper school children."**

Dr. Maria Montessori (1870 – 1952)

Maria Montessori is as controversial a figure in education today as she was almost a century ago. Alternately heralded as the century's leading advocate for early childhood education or dismissed as outdated and irrelevant, her research and the studies that she inspired helped change the course of education.

During her lifetime, Dr. Montessori was intent upon transforming adult beliefs about children and their education. She passionately believed each adult must develop her or his abilities to observe children deeply so as to witness the unfolding of each new human being. In order to discover a child's hidden potential or secret, a beginning step is to become an observer of children. Montessori discovered a number of "secrets" – aspects of young children never before observed. She described her experiences in terms of a profound transformation and believed this experience would occur for all other adults as well.

Those who studied and were influenced by her and went on to make their own contributions to education and child psychology include: Anna Freud, Jean Piaget, Alfred Adler, and Erik Erikson.

*Maria Montessori, *The Absorbent Mind*.

Many elements of modern education have been adapted from Montessori's theories. She is credited with the development of the open classroom, the role of teacher as a guide, multi-age classrooms, developmentally appropriate and individualized education, and the use of manipulative learning materials. In the last thirty-five years, educators in Europe and North America have begun to recognize the consistency between the Montessori approach and what we have learned from research in child development and best teaching practices.

Maria Montessori was an individual ahead of her time. She was born in 1870 in Chiaravalle, Italy, to an educated but not affluent middle-class family. She grew up in a country considered most conservative in its attitude toward women. Despite the considerable opposition of her father and teachers, Montessori pursued a scientific education and was the first woman to become a physician in Italy.

As a practicing physician associated with the University of Rome, she was a scientist, not a teacher. It is ironic that she became famous for her contributions in a field that she had rejected as the traditional refuge for women at a time when few professions were open to them other than homemaking, teaching, or the convent. The Montessori "Method" evolved almost by accident from a small experiment that Dr. Montessori carried out on the side. Her genius stems not from her teaching ability but from her recognition of the importance of that upon which she stumbled.

Dr. Montessori specialized in pediatrics and psychiatry. She taught at the medical school of the University of Rome, and, through its free clinics, she came into frequent contact with the children of the working class and poor. These experiences convinced her that intelligence is not rare and that most children come into the world with a human potential that is barely revealed unless adults create environments specifically designed for children to exercise their learning capabilities. Her work reinforced her humanistic ideals, and she made time in her busy schedule to support various social-reform movements. Early in her career, she began to accept speaking engagements throughout Europe on behalf of the women's movement, peace efforts, and child labor-law reform. Montessori become well known and highly regard-

(Below) Building the Pink Tower.
*A young student working with the **Pink Tower** materials, c. 1912.*

ed throughout Europe, which undoubtedly contributed to the publicity that surrounded her schools.

In 1900, Montessori was appointed director of the new orthophrenic school attached to the University of Rome. The children at the school were probably developmentally delayed or autistic. She initiated reforms in a system that formerly had served merely to confine youngsters with cognitive delays in empty rooms. Recognizing her patients' need for stimulation, purposeful activity, and self-esteem, Montessori insisted that the staff speak to each child with the highest respect. She created a program to teach her young charges how to care for themselves and their environment.

At the same time, she began a meticulous study of the available research. Her studies led Montessori to the work of Jean Jacques Rousseau (1712-1778), who believed sensory experience was the basis for all knowledge. He argued that teachers must begin with "knowing" learners and that a teacher's role is to assist learners with fully developing their own natures. To do this, teachers must begin with the concrete and real – sensory experiences rather than lecture-based recitations. From the Swiss educational reformer Johann Heinrich Pestalozzi (1746-1827), Montessori found further support for the idea that teachers develop the capabilities of learners rather than impart information. Pestalozzi defined observation as the method of teaching. Teachers must observe their pupils in order to know them, their interests, and how they learn. Like Rousseau, Pestalozzi's curriculum was based on engaging children in direct experiences involving physical activity, making collections, and outings beyond the confines of the classroom. He sequenced learning experiences from simple to complex; from concrete to abstract.

Friedrich Froebel (1782-1852), the German educator and originator of the kindergarten, bridged the ideas of Pestalozzi and Rousseau. Froebel studied with Pestalozzi from 1806 to 1810 before opening his own school in 1816. Froebel believed that education was a process of self-activity and self-discovery, leading to self-fulfillment.

The goal of an educator was to discover the universal principles that guided this process. Teachers should guide, not coerce, and teachers should never interfere with children's spontaneous learning activities. Froebel developed a series of "gifts" — balls, cubes, cylinders, and blocks — that heightened children's awareness of relationships among things.

Montessori also made a thorough study of two almost forgotten French physicians of the eighteenth and nineteenth centuries: Jean Marc Gaspard Itard (1774-1838) and Edouard Seguin (1812-1880). Itard is most famous for his work with the "Wild Boy of Aveyron," a youth who had been found wandering naked in the forest, having spent ten years living alone. The boy could not speak and lacked almost all of the skills of everyday life. Here, apparently, was a "natural man," a human being who had developed without the benefit of culture and socialization with his own kind. Itard hoped from this study to shed some light on the age-old debate about what proportion of human intelligence and personality is hereditary and what proportion stems from learned behavior.

The experiment had limited success, for Itard found the boy uncooperative and unwilling or unable to learn most things. This led Itard to postulate the existence of developmental periods in normal human growth. During these "sensitive periods," a child must experience stimulation or grow up forever lacking the adult skills and intellectual concepts he missed at the stage when they can be readily learned!

Although Itard's efforts to teach the "wild boy" were barely successful, he followed a methodical approach in designing the process, arguing that all education would benefit from the use of careful observation and experimentation.

This idea had tremendous appeal to the scientifically trained Montessori and later became a cornerstone of her Method. From Edouard Seguin, Montessori drew further confirmation of Itard's work, along with a far more specific and organized system for applying it to the everyday education of the handicapped.

Today, Seguin is recognized as the father of our modern techniques of special education. Seguin outlined an active sensory education that included graduated exercises in motor education, sorting geometric shapes, and explorations of textures, colors, and sizes.

From these predecessors, Montessori refined the idea of a scientific approach to education, based on observation and experimentation. She belongs to the "child-study" school of thought, and she pursued her work with the careful training and objectivity of the biologist studying the natural behavior of an animal in the forest. She studied children with special learning needs, listening and carefully noting everything that they did and said.

Slowly, she understood who they really were and what methods worked best. Her success was given widespread notice when, two years after she began, many of Montessori's students were able to pass the standard sixth-grade tests of the Italian public schools. Acclaimed for this "miracle," Montessori responded by suggesting her results proved only that public schools should be able to get dramatically better results with typical children.

The San Lorenzo Discoveries

Unfortunately, the Italian Ministry of Education did not welcome Montessori's suggestion that her methodology, which worked well with children with special learning needs, would yield even more dramatic results when used with typical children. Consequently, she was unable to continue the experiment with public, school-aged children. Several years later, in 1907, Montessori accepted an invitation to coordinate a day-care center for the children of working-class parents — children who were too young to attend public school. This first Casa dei Bambini, "Children's House," was located in San Lorenzo, an extremely poor district of Rome. The conditions that Montessori faced were appalling. Her first class consisted of fifty children from two through five years of age, taught by one untrained caregiver.

The children remained at the center from dawn to dusk, while their parents worked. They were fed two meals a day, bathed regularly, and received medical care. The children themselves were typical of extreme inner-city poverty conditions.

They entered the Children's House on the first day crying and pushing, exhibiting generally aggressive and impatient behavior. Montessori, not knowing whether her experiment would work under such conditions, began by teaching the older children how to help with the everyday tasks that needed to be done. She also introduced the manipulative perceptual puzzles that she had used with children with developmental delays.

The results surprised her, for unlike her earlier experiences with coaxing children with special learning needs to use the learning materials, the children of San Lorenzo were drawn to the work she introduced. Children who had wandered aimlessly the week before began to settle down to long periods of constructive activity. They were fascinated with the puzzles and perceptual training devices. But, to Montessori's amazement, three- and four-year-old children took the greatest delight in learning practical everyday living skills that reinforced their independence and self-respect.

Each day they begged her to show them more, even applauding with delight when Montessori taught them the correct use of a handkerchief. Soon the older children were taking care of the school, assisting their teacher with the preparation and serving of meals,

(Above) A "server" carrying soup, c. 1912.

In this photo a young Montessori student carefully carries soup to the table. In her book, A Montessori Mother *(1913), Dorothy Canfield Fisher describes her amazement at the way in which Montessori students learn to care for themselves.*

As summarized by Dr. Maria Montessori's student and colleague, E. M. Standing, young children prefer:

- Work without compulsion;
- Spontaneous repetition;
- Work rather than play;
- Concentration and self-discipline.

maintening a spotless environment, and even learning to read and write. Their behavior as a group changed dramatically, from street urchins running wild to models of grace and courtesy. It was little wonder that the press found such a human-interest story appealing and promptly broadcast it to the world.

Montessori called her discoveries the "secrets of childhood." As she opened more schools, she discovered further that these "secrets" were found in children everywhere. Montessori also discovered that two other qualities were necessary for this response from young children: a carefully prepared teacher and an environment specifically prepared for the learning capabilities found in its children.

Montessori made a practice of paying close attention to their spontaneous behavior, arguing that only in this way could a teacher know how to teach. Traditionally, schools paid little attention to children as individuals, other than to demand that they adapt to the school's standards. Montessori believed that the educator's job was to serve the child, determining what each one needed to make the greatest progress. To her, a child who failed in school should not be blamed, anymore than a doctor should blame a patient who does not get well fast enough. After all, it is the job of the physician to help us find the way to cure ourselves, and the educator's job is to facilitate the natural process of learning.

In 1907, Montessori's children exploded into academics. Too young to go to public school, they begged to be taught how to read and write. They learned to do so quickly and enthusiastically, using special manipulative materials that Montessori designed for maximum appeal and effectiveness.

The children were fascinated by numbers. To meet this interest, the mathematically inclined Montessori developed a series of concrete math learning materials that have never been surpassed. Soon her four- and five-year-old students were performing four-digit addition and subtraction operations and in many cases pushing on even further. Their interests blossomed in other areas as well, compelling an overworked physician to spend night after night designing new materials to keep pace with the children's interest in geometry, geography, history, and natural science. The final proof of the children's desires came shortly after her first school became famous, when a group of well-intentioned women gave them a marvelous collection of lovely and expensive toys. The new gifts held the children's attention for a few days, but they soon returned to the more interesting learning materials. To Montessori's surprise, children who had experienced both preferred work over play most of the time. In her insightful book, *The Secret of Childhood*, she wrote:

"Although the children in our first school could play with some really splendid toys, none cared to do so … I decided to help them play with their toys … The children were momentarily interested, but then went off on their own … [A child] regards play as we would regard a game of chess or bridge. These are pleasant occupations for hours of leisure…[but] when we have some important business to do, bridge is forgotten."*

Montessori evolved her Method through trial and error, making educated guesses about the underlying meaning of the children's actions. She was quick to pick up on their cues and constantly experimented with the class. For example, Montessori tells of the morning when the teacher arrived late to find that the children had crawled through a window and gone right to work. At the beginning, the learning materials were expensive and hand made. Each was locked away in a tall cabinet. Only the teacher had a key and would open the cabinet and hand the materials to the children. In this instance, the teacher had neglected to lock the cabinet the night before.

Finding it open, the children had selected one material apiece and were working quietly. As Montessori arrived, the teacher was scolding the children for taking the materials without permission. Montessori recognized that the children's behavior showed that they were capable of selecting their own work, and she removed the cabinet and replaced it with low, open shelves on which the activities were always available to the children. Today, this may sound like a minor change, but it contradicted all educational practice and theory of that period.

One discovery followed another, leading Montessori towards understanding the learning capabilities of the young child. She found that young children enjoyed long periods of quiet concentration, even though they rarely showed signs of it in everyday settings. Although they were often careless and sloppy, they responded positively to an atmosphere of calm and order. Montessori noticed that the logical extension of the young child's love for a consistent and often-repeated routine is an environment in which everything has a place. Her children took tremendous delight in carefully carrying their work to and from the shelves, taking great pains not to bump into anything or spill the smallest piece. They walked carefully through the rooms, instead of running wildly as they did on the streets. Montessori discovered that the environment itself was an essential component in obtaining the results that she had observed.

---

*Maria Montessori, *The Secret of Childhood*

Not wanting to use school desks, she had carpenters build child-sized tables and chairs. She was the first to recognize the frustration that a little child experiences in an adult-sized world. Eventually, she learned to design entire schools around the size of the children. She had miniature pitchers and bowls prepared and found forks and knives that fit a child's tiny hand. The tables were lightweight, allowing two children to move them without adult assistance. The children learned to control their movements, disliking the way the calm was disturbed when they knocked into things.

Montessori studied the traffic pattern of the rooms as well, arranging the furnishings and the activity area to minimize congestion and tripping. The children loved to sit on the floor, so she bought little rugs to define their work areas, and the children quickly learned to walk around them. Over the years, Montessori schools extended this environmental engineering throughout their entire buildings and outside areas, designing child-sized toilets and low sinks, windows low to the ground, low shelves, and miniature hand and garden tools of all sorts.

Some of these ideas were eventually adapted by the larger educational community, particularly at the nursery and kindergarten levels. Many of the puzzles and educational devices now in general use at the early childhood and elementary levels are direct copies of Montessori's original ideas. However, there is far more of her work that never entered the mainstream, and today's educators who are searching for new, more effective answers are finding the accumulated experience of the Montessori community to be of great interest.

The first "Children's House" received overnight attention, and thousands of visitors came away amazed and enthusiastic. Worldwide interest surged as Montessori duplicated her first school in other settings throughout Europe, and then in the United States, with the same results. Her American tours between 1912 and 1918 were made with the support of the Washington Montessori Society, whose members included Alexander Graham Bell and Woodrow Wilson's daughter. Montessori gave lectures at the White House, Carnegie Hall, and numerous universities. She conducted teacher education programs and developed a classroom at the Panama-Pacific International Exposition.

Montessori captured the interest and imagination of national leaders and scientists, mothers and teachers, labor leaders and factory owners. As an internationally respected scientist, she had a rare credibility in a field where many others had promoted opinions, philosophies, and models that have not been readily duplicated.

(Below) Dr. Maria Montessori, c. 1912.

The Montessori Method offered a systematic approach that translated very well to new educational settings: calm, responsible behavior; a love for work with learning materials; and freedom and spontaneity.

Many political leaders of that time saw this as a practical way to reform the outmoded school systems of Europe and North America, as well as an approach that they hoped would lead to a more productive and law-abiding populace.

Scientists of all disciplines heralded its empirical foundation, along with the accelerated achievement of young children. Montessori rode a wave of enthusiastic support that should have changed the face of education far more dramatically than it has.

Montessori's prime productive period lasted from the opening of the first Children's House in 1907 through the years of the Second World War. During this time, she continued her study of children and developed a vastly expanded curriculum and methodology for the elementary level as well.

Dr. Montessori gave up her medical practice, devoting her life to advocate the rights and intellectual potential of all children.

(Above) Montessori Middle School students working together to enhance their outdoor environment.

Montessori's Legacy

"It was January 6th (1907), when the first school was opened for small, normal children of between three and six years of age. I cannot say on my methods, for these did not yet exist. But in the school that was opened my method was shortly to come into being. On that day there was nothing to be seen but about fifty wretchedly poor children, rough and shy in manner, many of them crying, almost all the children of illiterate parents, who had been entrusted to my care.

They were tearful, frightened children, so shy that it was impossible to get them to speak; their faces were expressionless, with bewildered eyes as though they had never seen anything in their lives.

It would be interesting to know the original circumstances that enabled these children to undergo such an extraordinary transformation, or rather, that brought about the appearance of new children, whose souls revealed themselves with such radiance as to spread a light through the whole world."

— Dr. Maria Montessori

Within the next year, news of Dr. Montessori's work stirred interest around the world. Literally hundreds of people began to travel to Rome to see for themselves the school in which young children — children of the deepest poverty and ignorance — taught themselves how to read, write, do mathematics, and run their own schoolhouse with little or no adult supervision.

In her book about educational reform, *The Schoolhome* (Harvard University Press, 1992), Dr. Judith Rowland Martin writes that she was not very impressed when she first encountered Montessori education.

"I understood that Montessori schools placed children in multi-age classrooms and used manipulative learning materials, which may have been unusual during Dr. Montessori's lifetime but has long since been incorporated into most early childhood and many elementary classrooms thanks to the Open Classroom movement of the 1960s."

However, Dr. Rowland Martin's understanding of the value of the Montessori approach was profoundly shaken when she came across a statement in one of the very first books written about Dr. Montessori's work in the United States (*A Montessori Mother*, by Dorothy Canfield Fisher, Henry Holt and Company, New York, 1913). "The phrase, *Casa dei Bambini*, is being translated everywhere nowadays by English-speaking people as *The Children's House*; however, its correct meaning, both linguistic and spiritual is *The Children's Home*" (or Children's Community, ed.). Canfield Fisher insisted upon this rendering, which she felt offered a much more accurate and complete insight into the character of the Montessori classroom.

Rowland Martin reflected:

"This misreading of the Italian word casa *as* house *has effectively cut off two generations of American educators from a new and intriguing vision of what school can and should be. If you translate the word* casa *as* house, *your attention will be drawn to the child-sized furniture, the Montessori materials, the exercises in Practical Life, the principal of self-education.*

But if you translate the word casa *as* home, *you will begin to perceive a moral and social dimension that transforms your understanding of Montessori's idea of a school. Once I realized that Dr. Montessori thought of school on the model of a home, the elements of her system took on a different configuration. Where before I had seen small children manipulating concrete learning materials, I now recognized a domestic scene with its own special form of social life and education."*

Rowland Martin realized that what Montessori had established was not simply a classroom in which children would be taught to read and write. The Casa dei Bambini represented a social and emotional environment, where

(Right) Students working in the garden of the Montessori School in the Convent of the Franciscan Nuns, Rome, c. 1912.

(Left) Gardening helps Montessori students become more aware of their natural environment. Even inner-city Montessori schools incorporate gardening projects into their curriculum. These elementary students are fortunate to have a large outdoor area to explore.

children would be respected and empowered as individual human beings. It was an extended family, a community in which children truly belonged and really took care of one another. Montessori described this sense of belonging as "valorization of the personality," a strong sense of self-respect and personal identity.

Within this safe and empowering community, the young child learned at the deepest possible level to believe in herself. In an atmosphere of independence within community and personal empowerment, she never lost her sense of curiosity and innate ability to learn and discover. Confident in herself, she opened up to the world around her and found that mistakes were not something to be feared but rather the endless opportunity to learn from experience.

This special relationship that is so common among Montessori children and their teachers and schools is, unfortunately, still very different from the experience most children have in school.

The Discovery of the Child

Montessori was absorbed with what she later called "The Discovery of the Child." She did not see the core of her work as a method or curriculum, *per se*, as is commonly thought, but as a dramatic discovery that children around the world share common, or universal, characteristics and tendencies, even though each child is a unique human being, who deserves the same respect we would give an adult.

In response to the pleas of so many earnest admirers, Dr. Montessori arranged to give her first training course for teachers in 1909. Expecting only Italian educators, she was amazed to find that her first course, and all of the courses offered since, attracted teachers from all over the world who had heard of her discoveries and were moved to make great sacrifices to learn from her personally.

Many people have the impression that Montessori is a centrally controlled business, from which schools can buy a franchise and learn to replicate the model consistently. Nothing could be further from the truth.

The name *Montessori* was never copyrighted or controlled by Montessori, and much to her dismay, many people attempted to profit from the familiarity and cachet of the "Montessori" name.

The Association Montessori Internationale (AMI), the organization established by Montessori herself to oversee the integrity of her work, openly expresses its concern over the uncontrolled dissemination and loose interpretation of Montessori's ideas on their website:

"Since the beginning, Montessori pedagogy has been appropriated, interpreted, misinterpreted, exploited, propagated, torn to shreds and the shreds magnified into systems, reconstituted, used, abused and disabused, gone into oblivion and undergone multiple renaissances."

As teachers from many countries carried her ideas back to their homelands, national organizations were established, many of which evolved independently of a continued close association with Montessori and her closest circle of colleagues. The United States is a perfect example.

Montessori made two extended trips to America, the first in 1913 and the second in 1915. The reception that she received must have been gratifying. Montessori was greeted by attentive crowds wherever she spoke. Her first book about the work in Rome, *The Montessori Method,* was translated into English by her American sponsor, C.W. McClure, publisher of the enormously popular *McClure's Magazine*. She was strongly encouraged to allow her work to be translated by the president and faculty of Harvard University, to whom she dedicated the first American edition.

Rather than simply translate the original title of Montessori's book, which would have roughly translated as "Scientific Education in the Children's Houses (Communities) of Rome," C.W. McClure chose to give the book a title that was much more succinct, but quite different in perspective: *The Montessori Method*. The term has stuck for the last ninety-plus years in the United States and abroad.

During her visit, the first formal Montessori society, the Montessori Educational Association, was founded by Alexander Graham Bell, among many other nationally prominent supporters.

When Montessori returned to America in 1915, she arranged to have an entire class work in a special "schoolhouse" made of glass at the Panama-Pacific International Exposition in San Francisco. It attracted worldwide attention and publicity, as the children went about their tasks under the scrutiny of thousands of visitors from around the world.

Dr. Montessori also conducted a teacher training course in California and addressed the annual conventions of both the National Education Association and the International Kindergarten Union. That year a bill was introduced into the United States Congress to appropriate funds to establish several teacher education colleges across America to prepare educators to introduce the Montessori approach to American public schools. The one condition was that Montessori make her home in the United States, an offer that she graciously declined, remarking that her findings could never belong to just one country but must be introduced around the world.

Ultimately, her mother's untimely death and the intensified disruption to normal travel caused by World War I, led Dr. Montessori to leave America for Europe. In addition, Professor William Heard Kilpatrick published a scathing critique of her ideas entitled, "The Montessori System Examined." In it, he inaccurately accused her of being rigid and outdated in her psychological theories. Kilpatrick, a colleague of the highly popular American educational reformer, Dr. John Dewey of the University of Chicago, had a significant effect, leading many initially enthusiastic supporters back to the Progressive Education Movement led by Dewey.

Progressive Education, in turn, declined as America moved away from a child-centered perspective to a basic-skills focus, during the hard years of the Depression and Second World War.

Montessori was outraged at what she felt were false assertions made about her ideas by Dewey, Kilpatrick, and others. Whatever the true cause, over the next fifteen years, Montessori's influence in America slowly ebbed from its peak in 1920, when there were more than one thousand Montessori schools in America to the period from 1930 to the late 1950s, when only a handful of Montessori schools quietly worked without openly using her name.

In 1960, Nancy McCormick Rambusch, an American mother who had spent two years in Europe studying Montessori education, was given the support of the Association Montessori Internationale (AMI) to organize a

(Below) Although you will not find rows of desks in a Montessori classroom, you will find comfortable, child-sized furniture. In this photo, two elementary students enjoy the companionship of working together.

Most classrooms have quiet, cozy spaces, where children can read or think.

branch of the Association in the United States. The group that she founded was the American Montessori Society (AMS), which originally operated under the auspices of the AMI central office in Holland.

A teacher preparation program began at the Whitby School in Greenwich, Connecticut. Thanks to the untiring efforts of McCormick Rambusch, the American media became fascinated with the Montessori approach all over again. Determined to develop a specifically American interpretation of Montessori's work, differences over practice and policy eventually led the two organizations (AMS and AMI) to separate.

Montessori's Later Years in Europe and India

After Dr. Montessori left the United States, she eventually moved to Barcelona, Spain, where a liberal and enlightened provincial government was setting out the ideas that eventually blossomed into the Republic of Spain before the Spanish Civil War. She established an international training center and research institute in Barcelona in 1916.

In 1919, Montessori began a series of teacher-training courses in London. During the next three decades, she and her colleagues refined the Elementary Montessori program and began to open classes for older children across Europe.

That same year, she was invited to give a series of lectures on the issue of education for the young adult (secondary). These talks, later published as the *Erdkinder Essays*, reflected a strong theoretical basis for her thoughts about the reform of secondary education; however, she was not to develop them herself during her lifetime. Others did pursue this path, and the first secondary schools following the Montessori approach opened in the Netherlands in the 1930s. Today, after many years of fits and starts, Montessori Secondary programs have begun to be established around the world. (See the section on Montessori Secondary education, which begins on page 147.)

In 1929, Dr. Montessori was invited by Italian dictator Benito Mussolini to introduce her ideas throughout the Italian national school system. Having left Italy after her mother's death to find a more liberal-thinking home abroad, Mussolini's invitation was irresistible to the Italian-born, self-declared citizen of the world. Montessori arrived back in Rome with much fanfare in January of 1930 and re-established her teacher-training center.

It is fascinating to consider what each of the two, liberal Maria Montessori and fascist Benito Mussolini, were thinking. He certainly sought to add Montessori's worldwide acclaim to the glories of the modern Italy. We assume that she believed that she could quietly do her work without getting involved in politics. Ultimately, the two clashed publicly when Mussolini demanded that all students in Italy join the Young

Fascists and wear a special student uniform. In 1934, she was forced into exile once again, returning to Barcelona, Spain.

The years leading to World War II were tumultuous for Maria Montessori, who was then sixty-six years old. In 1936, as the Spanish Civil War broke out across Spain, she escaped the fighting on a British cruiser sent to rescue British nationals. She traveled to the Netherlands, where she opened a new Montessori teacher education center and lab school.

As war approached, many urged her to leave Europe, and in 1938 she accepted an invitation to conduct a series of teacher training courses in India. When India entered World War II as part of the British Empire, Montessori and her son, Mario, were interned as "enemy aliens." She was, however, allowed to continue her work and over the next few years trained more than ten thousand teachers in India and Sri Lanka.

It was during this period that she wrote several of her most important works, including: *The Absorbent Mind; Education and Peace;* and *To Educate the Human Potential*. Having spent years educating teachers to grasp the "big picture" of the interdependency of all life on earth, she reflected on the global conflict and humankind's ultimate place within the universe, distilling them into her Cosmic Curriculum: The Lessons in Science, History, and Human Culture that has offered generations of Montessori students a sense of wonder and inspiration.

Returning to Europe after the end of the war, during her final years, Montessori became an even more passionate advocate of Peace Education. Maria Montessori died in 1952 at her home in the Netherlands. In her last years, she was honored with many awards and was nominated for the Nobel Peace Prize in 1949, 1950, and 1951.

Montessori was a brilliant student of child development, and the approach that has evolved out of her research has stood the test for nearly one hundred years in Montessori schools around the world. During her lifetime, Dr. Montessori was acknowledged as one of the world's leading educators.

Mainstream education, however, moved on, adapting only those elements of Montessori's work that fit into existing theories and methods. Ironically, the Montessori approach is not designed to be implemented as a series of piecemeal reforms. It requires a complete restructuring of the school and the teacher's role.

Today there is a growing consensus among many psychologists and developmental educators that Montessori's ideas were decades ahead of their time. Only recently, as our understanding of child development has grown, have we rediscovered how clear and sensible her insight was.

As the movement gains support and begins to spread into the American public school sector, one can readily say that the "Montessori Way" is a remarkably modern approach.

> *"Supposing I said there was a planet without schools or teachers, study was unknown, and yet the inhabitants — doing nothing but living and walking about — came to know all things, to carry in their minds the whole of learning: would you not think I was romancing? Well, just this, which seems so fanciful as to be nothing but the invention of a fertile imagination, is a reality. It is the child's way of learning. This is the path he follows. He learns everything without knowing he is learning it, and in doing so passes little from the unconscious to the conscious, treading always in the paths of joy and love."*
>
> — Dr. Maria Montessori

(Below) Older Montessori students often participate in seminars, more often seen at the university level than in a typical elementary or secondary school.

THE MONTESSORI WAY

The Montessori Philosophy

Over the last century, Dr. Maria Montessori's ideas have had a growing influence on education around the world. However, while individual elements of her program find their way into more classrooms every year, there is a cumulative impact when schools fully implement the entire Montessori model. When done well, something that is quite distinct for children is possible. Montessori schools are designed to help each student discover and fully develop her unique talents and possibilities. They treat each child as a unique individual, allowing her to learn optimally at her own pace and in the way that best suits her learning style. They strive to be flexible and creative in addressing each student's needs.

Learning the right answers may get a child through school, but learning how to become a life-long, independent learner will take her anywhere. Montessori teaches children to think, not simply to memorize, feed back, and forget.

Rather than present students with right answers, Montessori educators lead students to ask their own questions and to discover how to find the answers for themselves. Older students are encouraged to do their own research, analyze what they have found, and come to their own conclusions. Teachers encourage children to think for themselves and become actively engaged in the learning process.

Core Values

Today there are more than four thousand Montessori schools in North America. Each one is unique. There are variations in size, facilities, programs, and emotional climate. Within a school, each class may look and feel quite different from the others, reflecting the interests and personalities of the teacher; however, certain values will be found in all schools that are honestly following the Montessori approach.

Montessori schools are child centered and deeply respect children as unique individuals. All school activities are guided by a vision of complete development — cognitive, social, emotional, physical, and spiritual.

Taken together, a core set of values guides the daily practices of an "authentic" Montessori school.* These values must be shared by the entire school community and include:

- Children are intrinsically motivated, and they will succeed when their learning activities incorporate movement and opportunities for independence.
- Children will become self-disciplined when they are empowered to choose learning activities designed for specific developmental and learning needs.
- Each classroom is a respectful community of mixed-age learners.
- Classrooms and other school spaces are learning environments prepared with curriculum and materials.
- Teachers are educated and certified as Montessori teachers.
- Parents understand and support the purposes of the school; they are partners.

*Excerpted from *The Authentic American Montessori School: A Guide to the Self-Study, Evaluation, and Accreditation of American Schools Committed to Montessori Education* by Dr. Nancy McCormick Rambusch and Dr. John Stoops, published in 1992 by the Commission on Elementary Schools of the Middle States Association of Colleges and Schools and the American Montessori Society.

Intrinsic Motivation

One of Montessori's key discoveries is the idea that children are intrinsically motivated. They are driven by their desire to become independent and competent beings in the world. They naturally learn and master new ideas and skills. For this reason, outside rewards are unnecessary. Outside rewards create a dependency on external motivation. Far too many children become dependent on others to define their self-image or obtain permission to follow their dreams. In the process of making independent choices and exploring concepts largely on their own, Montessori children construct knowledge, their own sense of individual identity, and their own understandings of moral right and wrong.

Montessori saw children as far more than scholars. In her view, each child is a full and complete human being, the mother or father of the adult man or woman he or she will become. Even when very young, the child shares humankind's hopes, dreams, fears, emotions, and longings. From her perspective, this goes beyond mental health to the very core of one's inner spiritual life. Montessori programs offer consciously designed experiences that cultivate the child's sense of independence, self-respect, love of peace, passion for self-chosen work done well, and the ability to respect and celebrate the individual spirit within people of all ages and the value of all life.

Independence and Movement: Acquiring Self-Discipline

Montessori teachers share a conviction that success in school is directly tied to the degree to which children believe they are capable, independent human beings. Young children are shown how to pour liquids, write letters, and compute sums. Older children are shown research techniques, Internet search routines, and forms of expository writing. When children develop a meaningful degree of independence, they set a pattern for a lifetime of good work habits, self-discipline, and a sense of responsibility.

Children readily take pride in doing things for themselves carefully and well. All children learn through movement. They must actively explore and examine the world around them. Montessori environments encourage children to move about freely, within reasonable limits of appropriate behavior.

Much of the time they select work that captures their interest and attention, although teachers also help them choose activities that will present new challenges and new areas of inquiry. Montessori teachers also direct students to master the basic skills of their culture.

Children learn by doing, and this requires movement and spontaneous investigation. Children touch and explore everything in their environment. The mind is handmade, because through movement and touch, the child investigates, manipulates, and builds up a storehouse of impressions about the physical world around her. Children develop thinking through hands-on learning.

Montessori children enjoy considerable freedom of movement and choice. Montessori children freely move about, work alone, or with others at will. However, their freedom always exists within carefully defined limits on the range of their behavior. Free to do anything appropriate within the ground rules of the community, children are consistently redirected promptly and firmly if they cross over the line. Children may select an activity and work with it as long as they

If they knew the words, even very young children would declare: "Help me learn to do it for myself!"

wish, so long as they do not disturb anyone or damage anything. When finished, they are expected to put materials back where they belong. Becoming self-disciplined is a major goal of Montessori programs. Students are taught to manage their own community, and they develop strong leadership skills and independence.

Respectful Communities of Mixed-Age Groups

Montessori schools are warm and supportive communities of students, teachers, and parents. As children grow older and more capable, they assume a greater role in helping to care for the environment and meet the needs of younger children in the class. The focus is less on the teachers and more on the entire community of children and adults, much as one finds in a real family. A child experiences courtesy and trust, two important aspects for optimal learning conditions.

The number of students in a Montessori class is determined by: the physical size of the classroom; regulations governing children-to-adult ratios; and the beliefs of the school community. Originally, Montessori enrolled more than forty-five children in a classroom. Her purpose for this was to insure that her teachers would help children become capable, independent learners, children who would also turn to one another for lessons and guidance.

Classrooms today are typically much smaller (usually twenty-five to thirty-five), bringing children together in multi-age groups, rather than classes comprised of just one grade level. Schools that place children together into small groups assume that the teacher is the source of instruction, a very limited resource. They reason that as the number of children decreases, the time that teachers have to spend with each child increases. Ideally, we would have a one-on-one tutorial situation. But the best teacher of a three-year-old is often another child who is just a little bit older and has mastered a skill. This process is good for both the tutor and the younger child. In this situation, the teacher is not the primary focus. Instead, a larger group size puts the focus less on the adult and encourages children to learn from each other. By having enough children in each age group, all students will find others at their developmental level.

By consciously bringing children together in a group that is large enough to allow for two-thirds of the children to return every year, the school environment promotes continuity and the development of a very different level of relationship among children and their peers, as well as among children and their teachers. Classes tend to be stable communities, with only the oldest third moving on to the next level each year.

A strong community develops as teachers and children create close and

(Below) A class involved in the **Silence Game**.

MONTESSORI PROGRAMS

The levels usually found in a Montessori school correspond to the developmental stages of childhood:

▲ Infant (birth through eighteen months);
▲ Toddler (eighteen months to age three);
▲ Early Childhood (age three to six);
▲ Lower Elementary (age six to nine);
▲ Upper Elementary (age nine to eleven);
▲ Middle School (age eleven to thirteen); and
▲ High School (age fourteen to eighteen).

At each level, the program and curriculum are logical and highly consistent extensions of what has come before.

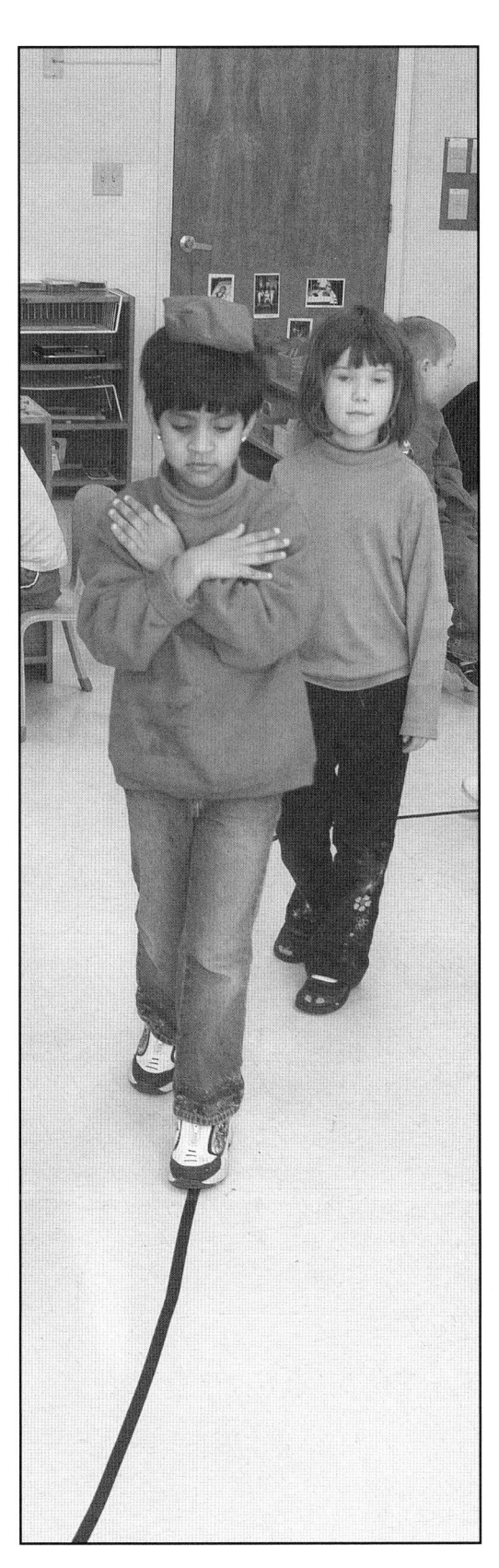

long-term relationships. Teachers know each child's temperament, personality, and learning style. Ideally, there would be an equal number of girls and boys evenly divided among the three age levels.

With the strong emphasis on international education, many Montessori schools attract a diverse student body representing many ethnic, religious, and international backgrounds. The curriculum is international in its heritage and focus and consciously seeks to promote a global perspective, promoting mutual respect. The intent is for children to regard diversity as a call for celebration and not a cause for fear. Older students learn to care about others through community service. The Montessori Peace Education curriculum supports this purpose.

Montessori's spiritual perspective leads Montessori schools to make a conscious effort to organize programs of community service, ranging from daily contributions to others within the class or school setting to community-outreach programs that allow children and adults to make a difference in the lives of others. The fundamental idea is one of stewardship. Students also develop a love for the natural world. Natural science and outdoor education are important elements of our children's experience.

(Left) Walking on the Line

This child is walking along a line on the floor, stepping carefully heel to toe, with a pillow balanced on his head. Many exercises at the early childhood level help children to develop control of their hands and large muscles.

The Prepared Environment: Curriculum and Materials

Montessori classrooms tend to fascinate both children and their parents. They are normally bright, warm, and inviting, with an abundance of plants, animals, art, music, and books. Shelves are filled with intriguing learning materials, fascinating mathematical models, maps, charts, fossils, historical artifacts, computers, scientific apparatus, a natural-science collection, and animals that the children are raising.

Montessori classrooms are commonly referred to as *prepared environments*. Each is a learning laboratory in which the children are allowed to explore, discover, and select their own work. The independence that the child gains is not only empowering on a social and emotional basis, but it is also intrinsically involved with helping the child become comfortable and confident in her ability to master the environment, ask questions, puzzle out answers, and learn continuously instead of waiting for adult direction.

The Montessori goal is less to teach the child facts and concepts, but rather to help her fall in love with the process of focusing her complete attention on some challenge and solving its riddle with enthusiasm and joy. Work assigned by the adult rarely results in such enthusiasm and interest as does work that children freely choose for themselves.

The classroom is organized into several curriculum areas, usually including: language arts (reading, literature, grammar, creative writing, spelling, and handwriting); mathematics and geometry; everyday living skills; sensory-awareness exercises and puzzles; geography; history; science; art; music; and movement. Most rooms will include a classroom library. Each area is made up of one or more shelf units, cabinets, and work tables with a wide variety of materials on open display, ready for use as the children select them.

Students are typically found scattered around the classroom, working alone or with one or two others. They tend to become so involved in their work that visitors are immediately struck by the peaceful atmosphere. It may take a moment to spot the teachers within the environment. They will be found working with one or two children at a time, advising, presenting a new lesson, or quietly observing the class at work. The focus of activity in the Montessori classroom is on children – who each one is, his or her interests and styles of learning. The teacher is a guide, providing direct learning experiences whenever possible.

A Montessori classroom is filled with vast arrays of sequenced learning activities known as the *Montessori materials*. The materials are displayed on open shelves sized for the height of the children. They are arranged to provide maximum eye appeal without clutter. Each object has a specific place on the shelves, arranged from the upper left-hand corner in sequence to the lower right.

The materials are arranged in sequence from the most simple to the most complex, and from the most concrete to those that are more abstract. Because of the order with which they are arranged in the environment, children can find precisely what they need whenever they wish.

When children choose a material, they develop an array of personal traits such as independence, responsibility, and time management. While investigating and using the materials to sort, arrange, build connections, and problem solve, they develop cognitive capabilities. Educational theorists now advocate learning through direct experience and the process of investigation and discovery. The child must be active and engaged, constructing her or his own knowledge. Most students do not retain or truly grasp much of what they "learn" through memorization. Instead, children need to manipulate and explore everything that catches their interest. Part of Montessori's contribution was her discovery of what is now assumed. But, she went further. Montessori developed a series of sequenced learning materials designed with incredible precision.

Each material is a concrete representation of an abstract idea. Depending upon the ages of the children, they will use the materials to explore and investigate ideas found in anthropology, art, astronomy, biology, botany, chemistry, earth science, geography, geology, geometry, history, language, mathematics, music, physics, and sociology.

Some materials isolate and teach one concept or skill at a time. Length, for example, is explored by three-year-olds arranging a set of ten rods. The first is 10 centimeters long; the second is twice this length. This progression continues until the tenth rod is in place with its length of 1 meter.

Students in a Montessori Elementary classroom use length to explore the concept of geological time. The arrival that our human species occupies is represented by the last centimeter of rope, which is two city blocks long.

Montessori teachers design and adapt the classroom environment with the specific community of children in mind, modifying the selection of educational materials available, the physical layout, and the tone of the class to fit the ever-changing needs of the children. Generally, young students will work individually or in small, self-selected groups. There will be very few whole-group lessons in the early childhood and lower elementary program levels.

(Right) As often as possible, Montessori materials and furniture are made of wood with beautiful natural finishes. Here, a student traces the cursive letter *y* in fine sand.

(Above) These two elementary students compose a song on the **Tone Bars.**

Children from ages two to six are interested in sequencing and sorting objects. They are drawn to the sensory properties of objects within the classroom: size, shape, color, texture, weight, smell, sound, etc. Children of this age tend to repeat exercises. With repetition, their movements slow and become more precise. Their attention to detail increases; they discover small details in the objects and classroom as they observe and appreciate their environment. This is a key in helping children discover how to learn.

Elementary and secondary students are interested in sequencing and sorting ideas. They are drawn to the interpretive meanings of literary works, social and historic events, scientific findings, and issues of moral justice.

Elementary and secondary classrooms are designed to facilitate student discussion and stimulate collaborative learning. In group discussions, students readily propose and debate solutions to open-ended problems. A goal is to pursue topics in depth rather than to "cover the material."

At the secondary level, an integrated thematic approach is used to connect the otherwise separate disciplines of the curriculum into studies of the physical universe, the world of nature, and the human experience. Literature, the arts, history, social issues, political science, economics, science, and the study of technology all complement one another.

The organization of the Montessori curriculum from early childhood through secondary programs could be thought of as a spiral of integrated studies rather than a traditional model in which the curriculum is compartmentalized into separate subjects, with given topics considered only once at a specific grade level. The Montessori curriculum is carefully structured and integrated to demonstrate the connections among the different subject areas. History lessons, for example, link architecture, the arts, science, and technology.

An especially important aspect of the materials is that they offer multiple levels of challenge and can be used repeatedly at different developmental levels. For example, the Trinomial Cube, which presents a complex and challenging twenty-seven-piece, three-dimensional puzzle to the five-year-old, is used to introduce the older elementary and secondary child to the algebraic concept of the exponential powers of polynomials.

The teacher presents the materials with precision and offers each child an initial exploratory procedure; the child is able to imitate what the teacher did. The teacher's presentation also enables children to investigate and work independently. A goal is for the children to become self-disciplined, able to use the materials and manage the classroom without direct adult supervision.

Children progress at their own pace, moving on to the next step in each area of learning as they are ready. Initial lessons are brief introductions, after which the children repeat the exercise over many days, weeks, or months until they attain mastery. Interest leads them to explore variations and extensions inherent within the design of the materials at many levels over the years.

The Montessori learning materials are not the Method itself; they are simply tools used to guide children into logical thought and discovery. The Montessori materials are provocative and simple; each is carefully designed to appeal to children at a given level of development.

In developing these materials, Dr. Montessori carefully analyzed the skills and concepts involved in each subject and noted the sequence in which children most easily master them. She then studied how children seemed to be able to grasp abstract concepts most easily and designed each element to bring the abstract into a clear and concrete form.

(Above) Working with the **Trinomial Cube.**

The Control of Error

The design of many of the materials gives children immediate feedback. Called the *Control of Error,* this feature makes it possible for Montessori students to determine for themselves if they have done each exercise correctly.

Children choose their learning activities within carefully defined limits as to the range of their behavior. Making mistakes is a vital part of the learning process. Discovery, investigation, and problem solving involve making wrong turns, getting stuck, and trying again. An important part of the learning experience is to recognize an error and learn how to make corrections. These experiences are part of the process of becoming self-disciplined.

A young child takes ten cylinders out of a wooden case; the cylinders vary in height and diameter. The control of error lies in the construction of the objects: a cylinder can only fit into one place in the wooden case. Another child learns the names of African nations. In this case, the control of error is initially found with the teacher, who uses the "Three-Period Lesson" to teach and re-teach the correct names of nations. Once the child knows these names, the control of error becomes his own knowledge.

Each repetition is not an exact copy of the previous use. Children continuously refine their work and learn more. The principle of control of error guides this process. In addition to the design of the materials, prior knowledge is also a control of error. Knowledge of colors, shapes, and size for younger children — knowledge of addition and multiplication for older children — results with self-corrected learning.

The Three-Period Lesson

Montessori teachers will use the Three-Period Lesson to help children develop a rich vocabulary in all areas of study. Children best learn the meaning for names when they can associate the name with an object. In the following example, a young child is taught the names of secondary colors.

During the first period, the child is shown an orange-colored tablet. The teacher names the color: "This is orange." The child is now shown a green-colored tablet. The teacher names this color: "This is green." Finally, a purple-colored tablet is shown, and the teacher states, "This is purple."

During the second period, the child makes a link between the language and her own experience. The teacher gives the name, and the child finds the object. The teacher asks, "Show me orange." The child points to the orange tablet. "Show me purple." The child now points to the purple tablet.

Considerable learning and teaching occurs during the second period. If the child is asked, "Show me green," but she points to the purple tablet, the teacher simply re-teaches. Returning to the first period, the teacher points to the purple tablet and restates, "This is purple." The teacher again points to the green tablet and restates, "This is green."

In the final period, the teacher points to one of the tablets and asks, "What is this?" The child answers, "Orange." If the child answers one of the other colors, the teacher will again re-teach the colors by renaming and reconfirming them using the first- and second-period lesson formats.

Maria Montessori understood that learning occurs best when stress and apprehension are removed from the learning situation. The Three-Period Lesson format is based on readiness. Complex vocabulary words are introduced when it is appropriate. Montessori educators believe that it is important for children to learn vocabulary, which is why so much emphasis is

(Above) A one-on-one lesson in long division in a lower elementary class.

placed on *nomenclature* (enhanced vocabaulary). The three- and four-year-olds do not merely identify *triangle;* our teachers name triangles precisely: *isosceles triangle* or *scalene right triangle*. A rich vocabulary is also taught to lower elementary students; such as terms from botany as well as the various land and water forms that make up our planet's surface. The more words children know, the more they actually see around them.

Certified Montessori Teachers

Montessori classes are taught by a certified Montessori educator teaching with one or more assistants or by two Montessori teachers. Montessori teachers know how to facilitate learning, develop learning communities, and relate to children as friends and mentors. Montessori classrooms are (after the toddler year) mixed-age groups in which children and teachers are together for three years. In this kind of learning community, children enjoy a home-like experience. The daily experience of being known, along with knowing familiar teachers and other children, renders Montessori classrooms remarkably peaceful and secure learning communities.

A Montessori teacher education program is an intense process leading to certification in the infant/toddler, early childhood, elementary, and secondary levels. Montessori teacher education programs are independent institutions or found in a university's department of education. Montessori teacher education programs are normally affiliated with the American Montessori Society (AMS), the Association Montessori Internationale (AMI), or one of the other organizations accredited by the Montessori Accreditation Council for Teacher Education Commission (MACTE). As defined by the MACTE Commission, a Montessori teacher education course is a post-secondary instruction designed to:

- Develop expertise in Montessori's educational system including philosophy, teacher roles, and the design of curricula and environments;

- Assure basic knowledge of child development; and

- Lead to certification in Montessori teaching within a specific age range.

THE ROLE OF MONTESSORI TEACHERS

Dr. Montessori believed that teachers should focus on the child as a person, not on the daily lesson plan. Montessori teachers are taught to nurture and inspire the human potential, leading children to ask questions, think for themselves, explore, investigate, and discover. Our ultimate objective is to help them to learn how to learn independently, retaining the curiosity, creativity, and intelligence with which they were born. Montessori teachers do not simply present lessons; they are facilitators, mentors, coaches, and guides.

To underscore the very different role played by adults in her schools, Dr. Montessori used the title *directress* instead of *teacher*. In Italian, the word implies the role of the coordinator or administrator of an office or factory. Today, many Montessori schools prefer to call their teachers *guides*. Montessori *guides* have four principal goals:

▲ to awaken the child's spirit and imagination;
▲ to encourage the natural desire for independence and high sense of self-esteem;
▲ to help children develop the kindness, courtesy, and self-discipline that will allow them to become a full member of society; and
▲ to help children learn how to observe, question, and explore ideas independently.

So, you would like to be a Montessori teacher? Where to begin ...

Montessori parents often make the best Montessori teachers, and with the constant increase in the number of Montessori schools throughout the world, a certified Montessori teacher is in great demand.

In the Appendixes, we have listed the contact information for many of the Montessori certification societies in the United States. The Montessori Foundation's website (www. montessori.org) also provides information and links for training programs and many other resources for Montessori educators and parents.

If you are searching for a Montessori teacher training program, you might also wish to contact the Montessori schools in your area. Through them, you will obtain information as to what is available in your region and what form of certification they require — especially if you are hopeful of obtaining employment with them in the future.

There are many good teacher education programs available in the United States and abroad. In the years to come, there will undoubtedly be even more, as the demand for Montessori teachers increases.

Montessori teachers do more than present curriculum. The secret of any great teacher is to help learners focus, not on getting good grades but, instead, on developing a basic love of learning. As parents know their own children's learning styles and temperaments, teachers, too, develop a sense of each child's uniqueness by developing a relationship over a period of years with the child and her parents. The Montessori teacher recognizes that her role is not so much to teach as to inspire, mentor, and facilitate the learning process. The real work of learning belongs to the individual child. Because of this, the Montessori educator remains conscious of her role in helping each child fulfill his potential as a human being and of creating an environment for learning within which children will feel safe, cherished, and empowered.

Montessori teachers closely monitor their students' progress, keeping the level of challenge high. Because they normally work with each child for two or three years, teachers will know their students' strengths, areas for growth, interests, and anxieties extremely well. They prepare the learning environment and use the children's interests to enrich the curriculum and provide alternate avenues for accomplishment and success. Montessori teachers play several roles:

Observer: Montessori teachers are trained observers of children's learning and behavior. They record observations and determine where their students are in terms of development. This information is used by teachers to know when to intervene in a child's learning with a new lesson, a fresh challenge, or a reinforcement of basic ground rules.

An Educational Resource: Montessori teachers facilitate the learning process by serving as a resource to whom the children can turn as they pull together information, impressions, and experiences.

Role Model: Montessori teachers deliberately model the behaviors and attitudes that they are working to instill in their students. Because of Montessori's emphasis on character development, Montessori teachers normally are exceptionally calm, kind, warm, and polite to each child.

Facilitates the "Match" between the Learner and Knowledge: Montessori teachers are trained to identify the best response to the changing interests and needs of each child as a unique individual. Because they truly accept that children learn in many different ways and at their own pace, Montessori teachers understand that they must "follow the child," adjusting their strategies and timetables to fit the development of each of their pupils.

Environmental Designer: Montessori teachers organize appropriate social settings and academic programs for children at their own level of development. They do this to a large degree through the design of the classroom, selection and organization of learning activities, and structure of the day.

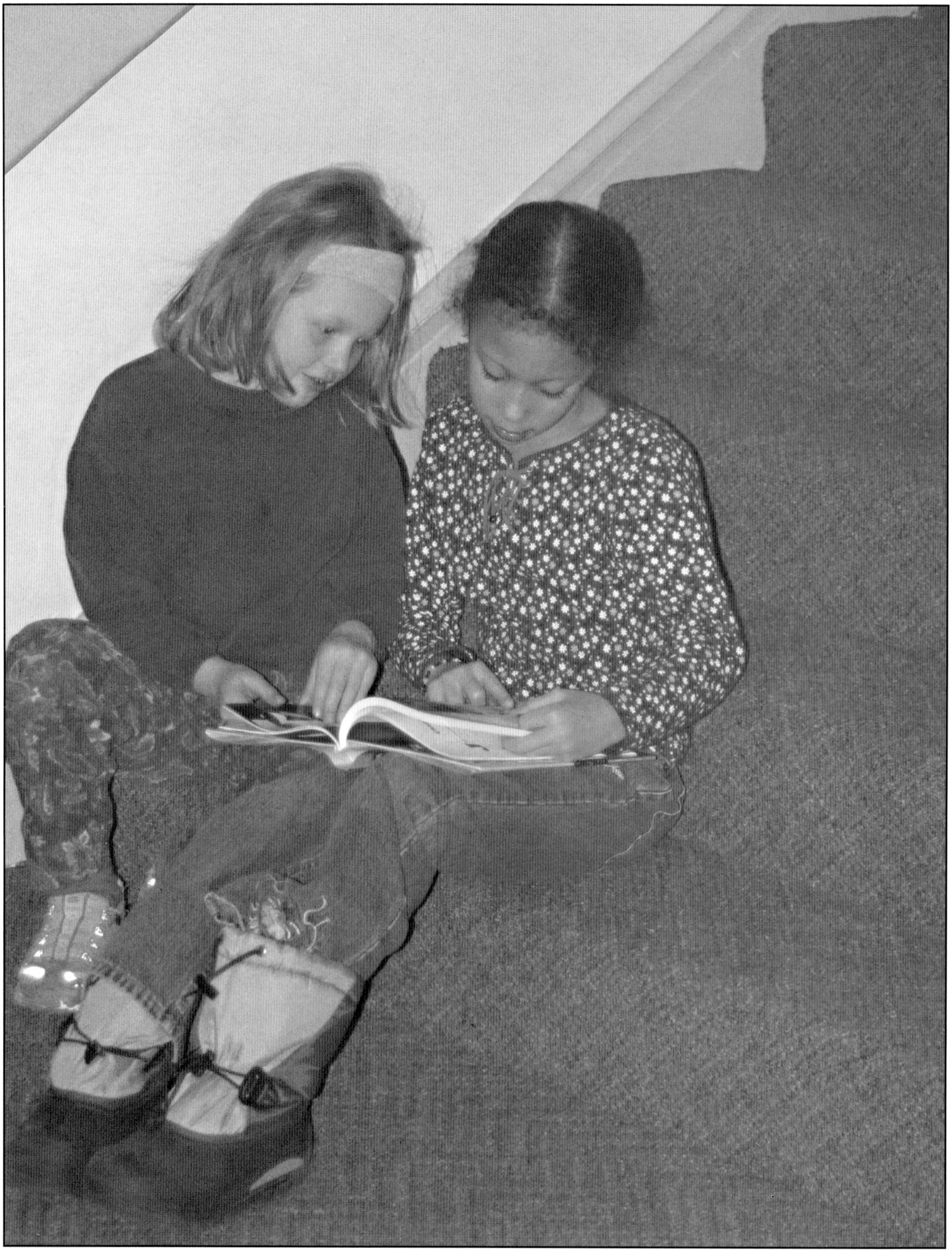

SECTION 2

MONTESSORI PROGRAMS

THE PLANES OF DEVELOPMENT
SENSITIVE PERIODS
THE METHOD OF OBSERVATION
THE NORMALIZED CHILD
A GUIDED TOUR OF EARLY CHILDHOOD &
ELEMENTARY MONTESSORI CLASSROOMS
MONTESSORI FOR THE KINDERGARTEN YEAR
ELEMENTARY PROGRAMS
MIDDLE AND HIGH SCHOOL PROGRAMS
INFANT-TODDLER PROGRAMS
MONTESSORI IN THE HOME FOR THE YOUNG CHILD
LEARNERS WITH EXCEPTIONALITIES

Montessori Programs

During a typical Montessori school day, children's developmental needs and learning characteristics are met while they engage in their learning activities. Montessori noted through her research that children's needs, interests, and abilities group into specific "planes of development."

A plane of development is a specific growth phase. Montessori taught teachers to design school classrooms to meet the needs and interests of children in each growth phase. Montessori also taught teachers to "follow the child" through careful observation. Through observation, teachers attend to each child's learning approaches, strengths and weaknesses, and interests and anxieties. The teacher next uses this information to prepare learning environments and learning activities that facilitate the development of each child's potential.

The Planes of Development

A plane of development is a specific phase of growth. Montessori educators typically talk about the first, second and third planes of development, corresponding to the ages birth to six; six to twelve; and twelve to eighteen. A fourth plane of development, from age eighteen to twenty-four years of age, is not of direct concern to this book but comprises the last stage of the journey from birth to adult maturity.

Because the specific characteristics of each plane is different from the others, Montessori referred to a child's development as a series of "rebirths," and she believed that schools should not be divided by grades (kindergarten, first, second, and so on) but according to each plane. For this reason, Montessori schools consist of mixed-age groupings divided into early childhood, elementary, and secondary programs.

Dr. Montessori's study of children led her to conclude that child development is not linear. Children do not, in other words, develop in a

---

(Below) An Early Childhood Montessori classroom.

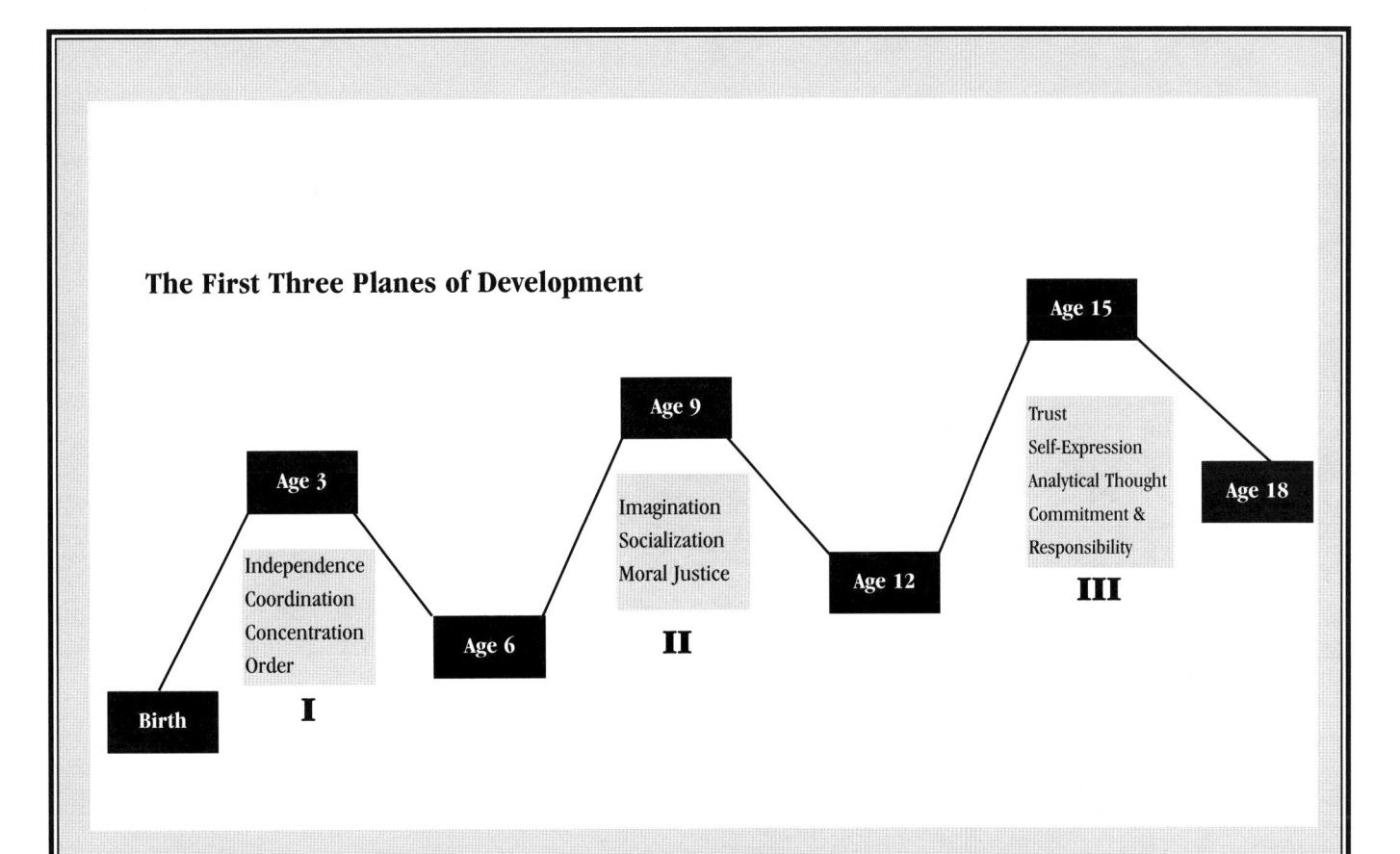

The First Three Planes of Development

- **Birth** → **Age 3**: Independence, Coordination, Concentration, Order — **I**
- **Age 3** → **Age 6** → **Age 9**: Imagination, Socialization, Moral Justice — **II**
- **Age 9** → **Age 12** → **Age 15**: Trust, Self-Expression, Analytical Thought, Commitment & Responsibility — **III**
- **Age 15** → **Age 18**

continual progression; instead, there are predominant years of attainment (as indicated by the rising line on the diagram) followed by predominant years of refinement (indicated by the falling line) within a period of approximately six years. However, the diagram should not be interpreted to mean that children do not attain new understandings and capabilities during periods of refinement. Instead, Montessori proposed that there is an overall tendency for attainment during the first three years followed by a tendency for refinement during the second three years.

Montessori educators teach in partnership with children. It is a partnership based on a guiding trust — a trust that each child will show us when she or he is ready to learn the next skill or concept. The fact that children are only ready when they are ready is well known by parents. Unless there is a developmental challenge, parents are usually not concerned with the particular day their sons or daughters first learned to walk and talk. If walking happened on a Monday, instead of a Wednesday, during the ninth month, rather than the tenth, parents may be proud.

Learning to read, however, can be a different matter. Parents may have an expectation for their children to begin reading before they turn five. It would be much simpler to educate children if learning to read, write, and compute arithmetic took place according to a specific schedule such as "in kindergarten," "in first grade," and so on. Children do, however, follow their own schedule. Despite national, state, and local performance standards and requirements for teacher accountability, learning to read, write, and compute arithmetic will occur only when the child is ready. Learning to balance and ride a two-wheel bicycle will only occur when the child is ready.

A fundamental Montessori principle is to respect each child as a real person. Respect includes expressing regard and esteem. Respect also involves honoring each child's readiness for learning. Children do not usually tell us when they are ready; instead, children respond to specially prepared learning environments. Montessori teachers are trained to prepare these environments and to observe for developmental signals that indicate readiness.

During each plane of development, children share similar inclinations. Each compels or focuses the child. Montessori discovered when children are empowered to follow their developmental inclinations, learning to read, write, and compute arithmetic will most likely take place.

During the years of the First Plane of Development, children develop independence, coordination, concentration, order and self-discipline. During the Second Plane of Development, a new set of characteristics becomes more predominant for elementary-aged children, including: exploring the natural and social worlds through imagination; engaging in learning and other social situations; and understanding moral justice. During the Third Plane of Development, adolescents engage in developing trust, using new forms of self-expression, exercising new ways of thinking, forming relationships involving commitment and responsibilities, and forming personal gender identities.

Montessori did not theorize the characteristics of each developmental plane. She wrote instead, "I must repeat that it is not that I first proposed these principles and then shaped my educational method around them. To the contrary, only the immediate observation of children whose freedom was respected revealed some of the laws of their inner being that I understand to be of universal value."

The First Plane of Development: Rapid growth and development take place during the first six years of life. From considerable dependence to independence, young children learn to feed themselves, walk, run, and ride bicycles. Infants, toddlers, and combined three-to-six-year-olds are the three Montessori classroom groups.

Young children are frequently heard to say, "I can do it!" Indeed, independence, helping a child do it for herself, is a key Montessori principle. In the classroom, children choose learning activities or materials to work with and explore.

Each activity is a set of age-appropriate materials specifically designed to attract a child's interest and attention. The materials are child sized, permitting success; for example, small pitchers for pouring. While children work with the learning materials, they satisfy their natural tendency to learn through movement. Repetitive movement results with children strengthening their muscular coordination.

Curiously, while young children develop coordination, their concentration lengthens from several minutes to more than an hour. As this occurs, the child's movements become slower, more precise, and controlled. The child becomes more ordered or self-disciplined.

The Second Plane of Development: Achieving independence, coordination, concentration, and order continue throughout life. Elementary children, six to twelve years old, take on several additional concerns. Montessori characterized the Second Plane of Development as the "metamorphic age." The body of the elementary child strengthens, and the mind is propelled with tremendous imagination and wonderment.

Whereas three- and four-year-old children readily pretend that a chair is a car, the elementary child wants to know the reasons for things. "Which is hotter?" asked a six-year-old. "The sun or a volcano?"

Younger children find what they need in carefully prepared classrooms. The elementary child, by contrast, is no longer content with only these surroundings. She, instead, requires going out into the world both to discover and understand it and to find her place in it.

The elementary curriculum is vast and includes, for example, grammar, literature, arithmetic computations, properties of geometry, techniques of laboratory science, principles of ecology, and lessons of cultural history. Elementary children prefer to learn and work together socially. They also become aware of moral values.

At first, a seven-year-old may complain that is it not fair that someone else got a turn or received something. Later, there is a concern for greater social injustices. Now nine or ten, the child may complain that is not fair that there are homeless or hungry people or that there is pollution.

Children in upper elementary (nine-to-twelve classes) are in an age of solidification and refinement; they pursue, in depth, topics which hold great interest to them.

The Third Plane of Development: By comparison with children who are ten or eleven, the young adolescent enters into a new developmental beginning. Individuals during this time of life may grow rapidly or gradually; often girls reach their adult height before boys. Cognitive and emotional development may take longer than physical growth. During the adolescent years, the child's cognitive capabilities begin to mature and become more similar to that of an adult.

Young children learn through movement; a pedagogical key is to help these children develop coordination. Elementary-aged children learn, in part, through imagination. At this age, one key is to offer holistic models of events on a larger scale. Young adolescents also require movement and can display tremendous imagination as well as great humor. They also prefer conversation; a key is to provide opportunities for them to design and implement personally meaningful and socially contributing experiences.

The young adolescent begins to understand interdependence — relationships of integrity and reliability involving trust, honesty, and commitment. These relationships involve learning to be responsible. Part of the Montessori experience is to help young adolescents plan and complete contributive experiences such as internships and service learning.

Montessori called children of the Third Plane the "earth children." She envisioned a farm setting as the prepared environment for young adolescents to mature safely. Montessori wrote, "There are two needs of the adolescent: for protection during the time of the difficult physical transition, and for an understanding of the society which he or she is about to enter to play his or her part as an adult." Although there are a few Montessori farm schools, most programs for adolescents are located in school buildings and offer academic studies involving interdisciplinary, thematic instruction with land-based learning, internships, and community service experiences.

Whether on a farm or in an urban setting, Montessori programs for the Third Plane of Development are guided to fulfill the compelling needs of adolescence. (See page 151 for a description of the Hershey Montessori Farm School.)

The Absorbent Mind and The Sensitive Periods

Montessori discovered two important characteristics of children before they reach the age of six. She called these the "absorbent mind" and the "sensitive periods." Unlike other mammals born with genetic programming for how to survive, human children begin with certain genetic predispositions and must also intentionally invent themselves through learning.

A child explores and interacts with an environment of people, other life forms, and things. Montessori believed children's explorations are guided by a set of innate sensitive periods in which children are predisposed to explore. Making sense of everything she or he has discovered is guided by the phenomenon of the absorbent mind.

Between birth until about the age of three, children unconsciously absorb sensory input from the environment. The absorption of sensory input forms connections between brain-cell neurons. In other words, children explore and form themselves.

The idea of the absorbent mind explains language acquisition. Infants, without the arduous study of language required by adults, become fluent. Infants hear language and/or observe sign language, and they naturally begin to talk or sign.

Sensitive Periods

Montessori believed in a necessary relationship between children and their environments. Children must find a properly prepared environment if they are to fully develop their unique human potentials. By analogy, consider the story of *Goldilocks and the Three Bears*. Goldilocks wandered off into the forest, despite warnings and admonishments from her parents to never ever leave home without their permission. Goldilocks, now very lost, arrived at the threshold of an inviting cottage-like house and (again, without permission) walked inside. Greeted by three bowls of porridge, a hungry and tired Goldilocks tasted the first one. It was too cold. The second was too hot. But the third was "just right."

Goldilocks next walked into the living room and tried each of three chairs. The first was too hard, the second too soft, and the third was "just right." Finally, she found her way to the bedroom of three beds, where the third was also "just right." This idea is the connection between Goldilocks and Montessori. In Montessori's Early Childhood programs, teachers are charged with providing learning environments in which everything is "just right."

Everything! Food, furniture, learning activities, social relations, clothing, routines, and rituals must all be "just right" in order for each young child to develop her or his fullest potential. No one knows what motivated Goldilocks to wander off into the forest. But for almost one hundred years, Montessori educators have observed a set of motivations shared by young children around the world.

What Dr. Maria Montessori discovered in the St. Lorenz Quarter in 1907 was that children are self-motivated to learn from their environment. Borrowing ideas from biologists and philosophers of her day, Montessori proposed that each child carries within himself his potential for physical and cognitive development.

In addition to determining the child's eventual height, hair color, and other physical characteristics, there is another cognitive plan which determines the unique emotional and intellectual qualities of each child. These qualities develop through what Montessori referred to as "the sensitive periods."

Each sensitive period is a specific kind of compulsion, motivating a young child to seek objects and relationships in his or her environment with which to fulfill his or her special and unique inner potentials. These cannot be directly known.

The young child is neither consciously aware of nor capable of directly communicating his or her potentials. Nevertheless, Montessori believed that each child will develop to his or her full human potential when everything in the environment is "just right."

Each sensitive period is:

- A period of special sensibility and psychological attitudes.
- An overpowering force, interest, or impetus directing the child to particular qualities and elements in the environment.
- A period of time during which the child centers his or her attention on specific aspects of the environment, to the exclusion of all else.
- A passion and a commitment.
- Derived from the unconscious and leads the child to conscious and creative activities.
- Intense and prolonged activity which does not lead to fatigue or boredom but instead leads to persistent energy and interest.
- A transitory state once realized, the sensitive period disappears.
- Never relived or regained, once passed.

Sensitive Periods

From Birth to Age Six

Dr. Montessori identified eleven different sensitive periods occurring from birth through age six. Each refers to a predisposition compelling the child to acquire specific characteristics as described below. When Montessori teachers speak about children being "inner directed," they are referring to an inner compulsion or sensitive period. A Montessori teacher would say, for example, "The child is in her sensitive period for order." These phrases point to each child's predisposition to follow her own daily classroom routine in which she chooses the same materials and in the same sequence. Ages of the onset and conclusion of each sensitive period are approximate and are indicated after the general description.

1. **Movement** — Random movements become coordinated and controlled: grasping, touching, turning, balancing, crawling, walking. (birth – one)

2. **Language** — Use of words to communicate: a progression from babble to words to phrases to sentences, with a continuously expanding vocabulary and comprehension. (birth – six)

3. **Small Objects** — A fixation on small objects and tiny details. (one – four)

4. **Order** — Characterized by a desire for consistency and repetition and a passionate love for established routines. Children can become deeply disturbed by disorder. The environment must be carefully ordered with a place for everything and with carefully established ground rules. (two – four)

5. **Music** — Spontaneous interest in and the development of pitch, rhythm, and melody. (two – six)

6. **Grace & Courtesy** — Imitation of polite and considerate behavior leading to an internalization of these qualities into the personality. (two – six)

7. **Refinement of the Senses** — Fascination with sensorial experiences (taste, sound, touch, weight, smell) resulting with the child learning to observe and with making increasingly refined sensorial discriminations. (two – six)

8. **Writing** — Fascination with the attempt to reproduce letters and numbers with pencil or pen and paper. Montessori discovered that writing precedes reading. (three – four)

9. **Reading** — Spontaneous interest in the symbolic representations of the sounds of each letter and in the formation of words. (three – five)

10. **Spatial Relationships** — Forming cognitive impressions about relationships in space, including the layout of familiar places. Children become more able to find their way around their neighborhoods, and they are increasingly able to work complex puzzles. (four – six)

11. **Mathematics** — Formation of the concepts of quantity and operations from the uses of concrete material aids. (four – six)

Note: Montessori identified additional sensitive periods that the elementary-aged child and the adolescent pass through on the road to adulthood. These are not discussed here at this time.

Montessori Programs

Children explore their classrooms, seeking and discovering objects and exercises which satisfy the compulsions of their sensitive periods. The sensitive period of order, for example, compels children to sort and sequence objects into just the right places. Younger children might choose the knobbed cylinders, pink cubes, or red rods. The sensitive period for order compels children to insist that events take place in exactly the right sequence. Parents of toddlers know that their children react loudly whenever anything is out of sequence or order. In *The Secret of Childhood*, Montessori wrote:

"A child's different inner sensibilities enable him to choose from his complex environment what is suitable and necessary for his growth. They make the child sensitive to some things but leave him indifferent to others. When a particular sensitiveness is aroused in a child, he is like a light that shines on some objects but not on others, making of them his whole world. It is not simply a question of having an intense desire for certain situations or certain things. Within the child there is a unique potentiality for using these objects for his own growth, since it is during the sensitive period that he makes his [cognitive] adjustments like that of being able to adapt himself to his environment or to move about with ever-increasing ease and precision."

If the environment does not contain what the child seeks, Montessori believed that the child would not obtain his or her full potential. The child's personality would become permanently stunted.

In addition to the environment being prepared with just the right objects, the environment must also be prepared at just the right time. Each sensitive period has its own beginning and ending, beginning and ending in its own time. This idea was powerfully expressed in Nikos Kazantzaki's novel *Zorba the Greek*:

"I remember one morning when I discovered a cocoon in the bark of a tree just as the butterfly was making a hole in its case and preparing to come out. I waited awhile but it was too long appearing and I was impatient. I bent over it and breathed on it to warm it. I warmed it as quickly as I could and the miracle began to happen before my eyes — faster than life. The case opened, the butterfly started slowly crawling out, and I shall never forget the horror when I saw how its wings were folded back and crumpled.

The wretched butterfly tried with its whole trembling body to unfold them. Bending over it, I tried to help it with my breath, in vain. It needed to be hatched out patiently, and the unfolding of the wings should have been a gradual process in the sun. Now it was too late. My breath had forced the butterfly to appear — all crumpled — before its time. It struggled desperately and a few seconds later died in the palm of my hand.

That little body I believe is the greatest weight I have on my conscience, for I realize today that it is a sin to violate the great laws of nature. We should not hurry. We should not be impatient, but we should confidently obey the eternal rhythm."

Early Childhood Montessori practice is largely based on the idea of sensitive periods, and teachers observe carefully for their presence as each child develops. The eleven sensitive periods have been observed in children from all socioeconomic backgrounds as well as in a large number of cultures, including (by co-author Paul Epstein) children living in an arctic town in Sweden, the slums of Brazil, and a mountain village in Nepal.

MONTESSORI PROGRAMS

Montessori teachers work with three powerful tools:

The first is their knowledge of child development and the sensitive periods.

The second is knowing how to prepare the classroom environment so that each sensitive period is satisfied.

The third is knowing how to observe.

Montessori Teachers Use Several Principles to Prepare a Classroom Environment ...

The Principle of Freedom: Children freely choose their own "work" — learning activities — based on their currently active inner sensitive period. But freedom is not a free-for-all. Instead, the principle here is that of freedom within limits. The Montessori teacher understands that for young children, freedom is an accomplishment of the development of inner self-discipline. Self-discipline is understood to be a result of succeeding independently of others. In other words, adults must never do for the child anything that the child can learn to perform for him or herself. Instead, the adult must protect each child's choice by ensuring that the child will be able to work with the chosen learning materials without interruption or interference from other children.

Beauty: Each learning activity is complete; everything needed is present and in good repair. Objects placed in the classroom are attractive and elegant, designed to attract the child's interest and attention.

Contact with Nature and Reality: The classroom objects also represent reality and nature. Children use real sinks and refrigerators instead of play ones. Because in real life everyone does not have the same thing at the same time, there is only one piece of material instead of multiple sets. Dr. Montessori taught that a child's direct contact with nature results with understanding and appreciating order and harmony. The Montessori classroom environment is a place of life. Children learn to take care of plants, animals, and fish. Magnifying glasses, microscopes, and simple experiments are available for children to observe and learn from nature.

50

The Method of Observation

Often people think of the Montessori materials as "The Montessori Method." The Montessori materials are, however, the *result* of the Method. The Method is *observation*.

Montessori taught that the purpose for observation is to assist children's growth and development. To accomplish this purpose, teachers engage in a process known as "scientific pedagogy." Teachers observe and then prepare the classroom environment with appropriate learning materials and activities.

According to Montessori philosophy, young children engage in specific patterns of behavior to explore and learn about their world. Described as the "sensitive periods," young children do not directly talk about these patterns of behavior. The task of the teacher is to discern each child's needs and interests as they explore the classroom.

Montessori teachers observe children's exploratory patterns of behavior with an implication of trust and respect. Teachers trust that a child will "know" and pursue what she or he most needs in order to become an adult. An often heard expression of this Montessori principle of trust is, "follow the child." Each child will explore that which interests him or her. Montessori once spoke to parents about children's interests and suggested:

"Those of us who have tried to learn the ways of childhood from children (instead of from our own ideas) have been amazed at the discoveries we have made. And there is one point on which we all agree – children live in a world of their own interests. The work they do there must be respected, for though many childish activities may seem pointless to grown-ups, nature is using them for her own ends. She is building mind and character as well as bone and muscle. The greatest help you can give your children is freedom to go about their work in their own way, for in this matter your child knows better than you."

Observing interests also applies to teachers of children in the elementary and secondary programs. The task of observation involves discovering and respecting children's pursuits of their interests, for each is following their needs in order to grow and mature.

Older children typically talk about and identify their interests; younger children may not. To discover the interests of young children, Montessori directed teachers to observe how long a child works with or stays involved with an activity.

The teacher also observes what the child does with the learning materials. An elaborate series of recordkeeping systems may be used by teachers to record children's uses of the learning materials and their learning accomplishments. Record keeping, a necessary classroom activity is not, however, observation.

With a focus on discovering and understanding inner needs and interests, Montessori directed teachers to understand what she called the psychic or spiritual development of children. This purpose still sets Montessori education apart from many other approaches. Psychic or spiritual development is not, in terms of Montessori philosophy, a religious experience. It is, rather, the development and expression of qualities such as compassion, empathy, kindness, gentleness, and respect.

Learning how to observe these qualities requires, according to Montessori, initiation and practice. Ordinarily, we think of observation as involving perceiving or seeing. What we see makes sense to us through a process of comparing, interpreting, and reasoning.

Very young children can compare quantities. They learn, for example, that things are big because they are not small; things are bright or fast because they are not dark or slow. In Montessori Early Childhood classrooms, children sort a series of ten red rods; each successive rod is 10 centimeters longer than the previous one.

By comparing lengths, children can sort the rods from smallest to longest. For older children and adults, observation involves comparison, interpretations, and reasons; things are meaningful and make deep and rich sense. Elementary and middle school students, for example, readily interpret and debate the meaning of a passage of literature. A humorous expression of this natural capability of observation, interpretation, and reasoning is described by A. A. Milne:

> "Winnie-the-Pooh sat down at the foot of the tree, put his head between his paws and began to think.
>
> First of all he said to himself: 'That buzzing-noise means something. You don't get a buzzing noise like that, just buzzing and buzzing, without its meaning something. If there's a buzzing noise, somebody's making a buzzing noise, and the only reason for making a buzzing noise that I know of is because you're a bee.'
>
> Then he thought another long time, and said: 'And the only reason for being a bee that I know of is making honey.'
>
> And then he got up, and said: 'And the only reason for making honey is so I can eat it.' So he began to climb the tree."

To see within, however, involves a very different quality and experience of ourselves as observers. The quality of observation that Montessori teachers must aspire towards is that of intimacy, for it is during these moments that we know and are known well. Throughout her writings, Montessori indicated this experience was the purpose of observation. She described, for example, a teacher's composure while observing:

> "[A] teacher must be calm ... a deeper calm, an empty, or better, unencumbered state that is a source of inner clarity. This calm consists in a spiritual humility and intellectual purity necessary for the understanding of a child, and which, as a consequence, must be found in the teacher." (Montessori, *The Secret of Childhood*)

Montessori described a process for how teachers become skilled observers:

> "We insist on the fact that a teacher must prepare himself interiorly by systematically studying himself so that he can tear out his most deeply rooted defects, those in fact which impede his relations with children. In order to discover these subconscious failings, we have need of a special kind of instruction. We must see ourselves as another sees us.
>
> This is equivalent to saying that a teacher must be initiated. He must begin by studying his own defects, his own evil tendencies, rather than by being excessively preoccupied with a child's tendencies..." (Montessori, *The Secret of Childhood*)

The process of becoming initiated includes becoming a "joyous observer":

> "The first step to take in order to become a Montessori teacher is to shed omnipotence and to become a joyous observer. If the teacher can really enter into the joy of seeing things, being born and growing under his own eyes, and clothe himself in the garment of humility, many delights are reserved for him that are denied to those who assume infallibility and authority in front of a class." (Montessori, *To Educate the Human Potential*)

Here lies the essential point; from her scientific preparation, the teacher must bring not only the capacity, but the desire, to observe natural phenomena. In our system, she must become a passive, much more than an active influence, and her passivity shall be composed of anxious scientific curiosity, and of absolute respect for the phenomena she wishes to observe. The teacher must feel her position of observer; the activity must lie in the phenomenon." (Montessori, *The Montessori Method*)

A focus for observation is an appreciation of life and the phenomena of children's spontaneous activities or "life acts of itself":

> "This idea, that life acts of itself and that in order to study it, to divine its secrets or to direct its activity, it is necessary to observe it and to understand it without intervening — this idea, I say, is very difficult for anyone to assimilate and to put into practice." (Montessori, *The Montessori Method*)

Having observed in this manner, Montessori teachers would be able to prepare classrooms in which children can find activities that allow them to exercise fully their inner needs and interests. If children were interested in the classroom activities, the teacher observed accurately. Observation continues, however; children do grow, and their interests do change. Observation and re-preparation of the classroom are perpetual.

The Normalized Child

A Montessori classroom is an exciting learning environment for young children. Low shelves are filled with boxes, trays, and baskets, and each of these is filled with colorful, intriguing objects for sorting, sequencing, mixing, and arranging. In time, each child learns about sizes, shapes, colors, sounds, mathematics, reading, writing, science, and geography.

At first, a child may select one, then another tray, explore its contents, and return it to its shelf location. Gradually, however, the child lengthens the time spent exploring and discovering. Movements slow, becoming precise and disciplined. Her concentration extends, and she is able to maintain her focus and attention. She begins to locate the ideas embedded in the learning materials and in her surrounding environments. This is the process of *normalization*.

Not long ago, a mother wrote: "My daughter attends a Montessori school. She loves school and tells me about all the wonderful things she does. I just have one question: Could someone please explain the term *normalization?*"

Normalization is a Montessori term that causes a great deal of confusion and some concern among many Montessori parents. *Normalization* is a terrible choice of words. It suggests that teachers will help children who are not normal to become *normal*. This is not what Dr. Montessori meant to suggest at all.

Normalization describes the process that takes place every year in Montessori classrooms around the world, in which young children, who typically have short attention spans, learn to focus their intelligence, concentrate their energies for long periods, and take tremendous satisfaction from their work.

Another mother put it this way: "My child just does not act the same now that he's been in Montessori for a while. He is usually happy, laughing, and running from one thing to another. In Montessori, he looks interested, sometimes puzzled, and often completely absorbed. I think of *normalization* as a kind of satisfaction that he seems to take from what he calls hard work."

Kay Futrell, in her classic little book, *The Normalized Child*, describes Dr. Montessori's amazement when the fifty frightened and ill-disci-

---

In his book, *Maria Montessori: Her Life and Work,* E. M. Standing described the following characteristics of *normalization* in the child between the age of three and six:

▲ A love of order
▲ A love of work
▲ Profound spontaneous concentration
▲ Attachment to reality
▲ Love of silence and of working alone
▲ Sublimation of the possessive instinct
▲ Obedience
▲ Independence and initiative
▲ Spontaneous self-discipline
▲ Joy
▲ The power to act from real choice and not just from idle curiosity

MONTESSORI PROGRAMS

plined inner city children of her first Children's House began to respond to the new environment.

"What followed seemed incredible even to Dr. Montessori, for the deprived children blossomed under this freedom, and the possibility of doing work suited to their needs. They revealed to her not only their enormous capacity for intellectual accomplishment but a strange character of sweetness and serenity.

They displayed a truly uncorrupted spirit, scorning rewards and punishment, and finding their joy in the prodigious work which involved them. They came from these labors refreshed, as from a creative experience, and as they worked, they grew in inner discipline and peace.

The sight of these children, who displayed the truly 'normal' characteristics of childhood, was the force which motivated Montessori for the remainder of her life. This secret of childhood she pursued with all the vitality of the genius who found her raison d'etre, *and from her tireless observations and efforts, evolved her perception of the child's psychic personality.*

As she traveled from country to country, lecturing, training teachers, helping to establish school after school, this same phenomenon was observed wherever conditions promoting its growth were perfectly realized.

This normalized child is the image which Montessori teachers keep uppermost in their minds. This is what we are striving for, what we hope to achieve. However, this child will appear only if we conscientiously prepare ourselves and our classrooms and if we can build on the proper preparation in the child's home."

A Guided Tour of Early Childhood & Elementary Montessori Classrooms

Together we are going on a tour of several Montessori classes. Along the way, we'll stop and take a look at children doing all sorts of things. We are going to focus most of our visit on classrooms of children age three through six; what Montessori schools commonly call the "Primary" or "Children's House" level (in Canada it is commonly called the "casa" level). However, we will also look in on the elementary classes to get a sense of how the Montessori curriculum extends upward at the higher level.

We wish to extend a very special thank you to the many Montessori schools that have provided us access to their classrooms over the years. Without their help, we would never have been able to compile the many excellent photos in this section.

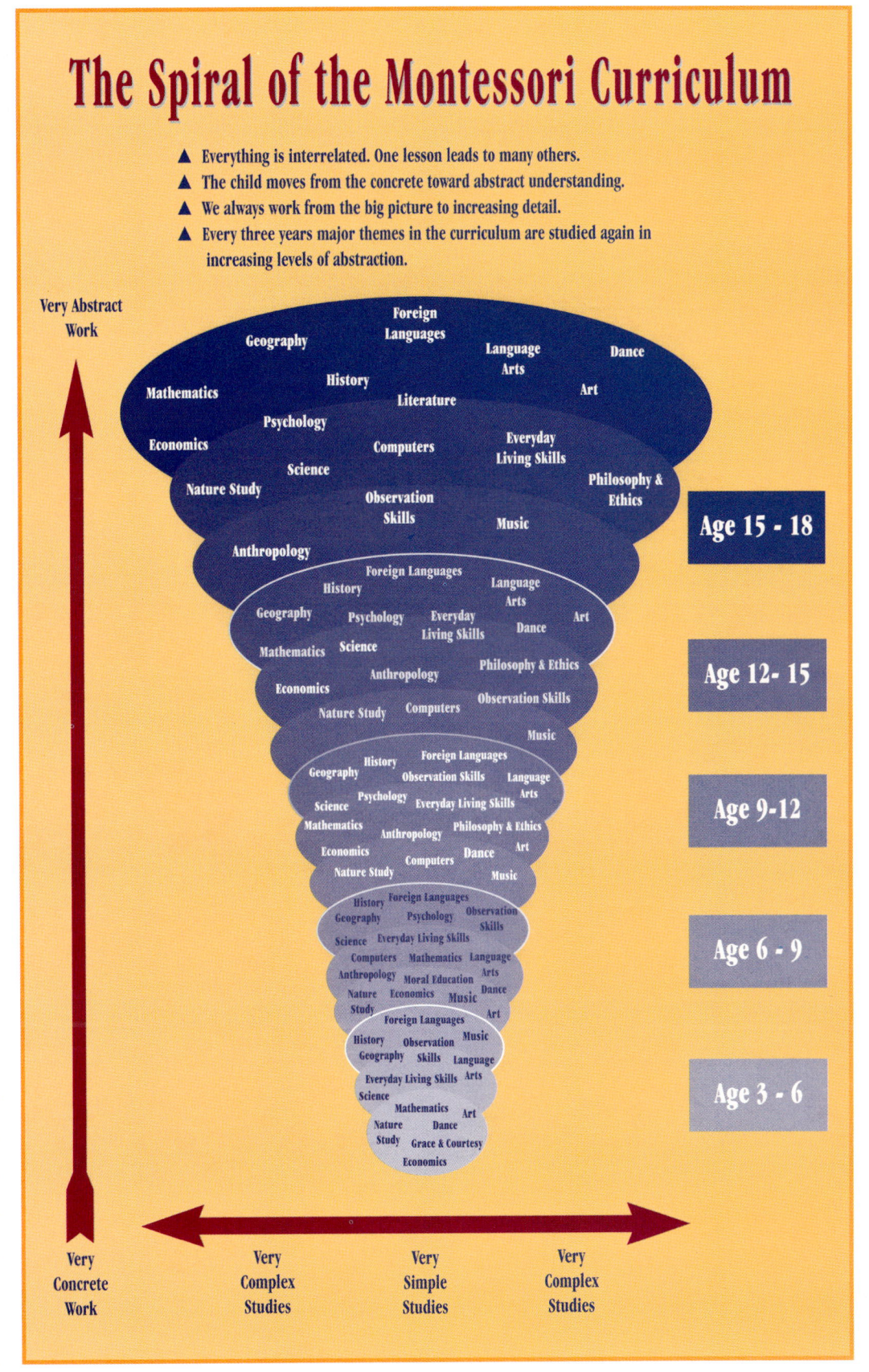

The Spiral of the Montessori Curriculum

▲ Everything is interrelated. One lesson leads to many others.
▲ The child moves from the concrete toward abstract understanding.
▲ We always work from the big picture to increasing detail.
▲ Every three years major themes in the curriculum are studied again in increasing levels of abstraction.

Age 15 - 18
Age 12 - 15
Age 9 - 12
Age 6 - 9
Age 3 - 6

Very Abstract Work
Very Concrete Work
Very Complex Studies — Very Simple Studies — Very Complex Studies

Montessori Programs

Practical Life

Success in school is directly tied to the degree to which children believe they are capable and independent human beings.

As we allow students to develop a meaningful degree of independence and self-discipline, we also set a pattern for a lifetime of good work habits and a sense of responsibility. In Montessori, students are taught to take pride in their work.

Independence does not come automatically as we grow older; it must be learned. In Montessori, even very small children can learn how to tie their own shoes and pour their own milk. At first, shoe laces turn into knots, and milk ends up on the floor. However, with practice, skills are mastered and the young child beams with pride. To experience this kind of success at such an early age is to build up a self-image as a successful person and leads the child to approach the next task with confidence.

Pouring

The children learn to pour from one container to another without spilling a single drop.

(Above and below) Transferring Materials

The hand movements needed to transfer liquids with a baster helps prepare the child for a wide range of later tasks.

More Transferring Exercises ...

(Right) This three-year-old is learning to transfer dried peas from one bowl to another with a large spoon.

(Far right) Many activities isolate one particular skill, allowing the young child to master it one step at a time. This young student is using a little spoon to transfer beads carefully from one bowl to another.

(Above) Children love to polish brass and silver, moving on to learning how to polish their own shoes.

(Above) In a very real sense, Montessori children are responsible for the care of this child-sized environment, which is why Dr. Montessori called it a children's "house" or "community."

(Above) They sweep, dust, and wash mirrors and windows.

"The essence of independence is to be able to do something for one's self."
— Montessori

(Background) The ability to control one's body and move carefully and gracefully around the room, often carrying things that must not be dropped, is an important aspect of the Practical Life lessons.

The children walk along a line on the floor, heel to toe, carefully balancing while carrying small flags, cups, or Montessori materials.

A GUIDED TOUR OF MONTESSORI CLASSROOMS — PRACTICAL LIFE

Table washing ...

(Left) To wash this table, this young student methodically gathers the bucket, little pitcher, sponges, scrub brushes, towels, and soap and proceeds to scrub a small table slowly and methodically. When she is finished, she will return everything to its storage place.

These lessons in Practical Life skills do much more than help children learn to wash tables. The process helps them develop an inner sense of order, a greater sense of independence, and a higher ability to concentrate and follow a complex sequence of steps.

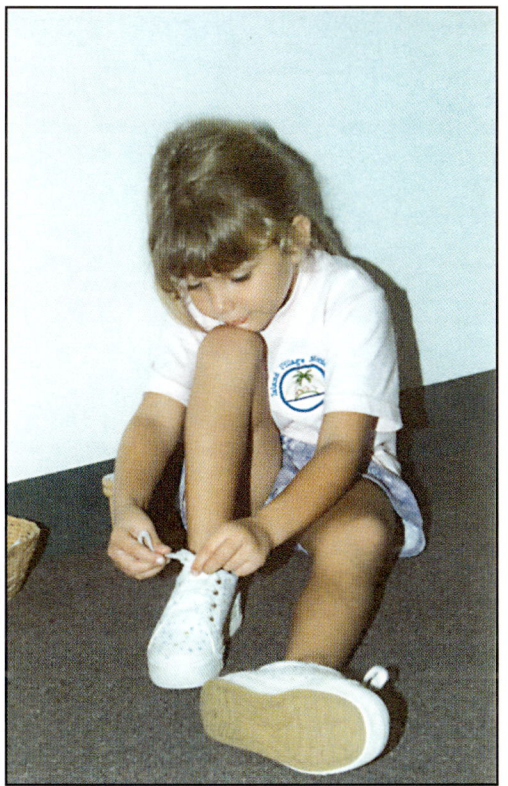

First steps towards independence ...

(Above) Young children work with the **Dressing Frames** *to master the dressing skills that classically challenge them as they begin to take their first steps toward independence: buttoning their clothes, working on a zipper, tying their shoe laces, and so on.*

Cleaning up ...

59

MONTESSORI PROGRAMS

Eating together ...

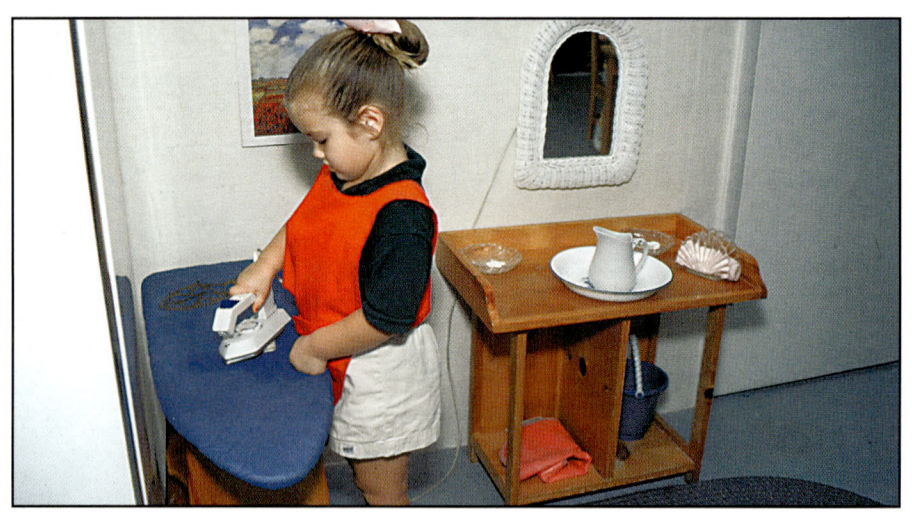

(Above) Washing and Ironing

Children learn to wash small polishing cloths and napkins. Once the cloths are dry, they learn to iron and fold them using a special low-temperature children's iron. Think of the pride that these young children take in doing **real** things, rather than pretending to help around the house.

(Left) Food Preparation

When the children are hungry, they prepare their own snacks. They pour themselves a drink from a little pitcher that is just right for their small hands. When finished they clean up and wash their dishes. When something spills, they help each other carefully clean up. In Montessori classrooms, you will find small children cutting raw fruit and vegetables.

Older Montessori students learn all sorts of everyday living skills, from cooking to balancing a checkbook. They plan parties, learn how to decorate a room, arrange flowers, garden, and do simple household repairs. Montessori builds many opportunities into the curriculum for students to learn from hands-on experiences. They learn to cook, set tables, eat together in a peaceful atmosphere, and steadily grow in their self-confidence and independence.

A GUIDED TOUR OF MONTESSORI CLASSROOMS — PRACTICAL LIFE

(Above) Sewing

By learning how to sew, children not only learn a Practical Life skill, they also develop fine-motor skills.

(Above) Animals in the Montessori environment

Children learn to care for the small animals being raised in or outside the classroom.

(Above and right) Gardening in and outside the Montessori classroom

A sense of beauty is a key element of Montessori. This young student, pictured above, is planting flowers in the class garden, which will later be cut to place in the bud vases on each table in her classroom. The boy to the right is helping to care for the plants in his indoor environment.

> "Adults work to finish a task, but the child works in order to grow and is working to create the adult, the person that is to be." — Montessori

61

Montessori Programs

Lessons in Grace, Courtesy, & Community Service

Learning how to work and play together with others in a peaceful and caring community is perhaps the most critical life skill that Montessori teaches.

(Above) The Silence Game

The **Silence Game** helps children develop a much higher level of self-discipline along with a greater awareness of the sounds around us that most people take for granted. In this group activity, the teacher will get the children's attention either by ringing a small bell or by hanging up a sign with the command "Silence." The children stop where they are or gather on the line, close their eyes, and try to remain perfectly still. The children sit still with their eyes shut and wait to hear the teacher whisper their name. When they hear it ever so softly spoken, they silently rise and join the teacher.

Sometimes the teachers will vary the Silence Game by challenging the children to carry bells across the room without allowing them to ring, or they may use the calm atmosphere to introduce the children to guided visualization. At first, the younger children may not be able to hold the silence for more than twenty or thirty seconds, but gradually their ability to relax, listen, and appreciate the perfectly calm environment increases. In many classes, the Silence Game is an important daily ritual. Montessori schools are almost always close-knit communities of people living and learning together in an atmosphere of warmth, safety, kindness, and mutual respect. Teachers become mentors and friends. Students learn to value the different backgrounds and interests of their classmates.

(Right) Community Service

Community service is an important element in most Elementary and Secondary Montessori programs. These girls, along with their teachers, spend part of their week delivering food to older people, who dearly appreciate not only the meal but the warmth of their company.

(Right) Teaching Peace

The Peace Table plays an important role in Montessori classrooms. Two children having a disagreement will normally decide to retreat to the Peace Table to solve their problem. Sometimes, children may not remember, and the suggestion might come from the teacher. When classmates observe an ongoing disagreement, somebody might bring them a peace rose with the reminder to solve their problem at the Peace Table.

Once arrived at the table, the child who feels wronged places her hand on the table, indicating that she wants to have her say without interruption. The other hand she places on her heart, indicating that she speaks the truth, from the heart. She then looks the other in the eye, speaks her name, "Lisa," and proceeds to state how she feels, "Lisa, I feel very angry ..." and continues to state why she feels that way, " ... because you didn't let me play with you and Lily!" She states how she wants to resolve the conflict: "And I don't want you to do that ever again if you want to be my friend!" Now that she has stated her case and opened the door for further discussion, she withdraws her hand from the table and from her heart and gives Lisa a chance to respond.

Lisa proceeds that same way. She places her hands on the table and her heart, looks Eleanor in the eye, and responds:

"Eleanor, I feel unhappy that you are angry, I did not mean to hurt your feelings. However, Lily is a good friend of mine also, and the game we played can be played by only two participants. Had I been playing it with you, nobody else could have joined us either. So, you see, it's just one of those things. I want to remain your friend."

With that, Lisa is finished and withdraws her hands. Now it is Eleanor's turn to agree or disagree. In any case, they continue the dialogue until they reach some kind of agreement, even if that means that they disagree. At least they are talking, without yelling, screaming, and blaming. They want to solve the problem. When they have reached an agreement, they ring the bell to let the others know. In case they cannot come to a positive conclusion, they may ask for a mediator. This may be one of the older children, who has been trained to be impartial and to listen well.

However, if the problem or conflict is too involved, then one of them may ask for a "pow-wow." During a "pow-wow," the entire class, or a large part of the class sits in a circle, listens to first one, then the other person's side of the story. The class members contribute what they can, either as facts of what they have seen or heard, as ethics (right and wrong), or in perspective to class rules upon which all have agreed previously. It is wise for the teacher to observe and monitor the entire process from the sidelines.

The core experience the students gain from these procedures is that it is necessary to solve disturbances honestly and with good will to maintain a harmonious and cooperative atmosphere in the community.

MONTESSORI PROGRAMS

(Left) Teaching Courtesy

Learning how to greet someone graciously is one of the first acts of courtesy learned in the Montessori classroom.

Everyday kindness and courtesy are vital practical life skills. Even the youngest child is treated by her teachers and classmates with dignity and respect.

Montessori students come to understand and accept that we all have responsibilities to other people.

These children learn how to handle new situations that they will face as they become increasingly independent.

They develop a clear sense of values and social conscience and absorb everyday ethics and interpersonal skills from the earliest years.

Helen Keller, inspired by Montessori, wrote:

"I believe that every child has hidden away somewhere in his being noble capacities which may be quickened and developed if we go about it in the right way, but we shall never properly develop the higher nature of our little ones while we continue to fill their minds with the so-called 'basics.' Mathematics will never make them loving, nor will accurate knowledge of the size and shape of the world help them to appreciate its beauties. Let us lead them during the first years to find their greatest pleasure in nature. Let them run in the fields, learn about animals, and observe real things. Children will educate themselves under the right conditions. They require guidance and sympathy far more than instruction."

Montessori proposed that we could accomplish world peace by healing the wounds of the human heart and by producing a child who is independent, at peace with herself, and secure. Montessori envisioned her educational reforms as essentially leading to a reconstruction of society. Montessori schools are different but not because of the materials that are used in the classrooms. Look beyond the maps, science charts, and geometry materials. Each classroom is a place where children really want to be because it feels a lot like home. Montessori schools give children the sense of belonging to a family and help children learn how to live with other human beings.

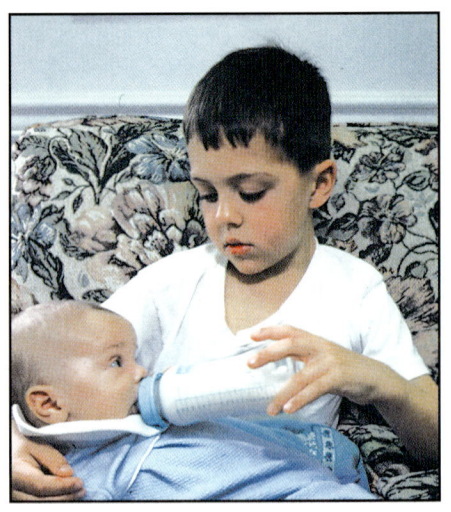

(Above) Learning to Care for Others

When we say that Montessori is not only a fine preparation for college but for life, we aren't exaggerating. Many Montessori schools teach elementary children how to care for infants, and some even train those who are interested to assist in the school's infant and toddler environments. The lessons of the heart that these children learn lasts a lifetime.

The Sensorial Exercises

*What's inside? Children use the **Mystery Box** to help develop their sense of touch.*

A child interacts with the physical world through her senses. From birth, she will look, listen, touch, taste, pick up, manipulate, and smell almost anything that comes into her grasp. At first, everything goes into the mouth. Gradually she begins to explore each object's weight, texture, and temperature. She may watch something that catches her attention, such as a butterfly, with infinite patience. The sensorial curriculum is designed to help the child focus her attention more carefully on the physical world, exploring with each of her senses the subtle variations in the properties of objects.

At first, the child may simply be asked to sort among a prepared series of objects that vary by only one aspect, such as height, length, or width. Other exercises challenge her to find identical pairs or focus on very different physical properties, such as aroma, taste, weight, shades of color, temperature, or sound. These exercises are essentially puzzles, and they tend to fascinate the children because they are just difficult enough to represent a meaningful challenge. Each has a built-in control of error that allows the child who is observant to check her own work.

The Sensorial exercises include lessons in vocabulary, as the children master the names of everything from sophisticated plane and solid geometric figures to the parts of familiar plants and animals. As the Inuits demonstrate to us with their many different words for *snow*, we observe that as the children learn the correct names for things, the objects themselves take on meaning and reality as the child learns to recognize and name them.

Why is it so important to educate the young child's senses? We certainly don't believe that we can improve a child's hearing or sight through training. However, we can help children to pay attention, to focus their awareness, and to learn how to observe and consider what comes into their experience. In a way, the Sensorial curriculum accomplishes something like a course in wine tasting or music appreciation; one learns to taste, smell, or hear what is experienced with a much deeper awareness and appreciation. These exercises can help children understand and appreciate their world more fully.

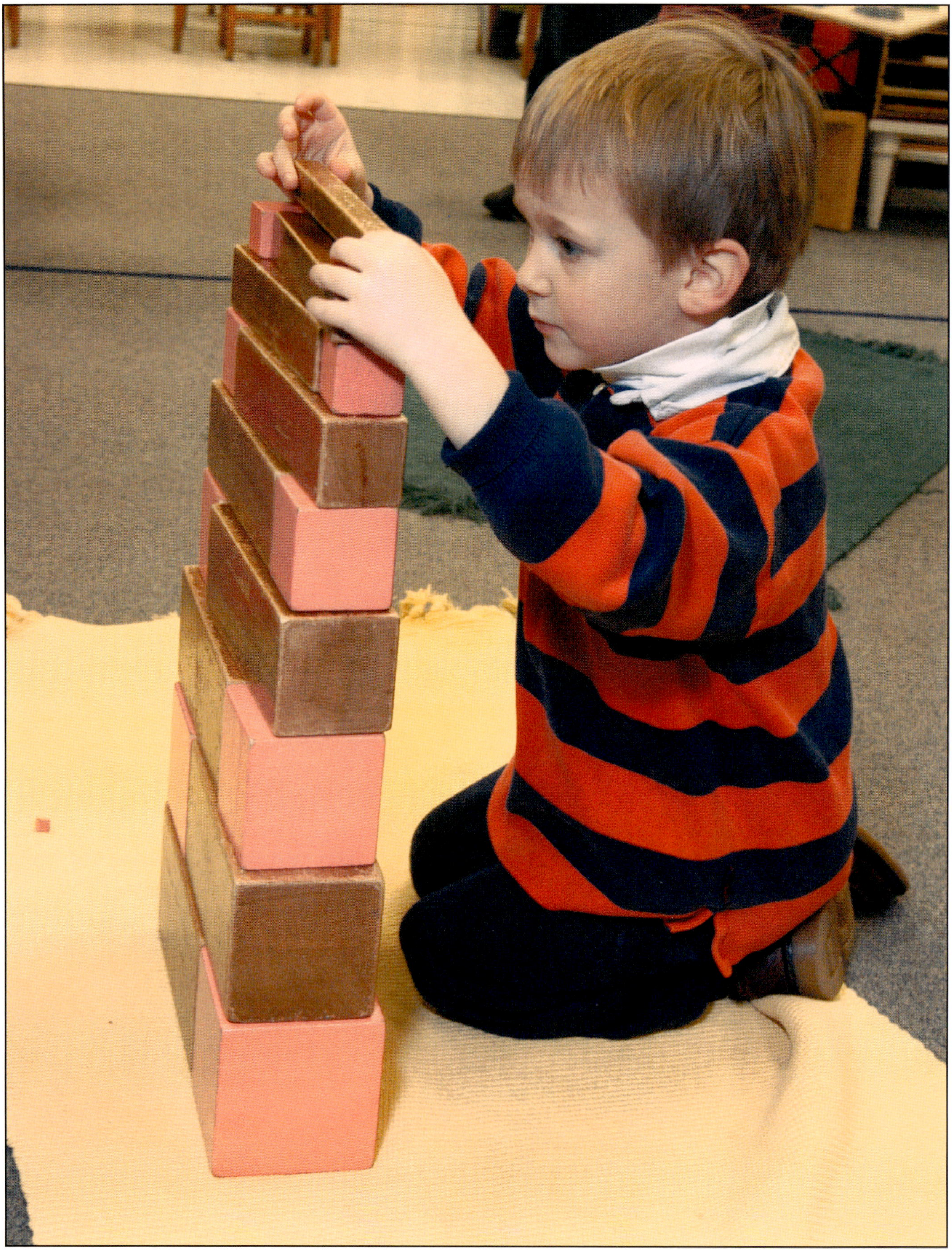

A Guided Tour of Montessori Classrooms — Sensorial Exercises

The Pink Tower is one of the Sensorial materials that children enjoy working with early in their Montessori experience. The Pink Tower, or "Tower of Cubes," is composed of a graduated series of ten wooden cubes. The largest cube has a square section of 10 centimeters per side and is 10 centimeters high. Thus, it measures 10 x 10 x 10 centimeters. The square section and height of each of the succeeding cubes decreases by 1 centimeter down to the smallest cube which measures 1 x 1 x 1 centimeter.

Children carefully carry the Tower, cube by cube, to the little rug that defines their work area. They carry each cube comfortably at waist height as they take the cubes and place them in random order upon the carpet.

As they manipulate the cubes and carry them across the room, the children get a very strong impression of size and weight. When all the cubes have been carried to the rug, the child looks for the largest one and begins to build the Tower, one cube at a time. At each step, he looks through the cubes that have not yet been added to the Tower to find the largest. As each is placed on the Tower, the child controls his movements to place the cube gently down right in the center of the larger cube on which it is rested. Once the Tower has been constructed, the child carefully takes it down and either begins again or returns the cubes, one by one, to their proper place on the shelf.

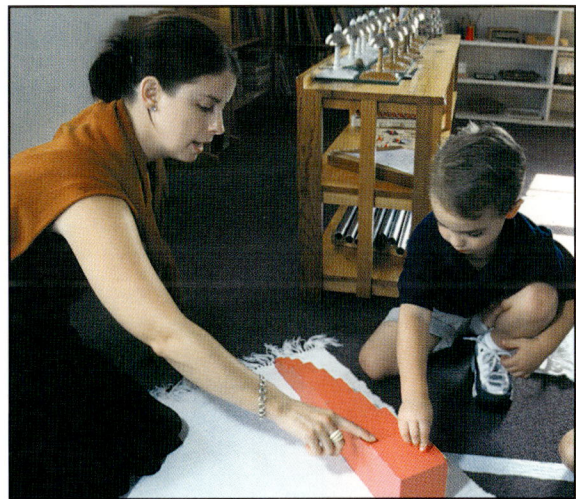

(Above and right) The Pink Tower

*Some people have heard that in Montessori, children are taught that there is only one way to work with each material. In truth, the children explore and discover all sorts of creative ways to work with them. For example, students will construct the Tower horizontally, or line up two edges to create a vertical stairway. The children will also build the **Pink Tower** in various combinations with the **Brown Stair** (described on page 68), along with some of the other Sensorial materials.*

Montessori Programs

The Brown Stair, which is sometimes called the Broad Stair, is made up of ten rectangular prisms with bases that have exactly the same graduated measurements as the cubes of the Pink Tower, but which are uniformly 20 centimeters long. The child is challenged to scatter them around her rug and then sorts them by size to place all ten prisms in proper order from thickest to thinnest. This results in a graduated series of rectangular prisms that resembles a little stairway. Because the squared sides of each prism correspond to the dimensions of the cubes of the Pink Tower, the two materials are often used together for all sorts of explorations and designs.

(Above) The Brown Stair

The Red Rods are a series of ten rods (thin rectangular prisms) in which the height and width are uniform; however, they range in length from 1 decimeter (10 centimeters) to a full meter (10 decimeters or 100 centimeters). The child scatters the rods around her rug and looks for the longest.

As each is arranged alongside the others in a series, they help the child discover the regular progression of length. The teachers introduce vocabulary: *short, shorter, shortest; long, longer, longest.*

The Red Rods are quite similar to the Red and Blue Rods in the Math area, which help the child learn to count by showing the growth of quantity as length, distinguished by alternating patterns of red and blue to represent each number.

(Above and left) The Red Rods

A Guided Tour of Montessori Classrooms — Sensorial

The Cylinder Blocks are a set of four naturally finished (unpainted) rectangular blocks of wood, into which have been cut ten cylindrical holes. Each hole is filled with a matching wooden cylindrical inset fitted with a little knob on the top to make it easy for a child's small hand to grasp and lift the inset out of its perfectly fitted hole.

Each set of cylinders is constructed to vary in a regular sequence by either diameter, length, or both. The children remove each cylinder in turn, carefully tracing its length and circumference and the depth and circumference of each hole with one finger.

Once all ten cylinders have been removed and placed on the rug, the children take each in turn and find the hole into which it fits perfectly, with the top of the cylinder flush with the top of the cylinder block. If they've made a mistake, the children can normally see it for themselves because all ten cylinders will not fit correctly.

The children quickly begin to challenge themselves by attempting to "see" which hole is likely to fit the cylinder in their hand rather than trying to fit each into one hole after the other. After a while, they will begin to do the same exercise with their eyes blindfolded, relying on touch alone.

When they are ready for a greater challenge, the children will mix the cylinders from two, three, or all four blocks together and try to fit them all into the corresponding holes.

(Above) The Knobbed Cylinder Blocks

*The child above is working with one set of the **Knobbed Cylinders**.*

(Above and right) The Knobless Cylinders

The Knobless Cylinders correspond to the four Cylinder Blocks. In this material, each of these sets is painted red, yellow, blue, or green.

With no cylindrical holes, the children depend upon sight or touch alone to arrange the cylinders.

Children will sometimes work with both the Knobless Cylinders and the more familiar Knobbed Cylinders from the Cylinder Blocks together, finding the match between each brightly painted and unpainted cylinder in turn.

By working with all four sets of Knobless Cylinders together, the children discover all sorts of geometric patterns and progressions within the material.

MONTESSORI PROGRAMS

The Color Tablets (left) help the child learn to distinguish among primary and secondary colors and shades, while mastering the words used to describe each color and shade. There are three separate boxes of Color Tablets. All of the tablets have the same shape and differ only in color. The first box of Color Tablets contains six tablets, two each of yellow, red, and blue. The children simply match the pairs and learn the spoken names of the colors.

The second box of Color Tablets contains eleven pairs of secondary colors, which the children match and name. The third box of Color Tablets contains seven different shades of nine different colors, which the children learn to sort in order from darkest to lightest shade. When all the tablets are laid out, they create a lovely display of color.

There are many ways in which the children and teachers can make the Color Tablets more challenging. For example, children can try to find the tablet that is closest in color to something in the environment. Another challenge is to give the child a Color Tablet from the third box and ask him to go to the box and, by memory alone, bring back the tablet that is just one shade lighter or darker.

Color, Touch, and Temperature ...

The Sandpaper Tablets

(photo courtesy of Nienhuis USA, Inc.)

Touch: The children commonly put on blindfolds to add an additional level of challenge as they sort or construct with the Sensorial materials. They love to explore their sense of touch.

One of the children's favorite activities is the **Mystery Bag**. Normally, it is simply a cloth bag or box with a hole for their hands in which they touch and manipulate objects that they cannot see. One activity is to place things that are familiar to the children inside, and challenge them to identify them by touch alone.

Another exercise begins with the **Rough and Smooth Boards**, which have a surface that alternates between the roughness of sandpaper and a smooth finished surface. The children wash their hands in warm water before beginning to make them more sensitive.

The Sandpaper Tablets (above) are a set of wooden tablets covered with several different grades of sandpaper. The challenge is to identify pairs that have the same degree of roughness, working by touch alone. An extension of these activities is commonly created by assembling a collection of pairs of cloth swatches cut from many different materials, each with its own texture. Again, working with eyes blindfolded, the children attempt to find the pairs by touch. Like all Montessori exercises, there is a built-in control of error. In this case, the children learn to check their work by removing the blindfold and seeing if the pairs have the same feel.

A Guided Tour of Montessori Classrooms — Sensorial

The Thermic Tablets and Thermic Jars: The thermic sense is the ability to distinguish among objects with different temperatures. The Thermic Tablets are a series of pairs of objects of identical size that are made from different materials, such as wood, stone, and metal. The materials tend to feel quite differently from each other at room temperature when lightly touched by a blindfolded child.

The challenge is to match them by temperature. The language of temperature is also taught: *hot, hotter, hottest, warm, warmer, warmest, cool, cooler, coolest,* etc. The Thermic Jars are a set of six little metal containers, which the teacher fills with water of varying temperatures to prepare the exercise. Two are filled with hot water, two with tepid water, and two with cold water. The child finds the matching pairs by touch alone, placing them in order from hottest to coldest.

The Baric Tablets: The baric sense is the ability to distinguish among different objects by weight. The Baric Tablets come as a box containing three pairs of little wooden tablets, identical in size, but made out of three different woods. One wood is very light, the next is made of a heavier material, and the third is quite heavy for its size. The child puts on a blindfold and sorts the scattered tablets to find identical pairs or to determine which in any given set of two is lighter or heavier.

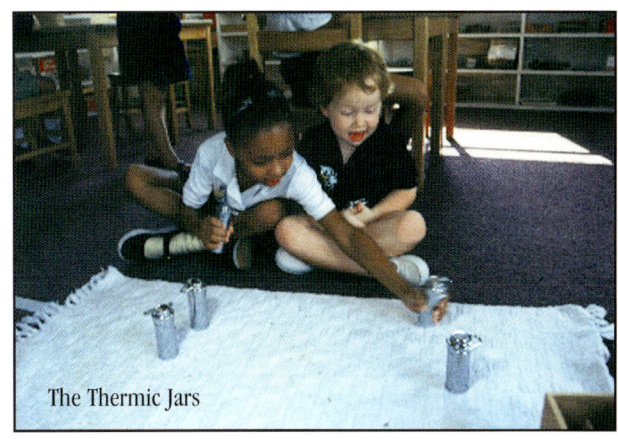

The Thermic Jars

Exploring the Sense of Smell ...

The Smelling Bottles resemble small spice containers with lids that have small holes through which the material inside can be smelled but not seen. The teacher prepares a set of six pairs. The children are challenged to find the identical pairs. Gradually, they learn to identify the source of the aroma. These exercises are extended beyond the classroom to the kitchen, garden, and nature walks. The children are blindfolded and asked to identify flowers, spices, and so on by their aromas. The materials inside the smelling bottles are varied every few weeks to give the child an ever-changing challenge.

(Above) The Smelling Bottles

MONTESSORI PROGRAMS

Sound ...

The Sound Cylinders (right) are designed to begin the process of teaching the child to listen attentively. It consists of a set of twelve hollow wooden cylinders, six of which have red caps, and six of which have blue. Each set of six appears identical except for the color of its cap. Inside each set, six different substances (such as sand, dry rice, or dried peas) create distinct sounds when the cylinder is shaken. The child arranges the cylinders into two sets according to the color of their caps and attempts to match the identical pairs by sound alone. Once children can accomplish this, they learn to grade them from the softest to loudest sound.

The Montessori Bells (below) extend the child's ability to distinguish sounds into the area of musical pitch. They are a lovely set of bells fixed to a little wooden base. Each bell is tuned to a different pitch. The set comprises one entire octave, including the eight-note scale and the five additional half steps commonly known as the "black notes."

The Sound Cylinders

The set includes one set of bells with tan-colored bases for all thirteen pitches and a second set in which the bases of the bells match the colors of the corresponding pitches on the piano (eight white and five black). At first, the children learn how to strike the bells with a small mallet to produce a clear note and damp them with a little felt-covered rod. Then the teacher sets out two or three pairs of bells from the two sets. The children match the pairs that produce identical notes. When they can do this easily, additional pairs are added until they can match the entire set.

A more difficult exercise challenges the children to grade the bells of just one set by pitch, from the lowest to the highest notes. As they become more familiar with the bells, children will commonly learn how to play and compose little melodies.

The Montessori Bells

Note: The Silence Game described in the section on Practical Life is also considered an activity in the Sensorial area.

A GUIDED TOUR OF MONTESSORI CLASSROOMS — SENSORIAL

The Geometry Cabinet is a set of plane geometric figures. It consists of six drawers, each of which is fitted with several wooden framed insets with a geometric form. In addition to the familiar circle, square, and rectangle, the child is introduced to a much broader array of complex figures, from the *right scalene triangle* to the *decagon*; and from the *ellipse* to the *curvilinear triangle* and the *quatrefoil*.

In addition to removing the pieces and replacing them in their frames, children sequence some shapes by size and classify other shapes by type. They also learn how to match them against three sets of printed cards that represent the same figures in increasing degrees of abstraction. The first set represents each shape completely colored in on the card in the same size as the piece from the cabinet. The children simply cover each card with the matching puzzle piece.

In the second set, the geometric shapes are printed as outlines drawn with broad lines that leave the inner area white. In the third set, the figures are simply traced with thin lines. As children gradually begin to recognize the more abstract representations of the three-dimensional objects, they are preparing themselves to recognize the little lines and squiggles of the written word.

Gradually, children learn the names of each of the geometric shapes. Once children begin to read and can verbally identify the shapes, they will begin to label them with pre-printed name cards. Eventually, the children will be able to prepare their own cards from scratch.

The Geometric Solids: (above) The logical basis for the Geometry Cabinet is the set of Geometric Solids. The children learn the names of these beautiful wooden forms, identifying them at first by sight and eventually when blindfolded. The set includes a sphere, cube, rectangular prism, a square-based and broad pyramid, triangular pyramid, ovoid, ellipsoid, and a cone. The children quickly begin to look for each geometric form in their environment. They also begin to discover the relationship between the two-dimensional figures and the solid forms: a circle is related to a sphere, a square to a cube, etc.

As they begin to read, children will learn to match Geometric Solids to a set of prepared label cards. Eventually, they will be able to prepare their own from scratch. This early introduction to geometry continues in the Elementary Montessori program. After years of hands-on experience with geometric figures and other mathematical exercises, children normally find it very easy to grasp more advanced concepts, from the definitions of geometric terms to the calculation of area, volume, and circumference.

Puzzles in the Montessori Classroom

Everyone who has worked with young children, whether as parent or teacher, knows how much children enjoy wooden puzzles; however, most of us take puzzles more or less for granted and fail to appreciate their hidden potential as an educational tool. The puzzles that we commonly give to children depict little animals or a cute scene. Dr. Montessori came to recognize that the attraction of fitting the pieces of a puzzle into the insets on their frames lies in the process of manipulating an object in all directions and finally discovering the one and only correct way that it will fit. There is more to all of this than simply the satisfaction of solving a puzzle. Somehow, we find that young children experience things that they can touch and manipulate quite differently from a picture of something printed on a piece of paper. In short, the positive and negative insets of a puzzle are much more real and interesting to a child than a simple two-dimensional picture. In the Montessori classroom, puzzles are used to help children learn to manipulate objects and assemble a complex whole from several parts. They are also used to introduce the children to a tremendous range of concepts and vocabulary, from geometric shapes to the countries of the world and the parts of a flower.

MONTESSORI PROGRAMS

The Binomial and Trinomial Cubes: These cubes are two of the most fascinating materials in the Montessori curriculum. At one level, they are simply a complex puzzle in which the child is challenged to rebuild the cubes and rectangular prisms contained in the box back into the form of a larger cube. Color coding on the outside of the box and the sides of certain pieces helps the child detect the pattern. The material is also an exercise in algebra and geometry, representing in concrete form the cube of a binomial $(a+b)^3$ and a trinomial $(a+b+c)^3$ where a=3 cm., b=4 cm. and c=5 cm.

(Above) The Trinomial Cube

*The young girl above is working with the **Trinomial Cube**, sorting the cubes and prisms.*

Editorial Note: The materials described on these two pages may not seem to the layperson to be Sensorial in nature. They are, however, included in the Sensorial curriculum, because this is where they are introduced to Montessori students in the early years.

Constructive Triangles

Constructive Triangles allow children to explore the geometric possibilities inherent within several different types of triangles. The material consists of six boxes, each of which contains a set of brightly colored flat wooden triangles, which can be manipulated like a puzzle to explore congruency and equivalence. For example, two right triangles joined together along the hypotenuse form a rectangle. To help the young child recognize the essential relationships, most of the triangles have a line drawn along those edges that join together to form new figures such as rectangles, squares, trapezoids, and polygons.

(Left) The Constructive Triangles

*Working with the **Constructive Triangles**, children explore how various triangles can form regular polygons in geometry.*

The Montessori Approach to Reading, Composition, & Literature

The process of learning how to read should be as painless and simple as learning how to speak. Montessori begins by placing the youngest students in classes where the older students are already reading. All children want to "do what the big kids can do," and as the intriguing work that absorbs the older students involves reading, there is a natural lure for the young child.

Montessori teaches basic skills phonetically, encouraging children to compose their own stories using the "Moveable Alphabet." Reading skills normally develop so smoothly in Montessori classrooms that students tend to exhibit a sudden "explosion into reading," which leaves the children and their families beaming with pride.

The Sandpaper Letters are a set of prepared wooden tablets in which each letter is printed in white sandpaper, glued down against a smooth colored background. Montessori's research confirmed what observant parents have always known: Children learn best by touch and manipulation, not by repeating what they are told. Her manipulative approach to teaching children to read phonetically is nothing short of simple brilliance and should have long ago become a basic element in every early childhood classroom around the world.

Typically, beginning at age two or three, Montessori children are introduced to a few letters at a time until they have mastered the entire alphabet. They trace each letter as it would be written, using two fingers of their dominant hand. As they trace the letter's shape, they receive three distinct impressions: they see the shape of the letter, they feel its shape and how it is written, and they hear the teacher pronounce its sound.

The teacher and child will begin to identify words that begin with the *kuh* sound: *cat, candle, can,* and *cap.* Seeing the tablets for the letters *c, a,* and *t* laid out before her, a child will pronounce each in turn, *kuh, aah, tuh: cat!* To help children distinguish between them, consonants are printed against pink or red backgrounds and vowels against blue.

The Writing Road to Reading

Another unusual result of the Montessori approach is that young children will often be able to write (encoding language by spelling phonetic words out one sound at a time), weeks or months before they will be able to read comfortably (decoding printed words).

The Sandpaper Letters

*Working with the **Sandpaper Letters** (shown here) leads to tracing the letters in the sand (below).*

Many Montessori classrooms use Sandpaper Letters that don't follow the traditional circle-and-line approach of teaching a young child the alphabet. Both cursive alphabets and D'Nelian letters (a modified form of italic printing that facilitates the jump to cursive) are available and used with excellent results.

When will children start to read?

There is typically a quick jump from reading and writing single words to sentences and stories. For some children, this "explosion into reading" will happen when they are four; for others when they are five, and some will start to read at six. A few will read even earlier, and some others will take even longer. Most will be reading comfortably when they enter first grade, but each child is different, and as with every other developmental milestone, it is useless to fret. Younger children are surrounded by older children who can read, and the most intriguing things to do in the classroom depend on one's ability to read. This creates a natural interest and desire to catch up to the "big kids" and join the ranks of readers. As soon as children, no matter how young they are, show the slightest interest, we begin to teach them how to read. And when they are ready, the children pull it all together and are able to read and write on their own.

(Left) The Moveable Alphabet

*Composing words (articles and nouns) with the **Moveable Alphabet**.*

The Moveable Alphabet: Once children have begun to recognize several letters and their sounds with the Sandpaper Letters, they are introduced to the Moveable Alphabet, a large box with compartments containing plastic letters, organized much like an old-fashioned printer's box of metal type. The children compose words by selecting a small object or picture and then laying out the word one letter at a time. As with the Sandpaper Letters, they sound out words one letter at a time, selecting the letter that makes that sound.

The phonetic approach, which has mysteriously fallen out of favor in many schools, has long been recognized by educators as the single most effective way to teach children how to read and write. However, we have to remember that, unlike Italian and Spanish, English is not a completely phonetic language. Just consider the several different sounds made by the letters *ough*. There is the sound *off* as in *cough*, or *ufff* as in *rough* or *enough*, or the sound *oooh* as in the word *through*, or the sound *ah* as in *thought*. Altogether, there are some ninety-six different phonograms (combinations of letters that form distinct sounds) in the English language (such as *ph, ee, ai, oo,* etc.).

It is not surprising that in the early years, as young children are beginning to compose words, phrases, sentences, and stories, their spelling can sometimes get a bit creative. For example, the word *phone* is frequently spelled *fon*. Montessori teachers deliberately avoid correcting children's spelling during these early years, preferring to encourage them to become more confident in their ability to sound words out rather than risk that they will shut down from frequent correction.

The process of composing words with the Moveable Alphabet continues for many years, gradually moving from three-letter words to four- and five-letter words with consonant blends *(fl, tr, st)*, double vowels *(oo, ee)*, silent *e*'s, and so on.

> Many parents find it curious that Montessori children are not taught the names of letters; instead, they learn the sounds that we pronounce as we phonetically sound out words one letter at a time. For a long time, children may not know the names of letters at all, but will call them by the sounds they make: *buh, cuh, aah,* etc. This eliminates one of the most unnecessary and confusing steps in learning to read: "The letter 'A' stands for apple. The sound it makes is *aah*."

Early Reading Exercises

As children begin to work with the Sandpaper Letters, teachers will lead them through a wide range of pre-reading exercises designed to help them recognize the beginning, and later the ending and middle, sounds in short phonetic words. One common example would be a basket containing three Sandpaper Letters, such as "c," "b," and "f." In addition, the basket will contain small inexpensive objects that are models of things beginning with these letters. The basket described above might contain little plastic objects representing a cat, cap, can, bug, bag, bat, flag, frog, and fan. In another exercise, we will substitute little cards with pictures instead of the small objects.

Cards with the names of familiar objects are commonly found in most kindergartens. However, in Montessori, children take this a bit further, learning the names of and placing the appropriate labels on a bewildering array of geometric shapes, leaf forms, the parts of flowers, countries of the world, land and water forms, and much, much more. Montessori children are known for their incredible vocabularies. Where else would you find four-year-olds who can identify an isosceles triangle, rectangular prism, the stamen of a flower, or the continent of Asia on a map?

(Right and below)
Metal Insets

*Working with the **Metal Insets** to develop control of the pencil (right).*

*After working with the **Sandpaper Letters** and the **Metal Insets**, the children practice writing on small chalk boards.*

The Metal Insets: First Steps to Writing

Montessori found that children in her schools were capable of encoding words months before they developed the eye-hand coordination needed to control a pencil. By using specially prepared moveable alphabets, Montessori separated the process of beginning to write from its dependency on the child's ability to write with paper and pencil.

To help children develop the eye-hand coordination needed to grasp and write correctly with a pencil, Montessori introduced them to a set of metal frames and insets made in the form of geometric shapes. When the geometric inset is removed, the children trace the figure left within the frame onto a sheet of paper. Then they use colored pencils to shade in the outlines that they've traced, using careful horizontal strokes.

Gradually, children become more skilled at keeping the strokes even and staying within the lines. As they get older, children begin to superimpose several insets over each other, creating complex designs which, when colored in, resemble stained glass. Montessori children will often prepare beautiful little books of their Metal Inset work.

Montessori Programs

(Above) The Verb Command Cards

*The **Verb Command Cards** have a simple one-word command (verb) printed on them. This little boy has just read the word* wave *and is acting out the command.*

The Verb Command Cards: One of the early reading exercises introduced to Montessori children once they have begun to read are the Verb Command Cards. This is a set of red cards on which a single one-word command (a verb) is printed.

Typically, two or three children will do this work together as a little game. They pick a card, read it, and perform the command: *hop, smile, yawn, sleep, clap, sit, stand, wave, eat, drink,* and so on. Once they can read these one-word command cards, later sets will use complete sentences to command them to, "Bring me the smallest cube from the Pink Tower," or, "Waddle across the room like a duck."

Command Cards are used with older children to suggest specific challenges in every area of the curriculum. For example, in Geography, a Command Card might challenge the child to look in the atlas to find the location of the largest inland lake on the Earth.

Teaching Children the Consonant Blends and Phonograms of the English Language

Montessori uses two sets of small Moveable Alphabets, each a different color, to help the children master consonant blends, such as *fl, st, ch, cl, cr,* or *tr*. A consonant blend requires the child to blend two distinct letter sounds together into one, as we do when we say *flag* or *train*. The child lays out several copies of the consonant blend with one color of the Moveable Alphabet.

Then she completes the small words by adding the remaining letters in the Moveable Alphabet printed in the second color. An example might be *tr...ip, tr...ade, tr...ain,* and *tr...iangle*.

    fl at
    fl eet
    fl ee
    fl ing
    fl ower

Phonograms are the combinations of vowels in the English language that form new sounds on their own, such as *ee, ai, oa, oo,* and *ou*. Some phonograms, such as *ough*, can make more than one sound. For example, *ough* has one sound in *cough*, another in *although*, and still another in *through*. The children construct words containing phonograms using two Moveable Alphabets just as they do the consonant blends.

Montessori teachers will normally prepare little booklets, each of which contains many examples of one particular consonant blend or "phonogram."

Puzzle Words: Some words, most of which have come to English from other languages, just don't follow the familiar rules. Examples of Puzzle Words are: *the, was, you, they,* and *their*. They have to be learned by memory.

The Study of Grammar & Sentence Analysis

We begin to teach children the functions of grammar and sentence structure to students as young as age five and six, just as they are first learning how to put words together to express themselves. This leads them to master these vital skills. Before long, they learn to write naturally and well.

Montessori created a set of symbols to represent each part of speech, which helps the children learn them easily during a time in their lives when it is a delight rather

(Below) Montessori Grammar Materials

Montessori children use geometric symbols to represent the parts of speech, as in the simple article, adjective, noun, verb, and adverb sentence pictured below.

78

than a chore. For example, the symbol for a noun is a large black triangle. Because they are related to the "noun family," the symbols for an article and an adjective are also triangles.

To distinguish them from the noun, which they modify, the symbol for an adjective is a dark blue triangle about one-third smaller than the larger symbol for the noun, and the symbol for an article is a much smaller light blue triangle.

The children will often call the noun a "naming word," an adjective a "describing word," a verb a "doing word," and so on. The symbol for a verb is a large red circle (implying a ball, or movement, since verbs describe action), and the symbol for an adverb is a smaller orange circle, showing that it is related to the verb.

Literature and Research: At this point, we begin a systematic study of the English language: vocabulary, spelling rules, and linguistics. The key to the Montessori language-arts curriculum is the quality of the material children are given to read.

Very young students are introduced to first-rate children's literature and fascinating reference materials on science, history, geography, and the arts. In an increasing number of Montessori schools, students begin the Junior Great Books Program in kindergarten, and literary studies continue every year thereafter.

(Left and below) Working with the Montessori Grammar Materials

Left: This seven-year-old has entered the correct grammar symbol for each part of speech for a series of short sentences.

Below left: These children are diagramming a simple sentence with the first sentence-analysis materials.

Below: This eight-year-old is diagramming a sentence with the sentence-analysis materials.

Elementary students write every day, learning to organize increasingly complex ideas and information into well-written stories, poems, reports, plays, and student publications. Montessori schools commonly teach elementary and middle school students how to use the computer to write, illustrate, and lay out their work. In recent years, many have begun to teach them how to use the Internet to gather information for their research.

Working with the Red and Blue Rods

Montessori Math Moves from the Concrete to the Abstract

Students who learn math by rote often have no real understanding or ability to put their skills to use in everyday life. Learning comes much more easily when they work with concrete educational materials that graphically show what is taking place in a given mathematical process.

Montessori students use hands-on learning materials that make abstract concepts clear and concrete. They can literally see and explore what is going on. This approach to teaching mathematics, based on the research of Drs. Maria and Mario Montessori, offer a clear and logical strategy for helping students understand and develop a sound foundation in mathematics and geometry.

The Montessori Math curriculum is based on the European tradition of "Unified Math," which is described in greater detail in the section on "Montessori for the Elementary Years" (page 115).

The concrete Montessori Math materials are perhaps the best known and most imitated elements of Dr. Montessori's work. These elegant and simply lovely materials hold a fascination for most children and adults alike.

They proceed through several levels of abstraction, beginning with concepts and skills that are the most basic foundations of mathematics, presented in the most concrete representation, up through the advanced concepts of secondary mathematics, which are represented in increasing levels of abstraction, until the student grasps them conceptually.

A Guided Tour of Montessori Classrooms — Math

The Red and Blue Rods (below and opposite page) are the child's introduction to mathematics. These rods have the same dimensions as the Red Rods found in the Sensorial area. Here, however, the rods are painted in alternating patterns of red and blue to distinguish their length in segments of one-tenth of a meter (a decimeter). The first rod is 1 decimeter long and is just painted red. The second is 2 decimeters long and is divided into two segments, one red and one blue. This continues through all ten rods.

As with the Red Rods, the children arrange the Red and Blue Number Rods into a stair from largest to smallest. Then they count each alternating colored segment. One of the insights that children gain from working with the rods is the nature of addition and the concept that two numbers can add up to another.

For example, when the children place the "one" number rod at the end of the "two" rod, they create a new rod that is the same length as the "three" rod just above. They explore similar relationships with all of the numbers from one to ten. They discover that the "four" and the "six" together are the same length as the "ten."

Montessori found that young children, in the beginning, find it difficult to grasp the concept of numbers by counting separate objects. While they can learn to "count" by rote, reciting the sequence of numbers from one to ten, most cannot easily grasp the difference between one quantity and another when looking at more than three or four objects. This is easily avoided by allowing children to visualize the concept of number and quantity by using this series of segmented rods of increasing length in the beginning, rather than trying to teach them to count sets of separate objects. The children also use the Sandpaper Numerals to label each Number Rod. These tablets are designed and used in the same way as the Sandpaper Letters described in the section on Language Arts.

(Right & opposite page)
Red and Blue Rods

The teacher and student to the right are working with a smaller "table-top" version of the **Red and Blue Rods.**

81

MONTESSORI PROGRAMS

(Right) The Spindle Boxes

The Spindle Boxes provide a nicely structured way for young children to make the next step in coming to understand the concepts of number and quantity. The material is made up of two wooden boxes, which together are divided into ten compartments. The compartments are labeled with the numerals from zero through nine. In a separate box or basket are forty-five wooden spindles used for counting. The exercise calls for the child to count the correct number of spindles to go in each compartment: one, two, three ... all the way to nine. Naturally, the compartment labeled "zero" is left empty, teaching the child at a very early age the concept of zero as an empty set. If the child has counted correctly, there will not be any spindles left over when she fills up the compartment labeled "nine." One lovely variation of this activity challenges the young child to create a distinct set for each number, while practicing bow-tying skills by tying a green ribbon (green symbolizes the concept of units — whole numbers less than ten) around the clustered spindles. Then this bundle is placed in the correct compartment.

(Left) Number Cards and Counters

The Numeral Cards and Counters:

After considerable experience with the more structured introductions to number and quantity created by the Red and Blue Number Rods and the Spindle Boxes, the child is finally ready to tackle the task of associating cards on which the numerals have been printed and objects to count. The child begins by arranging the numeral cards in order from one to ten. Then she begins to count out the appropriate number of counters, placing them in parallel rows of two after the number one. Even numbers end with an even number of counters in the bottom row; odd numbers only have one. This begins to focus the child's attention on the concept of odd and even numbers.

The Golden Beads — An Introduction to the Decimal System:

Dr. Montessori developed a wonderful educational material called the Golden Beads to illustrate concretely the nature of place value in the decimal system and its basic operations. The name comes from the beautiful color used for the enamel finish on this set of small glass beads.

(Below) The Number Cards and Golden Beads Materials

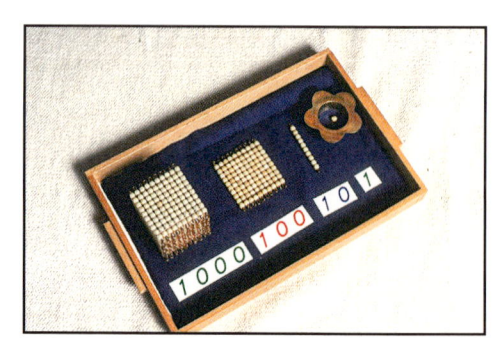

A Guided Tour of Montessori Classrooms — Math

(Right) The Bank Game

Preparing to exchange ten "10s" for one "100" in the Bank Game.

A single bead by itself represents a unit of one. Thus, the number 5 would be represented by a collection of five "unit" beads.

Ten "unit" beads strung together on a length of wire represents a unit of ten. Three "10" bars collected together actually consists of thirty "unit" beads, or three "10s". The children quickly discover that ten "unit beads are exactly the same as one "10" bar. They also begin to count not only the individual "unit" beads but by units of ten: 10, 20, 30 ... 100.

Ten "10" bead bars naturally equal the quantity of one hundred. Units of one hundred are made up of ten "10" bead bars laid side by side and wired together to form a square.

Ten "100" squares stacked one on top of the other form a cube containing one thousand "unit" beads. They are permanently wired together to form the thousand cube. Using these concrete materials, even very young children can build and work with great numbers. In a typical early lesson with the Golden Beads, the teacher might challenge the child to, "Bring me three '1,000s,' five '100s,' six '10s,' and one 'unit.'" While they will also work with prepared problem cards, children often enjoy thinking up numbers for themselves.

The Numeral Cards: This special set of numeral cards is used to help the children learn to read numerals up to 9,999. Used to label the units, tens, hundreds, and thousands in which the Golden Beads are laid out, they help children begin to understand the concept of the hierarchy of the decimal quantities and how we borrow and exchange from the next column in mathematical operations. The large size of the cards and the color coding used to represent units, tens, hundreds, and thousands makes it easy for children to understand how large quantities are constructed from right to left, read from left to right, and worked with in vertical columns.

3561

The Bank Game: The "bank" is a name given to a collection of Golden Bead materials, which includes enough "units," "10" bars, "100" squares, and "1,000" cubes to allow several children to create large numbers.

In one of the first exercises, the children explore the equivalencies of the decimal system. They learn that ten "units" can be exchanged at the bank for a "10" bar, and that a "10" bar can be exchanged for ten "units." They also find that ten "10s" can be exchanged for a "100" square, ten "100s" for one "1,000," and that each can, in turn, be broken down into its equivalent in the smaller quantity.

Using the Golden Bead material, the children can build two or more large numbers and add them together. By going through the steps of addition in this very

83

concrete manner, the children have a clear impression about what addition means. They also come to understand the process of exchanging, as they count the new quantities in each of the columns and trade in groups of ten "units" for one "10" bar, which they place in the "10s" columns; ten "10" bars for one "100"; and ten "100s" for one "1,000."

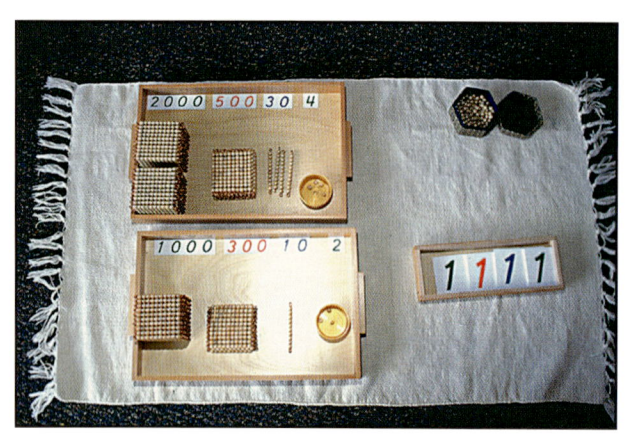

(Above) The Bank Game

*A problem laid out and ready to be solved with the **Bank Game**.*

Once they understand how to add with the Golden Beads, Montessori children begin to use them to multiply, subtract, and divide. For example, to divide the quality 3,333 by three, a child would set out three wooden skittles, and, beginning with the largest quantity, in this case the "1,000" cubes, he gives one "1,000" to each skittle. He continues on with the "100s," "10s," and "units."

If the child were challenged to divide this same quantity by four, he would begin by exchanging the three "1,000s" for thirty "100s" squares, add them to the stack of three "100s," and then he would distribute them equally. After placing eight "100s" beneath each of the four skittles, he exchanges the remaining one "100" for ten "10" bars. This process of exchanging continues until the final answer is derived: eight "100s," three "10s," three "units," with a remainder of one "unit."

The Short Bead Stair: Using the Golden Bead material, the child sees the numbers one through nine represented as individual units. But, as we mentioned above, although the child can count the beads one at a time, it takes many years before most children can recognize and really understand the idea of number except by one-to-one correspondence.

To help the child truly begin to grasp the idea of quantities from one through nine, Dr. Montessori prepared a set of colored glass beads, in which each quantity is represented by the appropriate number of individual beads wired together as a bar with a specific, easily recognizable color. In this material, a "1" is represented by a single red bead; a "2" by two green beads strung together; the "3" by three pink beads, and so on up through the ten Golden Beads that represent a unit of ten. The children work with the Short Bead Stair for many years, using the material to add and subtract, exchange, borrow, explore multiples, and for many other arithmetic processes. For example, to multiply 9 x 8, the children would lay out eight "9" bars or nine "8" bars. By counting the result, they can check their work.

The Teens and Tens Boards (Ten's Board is pictured on opposite page): This material is made up of two different sets of boards used by the child to explore the nature of quantities and numbers greater than nine. Each set consists of two boards, which are placed in a vertical row. The two boards are divided into nine sections, each of which is fitted with a thin frame into which the children can slide wooden cards on which the numerals 1 through 9 have been printed. Numerals have also been printed on the surface of the board, spaced so that when the cards are slid into the frame they will cover up one of the two digits.

On the **Teens Boards**, the numeral 10 is printed in the nine spaces created by the frames. The children arrange the numerals cards from 1 to 9 in order and slide them into the frames, creating the numerals 11, 12, 13 ... and so on through 19.

Using the Ten Bead Bars and the Short Bead Stair material described above, the children lay out the numbers 11 through 19 concretely. For example, the number 18 would be formed by placing one "10" bar in the "tens" column and one brown "8" bar in the "unit" column. This gives them a very clear picture of how the teens are formed and written: 10 + 1 is 11; 10 + 2 is 12; etc.

On the **Tens Boards**, the numerals 10, 20, 30, 40 through 90 are printed in the nine spaces created by the frames. They use the individual cards to form numbers in the "10s," such as 53, 24, 79, etc. and use the Golden Bead "10s" and "unit" beads or Short Bead Stair to build their concrete representations alongside.

A GUIDED TOUR OF MONTESSORI CLASSROOMS — MATH

The Tens Board

The Hundred Board challenges the young child who can count aloud from one to one hundred to lay out the numerals in the same sequence. The Board is a square divided into ten rows with ten small squares along each row. The children work with a set of one hundred wooden tiles that are labeled from one through one hundred.

Students spread the tiles out on the rug, arrange them in numerical order, and place them, one tile at a time, on the Hundred Board, working from the upper left-hand corner along each row to the right, down to next row, and so on until complete. When they are comfortable with this, they attempt the same exercise by filling in the squares on a blank chart drawn to duplicate the surface of the Hundred Board.

The Hundred Board

The Hundred and Thousand Chain: Another way that the children practice their counting and develop an increasingly clear concept of the size of one hundred and one thousand is by working with the Hundred and Thousand Chains.

These are long chains created by connecting ten "10" bars together to form a chain one hundred beads long, or in the case of the Thousand Chain, by connecting one hundred "10" bars together to form a chain of one thousand.

The children lay the chains out, duplicating them by creating a second line of individual "10" bars. At the far end, they place the "100" square or "1,000" cube, as appropriate. When working with the Thousand Chain, they also set out "100" squares after every ten "10" bars along the chain, representing that the next one hundred mark has been crossed.

In another exercise, they work with numeral cards printed with the numeral 1 to 100 or 1 to 1,000, counting by tens. The children sort them in order and place them along the chain. They tend to be quite impressed when they first see the Thousand Chain laid out across the classroom floor.

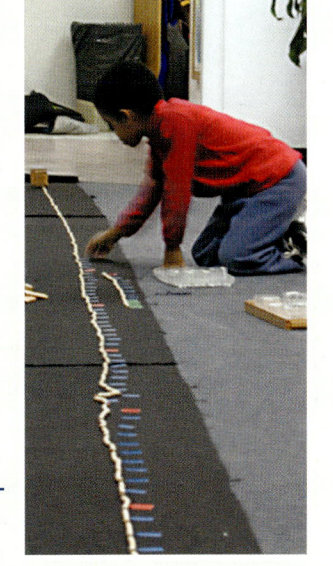

(Right) The Thousand Chain

85

The Square and Cube Chains: Following the same concept, the Square and Cube Chains introduce the child to the concept of skip counting by ones, twos, threes, fours, etc. through tens. Each chain is constructed by connecting multiples of the Short Bead Stair, using the same color scheme that the children learned before: red "units," green "2" bead bars, pink "3" bead bars, etc. The material also introduces the children to the concept of the squares and cubes of the numbers one through ten.

There are two chains for each number: one set representing the squares of the numbers one through ten, and the other representing the cubes. Thus, the square of five is shown as a chain of five "5" bead bars (the square of 5=25) and the cube as a chain of twenty-five "5" bead bars (5 cubed=125).

The material also includes a set of bead bars connected to show the squares and cubes of the numbers as actual squares and cubes. The children use the bead chains to skip count, working with number arrows similar to those used with the Hundreds and Thousand Chains.

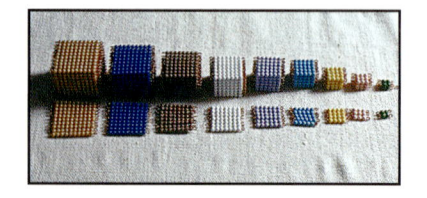

These students are skip counting using the Bead Chains.

(Above) The Squaring and Cubing Materials

*The **Squares and Cubes** of the numbers one through ten.*

The Stamp Game represents a next step toward abstract thinking in the Montessori Math curriculum. The Golden Beads and Colored Bead Bars concretely represent quantities as three-dimensional objects, the materials are essentially tokens, symbolic counters identical in size and differing only in color and in how they are labeled, but which represent different quantities. The Stamp Game is a box containing little wooden tiles (originally Dr. Montessori used paper squares that looked like postage stamps). Some are colored green and labeled "1" to show that they are units. Some are colored blue and labeled "10" to show that each represents a set of ten units. Some are colored red and labeled "100," and the last set is colored green and labeled "1,000" to show that each represents a unit of one thousand.

The children use the Stamps just as they did the Golden Beads, laying out quantities using the symbolic tokens to add, subtract, multiply, and divide. By this level, the children are normally writing their work on paper and using the stamps to help them visualize the process.

(Above) The Stamp Game

*Performing addition with the **Stamp Game**.*

For example, to subtract 822 from 1,000, the child would create four columns of stamps, beginning on the left with the "1,000s," then the "100s," the "10s," and the "units." Into the top row she would place a single "1,000" stamp in the "1,000" column. Below, she would place nothing in the "1,000" column, eight "100" stamps in the "100" column, two "10" stamps in the "10s" column, and two "units" in the "unit" column. Beginning with the "units," the child seeks to take two stamps away from the quantity above. Since the column is empty, she turns to the row to the left (the "10s"), which is also empty. Eventually she finds that her only choice is to exchange the one "1,000" stamp for ten "100," which she places in the "10s" column. Now she exchanges one of the hundreds for ten "10s," which she places in the "10s" column. Finally, she is ready to borrow from the "10s" column to solve her problem. She exchanges one "10" from the "10s" column and exchanges it for ten "units" and places them in the "units" column in the top row. From this ten, she takes away two, leaving eight "units." This process continues, until she finds that her top row contains the correct answer: zero "1,000s," one "100s," seven "10s," and eight "units" (1,000 - 822 = 178).

Fraction Work

The Fraction Materials: As the children become more and more comfortable with the Golden Beads, they eventually begin to ask whether there is anything smaller than the unit. The Fraction Skittles introduce children to the concept of a quarter, half, and whole. The Fraction Circles take this concept much further. It is a set of ten metal frames into which are set ten circles: one left intact; one divided into two parts; another into thirds, fourths, fifths through tenths.

The children learn the terminology, how to write fractions as figures, and begin to explore first the concepts of equivalence ($2/4 = 1/2$) and basic operations with fractions ($1/2 + 2/4 = 1$).

87

MONTESSORI PROGRAMS

The Short Division Board

Multiplication & Division

The Short Multiplication and Division Boards offer another pathway to abstraction with these two operations. In the Multiplication Board, the child lays out individual unit beads on a board organized into nine rows of nine shallow holes. The child lays out the beads in columns. For example, 4 x 8 would be eight columns of four beads in each column.

The Short Division Board is similar, except that here each vertical column of shallow holes represents one equal share, where a quantity is divided into two or more groups. The child places one small skittle at the top of each column to mark the number of shares that will be in the divisor. To divide twenty-four by six, she begins by placing six skittles along the top. Then she counts out the number of beads that she wants to divide and begins to distribute them, placing one bead in each hole from the top left to right and then down a row, until she finally has shared her quantity equally among the vertical columns. Any beads left over are her "remainder."

(Left) The Long Division Racks and Tubes

The **Long Division Racks and Tubes** help elementary students master division with the use of tubes, skittles, and beads with dividends up to the millions and divisors of up to four digits. It's not unusual for elementary students to work through problems using numbers much larger than a trillion.

(Below) The Multiplication Checkerboard

The **Multiplication Checkerboard** is used by elementary students to master multiplication with numerical hierarchies in the decimal system up to 100,000,000.

The Multiplication Board

88

A Guided Tour of Montessori Classrooms — Math

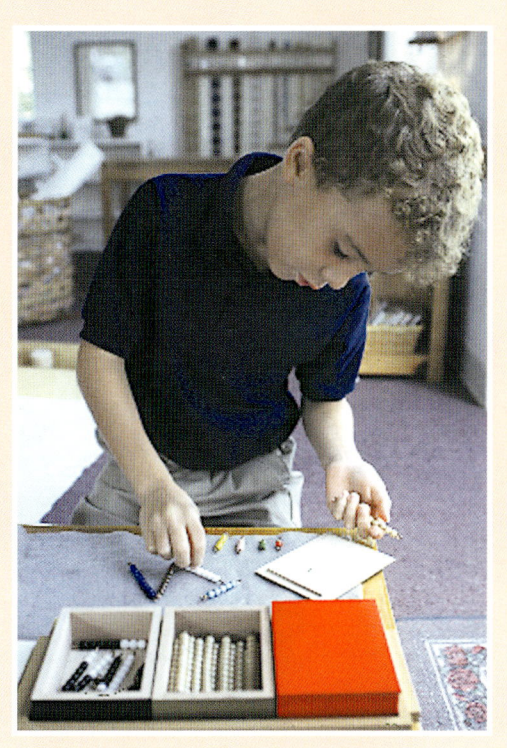

(Above) The Snake Game

The passage to abstraction: By this stage the children are recording their work on paper, although many won't be able to solve the same problems if asked to work with paper and pencil alone without the visual aid of the Montessori materials. Most young children under the age of seven or eight find it difficult, if not impossible, to grasp abstract quantities and what's really happening when we add, subtract, multiply, or divide. The concrete Montessori materials help the child to see and understand, slowly internalizing each concept until it becomes fixed and clear in her mind.

Naturally children can't depend on the materials forever. The entire purpose of the Montessori Math curriculum is to make the abstract concrete, until the child can close her eyes and visualize mathematical processes at work. Step by step, the materials become less concrete and more symbolic.

Step by step, children are challenged to demonstrate their understanding by teaching what they have learned to younger children, which also tends to reinforce and clarify their grasp of the subjects.

Montessori uses a wide range of parallel materials and exercises to help children extend their knowledge and gradually memorize the basic math facts that every one of us is expected to know. As parents, you will eventually begin to hear about materials with odd names like the **Snake Game**, the **Addition and Subtraction Strip Boards**, and the **Negative Snake Game**. Space doesn't allow us to describe every one of the Montessori math materials, but your child would probably be delighted to introduce them to you.

(Above) The Addition Strip Board

(Above) The Multiplication Memorization Chart

*This student is mastering his multiplication facts with the help of one of the **Memorization Charts**.*

Memorization Charts: There is also an involved series of Memorization Charts and associated exercises that help the children in their final stages of mastering addition, subtraction, multiplication, and division.

When the children have begun to show that they are ready for still more abstract exercises, they're introduced to another series of math materials. For example, the **Bead Frames** (or abacus) (pictured on page 90) challenge the child to solve problems in a still more abstract process.

The **Short Bead Frame** allows the child to work with quantities up to 9,999. The **Long Bead Frame** uses quantities as large as 9,999,999.

MONTESSORI PROGRAMS

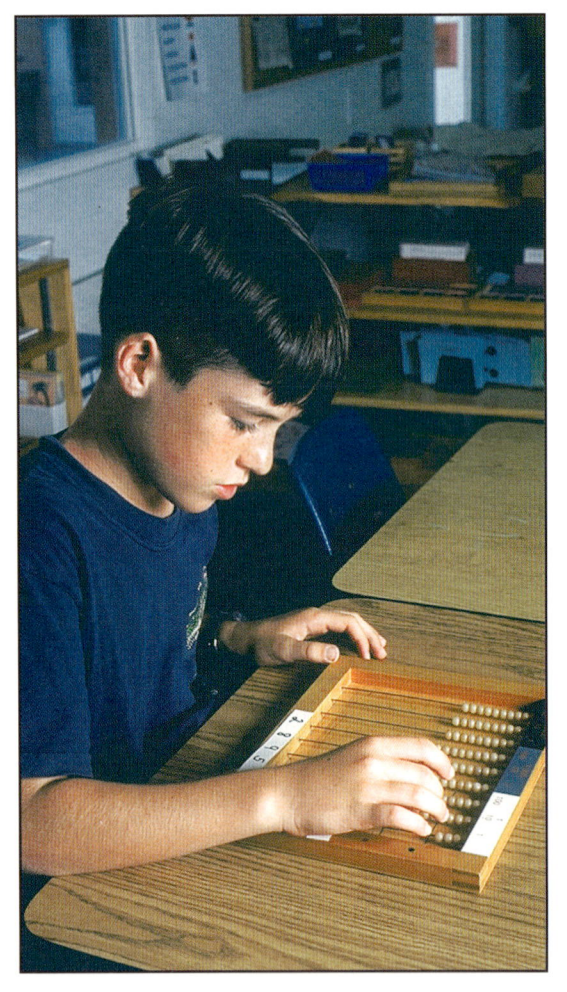

(Left) The Flat Bead Frame (Abacus)

The **Flat Bead Frame** represents the final step in the passage to abstraction with multiplication. It contains nine columns of Golden Beads with a zero at the base of each column. Color-coded dots representing the numerical hierarchies are found along the side of the Frame. The white, grey, and black strips along the top indicate the units of numbers: 1, 1,000, 1,000,000.

(Above) The Geometric Stick Materials

The **Geometric Stick Materials** are used to study angles and the construction of plane geometric figures.

(Below) The Long Bead Frame

(Left) Geometric Figures

At the elementary level, the children move on beyond learning the names of geometric figures to mastering the definitions as well. They also begin to construct geometric forms with protractor and compass.

90

History, Geography, & International Culture

We are all members of the human family. Our roots lie in the distant past, and history is the story of our common heritage. Without a strong sense of history, we cannot begin to know who we are as individuals today. Our goal is to develop a global perspective, and the study of history and world cultures forms the cornerstone of the Montessori curriculum.

With this goal in mind, Montessori teaches history and world cultures starting as early as age three. The youngest students work with specially designed maps and begin to learn the names of the world's continents and countries. Physical geography begins in the first grade with a study of the formation of the Earth, the emergence of the oceans and atmosphere, and the evolution of life. Students learn about the world's rivers, lakes, deserts, mountain ranges, and natural resources.

Elementary students begin to study world cultures in greater depth: the cus-

(Right) The Big Bang

Here is one student's artistic interpretation of the Big Bang.

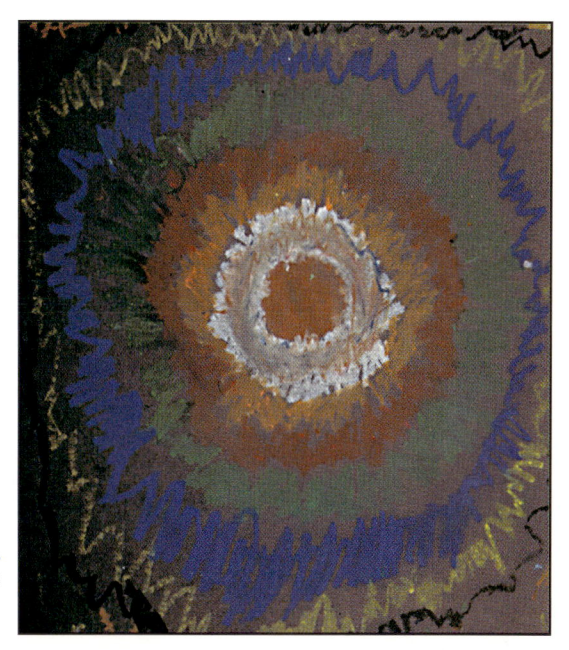

MONTESSORI PROGRAMS

toms, housing, diet, government, industry, the arts, history, and dress. They learn to treasure the richness of their own cultural heritage and those of their friends.

The children also study the emergence of human beings during the old and new stone ages, the development of the first civilizations, and the universal needs common to all humanity. For older elementary students, the focus is respectively on early man, ancient civilizations, and early-American history.

Montessori tries to present a sense of living history at every level through direct hands-on experience. Students build models of ancient tools and structures, prepare their own manuscripts, make ceremonial masks, and re-create all sorts of artifacts of the everyday life of historical eras. Experiences such as these make it much easier for Montessori children to appreciate history as it is taught through books.

While Montessori schools are communities apart from the outside world, in which children can first begin to develop their unique talents, they are also consciously connected to the local, national, and global communities. The goal is to lead each student to explore, understand, and grow into full and active membership in the adult world.

Field trips provide opportunities to explore the world outside the classroom.

(Above) Research Card Materials

Younger elementary children often use simplified research card material and charts in their studies.

(Left) The Imaginary Island Puzzle

The **Imaginary Island Puzzle** *introduces students in elementary classes to thirty-eight land and water forms. They study vocabulary and definitions of such words as isthmus, butte, tributary, archipelago, bight, lagoon,* and more.

Children also learn to plot longitude and latitude and analyze the flora and fauna of a region. With the use of eighty-four puzzle pieces, students are able to create an infinite variety of islands of their own design, modifying them at will, and reinforcing vocabulary words during the process.

GUIDED TOUR OF MONTESSORI CLASSROOMS — HISTORY, GEOGRAPHY, & INTERNATIONAL CULTURE

(Right) International studies continue at every age level in Montessori education. The curriculum integrates art, music, dance, cooking, geography, literature, and science. Children learn to prepare and enjoy dishes from all over the world. They learn traditional folk songs and dances in music and explore folk crafts in art. In Language Arts, they read the traditional folk tales and research and prepare reports about the countries they are studying that year. Units of study often culminate in marvelous international holidays and festivals that serve as the high points of the school year.

Foreign Languages

As part of the International Studies program, most Montessori schools introduce a second language to even their youngest children. The primary goal in a Foreign Language program is to develop conversational skills along with a deepening appreciation for the culture of the second language.

The student pictured here is researching colonial America.

MONTESSORI PROGRAMS

(Above) The Land and Water Forms

This student is working with the **Land and Water Forms**, a set of three-dimensional models that represent, in very simple terms, the nature of basic geographic features. This is also a pouring exercise, as the child adds water to the tray to create a higher level of sensory impression. Here she explores the idea that an island is a body of land surrounded by water, while a lake is a body of water surrounded on all sides by land.

The children learn to name each form, match the model with a photo of a real lake or island, place the correct printed label underneath each form, then prepare their own labels. They also learn the definitions of each form, continue to learn about the largest lakes or islands in the world, and research facts about specific places.

The first set includes such geographic forms as an isthmus, peninsula, cape, bay, *and* strait. Advanced exercises introduce more complex geographic features, such as mountains, mountain ranges, volcanoes, archipelagos, foothills, cliffs, mesas, prairies, river valleys, *and* river deltas.

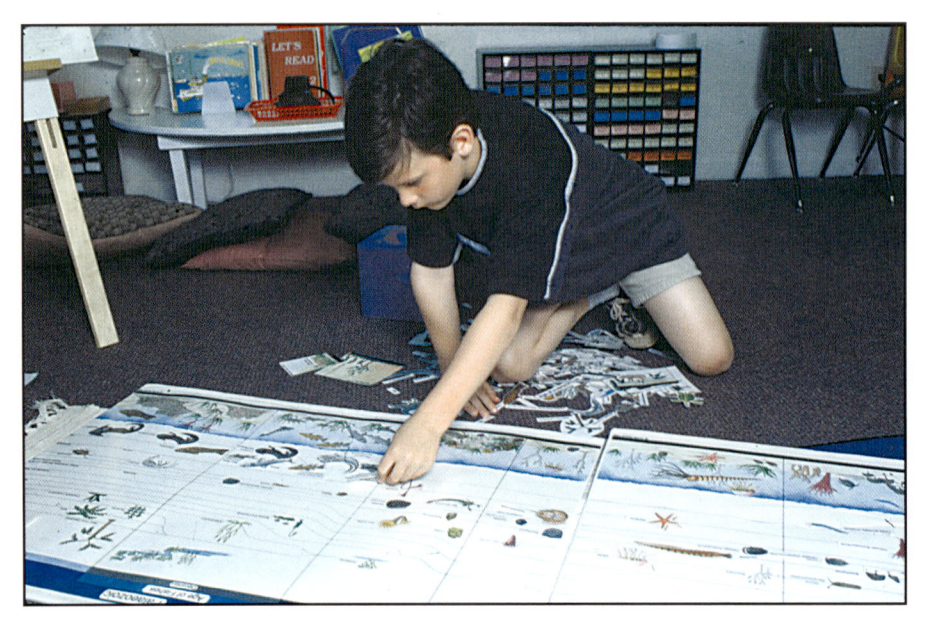

(Above) The Teaching Clock

Before a child can begin to understand history, she needs to begin to grasp the concepts of time. This child is learning to tell time, along with the other concepts of the passage of time, such as: How long is a minute, an hour, a day, a year? How old are the people that I know?

(Above) "Cuneiform" Tablets

A set of clay "cuneiform" tablets made by a class of elementary students who are studying ancient history.

(Left) Time Lines

A lower-elementary student at work with the **Time Line of Life on the Earth.**

A Guided Tour of Montessori Classrooms — History, Geography, & International Culture

Working with a section of the Time Line of Life on the Earth

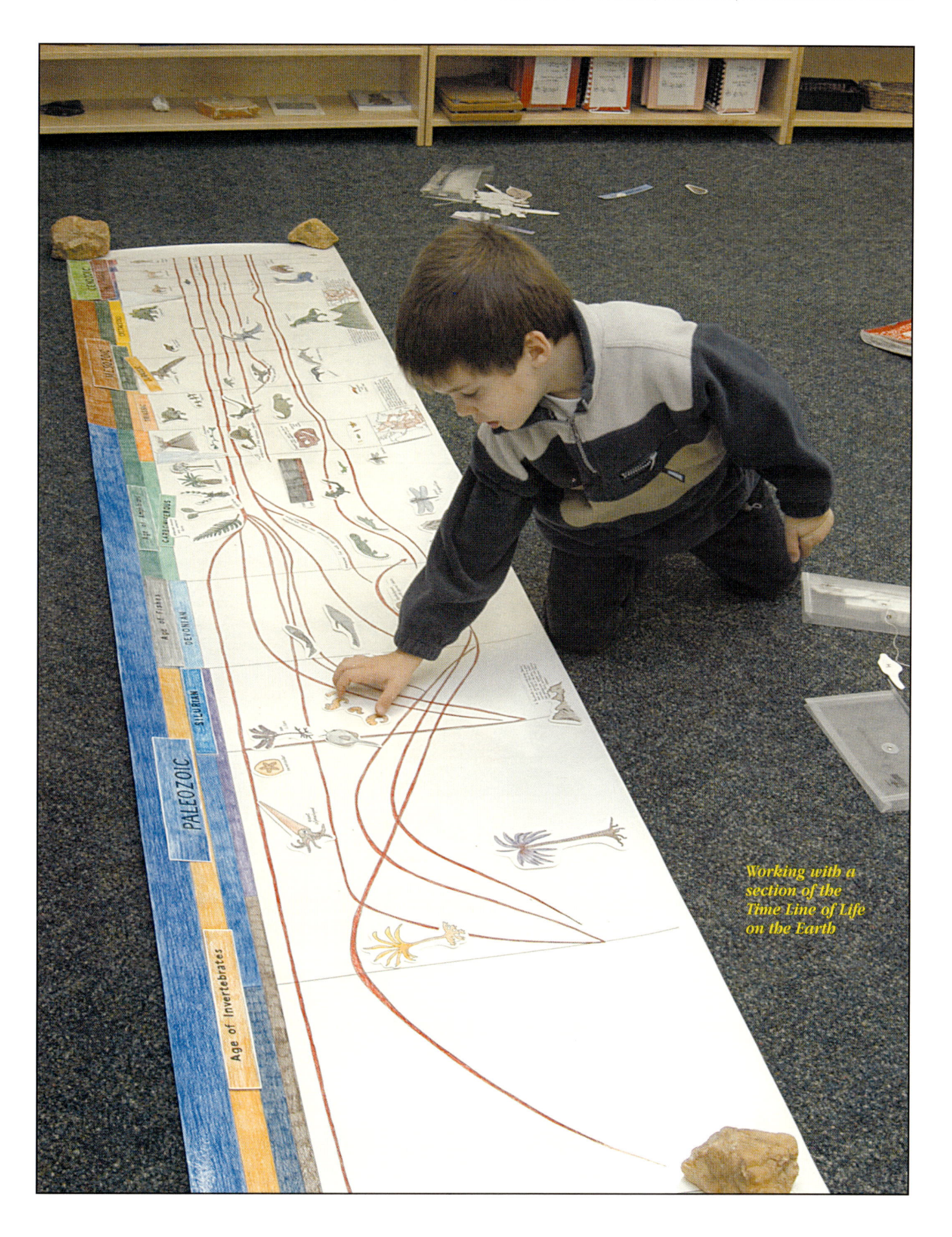

95

Montessori Programs

GUIDED TOUR OF THE MONTESSORI CLASSROOM — HISTORY, GEOGRAPHY, & INTERNATIONAL CULTURE

Montessori Maps & Globes

(Below) Puzzle Map of the Continents & Continent Globe

These children are beginning to grasp that flat maps, such as the Puzzle Map of the Continents, represent geographical features on a world that is a sphere. They note that the same color coding is used to show the continents on the Continent Globe and the Puzzle Map.

Primary children love to work with Puzzle Maps. At the beginning, they don't understand them to be maps of the Earth's surface; they are simply lovely puzzles. Gradually the children are taught the names of each continent and can identify a great many countries, states, and provinces. As they learn to read, they begin to label each piece.

(Above and below) Puzzle Maps

The student above is using a Puzzle Map to draw a map of North America.

(Left) Pin Maps

The Pin Maps challenge the upper elementary children to master the names of the countries, capital cities, and flags of the countries of several continents. Each label is printed on a card attached to a pin, which is placed in the appropriate hole on the map. A set of control charts allows these elementary children to check their own work.

Montessori Programs

Hands-On Science the Montessori Way

Science is an integral element of the Montessori curriculum. Among other things, it represents a way of life: a clear thinking approach to gathering information and problem solving. The scope of the Montessori Science curriculum includes a sound introduction to botany, zoology, chemistry, physics, geology, and astronomy.

Montessori does not separate science from the big picture of the formation of our world. Students consider the formation of the universe, development of the planet Earth, the delicate relations between living things and their physical environment, and the balance within the web of life. These great lessons integrate astronomy, the earth sciences, and biology with history and geography.

The Montessori approach to science cultivates children's fascination with the universe and helps them develop a lifelong interest in observing nature and discovering more about the world in which they live. Children are encouraged to observe, analyze, measure, classify, experiment, and predict and to do so with a sense of eager curiosity and wonder.

In Montessori, science lessons incorporate a balanced, hands-on approach. With encouragement and a solid foundation, even very young children are ready and anxious to investigate their world, to wonder at the interdependence of living things, to explore the ways in which the physical universe works, and to project how it all may have come to be.

For example, in many Montessori schools, children in the early elementary grades explore basic atomic theory and the process by which the heavier elements are fused out of hydrogen in the stars. Other students study advanced concepts in biology, including the systems by which scientists classify plants and animals. Some elementary classes build scale models of the solar system that stretch out over two miles!

(Above) The Clock of Eras

The elementary students shown above are working with the **Clock of Eras.** *This more advanced exercise presents the great geological eras of the Earth's history as a pie graph or clock face. The children label each geological era, from the formation of the Earth to the present day. In earlier exercises, they've begun to study what was happening on the Earth's surface during each era.*

"The secret of good teaching is to regard the child's intelligence as a fertile field in which seeds may be sown to grow under the heat of flaming imagination. Our aim is not only to make the child understand, and still less to force him to memorize, but so to touch his imagination as to enthuse him to his innermost core. We do not want complacent pupils but eager ones. We seek to sow life in the child rather than theories, to help him in his growth, mental and emotional as well as physical, and for that we must offer grand and lofty ideas to the human mind. If the idea of the universe is presented to the child in the right way, it will do more for him than just arouse his interest; it will create in him admiration and wonder, a feeling loftier than any interest and more satisfying."

— Maria Montessori

(Above) The Life Cycle of a Star

This eight-year-old is working with a model that depicts the life cycle of a star. This material is actually an introduction to the study of the chemical elements and how the more complex elements are "cooked up" in the nuclear furnace of the star's atomic fusion.

(Right) Model of the Solar System

Using this simple moving model, elementary students study the orbital relationships of the planets as they revolve around the sun.

MONTESSORI PROGRAMS

(Right) Exploring the Elements

This elementary student is exploring the elements. He is constructing models of the atomic structure of one element, placing protons and neutrons in the nucleus and electrons in the outer shells.

(Above) Constructing Molecules

These two elementary students are constructing models of common molecules, using wooden spheres to represent different elements.

(Above) Mendelev's Periodic Table of the Elements

*Working with this unique teaching version of **Mendelev's Periodic Table of the Elements**, elementary children begin to learn about the more complex elements, their symbols, and how various elements are grouped together according to their properties. At the same time, children are looking for examples of common elements in their daily environment and beginning to research information about the characteristics and uses of the elements.*

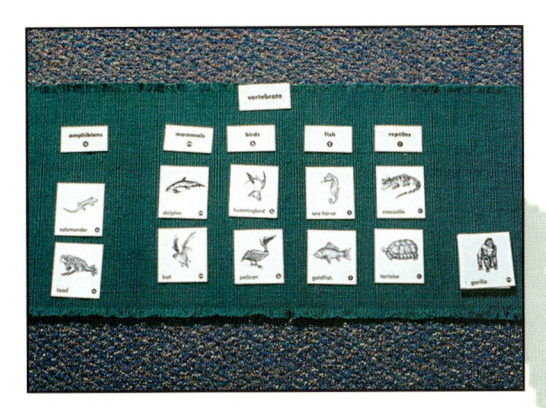

A GUIDED TOUR OF MONTESSORI CLASSROOMS — SCIENCE

(Above) Vertebrate Cards

The **Vertebrate Cards** help elementary children understand how to classify vertebrates into simple classes of amphibians, mammals, birds, fish, and reptiles.

(Right) Out of the Classroom ... Into the Garden

Working with nature, both in and out of the classroom helps Montessori students integrate conceptual science with practical life skills. Students of all ages experience the excitement of watching their seedlings develop into beautiful flowers for a floral arrangement to decorate their classroom or vegetables to prepare for a mid-morning snack.

(Left) Chart of the Plant Kingdom

These nine-year-old students are classifying cards with different plants on the **Chart of the Plant Kingdom** into their phyla and genera.

(Right) Three-Part Cards

Younger students use the **Three-Part Cards** to isolate each element as part of a system to learn correct terminology.

101

MONTESSORI PROGRAMS

(Above) A display of one child's research.

(Left) The study of basic chemistry continues with simple science experiments.

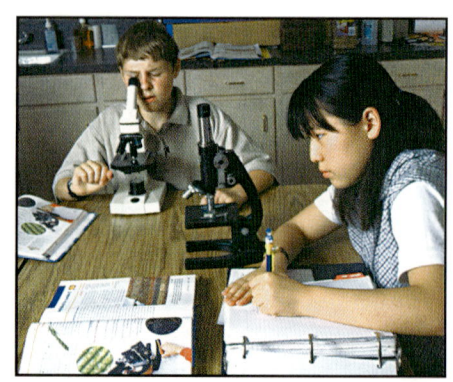

(Opposite Page) An elementary student receives a lesson in the anatomy of the human brain.

(Right) Using sophisticated scientific equipment, Montessori students explore the world around them.

(Left) Studying rocks and minerals.

A GUIDED TOUR OF MONTESSORI CLASSROOMS — SCIENCE

MONTESSORI PROGRAMS

The Arts

Art is not a separate area of the Montessori curriculum; it is an integral component. Throughout the day, even the youngest students are surrounded by the beauty of the materials and activities that Dr. Montessori developed for each developmental level. From the smooth, simple elegance of the Geometric Solids to the ever-increasing complexities of drawing using the Metal Insets, Montessori uses all of the children's senses to promote an awareness and appreciation of the beauty in all things — animate and inanimate.

In the early years, children are free to spend quiet moments in a special art corner of their classroom: painting, drawing, or working with age-appropriate crafts. Some, but certainly not all, Montessori schools will employ the talents of an art specialist, and many schools expand on their art programs through special after-school workshops.

Older students will incorporate art into their lessons when studying history, science, math, and international cultures. Art and music appreciation are re-introduced in greater depth throughout the years, and students of all ages enjoy performing in dramatic and musical productions for their families and at special school-wide celebrations.

MONTESSORI PROGRAMS
Health, Wellness, & Physical Education

Montessori schools are very interested in helping children develop control of their fine- and gross-motor movements. For young children, programs will typically include dance, balance and coordination exercises, and loosely structured cardiovascular exercise, as well as the vigorous free play that is typical on any playground.

With elementary and older students, the ideal Montessori Health, Physical Education, and Athletics program is typically very unlike that of the traditional model of "gym." It challenges each student and adult in the school community to develop a personal program of lifelong exercise, recreation, and health management.

A Guided Tour of the Montessori Classroom — Health, Wellness, & Physical Education

Montessori Programs

In Closing — The Role of Parents

Parents play a vital role in the development of "community" in Montessori schools. Through their presence at school as volunteers and through a wide range of social events and celebrations, students get to know the families of their friends and grow up with a sense of being part of an extended community. One of our common goals is to lead each of our students to explore, understand, and grow into full and active membership in the adult world.

Montessori for the Kindergarten Year

Every year at re-enrollment time, in thousands of Montessori schools all over North America, parents of four- and almost-five-year-old children are trying to decide whether or not they should keep their sons and daughters in Montessori for kindergarten or send them off to the local public schools.

The advantages of using the local schools often seem obvious; the advantages of staying in Montessori are sometimes not at all clear. When parents can use the local schools for free, why would they want to invest thousands of dollars in another year's tuition? It's a fair question, and it deserves a careful answer. Obviously, there is no one right answer for every child. Often the decision depends on where each family places its priorities and how strongly parents sense that one school or another more closely matches their hopes and dreams for their children. Naturally, to some degree the answer is also often connected to the question of family income as well. We are amazed, however, at how often families with very modest means place such a high priority on their children's education that they are willing to find the tuition dollars needed to keep them in Montessori.

So here are a few answers to some of the questions parents often ask about Montessori for the kindergarten-age child.

Q *In a nutshell, what would be the most important short-term disadvantage of sending my five-year-old to the local school?*

A When a child transfers from Montessori to a new kindergarten, she spends the first few months adjusting to a new class, a new teacher, and a whole new system with different expectations. This, along with the fact that most kindergartens have a much lower set of expectations for five-year-olds than most Montessori programs, severely cuts into the learning that could occur during this crucial year of their lives.

In a few cases, Montessori Kindergarten children may look as if they are not as advanced as a child in a very academically accelerated program, but what they *do* know, they usually know very well. Their understanding of the decimal system, place value, mathematical operations, and similar information is usually very sound. With reinforcement as they grow older, it becomes internalized and a permanent part of who they are. When they leave Montessori before they have had the time to internalize these early concrete experiences, their early learning often evaporates because it is neither reinforced nor commonly understood.

Q *What would be the most important advantages of keeping my five-year-old in Montessori?*

A Montessori is an approach to working with children that is carefully based on what we've learned about children's cognitive, neurological, and emotional development from several decades of research. Although sometimes misunderstood, the Montessori approach has often been acclaimed as the most developmentally appropriate model currently available by many experts on early childhood and elementary education.

One important difference between what Montessori offers the five-year-old and what is offered by many of today's kindergarten programs has to do with how it helps the young child learn how to learn.

Over recent years educational research has increasingly shown that students in many schools don't really understand most of what they are being taught. Howard Gardner, Harvard Psychologist and author of the best-selling book, *The Unschooled Mind,* goes so far as to suggest that, "Many schools have fallen into a pattern of giving kids exercises and drills that result in their getting answers on tests that look like understanding. Most students, from as young as those in kindergarten to students in some of the finest colleges in America do not understand what they've studied, in the most basic sense of the term. They lack the capacity to take knowledge learned in one setting and apply it appropriately in a different setting. Study after study has found that, by and large, even the best students in the best schools can't do that." ("On Teaching for Understanding: A Conversation with Howard Gardner," by Ron Brandt, *Educational Leadership Magazine,* ASCD, 1994.)

Montessori is focused on teaching for understanding. In a primary classroom, three- and four-year-olds receive the benefit of two years of sensorial preparation for academic skills by working with the concrete Montessori learning materials. This concrete sensorial experience gradually allows the child to form a mental picture of concepts, such as: *How big is a thousand? How many hundreds make up a thousand?* and *What is really going on when we borrow or carry numbers in mathematical operations?*

The value of the sensorial experiences that the younger children have had in Montessori has often been underestimated by both parents and educators. Research is very clear that young children learn by observing and manipulating their environment — not through textbooks and workbook exercises. The Montessori materials give the child a concrete sensorial impression of abstract concepts, such as long division, that become the foundation for a lifetime of understanding.

Because Montessori teachers are well trained in child development, they normally know how to present information in developmentally appropriate ways.

In many American schools, children do exercises and fill in workbook pages with little understanding. There is a great deal of rote learning. Superficially, it may seem that these children are learning the material. However, all too often, a few months down the road, little of what they "learned" will be retained, and it will be rare for the children to be able to use their knowledge and skills in new situations.

Learning to be organized and learning to be focused is as important as any academic work. Doing worksheets quickly can be impressive to parents, but there is rarely any deep learning going on. More and more educational researchers are beginning to focus on whether students, young or old, really understand or have simply memorized correct answers.

Q *In a class with such a wide age range of children, won't my five-year-old spend the year taking care of younger children instead of doing his own work?*

A The five-year-olds in Montessori classes often help the younger children with their work, actually teaching lessons or correcting errors. Anyone who has ever had to teach a skill to someone else may recall that the very process of explaining a new concept or helping someone practice a new skill leads the teacher to learn as much, if not more, than the pupil. When one child tutors another, the tutor often learns more from the experience than the person being tutored. Experiences that aid in the development of independence and autonomy are often very limited in traditional schools.

Q *Isn't it better for children to attend schools with the children from their own neighborhoods?*

A Once upon a time, people bought homes and raised their families in the same neighborhood. There was a real sense of community. Today, the average family will move two or three times before their children go to college. The relationships that once bound families living in the same neighborhood together into a community have grown weak in many parts of the country.

In many Montessori schools, families who live in different neighborhoods but who share similar values have come together to create and enjoy the extended community of their school.

Children growing up in Montessori schools over the last fifty years often speak of how closely knit their friendships were with their schoolmates and their families.

MONTESSORI PROGRAMS

Q *Since most children will eventually have to go to the neighborhood schools, wouldn't it be better for them to make the transition in kindergarten rather than in first grade?*

A The American Montessori Society tells of one father who wrote, "We considered the school years ahead. We realized a child usually does his best if he has good learning habits, a sound basis in numbers and math, and the ability to read. We realized that he has had an excellent two-year start in his Montessori school. If he were to transfer now to the local kindergarten program, he would probably go no further than he is now; whereas, if he stays in Montessori, he will reap the benefits of his past work under the enthusiastic guidance of teachers who will share his joy in learning."

Many families are aware that by the end of the kindergarten year, Montessori students will often have developed academic skills that may be beyond those of children enrolled in most American kindergarten programs; however, parents should remember that academic progress is not our ultimate goal. Our real hope is that children will have an incredible sense of self-confidence, enthusiasm for learning, and will feel closely bonded to their teachers and classmates. We want much more than competency in the basic skills; we want children to enjoy school and feel good about themselves as students.

Once children have developed a high degree of self-confidence, independence, and enthusiasm for the learning process, they normally can adapt to all sorts of new situations. While there are wonderful and exciting reasons to consider keeping a child in Montessori through elementary school and beyond, by the time they are in first grade, they will typically be able to go off to their new school with a vibrant curiosity and excitement about making new friends and learning new things.

Q *If I keep my child in Montessori for kindergarten, won't he/she be bored in a traditional first-grade program?*

A Montessori children, by the end of age five, are usually curious, self-confident learners who look forward to going to school. They are normally engaged, enthusiastic learners who honestly want to learn and ask excellent questions.

What teacher wouldn't want a room filled with children like that? Well, truthfully, over the years we've found some who consider these children "disruptive."

Remember that Montessori children are real human beings, and not all children who attend Montessori fit the idealized description; however, enough do that the generalization is often fairly accurate.

Montessori children by age six have spent three or four years in a school, where they were treated with honesty and respect. While there were clear expectations and ground rules within that framework, their opinions and questions were taken quite seriously. Unfortunately, there are still some teachers and schools where children who ask questions are seen as challenging authority. You can imagine an independent Montessori child asking his new teacher, *"But why do I have to ask each time I need to use the bathroom?* or *Why do I have to stop my work right now?"*

So the honest answer is that it depends on the teacher and school.

From an academic viewpoint, Montessori children will generally be doing very well by the end of kindergarten, although, once again, that is not our ultimate objective. The program offers them enriched lessons in math, reading, language, and a wide range of lessons in science, geography, and other cultural areas. If they are ready, they will normally develop excellent skills and become quite "culturally literate."

When one of these children enters a traditional first grade, they may have already mastered the skills that their new school considers first-grade curriculum. Some Montessori children are still more advanced. Some non-Montessori elementary schools are willing and able to adapt their curriculum to meet the needs of individual students who are ready for accelerated work, but check that this will occur daily rather than occasionally.

The key concept in Montessori is the child's interest and readiness for advanced work. If a child is not developmentally ready to go on, she is not left behind or made to feel like a failure. Our goal is not to ensure that our children develop at a pre-determined rate but to ensure that whatever they do, they do well. Most Montessori children master a tremendous amount of information and skills. Even in the rare case where one of our children may not have made as much progress as we would have wished, she will usually be moving along steadily at her own pace and will feel good about herself as a learner.

QUESTIONS FOR PARENTS TO PONDER

What were the most important factors that led you to select a Montessori education for your child?

What are the most important goals that you have for your child's education?

What skills, knowledge, and attitudes do our children need to be prepared as adults for living in the twenty-first century?

In what way does Montessori provide children with the skills, knowledge, and attitudes that they will need to succeed in the real world?

MONTESSORI PROGRAMS

Joyful Scholars: Montessori for the Elementary Years

During the early childhood years in Montessori classrooms, parents watch as their young children learn to read, write, and explore the world around them. The learning process seems painless and incredibly effective. It is both. What it is *not* is simple. The Montessori Method has been perfected over many decades, and it takes many years of dedication to become a Montessori teacher.

Montessori parents who are thrilled with their young children's progress often urge Montessori schools to expand their program to include the elementary years.

The Elementary Montessori program has also been proven to be painless and effective. Establishing a new elementary program, however, is not simple. It is not merely an extension of what came before. It is exciting, complex, and different!

Elementary Montessori teachers become certified after a rigorous course of study lasting a full year or longer. Qualified Montessori teachers at this level are in great demand and are often hard to find. Older students are also physically larger, requiring more classroom space. In addition to the Montessori materials that students at this level will continue to use, new research and teaching materials, such as encyclopedias, computers, and microscopes become exciting, necessary, and expensive educational tools.

Then there's the issue of accountability. This is the level when parents become increasingly focused on how their children compare to other students of the same age who have experienced a non-Montessori education. Issues of grading, test scores, and homework are raised much more often.

While these challenges should be carefully considered before expanding an existing program to include the elementary years, it is important to remember that Montessori at the elementary level works! It is the important next step in the lives of the "renaissance" adults we hope our children will someday become, and it is well worth the effort that it takes to produce a quality program.

As children near the end of their kindergarten year in Montessori, many parents struggle with the question of whether or not to keep their children in Montessori for the elementary program. On the one hand, the typical Montessori five-year-old's self-confidence and love of learning makes many families ask: "Why tamper with something that is clearly working?" On the other hand, since the children will be moving on to another class one way or the other, many parents feel that the first grade seems to be the logical time to make the transition from Montessori.

For many families, a major consideration will be the ability to save thousands of dollars a year by taking advantage of the local public schools. Others wonder if a more highly structured and competitive independent school would give their child a better preparation for college.

Although each family will analyze the issues in their own way, the family's final decision will involve an investment in their children's future. All of us want the best for our children, and the often unspoken concern of many parents is: "Will Montessori prepare my child for the *real* world?"

The answer, by the way, is *yes!* Montessori works! It has worked for years in thousands of Montessori schools around the world. Montessori has enjoyed the support of some of the leading personalities of our time, including President Woodrow Wilson, Alexander Graham Bell, Thomas Edison, Henry Ford, Mahatma Gandhi, Helen Keller, Sigmund Freud, Buckminster Fuller, Bertram Russell, Jean Piaget, Alfred Adler, Erik Erikson, Anne Frank (who was a Montessori student), and David Elkind, just to name a few. One elementary teacher responded to her parents' fears by describing "the Montessori Way" as follows:

"Many parents express the concern that Montessori at the elementary level may not prepare them for the 'real world.' I'm not exactly sure what that means. Is it that their Primary Montessori experience was too secure, too child-centered, too accepting? Surely, those qualities cannot be seen as negatives. Is it that there is a sneaking suspicion that all this Montessori stuff is fine up to kindergarten, but now it's time to face math tests and text

Authors' Note: For this chapter, we have drawn together some of Dr. Maria Montessori's thoughts about the foundation of education at the elementary years from three of her books, *To Educate the Human Potential*, *From Childhood to Adolescence*, and *Spontaneous Activity in Education*. In a few places, we have taken some liberty with the original translation for the purpose of clarity.

> "The passage to the second level of education is the passage from the sensorial, material level to the abstract. The need for abstraction and intellectual activity makes itself felt around the seventh year.
>
> Before age seven, the child focuses himself on a sensorial exploration and classification of the relationships among concrete objects — not exploration on the intellectual plane. The three- to seven-year-old generally is content to know **what** something is, along with a simplistic explanation of its function. The older child is oriented toward intellectual discovery and investigation.
>
> In the second period, the child needs wider boundaries for his social experiences. He needs to establish social relationships in a larger society and the traditional schools, as they have been conceived for so long, can no longer be sufficient for him. He feels the closed environment as a constraint, which is why children of this age may no longer go to school enthusiastically. He prefers to catch frogs or play with his friends without adult supervision. An education that suppresses the true nature of the child is an education that leads to the development of unhappy and socially immature adults.
>
> It is at age seven that one can note the beginning of an orientation toward the judgement of acts as right or wrong, fair or unfair ... This preoccupation belongs to a very special interior sensitivity – the conscience. The seven-to-twelve-year-old period, then, constitutes one of particular importance for moral education ... The adult must be aware of the evolution that is occurring in the mind of the child at this time and adapt his methods to conform with it.
>
> These three characteristics — the child's felt need to escape the closed environment, the passage of the mind to the abstract, and the birth in him of a moral sense — serve as the basis for a scheme at the elementary level."
>
> — Dr. Maria Montessori

books, standardized curricula and a real school? I suppose it is a question of examining one's own values regarding education. The observable fact is that the majority of children in Elementary Montessori programs achieve high-level academic standards because they are highly motivated and have been exposed to an extremely broad and integrated curriculum.

They may not have a weekly math test on which their grade is based, but they can prove to you that 'the answer in division is what one unit gets.' No, they won't have a multiple-choice quiz on Chapter 2 of their science or geography textbook. Rather, they can independently research topics using an encyclopedia, atlas, reference books, maps, microscopes, or magnifying glasses. Real school should engender a love of learning and an acceptance of personal responsibility for intellectual growth as well as social interaction. Real school attempts to shape long-term attitudes and concrete skills necessary not just to move up to the next grade, but to 'move up to' a successful and happy life."

Elementary children face new developmental challenges. A specially prepared learning environment is just as important now as it was before during the early childhood years if children are to fulfill their complete learning potential. More than school achievement test scores are at stake. Learning to identify, pursue, and communicate deep interests in the world leads children to self-mastery and to habits of lifelong learning.

Elementary Montessori students themselves are often the most compelling argument for the value of an Elementary Montessori education!

What makes Elementary Montessori different?

When you observe an Elementary Montessori class at work, you may find it difficult to get a sense of the big picture. Over here some students are working on math, some are reading, while others are working on science. In the corner, a teacher is giving a lesson to a small group of children, while occasionally glancing up to keep an eye on the rest of the class. The elementary classroom may appear to be unstructured, but these seemingly random, yet obviously purposeful activities, are basic to the independent learning and self-directed activity of the Montessori approach.

While there is a vast range in the level of curriculum on which the children are engaged, each child is considered as an individual. Montessori teachers strive to challenge each according to his or her developmental needs and abilities.

> Please keep in mind that, while Dr. Montessori developed a very specific model, individual Montessori schools and classrooms differ. These components, however, are typically found in most programs.

"Montessori Elementary gives children the opportunity to continue to progress at their own pace in an environment that nurtures a love of learning. Children take responsibility for their own learning and have daily opportunities to make decisions and choices in a child-centered classroom. They are exposed to many complex concepts at an early age through the use of wonderful concrete learning materials.

It is not unusual to see seven-year-olds in a Montessori classroom constructing atomic and molecular models. Nine-year-olds analyze the squares of trinomials, while ten-year-olds solve algebraic equations and twelve-year-olds compute the square root of large numbers.

What parent who has watched her children thrive both intellectually and socially in the Children's House would not want this to continue in the elementary years?"

— Judi Charlap
Elementary Montessori Teacher
The New Gate School, Sarasota, Florida

Basic Components of the Elementary Montessori Program

Multi-Age Class Groups

Elementary Montessori classes continue to bring children of different age levels together. Normally, classes will span three age/grade levels, with the common divisions being ages six to nine (grades one to three in the United States) and ages nine to twelve (grades four to six). Some schools may follow a somewhat different scheme of grouping their children. There are many reasons why Montessori classes group children of several grade levels together:

- Since Montessori allows children to progress through the curriculum at their own pace, there is no academic reason to group children according to one grade level.

- In a mixed-age class, children can always find peers who are working at their current level.

- To accommodate the needs of individual learners, Montessori classrooms have to include curriculum to cover the entire span of interests and abilities up through the oldest and most accelerated students in the class. This creates a highly enriched learning environment.

- In multi-level classrooms, younger children are constantly stimulated by the interesting work in which the older students are engaged.

- At the same time, in multi-level classrooms older students serve as tutors and role models for the younger ones, which helps them in their own mastery (we learn best when we teach someone else) and leaves them with a tremendous sense of pride.

- By working with children for three years, teachers get to know them extremely well.

- And, finally, there is a strong sense of continuity in the Elementary Montessori class, because two-thirds of the children return each year for either their second or third year with the same teacher(s). Most of the children know one another and understand the culture of the class. This makes it much easier to orient new children into the group.

Friendships and Community

One of the things that you will normally see when you enter an elementary classroom is joy, excitement, and enthusiasm. These are not children

(Above) Students participate in a lesson on the geological folding of the Earth's crust.

who are given worksheets over and over again. These are children who are engaged.

Montessori schools are normally small close-knit communities of children, teachers, and parents. They are like an extended family. Everyone knows everyone else. Children become close and remain friends with their teachers and both younger and older classmates. They grow up and study together for many years. While there may not be as many other children in the school as they would find in a larger school, their friendships will tend to be closer.

Elementary Montessori students can move around. They don't have to sit at a desk all day long. Students work together most of the time, either helping one another master skills and information or on group projects.

Parents are normally very involved at the elementary level as partners in supporting their children's education. They may come in to teach lessons, take small groups out into the community for field trips, and help with celebrations and performances.

Elementary Montessori Teachers Serve as Mentors, Friends, and Guides

The Elementary Montessori educator is not so much a "teacher" in the traditional sense as a "guide." In more and more schools, this title is actually used to describe their role.

The Elementary Montessori curriculum is very broad and requires the teacher to have a broad and thorough education of his or her own. With lessons that range from the history of mathematics to the physics of flight, mineralogy, chemistry, algebra, geometry, and literature, to name just a few, the average teacher would be lost.

The best Elementary Montessori teachers are "renaissance" men and women; individuals who are equally interested in mathematics, the sciences, the arts, architecture, literature, poetry, psychology, economics, technology, and philosophy. Beyond this, the Elementary Montessori educator needs patience, understanding, respect, enthusiasm, and a profound ability to inspire a sense of wonder and imagination. Such teachers are very rare, but they are absolutely magical!

Becoming an Elementary Montessori teacher requires a year of graduate study and student teaching and countless hours of hard work to gather or create the curriculum materials that constitute a prepared Elementary Montessori environment.

Academics

The Elementary Montessori classroom offers an environment in which children tend to blossom! This may sound like propaganda, but it's true!

Dr. Montessori was convinced that children are born curious, creative,

(Right) Elementary students often prefer to work on the floor with their friends.

and intelligent. In designing the elementary program, she was attempting to cultivate this human potential, nurture the spontaneous curiosity with which all children are born, and inspire a sense of wonder in their spirits.

The elementary years are the primary sensitive period for the acquisition of what has recently come to be known as "cultural literacy." Older children want to know the reason why things are as they are found in the world. They are oriented toward intellectual investigation and discovery.

Here lies one of the significant differences between Montessori education and the schools most children attend. In many classrooms, the primary focus is spent on teaching the *basic* skills of reading, writing, spelling, and mathematics.

From the Montessori perspective, the *basics* are not basic curriculum at all; they represent enabling skills which make it possible for the child to gain access to the real focus and substance of a Montessori education: science, history, the arts, great literature, world culture, politics, economics, and philosophy.

The Elementary Montessori Curriculum

The Elementary Montessori curriculum is highly enriched and challenging. It is organized into three elements:

1. Mastery of Fundamental Skills and Basic Core Knowledge

Montessori evolved out of the European tradition of academic excellence, and offers a rigorous course of study even in the elementary years. Elementary Montessori students explore the realm of mathematics, science and technology, the world of myth, great literature, history, world geography, civics, economics, anthropology, and the basic organization of human societies. Their studies cover the basics found in traditional curriculum, such as the memorization of math facts, spelling lessons, and the study of vocabulary, grammar, sentence analysis, creative and expository writing, and library research skills.

2. Dr. Montessori's Great Lessons

The Great Lessons are five key areas of interconnected studies traditionally presented to all Elementary Montessori students in the form of inspiring stories and related experiences and research projects.

The Great Lessons include the story of how the world came to be, the development of life on Earth, the story of humankind, the development of language and writing, and the development of mathematics. They are intended to give children a *cosmic* perspective of the Earth and humankind's place within the cosmos. The lessons, studies, and projects surrounding each of the Great Lessons normally span many months, and the questions that the children pose and their efforts to find the answers to their own questions may continue for many years.

> *"The Great Lessons are so exciting. They engage the children and then send them off to do all kinds of research that they are allowed to do at their own rate and their own pace. When children are excited about something, real learning takes place, and that's where Montessori shines."*
>
> — Valaida Wise, Headmistress,
> Henson Valley Montessori School
> Camp Springs, Maryland

Montessori Elementary: Giving Imagination a Chance

by David Kahn, Executive Director of the North American Montessori Teacher's Association

Although folk and fairy tales have their place in the elementary classroom, Montessori's vision of imagination — its power and centrality to emotional and intellectual life — is the basis of Montessori's Elementary education and why it works. Nothing compels the six-year-old learner like the canopy of stars overhead or, for that matter, the anatomy of a cell or an inside view of sub-atomic physics. Imagination creates a vision that expands and contracts, while fueling the mind to explore and to create a still bigger view with a deeper enthusiasm. "Human consciousness comes into the world as a flaming ball of imagination ... The secret of good teaching is to regard the child's intelligence as a fertile field in which seeds may be sown to grow under the heat of flaming imagination." (*Montessori*, 1948, pg. 15)

Imagination through Space and Time

The "flaming ball" of human consciousness travels on the first day of the Montessori Elementary experience back to the Big Bang, to the story of the universe as an "encompassing reality" and a "vision of the whole." This story captures the imagination; the child participates in the mystery of the "first cause," which is a whole spectacle of the beginning of self: "We shall walk together on this path of life, for all things are part of the universe and are connected with each other to form one whole unity." (*Montessori*, 1948, pg. 8)

Explaining the child's imagination and its attraction for a plausible story about the origin of the universe, Montessori writes that contemplating the cosmos in fact goes to the universal center of the child in connection with all things. (*Montessori*, 1948, pg. 8) It is clear that the imagination travels beyond the narrow bounds of the world we touch, hear, feel, and see. The elementary child experiences total immersion in a conception of all things. The imaginative ability to grasp the whole generates an emotion, the emotion of wonder and gratitude for large-scale diversity. Wonder is a magnet; it impels from within. Gratitude fosters well-being and harmony; it bonds with the universe. The child feels all at once directed in her learning.

The zest of the six-year-old's work is elicited by the imaginative lure of the concept, not necessarily by the hands-on experience, the physical aspects of a piece of material. For example, a mechanized model of the solar system with simultaneous revolving planets may have appeal as an impressionistic gadget, but the lasting emotion for the child is the realization of the planets' location in space, their mathematical distances, their scale in relation to the Earth. The imagination goes beyond the physical limits of the prepared environment and builds the child's critical attention around the span of the concept. It is important then not to circumscribe lessons, learning kits, or workbook sheets.

Imagination As a Medium for Inductive and Deductive Reasoning

The extension of the mind is further supported by scientific classification, as Montessori suggests when she says, "The world always repeats more or less the same elements." Thus, it is with the aid of both imagination and abstraction that the elementary child can expand the idea of "protozoa" to all unicellular life or extend the definition of "insect" to all insects of the world. "Reality is studied in detail, and then the whole is imagined. The detail is able to grow in imagination, and so total knowledge is attained." (*Montessori*, 1976 [1948], pg. 34)

Thus imagination represents the motion of reason — the impetus that moves the mind from the general to the particular and back again. A child experiences the general "story of the coming of life" and moves to the specific, a coral reef, researching it and then putting it in the context of the whole story once again. Or consider the possibilities inherent in a chunk of obsidian. Just a rock? Hardly. The child's mind can travel from obsidian to lava to volcano to the formation of the Earth's crust. Obsidian can also suggest the Native American's biface tool for scraping. Obsidian can also be classified into one of three categories: igneous, metamorphic, or sedimentary. The experience of obsidian builds connections, explorations, relationships. The whole impetus of science is fostered by an energized medium of detail connected to the whole — all propelled uniquely by the child's imagination, not teacher assignments.

"To do well, it is necessary to aim at giving an idea of all the sciences, not in precise detail but only as an impression. The idea is to 'sow the seeds of the sciences' at this age, when a sort of sensitive period for the imagination exists. Once the idea has been presented, we must show that a science extends from each branch: mineralogy, biology, physics, chemistry, etc. And, as we have seen, an examination of a detail triggers the study of the whole." (Montessori, 1976 [1948], pg. 40)

Imagination As a Love of Interdisciplinary Abstraction

Imagination works hand in hand with the emotional, the beautiful, and the essentially true. It should not be cluttered with small tasks that come from the teacher's preconceived notions.

"Whatever is presented to [the child] must be made beautiful and clear, striking his imagination ... Once this love has been kindled, all problems confronting the educationist will disappear. The great Italian poet Dante has said ... 'The greatest wisdom is first to love' ... Children can and do love abstract subjects, such as mathematics, so love can exist for the mental work, and the psychologist's dream for the future has already been achieved ..." (Montessori, 1948, pg. 24-25)

The emotional attachment once inspired by love of the immediate environment at the primary level expands at the elementary level to love of ideas and abstraction. A "sentiment of love" for all subjects is fostered by this flexible and illuminating grasp of reality, which is activated by imagination. The nature of the imaginative investigations is a passion demonstrated within and among all subjects as a way of experiencing the disciplines in a common world, a seamless web of interconnected knowledge to be explored uniquely by each teacher and child: "The mental and emotional growths are linked." (*Montessori*, 1948, pg. 24) The imagination's ability to see each discipline as a whole works towards building the interdisciplinary approach.

I remember, for instance, my first elementary class taking their geologist's picks and removing from a limestone matrix a horn coral — their first horn coral. "Look what I found!" And in the very next hour the same child chomps into his sandwich and compares it to a geological matrix. "Look! My sandwich is a sedimentary sandwich." The imagination is fluid; it allows knowledge to transfer within a discipline and between disciplines.

3. Individually Chosen Research

Elementary students are encouraged to explore topics that capture their imagination. Most former Montessori students look back on this aspect of the elementary program with particular fondness.

The approach is largely based on library research, with children gathering information, assembling reports, teaching what they have learned to their fellow students, and assembling portfolios and handmade books of their own.

Beginning by simply using an encyclopedia to find the answers to a list of questions prepared by

(Below) The **Hierarchy of the Decimal System** is an excellent example of how Montessori materials make abstract concepts concrete. The largest green cube represents the number one million. The red square prism is 100,000, the blue rectangular prism 10,000, and the small green cube 1,000. In the box are even smaller figures representing 100, 10, and 1 unit. *Photo courtesy of Nienhuis Montessori USA, Inc.*

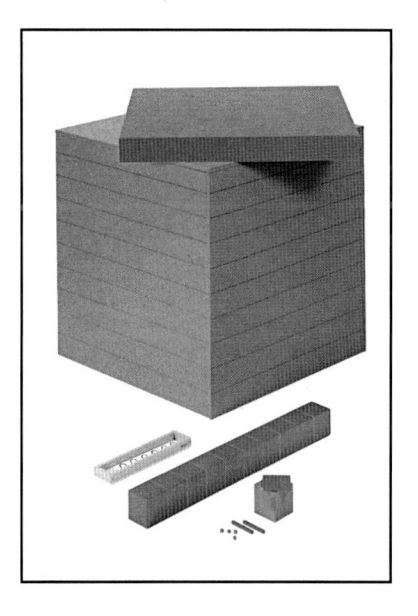

their teachers, Montessori students are taught how to use reference materials, libraries, and the Internet to gather information and uncover the facts. Their oral presentations and written research reports grow in sophistication and complexity over the years.

The Montessori Materials and the Passage to Abstraction

At the elementary level, learning continues to be a hands-on experience, as students learn through inquiry.

The advanced Elementary Montessori materials provide children with more complex and abstract concepts in mathematics, geometry, and pre-algebra. The goal is to lead the child away from a dependency on concrete models that visually represent abstract concepts towards the ability to solve problems with pen and paper alone. Part of this is made possible by the older child's ability to grasp abstract concepts, but it has been greatly enhanced over the years by countless hours of work with the concrete materials that made the abstract real and helped him visualize the abstraction.

Similar hands-on materials help students understand grammar, sentence analysis, geographical facts, and concepts in science.

Learning How to Learn

At the elementary level, Montessori students learn to think for themselves. They are encouraged to do their own research, analyze what they have

Likewise, imagination inspires the miraculous discovery when the logical layout of the binomial square yields the vision of a trinomial square. The child exclaims at the elementary age: "Nobody taught me." The elementary mind takes its own cognitive steps: the passages are self taught. The child creates the trinomial square by visualizing from the binomial square. There is an inner appreciation from the light of discovery, propelled by the ability of the mind to leap to something new, something not presented, something not demonstrated. The order of abstraction collaborates with the invention of imagination.

Imagination can ease the production of research by combining two ideas: constructiveness and writing. Children study history, for example, in the context of the needs of humans, producing a classroom lined with dioramas, tapestries, history fairs, murals, clay models, 'Needs-of-Humans' charts, day-in-the-life fiction. The children invent, through the making of things they need, the opportunity to establish what is their work, their interests, their ideas.

Imagination as the Basis for Philosophy of Life and Service

The imagination is the engine that drives the elementary years; it powers the quest for knowledge across the disciplines. It builds towards philosophy and great speculations. There is an emotional quality to the question "I wonder if ...," which becomes a conscious resource as the child matures into adolescence. This Montessori thirteen-year-old-student expressed the power of imagination in what he called an "expository essay." His imagination had become focused and keenly aware of its majestic reach.

"The universe is a huge area occupied by mass in random spots. The word 'universe' has come to mean everything in human knowledge and even beyond, and so is very vague and is, in effect, a synonym for everything. Yet despite its vastness, the idea of a huge universe doesn't seem to satisfy the human mind. Either because our minds are too primitive to conceive a universe so vast that it is never ending or because our minds are convinced everything, even life, has an end, people feel that there must be something else."

Reflecting on imagination and enthusiasm, the adolescent forms an identity reflected in the following essay, written later in life by Molly McNamara, another Montessori child. The imagination, now a conscious resource in this teenager, formed her life vision while integrating her personality.

My Good Earth

Every human being has his Good Earth; mine is the wonderful world of imagination. My imagination is many things to me: my security; my future; my wealth. Without an imagination, life would be desolate, but with one, life is rich and full of joy.

Imagination provides for me an escape and sanctuary from the sometimes harsh realities of life. If I'm feeling friendless and my world has turned a dull blue-grey, I can escape at will to a dreamland which is bright and shiny, red and gold, with untapped stores of blithe merriment. With no equipment except my own mind, I can go anywhere — see, do, and experience anything I wish. When life gets me down, nothing can stop me from entering the world of imagination. I can always feel secure knowing that I have my separate world of imagination to fall back upon.

In addition, imagination is my future. I am only sixteen, but I already have hundreds, if not thousands, of alternate futures planned out for myself. I only have one true life to live, but in my dreams, I have been an actress, a singer, a millionaire, a lawyer, a teacher, a politician, an international traveler, a wife, and a mother much loved by her family and never ever disobeyed. I am still young, and it is conceivable that any one of these could come true. I don't know if dreaming about them will have the same thrill and excitement when my life has been set on a definite course, but however my life turns out, I shall have had the satisfaction of living many different lives before I 'settle down.'

Finally, having a healthy and well-developed imagination is wealth beyond human measure. It gives me many small gifts, such as the ability to entertain myself with stories while I am lying in bed and cannot sleep and not having too much trouble coming up with topics for stories and papers for English class. However, in my opinion, it has also given me some of the greatest gifts a person can have. It has bestowed upon me a love of literature which will remain with me until I die, for I can easily put myself in place of a character in one of my current favorite books or plays. An imagination makes it easier for me to see the ideas behind a story or a character. Most importantly, my imagination has given me the ability to appreciate the many wonderful things I have in my life. I can appreciate the beauty of nature and the love of my family, because I realize the emptiness of a life without these gifts. Without an imagination, I would soon take all I have for granted.

Imagination is one of the greatest gifts God can bestow upon man. Mankind received an imagination along with his soul to differentiate him from other animals. I have been blessed with a particularly strong imagination; it is my Good Earth, and I would not trade it for any amount of worldly wealth.

Although she implies much about imagination, primarily Molly says she can imagine what is other than herself. She can put herself into the context of service, of beauty, of nature, of her own future, or the discovery of new people and places. She equates imagination with the "Good Earth," the very fertile field that Montessori articulates over and over.

**Imagination as the Basis for Cooperative Vision:
The Classroom and Beyond**

Imagination also expands the child's perception of his social world community to global community. From the community of classroom, the elementary child can construct vision of the human family. Montessori writes in an essay entitled *Supernature and the Single Nation*:

"We could no longer live within nature if we could only walk with our feet and look with our eyes. Everything depends on the possibility of our going beyond our natural limitations ... All mankind forms a single organism, but man continues to live in an emotional world that is outdated. Humanity forms a single unit — a single nation. This single nation has opened the whole world and brought all men together."
(Montessori, 1972 [1949], pg. 116-117)

The necessary conservation of the Earth's resources can only be addressed by the "single nation." The new world order is converging towards an international collaboration to protect the ozone layer, to keep the air and water fresh and the rain forest intact, and to keep the peace. Thus, the imagination encompasses the whole task of mankind. As a vital part of education, imagination facilitates a new vision for each generation so that the human community may accomplish its work and express its recurring dream.

References
Montessori, Maria (1976; first published 1948) *From Childhood to Adolescence*.
Montessori, Maria (1948) *To Educate the Human Potential*, Kalakshetra.
Montessori, Maria (1972; first published 1949) *Supernature and the Single Nation. Education and Peace*. Chicago: Henry Regnery, 109-118.
Montessori, Mario M., Jr. (1976) *Cosmic Education. Education for Human Development*, New York: Schocken Books. 97-106.

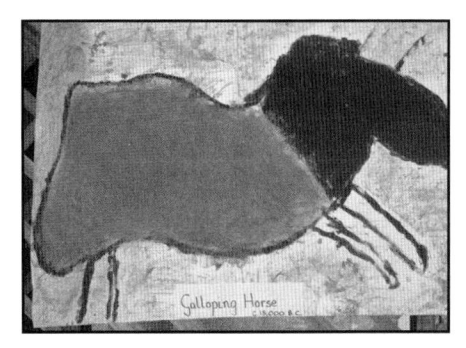

(Above) An elementary student's reproduction of a horse from a Neolithic cave painting.

found, and come to their own conclusions. Montessori teaches students to think, not simply to memorize, feed back, and forget. They literally learn how to learn, discovering that the process of learning can, and should, be as natural as breathing! Students become fully engaged in the learning process.

Rather than present students with all the "right answers," Montessori teachers ask the "right questions," and challenge them to find new solutions or discover the answers on their own. This is yet another element of the Montessori program that prepares children to succeed in the real world of ideas, enterprise, and challenging perspectives. Why? Because while learning the right answers may get children through school, learning how to learn will get them through life!

An Invitation to a Lesson

A Montessori teacher will invite her students to a lesson, consciously trying to attract and then capture their interest, knowing that at times she will "fail to make the sale." She attempts to make each lesson as interesting as possible. For example, she might say, "Today, I've brought in a live lobster, and I have room for eight of you who are interested in learning about crustaceans and how they live. If you are interested, you may join me." She invites her students to come over for a lesson voluntarily, knowing that there will be some days when no child will come.

(Right) Elementary Montessori students rarely use textbooks. They are encouraged to explore topics that capture their imagination. Students do a great deal of independent reading and library research. Children gather information, assemble reports, assemble portfolios and handmade books of their own, and teach what they have learned to their friends.

Intrinsic Motivation

Sometimes, because Montessori places so much emphasis on cultivating children's sense of curiosity and wonder, parents may have the impression that students can simply do whatever they wish, avoiding subjects that they dislike. This is certainly not the case in a well-run elementary class.

Montessori helps children learn how to learn. We help focus their attention, come into a setting willing to listen, ready to learn, and able to observe. Montessori students reflect and play with ideas until they figure out how things fit together, and they practice new skills until they are mastered.

We operate from the understanding that intelligence, creativity and imagination can be found in every child. A lot of Montessori education is simply about learning how to learn: observing life, listening, looking for patterns and connections, and reflecting on how things fit together and how they work.

Even though there may be some things that give them difficulty, or which they may do better than others, children can learn to recognize their best learning style. They can learn to pursue not only those things that they find interesting or which come easily, but as they become more organized and self-disciplined, they learn how to accomplish things that they would rather avoid.

The Junior Great Books Program for Montessori Classrooms

Montessori schools throughout the United States are discovering and implementing the Junior Great Books Program into their curricula.

The Junior Great Books Program is sponsored by the Great Books Foundation, a national nonprofit educational organization based in Chicago. Through their Junior Great Books Program, Montessori schools provide opportunities for students in kindergarten through high school to develop a love of reading by discussing some of the most engaging, most enduring works of literature ever written.

Children in this program read classic folk and fairy tales, along with outstanding contemporary works from all over the world. They are guided by a trained leader (usually a teacher or parent volunteer), who engages the children in "shared-inquiry" discussions about their reading.

The program teaches children how to think about what they read and how to discuss and develop their ideas about literature with others. Parents and Montessori guides value the program because it improves students' reading, thinking, speaking, and social skills.

Montessori schools throughout the United States have found the Junior Great Books Program to be very compatible with the Montessori Elementary program approach, because they both stress authentic, active learning and help children develop a lifelong appreciation for learning.

In keeping with Montessori's emphasis on developmentally appropriate learning opportunities, the Junior Great Books Program is also designed to employ activities that provide children with structure and flexibility, giving children the freedom to develop skills and capacities in their own way but within a definite structure and clear discipline. Both approaches are characterized by a balance between independent thinking and collaborative learning, which tend to be mutually reinforcing.

At the same time, this format instills a respect for diversity and differing viewpoints, since there is no attempt to reach consensus, nor is there any attempt to lead students to a "right" answer. Finally, students working with the Program are challenged to explore interpretive problems in a work of literature that is rich in language and full of meaning, helping children develop a genuine love of literature and reinforcing a habit of lifelong learning through reading.

Examples of Material from the Junior Great Books Read-Aloud Program for Grades K-1

Volume 1: Dragon Series

The Frog Prince, Brothers Grimm, as told by Wanda Gag

Guinea Fowl and Rabbit Get Justice, African folktale as told by Harold Courlander & George Herzog

Nature Speaks, Poetry by Carl Sandburg, James Reeves, & Frederico Garcia Lorca

Examples of Material from the Junior Great Books Series for Grades 2-6

Series 2: First Semester

The Happy Lion, Louise Fatio

The Tale of Squirrel Nutkin, Beatrix Potter

How the Camel Got His Hump, Rudyard Kippling

Kanga & Baby Roo Come to the Forest, and Piglet Has a Bath, A.A. Milne

Arap Sang and the Cranes, African folktale told by Humphrey Haman

Blue Moose, Daniel Manus Pinkwater

The Magic Listening Cap, Japanese folktale as told by Yoshiko Uchida

The Jackal and the Partridge, Punjabi folktale as told by Flora Annie Steel

Nail Soup, Swedish folktale as told by Linda Rahm

The Apple of Contentment, Howard Pyle

Series 5: First Semester

Charles, Shirley Jackson

Ghost Cat, Donna Hill

Turquoise Horse, Gerald Hausman

Maurice's Room, Paula Fox

Lenny's Red-Letter Day, Bernard Ashley

The Prince & the Goose Girl, Elinore Mordaunt

Tramp, Malcolm Carrick

Alberic the Wise, Norton Juster

Posbu and Aruwa, African folktale as told by Humphrey Harman

The Invisible Child, Tove Jansson

Activities for Grades 2 - 6

Text Opener: a pre-reading activity to help students connect with the story.

First Reading of the story followed by **Sharing Questions.**

Second Reading with Directed Notes: a method of taking notes that motivates students to read actively and reflectively.

Interpreting Words: vocabulary work that focuses on words that are thematically important, not just unfamiliar.

Shared Inquiry & Discussion

Writing after Discussion: creative writing and personal or evaluative essays.

Montessori does not just prepare children to make a living; it prepares them to make a balanced life. This will require a nurturing environment. We argue that if a child is emotionally handicapped by self-doubt, if he is afraid of looking foolish, afraid of failure, then the grade or approval of parents and teachers becomes an end in itself, rather than what is really important, the joy of exploring ideas and figuring things out. We want children to love learning not the petty external and artificial rewards that most schools use to motivate students.

No one needs to motivate an infant or a very young child; they are born motivated to learn. Two-year-olds are normally fascinated by the world. External motivation interferes. Curiosity and intelligence are just as vibrant in a student during the elementary, secondary, and university years. The true challenge of education is to keep the spark of human intelligence and curiosity alive. A vital part of being human comes from the sense that the world is vast and fascinating and that we should never be afraid to ask questions and wonder why things are the way they are, or how things might be *if . . .*

Children must never be afraid of asking questions, because that's how we learn. Human beings have always learned as much from their mistakes as from their successes. But when parents and teachers look at the early creative writing of the young child and find creative phonetic spelling or sloppy handwriting, they often shut her off when they focus on what she did incorrectly, rather than what she did right. When parents are disappointed at a child's early efforts, they subtly communicate that their expectations have not been met. Their children then learn to protect themselves by quietly pretending that they do not care or by choosing not to share information with their parents when they can avoid it. We need to help children discover their own unique talents and capacity to create and discover.

Above all, Montessori is an education of the heart. We look at each child as a unique human being. We know that each child has particular strengths and a distinct learning style. We know that each child's emotions and self-esteem play a critical role in whether or not they are ready to learn. We find it difficult to imagine any other way of teaching.

The Integrated Montessori Curriculum

In the Montessori program, subject matter is not separated into curriculum areas: *this is geography, this is social studies, this is science, this is math.* Everything is interrelated. The subjects weave in and out of each other (see chart on page 55). Literature, art, music, dance, drama, history, social issues, political science, economics, architecture, science, and the study of technology all complement one another in the elementary curriculum. This integrated approach is one of the Elementary Montessori program's great strengths. Studies come alive through a host of hands-on projects and activities.

Language Arts and the Humanities

The Elementary Montessori Language Arts program places great stress on the development of strong skills in composition and creative writing.

(Below) Montessori materials such as the **Fraction Skittles** and **Fraction Circles** help students grasp abstract concepts, such as the addition of fractions.

(Above) Younger elementary students often compose short essays with the **Small Moveable Alphabet.**

Students are asked to write continuously, emphasizing at first an enjoyment of the writing process, rather than the strict use of correct grammar and spelling. However, formal grammar, spelling, and sentence analysis are systematically taught.

Elementary children are normally very interested in words and sentences. They like to parse and analyze. In this way, they are clarifying their understanding of the structure of language that they absorbed unconsciously in the early childhood class. Montessori takes advantage of their natural interest and gives children a great quantity and variety of material. While they study the theory of grammar, spelling, and sentence analysis; they are also expanding their knowledge of written language.

During the elementary years, Montessori increasingly focuses on the development of research and writing skills. This overlaps into the other areas of the curriculum, from which students draw topics of interest. Gathering information from the encyclopedia and library reference books, they learn to prepare well written reports.

Creative writing continues to be equally important, as students are encouraged to write and share their stories, plays, poetry, and class newspapers with others .

Finally, and most importantly, the key to the elementary Language Arts curriculum is the quality of the material Montessori gives children to read. Instead of basal readers, they are introduced from an early age to first-rate children's books and fascinating works on science, history, geography and the arts. Many elementary classes follow the Junior Great Books Program (see page 124), with formal literary studies continuing every year through graduation. Literature is connected with all of the other areas of the curriculum, with students reading stories and plays about cultures and historical periods that they are studying. By introducing students to the very best literature available for young people, Montessori cultivates a deep love for the world of books.

Unified Mathematics

Montessori math is based on the European "Unified Math" model, which introduces elementary students to the study of the fundamentals of algebra, geometry, logic, and statistics, along with the principles of arithmetic.

Montessori students learn to recognize complex geometric shapes and figures. They learn to define, calculate, and draw all sorts of geometric relationships: angles, polygons, circumference, area, volume, squares and square roots, cubes of polynomials, to name just a few. In Montessori, arithmetic, algebra, and geometry are interrelated.

Elementary Montessori students learn from hands-on experience by applying math in a wide range of projects, activities, and challenges, such as graphing the daily temperature and computing the average for each

"When we study the history of Maryland, for example, we also look at the geography of the land to understand what the original colonists had to work with when they came here. We also look at the first Americans who lived here when the colonists arrived. We look at the geology and ecosystems of Maryland from our mountains to the Chesapeake Bay. We go to the Chesapeake Bay itself. It's one of the largest ecosystems in the world. As the children look at the Bay, they begin to realize that it's all interconnected."

— Marsha Jacques, Head
Evergreen Montessori School
Silver Spring, Maryland

Montessori Programs

(Above) Elementary students are shown working with the **Grammar Boxes and Symbol Materials**.

(Above) Many students use laptops or desktop computers to learn to write essays and short stories.

(Below) This student is using the **Stamp Game** to solve a problem in dynamic addition.

month, or adjusting the quantities called for in a recipe for a larger number of people. Because children love to work outdoors, we try to prepare tasks that use the school grounds whenever possible. For example, using simple geometry, students can determine the height of a tree, measure the dimensions of buildings, or calculate how much they will feed the school's animals in a year. They prepare scale drawings, calculate area and volume, construct three-dimensional geometric models, and build scale models of historical devices and structures.

Montessori Mathematics climbs in sophistication through the level of trigonometry and calculus. It includes a careful study of the practical application of mathematics in everyday life, such as measurement, handling finances, making economic comparisons, or in gathering data and statistical analyses.

(Above) The **Golden Mat** provides still another step on the passage to abstraction, as students solve basic math operations.

Computers

The computer is a basic tool used in many Elementary Montessori classes. On a fairly simple level, students use computers to help with their memorization of their basic math facts. Computers provide all sorts of simulation and problem-solving situations, calling on students to compete against the computer or make predictions while engaging in role-playing scenarios.

(Right) Students use the **Multiplication Checkerboard** to learn the principles of long multiplication.

Montessori Programs

(Above) Students use the **Racks and Tubes Division Materials** to solve problems in long division.

(Opposite Page - bottom left) Elementary students use the **Fraction Insets** to explore a wide range of concepts in geometry and mathematics, such as the principle of equivalence of fractions. **Montessori Fraction Circles** are also used to teach the concept of angles in elementary geometry.

(Left) The **Large Bead Frame** leads children toward the ability to solve math problems abstractly, using an abacus with representations of quantities into the millions.

130

MONTESSORI FOR THE ELEMENTARY YEARS

Older students work with spreadsheets, graphs, and logical analysis. Today they are also learning desktop publishing, multi-media presentations, digital photography, and video editing. And every year, more and more elementary classes teach children how to use their computers to access the world's largest library collection: the Internet.

History and Culture Come Alive in the Elementary Class

One of Montessori's key objectives is to develop a global perspective, and the study of history and world cultures forms the cornerstone of the curriculum.

Physical geography begins in the elementary program with the study of the formation of the Earth, the emergence of the oceans and atmosphere, and the evolution of life. Students learn about the

(Above) Materials used to help students learn the names of geological features in the landscape.

A model of the Inner Core of the Planet Earth.

131

MONTESSORI PROGRAMS

A student uses the Puzzle Map of South America to help him learn to identify and write the names of the countries of Latin America.

(Left) At a more advanced level, elementary students work with the **Pin Maps** to learn the names of the countries and capital cities of Africa.

(Below) Younger students use concrete materials, such as the **Land and Water Forms,** to continue their study of basic land formations in earth science.

MONTESSORI FOR THE ELEMENTARY YEARS

world's rivers, lakes, deserts, mountain ranges, and natural resources.

Elementary students study the customs, housing, diet, government, industry, arts, history and dress of countries around the world. They also study the emergence of the first civilizations and the universal needs of humankind. In the upper elementary class, the focus is usually placed on early man, ancient civilizations, and American history.

The elementary program teaches history through hands-on experiences. Students may build shelters, cook over a wood fire, churn butter, hike, work with map and compass, canoe, and camp out. They build models of ancient tools and structures, prepare their own manuscripts, and recreate everyday artifacts from the past.

International studies continue during the elementary years, integrating art, music, dance, drama, cooking, geography, literature, and science. The children learn to prepare and enjoy dishes from all over the world. They learn the traditional folk songs and dances in music and explore traditional folk crafts in art. They read folk tales, literature, and reference materials about the cultures they are studying and prepare reports about them. Units often culminate in marvelous international festivals.

Practical economics is another important element in the Elementary Montessori curriculum. Students learn how to compare prices against value, compute costs, maintain a checkbook, operate small school stores, and understand the stock market.

Citizenship is yet another element that weaves throughout the elementary curriculum. Students study the workings of the local, state, and federal governments and begin to follow current events.

During election years, they follow candidates, discuss the issues of the day, and sometimes even volunteer in

This student is working with a Time Line of Life on Earth, placing cards that show the plants and animals that thrived during different periods in the development of the modern Earth.

133

MONTESSORI PROGRAMS

the campaign of a local candidate of their choice.

The goal is to lead each student to explore, understand, and grow into full and active membership in the adult world.

Montessori's Hands-On Approach to Science

The Montessori Science curriculum is focused on the study of life, the laws and structure of the universe, and how humanity has struggled throughout history to put our understanding to practical use. It seeks to captivate children's imagination and fill them with a sense of wonder at the grandeur of the universe, the simple beauty of the

134

physical laws, and the miracle of life. It also teaches them the process and philosophy of science: how to ask testable questions, observe systematically, collect specimens, gather and analyze data, and conduct experiments.

Montessori Science often takes place outdoors. Classes grow flowers and vegetables in small gardens. They often raise class pets and sometimes even small farm animals.

Students are encouraged to learn to recognize and name local trees, flowers, birds, and animals. They learn to recognize familiar plants by their leaves, bark, and seeds. By looking at animal tracks, they can determine which animals live in the area.

In the spring, students may study the local wild and domestic flowers, comparing different species and counting petals, and stamens. They bring caterpillars back to their classrooms to be kept in terrariums so that the children can see the chrysalis that they form and the moth or butterfly that emerges. They hatch frog eggs and watch them turn into tadpoles before releasing them in the pond. In the fall, they look for fruits, nuts, and berries, noticing how they are distributed and what animals look to them as food.

Older children begin to keep journals of their observations of classroom animals and write poems and stories that attempt to capture the sense of wonder and beauty all around us. Back in the classroom, they pursue their investigations using a wide variety of charts and displays, "research" materials, and reference books.

Students collect specimens and bring them back to the classroom for identification, labeling, and display in a nature center. They collect leaves, which can be pressed or preserved as leaf skeletons. They learn the botanical names for the different leaf shapes. They prepare collections of dried plants, seeds, flowers, beehives, bird nests, eggs, snake skins, tree sections, samples of familiar tree woods, cocoons, mounted insects, and animal bones. In most classes you will find ant farms, perhaps a pet chameleon or gerbil, birds, turtles, and aquaria.

More formal elements of biology are taught as well, particularly at the upper elementary levels. Dr. Montessori found that systematic knowledge allows one to discriminate details among species, literally to see on a whole new level; therefore, we introduce the student to the classification of the plant and animal kingdom.

The study of the internal and external anatomy of plants and animals likewise gives children a new level of awareness and sensitivity in their observation and study of life. They compare different anatomical systems among species, such as the eyes, teeth, hooves, and claws of various animals.

(Opposite Page/Top) Chemistry plays a significant role in the Elementary Montessori curriculum. In many ways, it overlaps into the area of Practical Life as well as Science, requiring students to follow careful procedures, measure accurately, control temperatures, and carefully clean glassware after use.

(Opposite Page/Bottom) Students commonly work with powerful microscopes normally only found in secondary science labs.

(Above) This child is studying the life cycle of a star. It is part of an introduction to the study of stellar nuclear synthesis, the process by which complex elements are created by fusion in the heart of the stars.

They come to ask questions: *"Why did the horse evolve this sort of teeth or this form of foot?"*

Elementary students also learn a wide range of important basic concepts of physics and chemistry, such as the structure of atoms and molecules, the difference between elements and compounds, the chemical composition of familiar compounds, the three states of matter, and chemical and physical change. Students also enjoy doing research about the elements, and a first exposure to Mendelev's Table of the Elements.

Elementary children love to work with scientific apparatus and delight in seeing mixtures change color, testing liquids with litmus paper, experimenting with small electrical circuits, or building models of atomic compounds. Students learn to observe and record what takes place during their experiment. The goal is to teach both the scientific method and techniques for safely working with science equipment.

Foreign Languages

As part of their International Studies program, most Montessori schools offer a second language. The goals in a foreign language program are to develop conversational skills, expand vocabulary, understand basic written information in the second language, and have a better appreciation for the culture of the countries where the language is spoken.

The Arts Are Integrated into Every Subject

In Montessori Schools, the Arts are normally integrated into the rest of the curriculum. They are modes of exploring and expanding lessons that have been introduced in science, history, geography, language arts, and mathematics. For example, students might make a replica of a Grecian vase, study calligraphy and decorative writing, sculpt dinosaurs for science, create dioramas for history, construct geometric designs and solids for math, and express their feelings about a musical composition through painting.

Art and music history and appreciation are woven throughout the history and geography curricula. Traditional folk arts are used to extend the curriculum as well. Students participate in singing, dancing, and creative movement with teachers and music specialists. Students' dramatic productions make other times and cultures come alive.

Health, Wellness, and Physical Education

The ideal Elementary Montessori Health and Physical Education program challenges students to develop a personal program of lifelong exercise, recreation, and health management.

The Montessori approach to health and fitness helps children to understand and appreciate how our bodies work and the care and feeding of a healthy human body. Students typically study diet and nutrition, hygiene, first aid, response to illness and injury, stress management, and peacefulness and mindfulness in our daily lives.

Daily exercise is an important element of a lifelong program for personal health. Instead of one program for all, students are typically helped to explore many different alternatives. Students commonly learn and practice daily stretching and exercises for balance and flexibility. Some programs introduce students to yoga, *Tai Chi*, or aerobic dance. They learn that cardiovascular exercise can come from vigorous walking, jogging, biking, rowing, aerobic dance, calisthenics, using stationary exercise equipment, through actively playing field sports, such as soccer, or from a wide range of other enjoyable activities, such as swimming, golf, or tennis. With older students, the goal is to expose students to many different possibilities, encouraging them to develop basic everyday skills and helping them to develop a personal program of daily exercise.

Many schools have limited space and facilities, but where funds and facilities are available for older students, the ideal Montessori environment offers a variety of facilities and programs, which can potentially include a room with stationary bikes and other exercise equipment designed for children, an indoor track, a basketball court, a room for aerobic dance, and perhaps even an indoor pool and tennis courts. Again, ideally, this fitness center would not be reserved for the children alone; school families would be able to use the facilities after hours, on weekends, and during school hours when it didn't interfere with student programs.

An Education in Practical Life Skills

One of the keys to understanding Montessori's success can be found in the way in which it carefully encourages the development of children's self-esteem and independence.

Elementary children are ready to take on a much higher level of challenge and responsibility. The elementary classroom is a small community run almost entirely by the students. They keep the room in order, care for classroom animals, tend to the plants and perhaps a small garden, set up for lunch, organize special events, and generally move about the school much more independently.

Where the early childhood children enjoyed washing dishes and scrubbing tables for the sheer joy of the process, elementary children simply work to get the job done. However, the knowledge that they are responsible for their classroom, and to some degree the entire school, gives Elementary Montessori children a tremendous sense of pride.

The lessons in Practical Life skills found in an Elementary Montessori class are diverse. Children learn how to cook and bake, use a washing machine, iron a shirt, arrange flowers,

(Right) Montessori students routinely help to maintain their classroom and the school grounds.

(Below) Elementary students learn how to use tools and perform routine household repairs.

fix a bicycle, tie knots, use hand tools, plan a party, balance a checkbook, comparison shop, train a dog, dress appropriately for any occasion, write thank-you letters, prepare for a long hike, pack a suitcase or backpack, swim, perform first aid, babysit, learn self-defense, and observe everyday rules of etiquette. Many will serve as school safety patrols or will assist in the preschool classrooms.

Field Trips: Going Out Into the Community

Elementary children are normally anxious for a much higher level of personal challenge. They may enjoy vigorous games and organized sports, daily exercise, long hikes, horseback riding, gymnastics, or dance. They often ask to write and produce their own plays, designing their own costumes and scenery with as little help from adults as possible.

Field trips are often an integral part of Elementary Montessori programs. Students take trips to planetariums, art galleries, the zoo, museums, and many other destinations. They visit the centers of local government, colleges, hospitals, veterinary clinics, wildlife refuges, libraries, laboratories, factories, and businesses.

Elementary Montessori children typically suggest and organize their own field trips for the class or a small group of children who share a common interest. By initiating a proposal, developing the plan, making all arrangements, and carrying them through, they gain a great sense of individual power and dignity.

(Above) Environmental education or Practical Life skills? Perhaps a bit of both.

Social Skills, Character, Ethics, & Community Service

"It is at this age also that the concept of justice is born, simultaneously with the understanding of the relationship between one's acts and the needs of others. The sense of justice, so often missing in man, is found during the development of the young child."

— Dr. Maria Montessori

The elementary classroom is not only a community of close friends, it is a source of countless "life lessons" in social skills, everyday courtesy, and ethics. Montessori noted that elementary children not only enjoy each other's company, they naturally form little social groups of friends, each with its own internal hierarchy and rules of conduct.

"It is self-evident that the possession of and contact with real things bring with them, above all, a real quantity of knowledge. Instruction becomes a living thing. Instead of being illustrated, it is brought to life. In a word, the outing is a new key for the intensification of instruction ordinarily given in the school.

There is no description, no image in any book that is capable of replacing the sight of real trees, and all of the life to be found around them, in a real forest. Something emanates from those trees which speaks to the soul, something no book, no museum is capable of giving."

— Dr. Maria Montessori

(Above) Elementary students commonly organize their assignments and receive feedback from their teachers and parents in notebooks like the one this student is holding.

The elementary classroom takes advantage of this tendency by operating as a small social community in which children learn to work together, resolve conflicts peacefully, encourage and acknowledge each other, and work as committees to complete complex tasks. Dr. Montessori also noted that the elementary years are a time when children develop their sense of justice and moral reasoning. Most classes go beyond simple lessons in grace and courtesy to begin a serious exploration of moral philosophy. It is common to find Elementary Montessori students discussing difficult questions such as: *Why are some things considered a sin? What happens to us when we die? Why is it important for the fortunate to lend a hand to the poor? If kindness is so important, what can I do when I feel angry?*

During the elementary years, Montessori children begin to address the question of aid to the elderly, handicapped, critically ill and economically disadvantaged. They explore international issues from the perspective of building bridges toward world peace. They study ecology, wildlife preservation, and conservation of natural resources. Elementary classes almost always become directly engaged in acts of charity: gathering food, toys, and clothing for the poor; raising funds for local shelters; assisting in food kitchens for the homeless. Through personal experience, investigation, research, and exploration of these themes in literature and film, students make their first efforts at trying to understand war, violence, poverty, and the crisis of the homeless. More importantly, they struggle with what they, as individuals, can do to make the world a better place.

It is quite common to find elementary classes engaged in community service projects. Classes often recycle and prepare compost. They will commonly clear streambeds, plant wildflowers, and participate in erosion-control programs. Most will raise funds for charities or to support a child through one of the overseas aid organizations.

One thing that Montessori Elementary students tend to do is write letters; hundreds of lawmakers and decision-makers in industry know what Montessori students think about a wide range of social and environmental issues. These students talk about the issues of the day with their friends and families.

Through these and many other efforts, we begin to introduce Montessori children to moral questions in personal relationships and encourage the awakening of their social conscience. They engage in a gradual process of self-discovery and start to ask the larger questions: *What do I do well? What do I stand for? What is the purpose of my life?*

Is Montessori opposed to homework, tests, and grades?

Many parents have heard that Montessori schools do not believe in homework, grades, and tests. This is a misunderstanding of Montessori's insights.

Most Montessori schools do not assign homework at all below the elementary level. When it is assigned to older children, it rarely involves page after page of busywork; instead, Montessori students pursue meaningful, interesting assignments that expand on the topics that they are studying in class. Many assignments invite parents and children to work together.

A Student's Story: What Not Getting Graded Has to Do with It

by Wendy Smith

As a product mostly of liberal, private school education, my experiences have varied drastically from those of most American school children. One kind of experience stands out from the rest because it has continued to make an impact on my life: my time in a Montessori school from kindergarten through fifth grade.

The Montessori Method teaches children to be free and independent thinkers and emphasizes the joy of learning. But the most valuable idea received was the belief that I was a unique and important person. I was given a wonderful sense of worth, while at the same time I was taught to recognize the worth in everyone else. There were several reasons why this idea could grow: I was never compared to other children, my teachers urged me to develop my individual talents and skills, and mostly there was no grading system.

A student writes out the day's schedule in a class at the Montessori School of Raleigh.

These experiences helped me to make the transition to a new school. After graduating (reluctantly!) from fifth grade, I went on to another private school — much more structured than my Montessori school, but still by no means typical (like "traditional" public school). My new school did use a grading system, and this was really difficult for me at first. Failing a math test when I had never failed at anything before was a bitter pill to swallow. It knocked me flat! But with the strong self-concept that Montessori had given me, I was able to find the courage inside to recognize that this was OK, that everyone has to fail sometimes in their lives. I concluded that I was going to have to work harder at math, but that I was not a failure as person. I doubt very much that I could have bounced back as quickly had it not been for my Montessori experience. It didn't take long for me to find my place at my new school. I soon noticed that the same basic ideals were emphasized: the importance of the individual and the focus on the fun of learning. Both of these things prepared me for what was to come next.

Faced with my first year of public high school, I had never felt more terrified. Coming from a class of twenty-three students, I was convinced that I'd never be able to handle a freshman class of three hundred. In the first month or so, I panicked when a test was given. Anything lower than a B+ made me think that the world was coming to an end! But again, I think because of the positive self-image I experienced in my early years, I came to feel that I could handle any challenge given to me in high school. And those beginning years have also prepared me for college.

It is amazing to me that the type of schooling I received when I was younger can still have such an impact on my life today. My Montessori education gave me confidence — by not using a grading system and by not comparing me to the other children. This allowed me to enjoy learning everything, even subjects that were difficult for me. Learning was always a positive experience, never frightening. Though at first I was intimidated by the evaluation systems of those later schools, after only a short time I was able to adopt them and feel even more assured. I owe that security and sense of self-worth mostly to my early education. It has helped me in the past, and I am certain it will continue to do so in the future.

Wendy Smith attended a Montessori school in the Washington, D.C. area. She went on to Washington University in St. Louis, Missouri. Wendy's reflections first appeared in the Summer, 1990 edition of Montessori Life, *the Journal of the American Montessori Society. Reprinted with permission.*

Homework should never become a battleground between adult and child. One of our goals as parents and teachers is to help children learn how to get organized, budget time, and follow through until the work is completed. Ideally, home challenges will give parents and children a pleasant opportunity to work together on projects that give both parent and child a sense of accomplishment. They are intended to enrich and extend the curriculum.

Montessori challenges children to think, explore, and pursue tangible projects that give them a sense of satisfaction. Homework is intended to afford students the opportunity to practice and reinforce skills introduced in the classroom.

Moreover, there is a certain degree of self-discipline that can be developed within the growing child through the process of completing assignments independently.

For example, many elementary classes will send home a packet of "At-Home Challenges" for each age group in the class. The children have an entire week, through the next weekend, to complete them. The following Mondays, teachers sit down with the children to review what worked, what they enjoyed, and what they found difficult or unappealing.

Depending on the child's level, assignments normally involve some reading, research, writing, and something tangible to accomplish. They may be organized into three groups:

1. **Things to be experienced**, such as reading a book, visiting a museum, or going to see a play;

2. **Things to learn**, stated in terms of skills and knowledge, such as *See if you can learn how to solve these problems well enough so that you can teach the skill to a younger student*; and

3. **Products to be submitted**, such as a play, essay, story, experiment, or model.

When possible, teachers will normally build in opportunities for children to choose among several alternative assignments. Sometimes teachers will prepare individually negotiated weekly assignments with each student.

Whenever students voluntarily decide to learn something, they tend to engage in their work with a passion and attention that few students will

Homework ... Montessori Style

Here are just a few examples of assignments that students and families have found to be both interesting and challenging:

* Perform an act of charity or extraordinary kindness.

* Plan and prepare dinner for your family with little or no help from your folks.

* Plan and prepare a dinner for your family typical of what the ancient Greeks might have eaten.

* Read together books that touch the soul and fire the imagination. Discuss the books that the children are reading in class on Fridays.

* Visit a church or synagogue of a different faith than yours. Meet the rabbi, priest, or minister and learn as much as you can about this other faith.

* Go to a boatyard and learn what you can about different kinds of boats, their purpose, cost, advantages and disadvantages.

* Buy some stock and follow its course over time. Pretend that you have a thousand dollars to invest ... ten thousand, a million.

* Calculate how many square feet of carpet it would take to cover your entire house. Convert this number into square yards. Call two carpet dealers. What kinds of carpet do they offer and what would it cost to carpet your house?

* Build a model of the floor plan of your house out of cardboard, one floor at a time. Be as careful and exact as you can.

* Develop a pen pal in another Montessori school.

* Prepare a list of all the things that you would like to do with your life: career, cities to visit, mountains to climb, things you want to learn, etc.

* Teach your dog a new trick.

* Build a model of the Parthenon, an aqueduct, or some other historical structure.

* Plant a garden, tree, or some bulbs around your house.

* Write a play and perform it with some friends for your class.

* Make puppets with your folks, build a puppet theater, and put on a performance.

ever invest in tasks that have been assigned.

Providing Structure: Setting High, Individually Tailored Expectations

Individually tailored expectations doesn't mean that students can do whatever they want academically. They cannot elect whether or not to learn to read. Montessori students have to live within a cultural context, which for us involves the mastery of skills and knowledge that we consider basic.

Montessori gives students the opportunity to choose a large degree of what they investigate and learn, as well as the ability to set their own schedule during class time

Montessori children normally work with a written study plan for the day or week. It lists the basic tasks that they

(Above) An Elementary Montessori student taking her weekly spelling test.

* Learn about magic and master a new trick.

* Build a bridge out of popsicle sticks held together with carpenter's glue that will span a three-foot chasm and support several bricks.

* Interview your grandparents about their childhood. Write a biography or share what you learn with your class.

* Using one of the better books on children's science projects, select an experiment or project, carry it out, and prepare a report that documents what you did.

* Build a model sailboat using different types of sail plans. Race them on a pond with your class.

* Select a city somewhere in the world where you have never traveled. Find out everything that you can.

* Learn something new and teach it to someone in your class.

* Meet a real artist and visit her studio.

* Learn first aid.

* Prepare a time line of the presidents of the United States, along with picture cards, name tags, and fact cards. Study until you can complete the timeline on your own.

* Make your own set of constructive triangles, golden beads, or some other familiar Montessori material.

* Using 1 cm. as a unit, build out of clay, wood, or cardboard pieces to make up units, tens, hundreds, thousands, ten thousands, hundred thousands, millions up to one billion.

* Prepare a scale model of the solar system in which the distance from the sun to Pluto will be two miles. Prepare carefully measured models of the planets and sun and calculate the distance that each will need to be placed on the scale away from the sun.

need to complete, while allowing them to decide how long to spend on each and what order they would like to follow. Beyond these basic individually tailored assignments, children explore topics that capture their interest and imagination and share them with their classmates.

Tests

Montessori children usually don't think of our assessment techniques as "tests" so much as "challenges."

Early Childhood Montessori teachers observe their children at work or ask them to teach a lesson to another child to confirm their knowledge and skill.

Most Elementary Montessori teachers will give their students informal individual oral exams or have the children demonstrate what they have learned by either teaching a lesson to another child or by giving a formal presentation. The children also take and prepare their own written tests to administer to their friends.

Rather than being graded using a standard letter-grade scheme, students are normally working toward mastery.

Standardized Tests

Very few Montessori schools test children younger than the first or second grades; however, most Montessori schools regularly give elementary students quizzes on the concepts and skills that they have been studying. Many schools ask their older students to take annual standardized tests.

While Montessori students tend to score very well, Montessori educators frequently argue that standardized testing is inaccurate, misleading, and stressful for children. There are many issues, including how well a given test captures a sense of someone's true skills and knowledge.

Any given testing session can be profoundly affected by the student's emotional state, attitude, and health, and to a large degree, what they really demonstrate is how well a student knows how to take this kind of test. Montessori educators further argue that formal tests are unnecessary, since any good teacher who works with the same children for three years and carefully observes their work, knows far more about students' progress than any paper-and-pencil test can reveal.

The ultimate problem with standardized tests in our country is that they have often been misunderstood and misinterpreted in other schools. Tests can be fairly useful when seen as a simple feedback loop, giving both parents and school a general sense of how students are progressing.

Although standardized tests may not offer a terribly accurate measure of a child's basic skills and knowledge, in our culture, test-taking skills are just another Practical Life lesson that children need to master.

Reporting Student Progress

Because Montessori believes in individually paced academic progress and encourages children to explore their interests rather than simply complete work assigned by their teachers, we don't assign grades or rank students within each class according to their achievement. Parents, students, and guides give and receive feedback in several different ways:

Student Self-Evaluations: At the elementary level, students will often prepare a monthly self-evaluation of their previous month's work. When completed, they meet with the teachers, who will review it and add their comments and observations. Students also prepare self-evaluations of the past three month's work: what they accomplished, what they enjoyed the most, what they found most difficult, and what they would like to learn in the three months ahead.

Portfolios of Student Work: In many Montessori schools, two or three times a year, teachers (and at the elementary level, students) and sometimes parents go through the students' completed work and make selections for their portfolios.

Student/Parent/Teacher Conferences: Once the students' three-month self evaluations are complete, parents, students, and teachers will hold a family conference two or three times a year to review their children's portfolios and self-evaluations and go through the teachers' assessment of their children's progress.

Narrative Progress Reports: Typically once or twice a year Montessori teachers will prepare a written narrative evaluation of the student's work, social development, and mastery of fundamental skills.

Some final thoughts in closing ...

We invite you to take a close look at the kind of person your child has become today at four or five and ask yourself how would you like her to be when she's eighteen? By what set of values do you hope she will live? Do you hope that she will still love school and be excited about learning? If so, then you have laid the right foundation by sending her to Montessori thus far. Like our families and so many millions of others like us, you've taken the first step. And now the question is what's next? We invite you to follow those of us who have gone before down the Montessori path. We have discovered it to be the best decision that we could have made for our children. What your son or daughter has experienced thus far is just the first step in the journey, and the best is yet to come.

MONTESSORI PROGRAMS

Montessori At The Secondary Levels

Your children have been in Montessori all their lives. They love school and learn enthusiastically. Montessori has been the perfect match, but your children are approaching the age where they will have to leave Montessori if their school doesn't do something soon! And so you ask, "Why aren't there any Secondary Montessori programs in our town? What would it take to start a middle school class at our school?"

Most Americans have the impression that Montessori is just for early childhood. Even though Montessori schools have spread all over the world during the last century, most schools in the United States stop after kindergarten. Some schools run through sixth grade, but Secondary Montessori schools are very rare. This is beginning to change as more and more Montessori schools open elementary classes, and many have either opened or are exploring the possibility of developing middle school programs.

This is important to the entire Montessori community because, unfortunately, in the eyes of many people around the world, "real education" begins with high school. Just consider the relative respect given to high school teachers compared to the level of respect given to those who teach preschoolers. Consider the dollars contributed annually to high schools compared to the relative pittance given to early childhood programs.

> *"The need that is so keenly felt for a reform of secondary schools is not only an educational but also a human and social problem. This can be summed up in one sentence: Schools as they are today are adapted neither to the needs of adolescence nor to the time in which we live."*
>
> — Maria Montessori

Today, we know that this prejudice is illogical, as research supports the premise that the most important years of a child's education are not the years of high school and college but those of the first six years of life. This is the foundation of everything that will follow.

Illogical as this prejudice may be, it is a fact of life that Montessorians have not been able to escape. Parents invariably look for evidence that Montessori works, and the evidence that parents would find ultimately compelling is a track record of Montessori preparing students to gain admission to the finest colleges and universities.

For this reason, as Montessori education slowly develops at the high school level, it will finally be able to take credit for those terrific young men and women that we have been sending off for generations to the finest public and private high schools. Think back. Do most people give credit to the preschools and elementary schools that they attended, or do they look back fondly on their high school years? For this reason alone, the expansion of Montessori at the high school level is an important and essential trend in the future development of Montessori around the world. Only the establishment of successful Montessori High Schools can validate the effectiveness of Montessori as a "whole" in the eyes of the average person.

The Emergence of Secondary Montessori Programs

The first secondary schools organized along Montessori principles were founded in Europe in the 1930s. Anne Frank, the young girl made famous by her poignant diaries, was a student in the first Montessori high school in Amsterdam when it was closed by the Nazis. At last count, there were eight large, highly regarded Montessori High Schools in the Netherlands.

The first American secondary programs influenced by Dr. Montessori's ideas, but not openly identified as "Montessori" began to appear in the 1940s and 1950s. Co-author, Tim Seldin, attended one of the first of these programs at the Barrie School in Silver Spring, Maryland, which established its upper school in the 1950s.

In the late 1970s, a small group of Montessori leaders, interested in the development of an American Montessori secondary model, founded the *Erdkinder* Consortium. This group's discussions led to a consensus that while Dr. Montessori's vision of a residential, farm-based learning community would be a model to work toward, schools interested in developing a modified middle school program in the interim should be encouraged to do so. These schools became known as "urban-compromise" programs.

In the 1970s, a number of early adolescent programs openly identified as being "Montessori influenced," were established in the United States, including Near North Montessori in Chicago, the Ruffing Montessori School in Cleveland, Ohio, and two that are no longer in operation: the Montessori Farm School in Half Moon Bay, California and the Erdkinder School near Atlanta, Georgia.

In 1982, the Barrie School became the first Montessori Junior and Senior High School program officially recognized by the American Montessori Society. That year, the Institute for Advanced Montessori Studies in Silver Spring, Maryland, and the Dallas Montessori Teacher Education Program in Dallas, Texas, opened the first Montessori Secondary teacher education programs.

During the 1980s, a number of other programs for young adolescents opened in the United States and Canada, including the Franciscan Earth School in Portland, Oregon; the School of the Woods in Houston, Texas; St. Joseph's Montessori in Columbus, Ohio; the Toronto Montessori School in Ontario, Canada; and the Athens Montessori School in Athens, Georgia.

Today, perhaps half the Montessori schools in America stop after kindergarten, while most of the rest extend to the third or sixth grade. Montessori Middle and High School programs, however, are still very rare. We estimate that there

"My vision of the future is no longer of people taking exams, earning a secondary diploma, and proceeding on to university, but of individuals passing from one stage of independence to a higher, by means of their own activity, through their own effort of will, which constitutes the inner evolution of the individual."
— Maria Montessori

are now more than two hundred Montessori Middle School programs in North America with numerous others in various stages of development. There are approximately twenty high schools openly identifying themselves as Montessori, and a growing number under development.

Montessori's Vision of the *Erdkinder*

Maria Montessori first proposed her ideas for the reform of secondary education in a series of lectures given at the University of Amsterdam in January 1920. They were later published during the 1930s as part of her work *From Childhood to Adolescence*.

Dr. Montessori's model of secondary education is based on her understanding of the developmental needs and learning tendencies of early adolescents. In addition to conceiving many of the reforms incorporated into today's most innovative programs for early adolescents, Montessori added a unique idea: she recommended a residential school located in a country setting.

Montessori believed that by living independently of their families for a few years in a small rural community, young people could be trained in both the history of technology and civilization, while learning the practical habits, values, and skills needed to assume the role of an adult in today's society.

Envisioning a school where children would grow their own food and live close to nature, she called her program the *Erdkinder*, which translates from the Dutch as "the children of the Earth" or "children of the land."

Dr. Maria Montessori proposed living and working on a residential farm school as the best possible educational setting for young adolescents (twelve- to fifteen-year-olds) as they transitioned physically, cognitively, socially, emotionally, and morally to adulthood.

Montessori believed the demands of puberty warranted a holiday from traditional lecture-based instruction. Instead of confining students to classrooms, she proposed a program that would help them accomplish two key developmental tasks: becoming psychologically and economically independent. Only then, she argued, would young adolescents escape from the pettiness of traditional schooling and engage seriously in the realities of life in society.

Montessori envisioned the *Erdkinder* as a small community of teenagers and adults located in a rural setting. Here teachers and students would live and work together throughout the year, growing much of their own food and manufacturing many of the things they would need for life in the country, thereby developing a deep sense of their connection to the land and the nature and value of work.

She envisioned students, under adult supervision, managing a hostel or hotel for visiting parents. The students would sell farm goods and other products in their own store. These farm management and store economics would form the basis of meaningful academic studies.

The *Erdkinder* curriculum would encourage self-expression through music, art, public speaking, and theater. Students would also study languages, mathematics, science, history of civilizations, cultures, and technological innovations. The *Erdkinder* would possess a "museum of machinery," where students could assemble, use, and repair their own farm equipment.

For many years the idea of a residential farm school was explored, but considered impractical. Montessori Secondary schools are now found in urban and suburban settings in the United States, with enrollments ranging from fewer than ten students to public school programs with more than 250 students.

The cost of organizing a residential *Erdkinder* program has been considered far too high for any one school to attempt; instead, Montessori Middle School programs attempt to incorporate as many *Erdkinder* components as possible.

The Montessori community looked on with considerable interest in 2001 when David Kahn, Director of the North American Montessori Teacher's Association (NAMTA), opened the Montessori Farm School in Huntsburg, Ohio in conjunction with the Hershey Montessori School. Serving students from ages twelve to fifteen, the Montessori Farm School is a lovely facility and an exciting project that has attracted widespread attention, including a substantial article in the *London Times*.

Many leaders in Secondary Montessori education believe that the future will lie primarily with non-residential programs. The opening of the Farm School, and others like it that may follow, provides an opportunity to test one of Dr. Montessori's hypotheses. She proposed that the residential community, with its artificially created social laboratory, will prove to be of most value in the completion of the development of mature, well adjusted young adults.

A piece prepared by David Kahn describing the Montessori Farm School in greater depth follows.

The Hershey Montessori Farm School

The Hershey Montessori Farm School is located in Huntsburg, Ohio, one hour east of Cleveland. An outgrowth of over twenty years of Montessori adolescent practice, the Farm School is guided by Maria Montessori's vision of a farm-based community as an optimal place for adolescents to unlock their potential as self-motivated, independent, and fulfilled young learners. The Farm School vision, specifically built according to Maria Montessori's concept, focuses on human interdependency with the natural world. In cooperation with the farm and its related activities, and through participation in surrounding rural life and commerce, students experience practical roles that integrate and engage academic studies, while building a greater connection to society and the world. The Farm School represents the next stage of development that begins with the prepared environment of the "Young Child Community" (age 0-3); Children's House (age 3-6); continues through the culturally expanded program of Montessori Elementary (age 6-12); and culminates with the "Adolescent Community on the Farm" (age 12-15).

Why a Farm School for the Adolescent?

The Hershey Montessori Farm School serves a vital need for adolescents: the need for developing intellectual abilities — abilities to abstract, conjecture, predict, and create; the need for peer interaction and acceptance as well as mentor relationships with adults who are not their parents; the need to form a personal identity, to know how one fits into the world.

Adolescents can meet these needs through a real community experience that will offer them meaningful work — work that will be valued by the community itself. Real work. Work that challenges both the mind and the body. Work that the culture recognizes as legitimate. Work that is made noble by being done with integrity and passion.

The Hershey Montessori Farm School integrates these needs into both academic and work interests. The farm is an exercise in social independence; it teaches lessons of self-sufficiency. At the same time, it provides goods and services to the community. It provides the highest expectations of challenge in both academic and social development, appealing to the very different contributions each individual adolescent has to offer.

The Hershey Montessori Farm School

The Montessori Farm School is a serene, awe-inspiring place, on 97 beautiful, forested, rolling acres. It houses approximately 45 local, national, and international boarding and day students, ranging in age from twelve to fifteen, and acts as a resource center for local and national Montessori schools. As a program of the Hershey Montessori School, an Association Montessori Internationale (AMI) school established in 1978 and located in Concord Township, Ohio, The Hershey Montessori Farm School is connected to a warm and cohesive community of parents, teachers, and infants through children aged twelve.

The 24,000 square-foot main farm building is an intimate, homelike space designed to resemble an historic farmhouse structure. In addition to living, eating, and sleeping areas, the farmhouse has ample study, utility, and recreation space. The house is designed to allow the students to run the household: to cook, clean, process and preserve food, study, do artwork, reflect, socialize, and be members of a healthy community of adolescents and adults. Two families live on the farm to help build a familial atmosphere.

Students also have the use of barns that house a woodworking shop, performing arts-and-crafts center, and farm animals. A bio-shelter, or alternative energy greenhouse, provides shelter for plants and serves as an educational laboratory. Specialized structures designed and built by students, including barnyard sheds, a maple sugar house, creek bridges, and a produce stand, provide further laboratories for study. Students also run a bed-and-breakfast for visitors. The Farm School is a microeconomy, and all economic activities are tallied, including the harvest. Students may apply for one of nineteen managerial positions, assuming major responsibility for farm operations.

The Educational Program

The Hershey Montessori Farm School has a work and study process that emerges from direct contact with the land. The vast acres of woods and farm at Huntsburg become the "prepared environment" for the adolescent. The farm activities lead the students to a study of farm science, land management and ecology, biology and chemistry, mathematics, accounting, geometry, civilization, economic systems, algebra, physics, energy, environmental issues, and technology and information. In short, the farm activities and their features are the points of departure for formal studies, but the educational syllabus goes well beyond immediate academic extensions that arise out of farm work.

The Hershey Montessori Farm School's curriculum and instructional design are developed so that, within the farm environment, each student is exposed to and well versed in knowledge and skills common to pre-collegiate curricula. Courses of study necessary to meet these standards are available to the students if they are not accomplished through the farm's integrated plan of study. When students graduate from The Hershey Montessori Farm School at ninth grade, they will find themselves more than adequately prepared for their remaining years of high school.

The Administration and Faculty

The Hershey Montessori Farm School has assembled a faculty of AMI Montessori visionaries balanced by academic, art, music, and trade specialists from the surrounding area. Researched and designed since 1996 by some of the best and brightest in the Montessori field, The Hershey Montessori Farm School prototype design work has since received input from the Pedagogical Committee of the Association Montessori Internationale, and the Program Director is in direct consultation with the International Center for Montessori Studies in Bergamo, Italy.

The Course of Study

Humanities (World History and English)

Montessori has three thematic approaches to history: The Study of Living Things; The Study of the History of Mankind; and The Study of Human Progress and the Building Up of Human Civilization (*From Childhood to Adolescence*). Following the orientation to culture suggested by these themes, four representative cultures that form a span of social communities extending from ancient to modern times are selected for study each academic year. The program places strong emphasis on the evolving stages of civilization — from village to megalopolis — with a final goal of seeing our time, place, and culture as part of a continuing endeavor of the whole of humanity. Literary works are included.

The course of study uses period readings for the art of discussion (seminar technique); visual arts, drama, and writing for the internalization and expression of philosophical values; time lines for chronological emphasis; and research papers and essay tests for challenging students to demonstrate their understanding.

Science, Occupations, and Learning by Doing

Occupations are points of engagement for the adolescent on the land. They are a source of meaningful work valued by the community, work that challenges both mind and body, work that is recognized as legitimate by the culture, work that has economic validity, noble work done with integrity and passion. Occupations not only fulfill the adolescents' need to belong and be valued, but they also provide the motivation for academic study.

"Work on the land is an introduction both to nature and to civilization and gives a limitless field for scientific and historic studies." — Maria Montessori

The science demanded for project-based, experience-based learning is not a subject to be covered, but rather it is knowledge to be applied for the greater good of the operating farm throughout the seasons. Care of plants and animals, nutrition, small building construction, and simple machines are examples of specific interest centers which can generate specific academic contexts that include zoology, geology, physics, ecology, chemistry, meteorology, history, and archeology and add up to a well-rounded and integrated learning experience.

Thus, the occupation's meaningful work extends to all areas of study and at the same time provides adolescents with the motivation to become "experts" in specific occupational areas. Experts can apply for management positions that follow their expertise and give them a higher profile role in the farm's micro-economy. The beekeeper becomes the beekeeping manager. The pond tester becomes the pond manager. The occupation converts into a "role," and the adolescent learns what it means to make a contribution to society.

The ninth graders experience a "place-based" biology course, the goal of which is to integrate land-based activities with high school biology content, including such subject areas as evolution, genetics, taxonomy, physiology, cell structure, animal and plant behavior, environmental science, and biochemistry.

Fine Arts: Opportunities for Self-Expression

Montessori's original educational syllabus included a category for self-expression through language, music, drama, and art. Adolescents must be given opportunities to channel their natural tendencies to talk, to express, and to create. The Hershey Montessori Farm School facilitates creative projects in which the students set up their own projects in music, videography, photography, drawing, drama, etc. Since coordination of operations in the farm cooperative depends on sharing information, oral presentation, visual display, video recording, and photography are a serious part of the curriculum.

Mathematics (Theoretical and Real World)

Mathematics is an applied science focused on the opportunities for problem solving that arise in the farm experience. At the same time, mathematics is a theoretical discipline exploring relationships between abstractions. Both theoretical mathematics and applied science address patterns and relationships, and the two studies contribute to one another. For example, science provides mathematics with problems to investigate.

Mathematics provides symbolic systems to help science organize data. Mathematics also provides the structure of scientific laws and formulae. Technology opens up new mathematical explorations, while mathematical operations improve understanding of technology.

The general goals for the utilization of both Algebra I, Algebra II, and Geometry are:

1. to utilize mathematics and real-life problem solving;
2. to increase the application of mathematical reasoning and skills to tasks and occupations on the farm; and
3. to model real-world phenomena with a variety of mathematical functions.

The basis for applied mathematics is the farm. Many jobs on the farm entail specific measurement: for example, quantitative analysis for feed and rate of animal consumption; computation of square footage for pasture in relation to livestock inventory and rate of reproduction; use of computers for producing bar graphs, circle graphs, and line graphs to summarize productivity, etc. The farm micro-economy will also use business math to measure the extent of the enterprise's self-sufficiency and profit.

Physical Education

Physical Education at the Farm School is found in many areas, physical work being integral to daily living. Generally, the Farm School promotes physical activities at several levels:

Work: Farm work involves physical chores and projects that require significant body exertion, such as animal feeding, stall cleaning, planting, cultivation, trail maintenance, harvesting, building structures, etc.

Sports: Coached team sports are available based on season and student interest.

Specialty Electives: Running, hiking, weight-lifting, fencing, dance, tennis, biking, and horseback riding are examples of rotating options to be selected by students according to their interests.

Vocational Arts

Although farm-based education includes aspects of agricultural education, the essence of the operating farm lies in the experience of community living and community enterprise, which provides a comparison to the history of civilizations both in role playing and economics. In order to be a microcosm for society, the farm must be an operating economy, a true exercise in a challenging life style, and a real attempt at self-sufficiency. The students learn to sew, grow and cook their own food, and build their own special tools and artifacts.

Computers

Computers in the Montessori environment are treated as tools and, generally speaking, are not used for assisted instructional purposes. At the farm, computers interface with the agricultural business (micro-economy), with Global Information Systems and global positioning on the land, and with fine arts especially videography, sound engineering, and photography. They are also used for Internet research and communications. The computer in the context of the Hershey Montessori Farm School is intended to serve agricultural, social, and ecological goals.

Foreign Languages (Spanish)

Spanish is taught in a multi-age classroom, consisting of seventh, eighth, and ninth graders and covers basic information appropriate for beginning and intermediate learners. Lessons are conducted in small groups and are based on both a textbook and multimedia approach. Other languages, including classical languages, may be available for small group work, upon request, depending on personnel availability.

— *by David Kahn, NAMTA**

---

*Contact information: David Kahn, North American Montessori Teacher's Association (NAMTA), 13693 Butternut Road, Burton, OH, 44021; (440) 834-4011.

A number of independent Montessori schools around the world are currently establishing high school programs, including: The Toronto Montessori School in Toronto, Canada; The Claremont School in Boca Raton, Florida; The School of the Woods in Houston, Texas; the New Gate School in Sarasota, Florida; the Brisbane Montessori School in Brisbane, Australia; and the Athena Montessori College in Wellington, New Zealand. Clark Montessori Secondary School, the first American public Montessori High School (located in Cincinnati, Ohio), recently graduated its first senior class.

The parents of students at Clark Montessori Secondary School speak enthusiastically about the quality of the program and the success of its graduates.

These Secondary Montessori schools are developing their middle and high school programs based on the model of adolescent development Dr. Montessori described in her work *The Erdkinder*. Other design elements for today's Montessori Middle and High School programs have come from secondary school reform efforts of the past decade and recent insights regarding adolescence.

Observations on the Nature of Adolescence

The term *adolescence* is a recent social category. The idea of adolescence as a distinct age group within our population developed during the late 1800s and early 1900s as western countries industrialized, established laws forbidding the use of cheap child labor, and required compulsory school attendance. Unlike our society, few non-western cultures recognize young adolescence (the years from eleven to fourteen) as a social category distinct from middle adolescence (the years of early sexual maturity between fifteen and eighteen) and later adolescence (now thought to extend to as late as twenty-five or twenty-six). In some cultures, childhood is followed by a young adult stage of life. Many societies traditionally marked the transition from childhood to youth with an initiation ceremony or rite of passage. By comparison, our society offers few benchmarks that either children or adults see as particularly meaningful, other than perhaps passing the driver's test or graduating from high school.

Montessori described the young adolescent years as a period of vulnerability and self-construction. It is a time marked by uncertainty and self-consciousness; it can also be an awkward time. They have to cope with emerging sexuality and hormonally driven conflicting emotions. More recently, adolescent psychologists have described the pattern of physical growth as generally "outside-in." The child's feet and hands grow before the arms and legs; the nose and ears grow before the face. There is an increase in weight, height, heart size, lung capacity, and muscular strength. Coordination is a challenge for many young adolescents as bones lengthen prior to muscular development. Some young adolescents are physically awkward as their body's center of balance is thrown off. As their muscular development proceeds, many literally don't know their own strength.

Recent studies of adolescent development also suggest there are several "normal" overall patterns of physical growth. In general, while physical growth occurs in girls before boys, cognitive growth may occur similarly across gender. Young adolescents may grow rapidly and attain their adult height after several months. Still at twelve or thirteen, they have to learn to deal with a "new" body of a sixteen-year-old and the way that it affects their social relationships with peers and older teens. Others grow very gradually and require several years to reach their adult height and body proportions.

Young adolescents have the potential for new thinking capabilities. They are learning to reason hypothetically, plan ahead, understand analogies, and construct metaphors. Concentration is, however, often difficult; young adolescents are easily distracted.

Young adolescents are also concerned (and sometimes overly preoccupied) with justice and fairness. It matters and bothers them when injustice (as they define it) occurs. They have a strong desire to contribute to and help others. It's an age of idealism; they assume friends, family, and society can and should be perfect. Finding their place in the world is an enormous undertaking, and they will try on many roles and activities as a way to create personal identities.

Friends are exceedingly important for most young adolescents. Friends provide one another an emotional safety net as they venture out of childhood and try out new ideas, roles, and behaviors. Friends will take new risks. To them, the gravest wrong that can occur is to have their trust betrayed by someone whom they consider a true friend. As a result, young adolescents often test one another's friendship to determine whether or not a secret will be broken, whether a practical joke or teasing will end a friendship, or whether their friends will stand by them. Many are also anxious to make and keep commitments to friends.

Young adolescents are consciously beginning to learn how to choose to live and work interdependently. In adult terms, interdependence involves being trustworthy and being trusted. Interdependence requires being able to give and keep your word; to be someone who can be trusted and depended on. Effective communication skills, shared inquiry, problem definitions, and multiple approaches to generating and adopting solutions rest on reliability.

Young adolescents seek to develop interpersonal reliability. Their chief approach for this is through self-expression. Amongst themselves they talk, write notes, and also write and exchange emails. Psychological research documents that when teenagers talk and pass notes to one another, they are exchanging personal information that is understood to be communicated in strict confidence. Young teenagers often fail, however, to keep their word; young adolescents do not keep all of their promises. Young adolescents require caring and respectful adults who prepare environments in which the promises young adolescents keep result with successful activities that truly matter. For new beginners in living interdependently, their environment must allow for moments of not keeping promises as key opportunities for examining intentions, commitments, and forgiveness — qualities of an interdependent life.

Secondary Montessori programs are primarily intended to serve as the logical next step for a child who has come up through the Early Childhood and Elementary Montessori programs. One Montessori Secondary program might even serve an entire community, drawing students from several different Montessori Elementary schools. It is possible to accept a limited number of older students who are coming from other more traditional schools, but only after consideration for their potential success in the Montessori Secondary program.

The Basic Elements of a Secondary Montessori Program

Montessori Middle and High Schools today blend various aspects of the *Erdkinder* model with elements developed by exemplary secondary schools during the past twenty years. For example, middle school students at the School of the Woods in Houston, Texas, spend one week out of every six living at the school's Land Lab, where they study, build shelters, cultivate crops, and recycle. Students in another program run a baby-sitting business. These kinds of "Practical Life" activities are essential. They provide direct learning experiences that involve the young adolescent with meaningful learning activities.

Other basic elements of Montessori Secondary programs include interdisciplinary, thematic instruction; discovery-based learning; individual and small-group learning projects; authentic and performance-based assessment; small advisory groups; community service, internships, and land-based studies. In addition, you should find the following specific program elements in a Montessori Secondary program:

- The curriculum is developmentally based and appropriate to meet the growing intellectual, social, emotional, and physical needs of adolescents.

- Students need ample opportunities for self-expression as they construct personal meaning about their studies and themselves.

- Students should solve meaningful problems and develop logical reasoning, research skills, and higher-order "formal" thinking skills rather than only memorize predigested concepts, theories, and information presented in lectures and textbooks. The curriculum should allow students to learn through experience and practical "hands-on" application.

- The curriculum should offer a broad view of the world, emphasizing ecological interdependency, the historical development and interconnectedness of ideas and events, and an international/multicultural perspective.

- The curriculum should be organized as an "integrated thematic approach" connecting separate disciplines of the curriculum into studies of the physical universe, the world of nature, and the human experience.

- Montessori Secondary programs do not emphasize academic competition among students. The program should evaluate students on a logical, objective basis. Students should not be graded on a curve but rather should be evaluated individually against clearly stated academic objectives through a wide variety of authentic assessment techniques, including portfolios, long-term projects, and self-evaluation.

- The faculty should use a variety of teaching styles and modify assignments and assessment strate-

(Below) The Adolescent Center at the Montessori School of Raleigh (North Carolina)

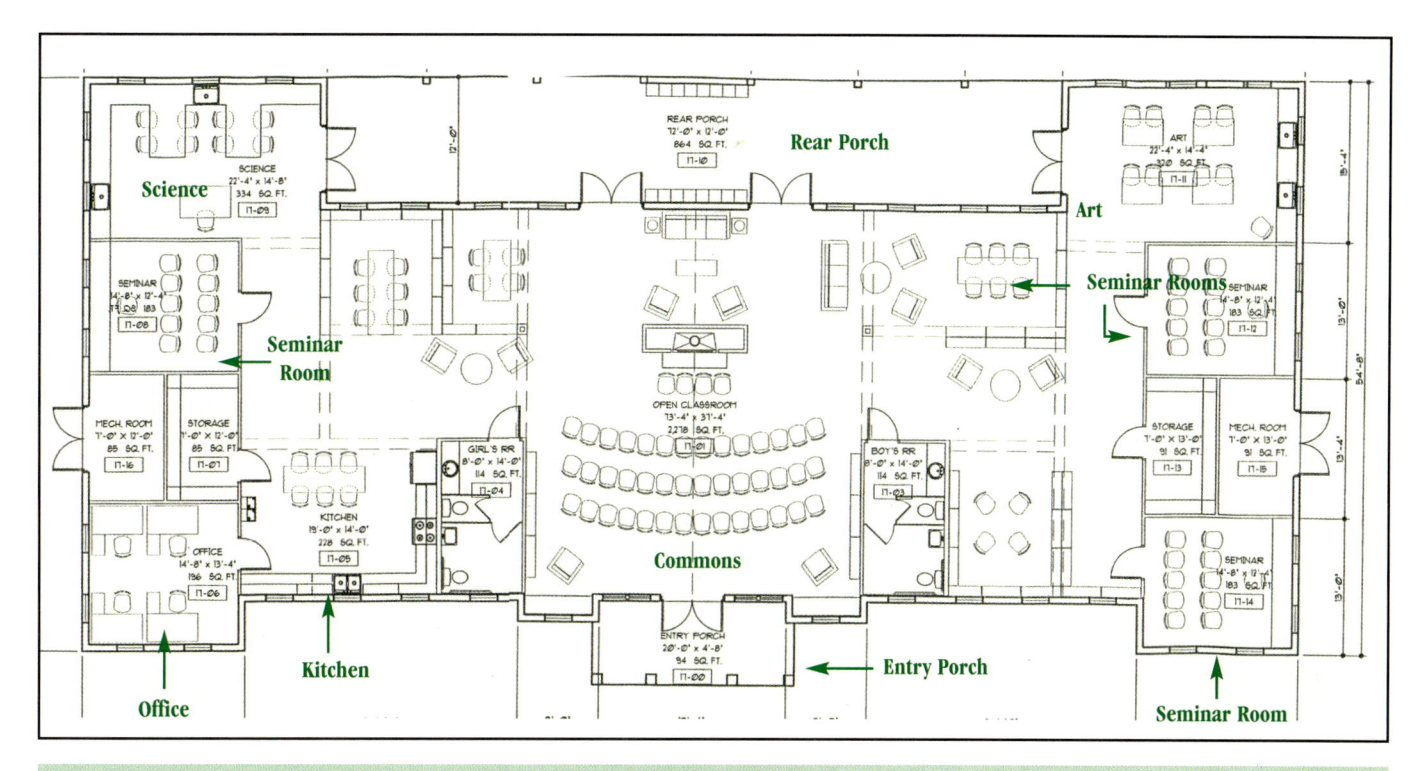

**New Gate School
Design for an Upper School House
45 Students — Grades 7 & 8, 9 & 10, or 11 & 12**

(Above) Working draft of the design for a Montessori Upper-School "House" developed for the New Gate School in Sarasota, Florida. New Gate's master plan calls for the construction of several of these Houses as enrollment growth warrants. At the time this book went to press, these particular structures are scheduled for the next phase of construction.

gies to meet individual student's learning styles and special interests.

■ The faculty should serve as mentors and facilitate the process as their students learn how to observe, listen, read critically, gather information, and learn from hands-on experience.

■ The faculty should consciously strive to help their students develop self-esteem, independence, responsibility, compassion, openness to new experiences and learning, patience and self-discipline, acceptance of others, and effective and satisfying social relationships.

■ The school should be a community of young people and adults based on kindness, trust, and mutual respect. The school should support young adults learning the skills of living in the adult world within a safe environment.

■ There should be many opportunities for student participation in the planning and operation of the life of the school community.

■ Students should be introduced to social issues of the community in which they live, both through the curriculum and through field experiences, volunteer efforts, and internship projects. The school should consciously promote students' personal spiritual and ethical development and encourage service to the community.

■ The school should consciously promote entrepreneurial spirit.

New Montessori Middle School programs typically begin with a small group of seventh graders. The enrollment gradually builds in size over the years as more families and their students elect to continue with the school through the upper level(s). This presents a tremendous challenge for many schools, because parents and students are normally reluctant to be part of what they perceive as a fragile new program.

Many factors contribute to this, all of which are tied to our culture's image of what a middle or senior high school should look like. For example, parents and students alike tend to expect a fairly large enrollment of several hundred to more than a thousand students in which students can choose among a wide range of friends and extra-curricular activities. And yet, school-reform efforts in these large institutions are heading in the direction of creating smaller learning communities called "houses" or "academies."

Although mixed-age groups within a classroom is an essential component of all Montessori programs, there is no agreement as to the mix of ages in the middle school. Some schools combine grades seven through eight only.

Other schools define the middle school as grades six through eight or grades seven through nine. Schools that extend to grade twelve may offer three mixed-age levels: grades seven to eight; nine to ten; and eleven to twelve. Still other schools offer two levels: grades seven to nine and ten to twelve.

Ideally, each house will have its own suite of classrooms and meeting areas. Most programs are forced by budget or limited space to adapt themselves to existing facilities.

The facilities that The Montessori Foundation helped to design for the New Gate School in Sarasota, Florida are one example of what would be appropriate for an established "house" of perhaps forty-five to sixty students. This model is drawn from a blend of many upper-school facilities that the authors have visited over the years.

Each house is centered around a commons room of approximately 2,000 square feet. This space is designed for reading and quiet study. Each commons room also contains part of the library. At one end of the commons there might be a small stage used for debates, student presentations, guest speakers, and performances.

Several smaller rooms are adjacent to the commons. Three are designated as seminar groups; each has a large conference table and seats up to ten participants. Another room is designed as a math lab. Students work alone or in small groups, and the room is equipped with a wide range of mathematical apparatus.

A fifth room serves as a science lab with a large attached greenhouse. The lab is equipped for the life and physical sciences, with corrosive-resistant work surfaces, sinks, Bunsen burners, aquaria, animal cages, and secure storage for chemicals and equipment. For safety, the labs will have an emergency shower, eye wash, and a ventilated fume hood in which students can safely work with potentially noxious chemicals. A sixth room houses an art studio and craft workshop. Creative self-expression is particularly appealing to many adolescents. In addition to formal lessons, students should be able to engage in the arts as their interest, workload, and schedule allow.

The craft workshop provides tools for building model structures from wood, paper, and other materials. Older students often construct dioramas, models of ancient buildings, little machines, or re-creations of historical artifacts.

Finally, a small but complete kitchen is important, allowing students to prepare their own meals. Many Montessori Middle School programs operate a small lunch business. Students purchase the ingredients, prepare the day's meal, serve and clean up, collect lunch fees, and keep the business books.

In the following description, Melody Mosby describes her Montessori Middle School program in Athens, Georgia, which combines many aspects of the *Erdkinder* model with recent middle school innovations.

(Below and opposite page) Students working and dining in the Commons Room in the Adolescent Center at the Montessori School of Raleigh (North Carolina).

In addition to its other functions, students and teachers normally eat lunch in the Commons Room.

Athens Montessori Middle School:

A Place for the Adolescent

by Melody Mosby

Imagine a place where young adolescents have an opportunity for practicing their future role in society, where meaningful work extends outside, where blue skies replace bulletin boards, where historic artifacts and experiential studies replace worksheets, and textbooks become resources. If you can imagine such a place, then you have imagined the learning environment at Athens Montessori Middle School.

Athens Montessori Middle School* is a land-based model for young people, ages twelve to fifteen, who wish to continue their Montessori experience in a place where love of learning is nurtured, and the skills essential for optimal development of the adolescent are realized. The school is located in a residence on four acres of land featuring a wood lot, an active stream-bed, organic gardens, and an open field, where students enjoy life in the open air and take on the responsibilities and maintenance of the land.

This natural setting provides a quiet, serene environment for the adolescent to balance the extremes of emotions characterizing the age. Besides the calm surroundings, the work on the land provides, as Dr. Montessori suggested, "an introduction to nature and to civilization" (Montessori, *From Childhood to Adolescence,* pg. 69)

Students at Athens Montessori Middle School are not confined to a desk; rather, their role is very active, placing them in purposeful work and study that captivates the mind and body of the young adolescent. The activities that arise from the diverse geographical features on our four-acre property provide students with unlimited valuable lessons in a range of topics from botany to chemistry, geology, anthropology, anatomy, physiology, geometry, physics, and beyond. Academic studies are tied to projects and offer a balance of both manual and intellectual application.

The streambed is rich in micro-organisms and macro-organisms that provide a wealth of information about the life cycle. If the rains push debris and sediment into the stream, it has to be cleared. Paths through the woodlands have to be maintained in order to prevent further erosion. When it is time to plant, the soil requires preparation, and a soil test is taken to determine what nutrients are needed. The garden requires tilling, mulching, weeding, and certainly water in times of drought. Our nature reserve is filled with a variety of native species and some that are endangered. With field guides in hand, and experts to help with plant identification, we have begun the process of documenting, mapping, and labeling the numerous species thriving in our reserve. After a recent visit to the Museum of Natural History at the nearby university, our interest in endangered species was heightened. Now, we are working with a wildlife specialist to track and survey the various species of animal life that inhabit our property.

In this way of working with our academic studies, the topics of biology, zoology, soil chemistry, stream

---

Contact information: Melody Mosby, Athens Montessori School, 3145 Barnett Shoals Road, Athens, GA 30605; (706) 549-8490.

ecology, botany, and geology become relevant, and a wider understanding of the subject matter is apparent. We are not learning for learning's sake; we are truly receiving a preparation for life.

Besides the intellectual pursuits this work on the land offers, many social experiences arise, giving the adolescent further opportunity for nurturing the social interest of the age. Decisions have to be made about the division of labor: Who is going to do what, and how much?

Adolescence is a very social age when important lessons in responsibility and acceptance are learned. Working closely with peers on a project is a real lesson in character building and social consciousness. You find out very quickly on whom you can count, and who is going to give the best effort possible. Athens Montessori Middle School is not a boarding school, nor is it an environmental camp, but students do collaborate and cooperate with each other on the daily maintenance of the school and, if asked, they will express a deep sense of stewardship for their land-based environment. Adolescents need a sense of place. Just as the children's house was significant to the growth of the young child, a special place that creates a sense of ownership is critical to the optimal growth of the adolescent. Our adolescents work in community with each other every day, immersed in the operations of running a school program. Routines are important, and we have them, but we also remain flexible and open ended.

To begin the day, students prepare by setting up the environment, both inside and on the land. Inside, the furnishings are arranged, fresh towels are laid out, fruit is washed and placed in a ceramic bowl, flowers are arranged in glass vases, the technical equipment is turned on, attendance is taken, academic work is checked and filed, the store is opened for business, and everyone prepares themselves for a productive day. On the land, readings from the weather station are taken and recorded, the seed flats in the greenhouse are watered, the garden is tended, flowers are cut for the vases, and any necessary work to prepare our land for the day is done at this time.

Our plan of work and study is not restricted by a fixed curriculum but an evolving plan, which includes adolescent input and interest. This year, the study of our state's history and geography has been taken on the road. Students divided themselves into groups for this study and chose a particular geographical area. After researching the features unique to that area, students made plans and arrangements for a regional tour. Our studies have taken us to small towns, a granite outcropping, a rural sod farm, a coastal city, and the Appalachian trail.

Because our Georgia winters are not extreme and the weather conditions are some of the best our southern skies can offer, we enjoy our meals together in the open air year round. In fact, the weather allows for a long growing season that enables us to produce a bounty of food, which we can sell at the farmer's market on Saturday mornings. With the profits, we are able to purchase more seed and supplies to keep the garden going.

Dr. Montessori emphasized the importance of economic enterprise for the enhancement of the adolescent's self-worth. At age twelve to fifteen, most adolescents are unable to hold a job and earn a wage, yet the adolescent has reached a level of capability that can enable them to undertake many vocations in the labor force. In fact, adolescents were the primary labor force less than a century ago in the farming community and in industry. By taking part in a business enterprise that compensates adolescents for their efforts, they can feel a sense of self-worth and realize the value of work.

The adolescents at Athens Montessori Middle School provide a pizza lunch service each week for our school. The students, with teacher guidance, are responsible for recording orders, serving the lunch, and accounting for income and expenses. The profit from the business is used to finance supplies, special projects, and our end-of-the-year road trip. There is a great deal of satisfaction gained from this enterprise, as well as life skills practiced.

Additionally, students intern for one week during the year in a local business. This intern week is a highlight for the adolescent. The self-confidence, enthusiasm, and experience they gain from this endeavor is immeasurable. Our parents are very supportive of this real-life experience and recognize the valuable lessons learned.

During the intern week, one of our students worked in a retirement home and made some strong connections with the residents. Since then, she has created an inter-generational community service project for interested students who want to spend one day a week with the retirement community.

The power of the adolescent for their growth and self-knowledge is phenomenal. They are very capable of compassion, empathy, and acts of an heroic nature. When they are placed in an environment that meets their needs, the noble characteristics belonging to this age emerge. As program director and teacher in our land-based model at Athens Montessori Middle School, I am in very close contact with the adolescents. I have observed in them the highest level of personal growth and academic achievement.

This learning environment, where our student enrollment is small, where there is personal, individualized learning, and where community and social interaction with peers and teachers is possible provides a positive, empowering climate for learning and a true place for the adolescent.

A typical day looks like this:

8:15 A.M. - 8:30 A.M.	Start of the school day Prepare environment and self Community Meeting
8:30 - 10:15 A.M.	Small-group lessons (Math and Language Arts) Personal work, which includes land management
10:15 - 10:30 A.M.	Mid-morning snack break
10:30 - 11:45 A.M.	Thematic lessons (cultural studies, science, history) More open-work period Spanish studies. Community work is done during this time, for example: accounting for lunch service, planning field trips, etc.)
11:45 - 12:00 NOON	Prepare for lunch; inspiration is read
12:00 NOON - 12:30 P.M.	Lunch (we provide a lunch service on Friday — one of our business enterprises)
12:30 - 1:00 P.M.	Personal reflection (music is played) Creative expression
1:00 - 1:45 P.M.	Occupational studies (wood lot, stream-bed, garden, nature reserve, maintenance on weather station or grounds.) (This time is extended on most days.)
1:45 - 2:00 P.M.	Clean environment and prepare for dismissal
2:00 - 3:00 P.M.	Outdoor education
3:00 - 3:15 P.M.	Gather together at log circle for saying goodbye

Secondary Montessori Teachers

Certified and experienced Secondary Montessori teachers are quite rare at this time. Schools contemplating a new program should plan on sponsoring one or more teachers through Secondary Montessori teacher training. The obvious alternative is to open the program with a staff that is not trained at the secondary level. Although this is not something that we would recommend, new secondary programs may see it as their most realistic option.

Today there are only a few programs preparing Montessori Secondary teacher educators. Dr. Betsy Coe offers a MACTE-accredited, AMS-Certified Secondary Montessori teacher education program at the Houston Montessori Center in Houston, Texas; Melody Mosby is inaugurating a new program in Athens, Georgia, to train middle school teachers; and more are under development. Also, for some years, the North American Montessori Teachers' Association (NAMTA) has offered a highly regarded summer workshop in Secondary Montessori education.

Secondary Montessori teachers should not be thought of as specialists in one area of the curriculum. Instead of teaching science, math, or history in isolation, they integrate aspects of these courses of study into thematic units. In small programs, one teacher will teach all of the major subjects, much as elementary teachers do. Two to four teachers may form a team in larger programs.

The teaching team will be much more than just teachers of specific subject matter; they are also mentors, counselors, and guides through the learning process. A program may supplement the skills of the full-time core teachers by bringing in part-time specialists for such areas as, for example, physical education, foreign languages, drama, music, and the arts.

The teacher's personality and ability to relate to adolescents is perhaps the most important element in predicting potential success. At no stage of education is it more important that the teacher become the students' mentor, confidante, and trusted friend.

In traditional secondary schools, teachers tend to see helping students absorb the curriculum as their fundamental goal. In a Montessori program, academic studies are balanced with emotional, social, and moral growth. The Secondary Montessori educator must recognize the crucial role played by this process of social and emotional growth.

Group process and lessons in everyday living skills are not supplemental activities to enrich the real curriculum; they are in many ways the most important element of the curriculum. The Montessori Secondary teacher should have a thorough understanding of:

▲ Montessori's concept of *The Erdkinder;*

▲ Montessori Early Childhood and Elementary philosophy and curriculum;

▲ Adolescent psychology and development;

▲ Today's most promising and innovative secondary curriculum elements and teaching methods;

▲ Individual and group counseling techniques;

▲ Field studies, including running a small business, community-service programs, land-based studies, and internships;

▲ The practical issues of organizing, structuring, and administering alternative secondary school programs; and

▲ Contemporary high school and college admission requirements.

A Typical Day

Secondary Montessori programs normally do not look very much like Elementary Montessori classrooms because of the very different personality of the adolescent. Adolescents prefer interactions with their friends.

In most programs, students and teachers gather every day in Town Meetings, where they learn how to work together, express their thoughts clearly and honestly, resolve disagreements, compromise, and reach consensus. There is a real sense of community.

The familiar Montessori materials are not noticeable. When they were ten, Montessori students may have enjoyed working with the Montessori materials, but at twelve they don't want to be reminded of the years when they were "just kids," and they may reject the Montessori materials as "babyish."

On the other hand, learning rarely involves passively sitting back and listening to a teacher talk. Students learn from participating in seminars, meeting with guest speakers, conducting research, performing historic re-enactments, building models and dioramas, and organizing field trips and internships. These experiences engage learners in constructing a personal and meaningful education and invite students to get involved, ask questions, and think.

Teacher-initiated group lessons are usually brief — rarely lasting more than thirty minutes. Seminars and specialist classes are scheduled in such a way as to allow students large blocks of time to work without interruption. The schedule for group activities is flexible and allows the teachers to set aside the amount of time most appropriate for given activities.

Many Secondary Montessori programs give students study guides to help them organize their work. A study guide describes the interdisciplinary theme and organizes learning experiences. Ideally, these guides are not prepared by the teachers alone. Teachers and students should work together to set goals and suggest a learning path that is defined in accordance with each student's individual learning style. Study guides typically identify three elements:

- Skills and knowledge that the students are expected to learn;

- Learning experiences in which students engage, such as attending seminars or lectures, books that need to be read, movies that must be viewed, field trips to be taken, presentations given, lab experiments completed, tests taken, etc.

- Essays, reports, and other assignments or projects students complete.

Many programs expect students to demonstrate a given level of mastery before they are allowed to move on to the next level. Unacceptable work or performance on tests of skills and knowledge must be resubmitted after additional lessons or coaching.

It is common for Secondary Montessori programs to allow students to select from among several optional learning strategies and assignments or to propose another option.

Using this approach, Secondary Montessori students continue to learn how to prioritize, pace themselves, and take responsibility for their work. These are skills that are critical to success in university and life.

(Above) A Town Meeting.

The World is Their Classroom

Montessori Secondary programs will normally go out into the community to give their students a wide range of projects and experiences that would never be possible in a traditional schedule. Some schools go out as opportunities arise; others schedule one day a week for academic extensions, breaking off into small groups to visit museums, galleries, the theater, university libraries, the courts, government offices, and scientific laboratories.

Students also use "Extension Days" to work on special projects or to study issues in depth. They contact and visit government agencies, public interest groups, and relevant industries, pour through public records, and interview key public figures. Gradually, they assemble information and attempt to interpret the "big picture."

Example of a Middle School Assignment:

Study Guide: Presidential Politics, Cultural Revolutions, and the Korean War Cycle: Expectation
Chiaravalle Montessori Middle School Program

Quotation: "He hath indeed better bettered expectation." — William Shakespeare (1564-1616): *Much Ado about Nothing.* Act 1, Sc. 1

Essential Questions:

1. What are personal characteristics?
2. What are the characteristics of a president?

Habits of Mind:

1. Evidence: How do I know this? What is the proof?
2. Persistence: What are some alternative ways of accomplishing goals?
3. Managing Impulsivity: Have I considered all options and consequences before acting?

Learning Goals:

1. Compare and contrast the presidential elections of 1948, 1960, and 2000.
2. Identify major decisions made by Presidents Truman and Bush.
3. Describe the purposes of the Chinese Cultural Revolution.
4. Define the goals of the United States during the Korean War.

Investigations:

1. Define "personality trait." What are some of yours?

2. Two signs sat on President Truman's desk in his White House office. One said, "The buck stops here." The other was a quote from Mark Twain, "Always do right. This will gratify some people and astonish the rest."

   a. What difficult decisions do presidents make?

   b. Suppose these signs were on your desk. What decisions do you make each day? How does the buck stop with you? How do you know what is right? Is it hard to "always do right?"

3. Read the following sayings from President Truman. What does each mean? How does it fit your life?

   a. "If you can't stand the heat, stay out of the kitchen."
   b. "Children nowadays have too many gadgets to fool with and not enough chores."
   c. "I always tell students that it is what you learn after you know it all that counts."

4. Write your own saying and its meaning.

5. Define the following terms, persons, and events:

   a. Mao Zedong
   b. Jiang Jieshi
   c. the red army
   d. the nationalist army
   e. the "Great Leap Forward" plan of 1958
   f. communes
   g. the Red Guards
   h. the Cultural Revolution

6. What evidence did the *Chicago Tribune* use to proclaim on November 3, 1948: "DEWEY DEFEATS TRUMAN"

7. Define the circumstances that led to the creation of the *Washington Post* political cartoon caption: "REPORTS OF MY POLITICAL DEATH WERE GREATLY EXAGGERATED"

8. Compare the 1948 Democratic and Republican platforms. For whom would you vote and why?

MONTESSORI PROGRAMS

Study Guide: Presidential Politics, Cultural Revolutions, and the Korean War Continued ...

9. Examine polling predictions of the 1948 presidential election. What evidence were these predictions based upon?

10. Truman made numerous decisions including: dropping the atomic bomb; desegregating the Armed Forces; promoting Truman Doctrine; enforcing the Marshall Plan; recognizing Israel; and fighting in Korea. What are some of President Bush's decisions?

    a. In carrying out these decisions, how did each president demonstrate persistence and resist acting impulsively?

11. React to the following political satire piece: *"2004 Presidential Election Cancelled."*

12. Research:

    a. Who decided to divide Korea at the 38th parallel?
    b. What was China's role during the Korean War?
    c. How did Truman's views differ from MacArthur's? Was Truman's decision to fire his general a good one?
    d. How did the Korean War end?
    e. What is the relationship between North and South Korea today?
    f. What is the relationship between the United States and these two countries today?

A culminating project:

Your final project involves speculation. Imagine President Roosevelt completed his fourth term. What effect would this have had on the ending of World War II, the election of 1948, China, and Korea? What evidence supports your hypotheses?

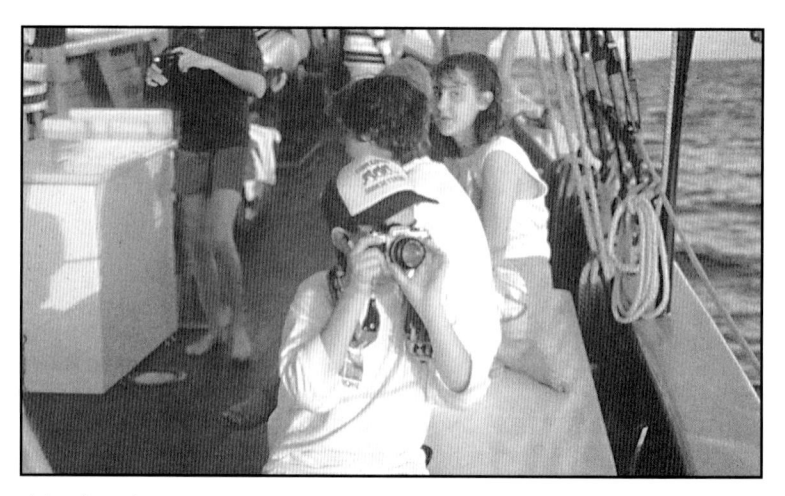

(Above) Students study marine biology in the Caribbean in this archive photo from the Barrie School in Silver Spring, Maryland.

Secondary Montessori programs also arrange for their students to participate in field work — a combination of land-based studies, community service, and internship experiences. At certain points of the year, students will engage in internships in the business, professional, or public-interest communities. Students develop their own resumes and are expected to find their own internship position. Montessori High School students have interned in government offices; worked for Greenpeace; studied at the zoo; and assisted in doctors' offices, architectural firms, veterinary clinics, radio stations, newspapers, hospitals, retail businesses; or volunteered in shelters for the homeless. Many internships develop into long-term relationships. One of the unique programs in a Montessori High School is the opportunity for a wide range of international study and travel. Montessori education is worldwide, and each program has sister schools across America and in Europe, Asia, Australia, and South America. There are invaluable opportunities for correspondence and student exchange experiences. Again, using Barrie as an example, students have engaged in travel/study programs in Israel, Canada, France, Spain, Italy, Greece, Mexico, Costa Rica, Russia, the Caribbean, Japan, and China. Montessori High Schools also sponsor camping, canoeing, and sailing expeditions.

Montessori High Schools

A number of independent and public schools now offer Montessori at the high school level. At this time, however, there is no agreement as to what defines a Montessori High School. The following insert about Clark Montessori Secondary School in Cincinnati, Ohio, offers one description.

A Montessori University

In keeping with her philosophical focus on designing learning environments to satisfy developmental needs, Montessori noted that university studies must help students become autonomous and

Clark Montessori Secondary School
Cincinnati, Ohio

Clark Montessori Secondary School is located in Cincinnati, Ohio*

Author's Note: Our thanks to Program Director, Marta Donahoe, for her description of Clark Montessori Secondary School.

Clark Montessori Secondary School* is the first public Montessori High School in the nation. In 2003 Clark, which is located in Cincinnati, Ohio, graduated its fourth class with 98 percent of its students college bound and one National Merit Finalist. The Bill and Melinda Gates Foundation, in the publication *Small, Safe, Sane, Successful Schools*, recognized Clark Montessori as an exemplary secondary model. The small-school design provides opportunities for students to learn the skills and values involved in teamwork and group decision making, long-term project management, and service to the community. These skills in human development are imbedded within the challenging academic courses required of all students.

In keeping with Montessori philosophy, "Clark places a priority on developing students' emotional competencies, building a caring community in which students feel respected, cared about, and bonded to classmates. Adolescents need to feel responsible for learning and their social life. They want to be with peers, but they need support and clear expectations from adults. They need to enhance their personal self-esteem, communication skills, sense of community, and ability to engage in meaningful learning experiences." (Mckenzie, G. K. [2003]. "A High School Model: Inside Cincinnati's Clark Montessori School." *Public School Montessorian*/Spring 2003.)

These developmental needs are met with a number of planned experiences including community meetings, peer counseling responsibilities, immersion weeks, community service, independent study, and job internships. Students are expected to participate in each of these experiences as well as maintain their studies in Clark's rigorous academic program. Clark Montessori Secondary School has earned "School Achievement," the school district's highest academic ranking.

During regular community meetings, students discuss issues and concerns. Peer counseling began at Clark in 2001, after students read Montessori's essay. Teachers, along with a group of

(Right) Work with the land incorporates some of the basic elements of Montessori's proposed *Erdkinder* approach.

Contact information: Marta Donahoe, Clark Montessori, 3030 Erie Ave., Cincinnati, OH 45208; (513) 533-7380.

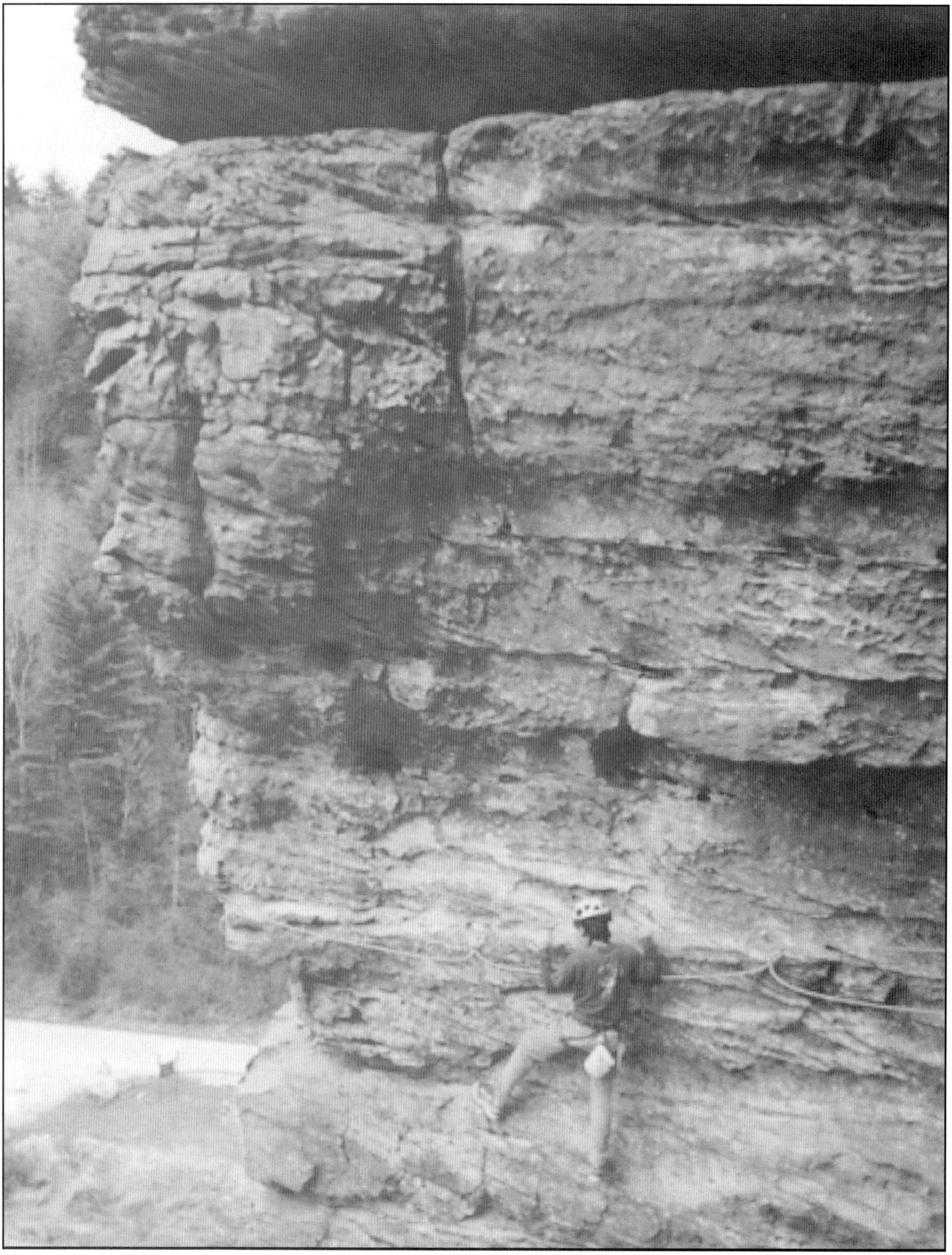

junior students, now counsel and advise freshman; other teachers, along with a group of seniors, counsel sophomores. Advising begins with a fall camping trip and continues during the school year with twice-a-week meetings.

Intersession courses are held twice a year when the entire high school stops the routine of regular coursework and holds immersion courses for two weeks. Each course has both an academic and service component. For example, a trip to Appalachia involves hiking, camping, and biological and historical studies. In a civil-rights course, freshman and sophomores travel to locations in Alabama, Georgia, and Mississippi. Other courses take place at Clark School. As if the academic coursework were not compelling enough, students are coached during these immersion courses in leadership skills such as group development, decision making, and dealing with conflict.

Students are required to complete two hundred hours of community service during their four years of high school. Students also complete two job internships prior to graduation. The immersion weeks, community service, and internships give students opportunities for "real-world" learning experiences. This is "Practical Life" at the secondary level.

Students' high school experiences culminate with a year-long senior project involving an in-depth study of their choice, long-range planning and implementation of the project, and a culminating exhibition. The senior project showcases the students' individual skills acquired during their twelve to fifteen years in Montessori classrooms.

Twice a year the entire high school participates in immersion courses, which involve activities outside the classroom, such as hiking the Appalachian Trail (shown here) or rock climbing (shown opposite page).

learn how to adapt to rapidly changing global natural and social conditions. Montessori further believed that university students should know how to achieve moral equilibrium and become economically independent.

At this time there are no Montessori universities; developing a Montessori university experience is work still to be done. There are, however, a number of colleges and universities that offer undergraduate and graduate programs in Montessori teacher education. Students complete a rigorous course of study involving Montessori philosophy, curriculum, methods of instruction, classroom leadership, and classroom teaching under the supervision of an experienced Montessori teacher.

The Challenge Facing Montessori Secondary Education

Ironically, as interest in Secondary Montessori education in the United States has begun to expand, many of the most established Montessori schools find themselves facing what may prove to be the greatest challenge to Montessori education. Despite decades of well-prepared young men and women who have graduated and gone on to succeed at highly competitive high schools and colleges, more and more contemporary parents express fear that their own sons and daughters will not adequately be prepared by anything less than a traditional, highly structured, and competitive college-prep program.

The experience of one very old and venerable Montessori school stands as a prime example of this trend. The school was founded and led for more than sixty years by a family devoted to strong ideals and a clear educational philosophy. Under the founding family's leadership, the school enjoyed a worldwide reputation and was recognized as one of the first Montessori Junior and Senior High schools in North America. However, when the founding family turned the school over to the care of a parent board of trustees, the board decided to replace the former head with a traditionally oriented and non-Montessori-trained head of school. With no one at the helm to articulate the school's core values and vision, there was no longer a strong force to address the concerns expressed by some leading families about the effectiveness of a Montessori education at the secondary level. As a result, despite many years of successful graduates, the school transformed its Montessori Junior and Senior High School into a more traditional college-preparatory program.

This decision was apparently based on the school's desire to maintain the confidence and support of parents who were primarily focused on college admission. Presumably with the goals of increasing upper school enrollment and fund raising, the school entered into an odd dichotomy in which it now describes itself as offering a Montessori program through grade five, with a rigorous college-preparatory program for grades six through twelve. Sadly, as the United States has become more obsessed with tests and *accountability*, some leading Montessori schools have followed a similar path to become less *Montessori* and more conventional in their public image.

The basic premise of this book is that the two approaches reflect completely different perspectives on education and human development: the conventional approach of the highly competitive school and the *Montessori Way*. We believe that while both perspectives have merit, they cannot exist in one school without leading to a confused institutional identity stemming from this sort of inconsistent and illogical educational philosophy.

Jamie Wheal, Head of the Upper School at the Telluride Mountain School in Telluride, Colorado described the challenge to Montessori Secondary education this way:

"If Montessori is an effective and positive approach for young children, as has been well documented for ninety-six years, then why, at the crucial juncture of adolescence, would it suddenly become less effective?

If independence, curiosity, values of self-direction, inquisitiveness and responsibility are important for a five year old, are they any less so for a sixteen year old? If 'following the child' can be an effective maxim for a decade of schooling, should we doubt that same child's lead when he becomes a teen?

We do not even need to cite the drumbeaters of the crisis among American adolescents to make the case for Montessori high schools today. Dr. Montessori's approach always seemed to be more visionary than alarmist and focused on the potentials of the human experience more than its pitfalls. A quick survey of adolescent life today, however, with its intense emotional and social pressures, alienation and sometimes tragic violence, would suggest that, if nothing else, the need for meaningful education of young adults is as strong as ever.

In the past five to ten years, it seems that many Montessori communities have perceived that need and have taken steps toward meeting it. Drawing on the examples of Montessori High Schools developed from the 1930s around the world, as well as from Dr. Montessori's own essays, over the last twenty years Montessori schools from New England to British Columbia have begun to create exciting new visions of this final stage of Montessori education."

— Jamie Wheal, New Directions for Montessori Secondary Education

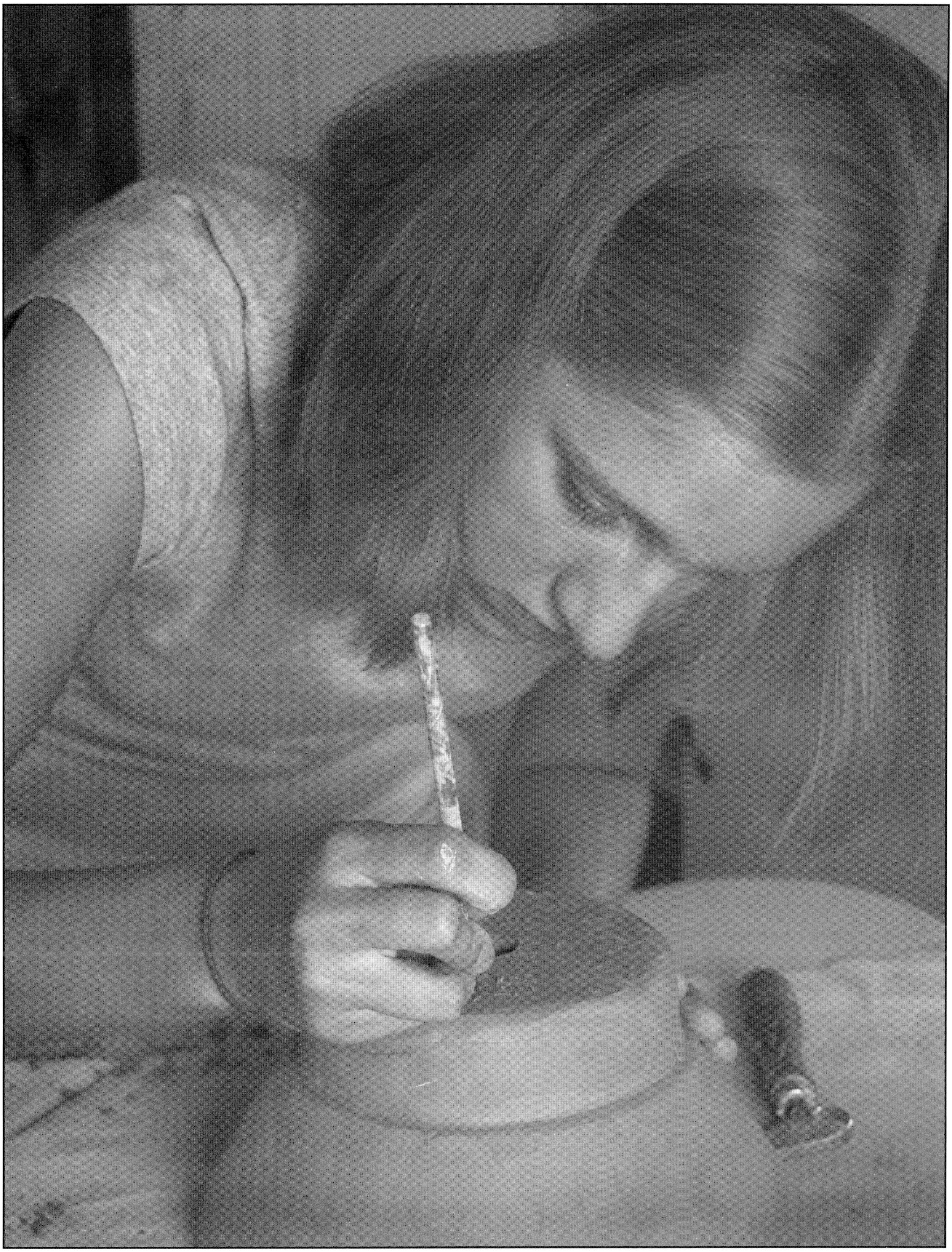

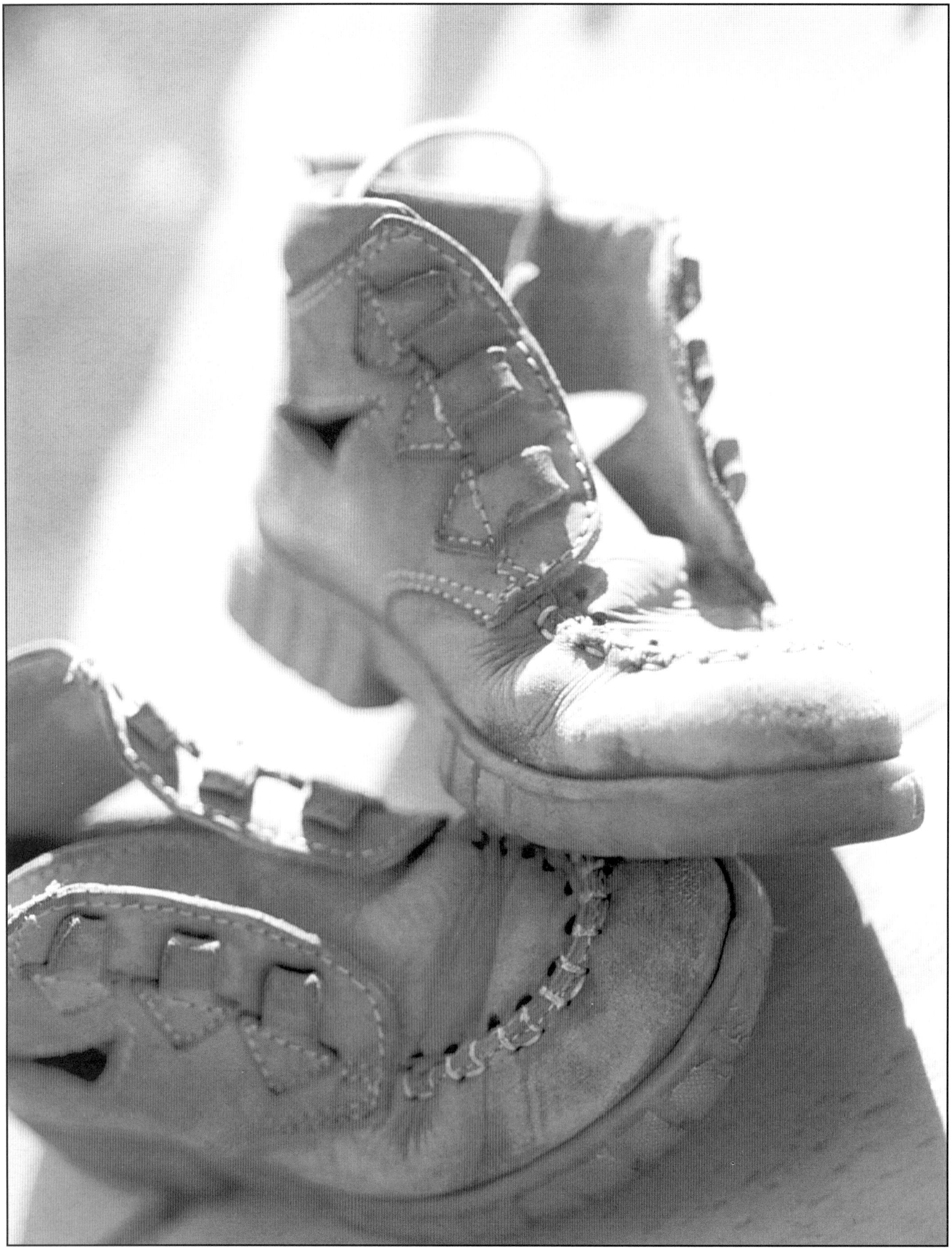

Montessori Infant-Toddler Programs:

The Best Beginning

There is an ironic prejudice about education found in almost every country: the older the students are that one teaches, the higher the pay and respect for the teacher. We take it for granted that a professor in a graduate school is a more prestigious position than that of a high school teacher, which is, in turn, considered a more sophisticated position than teaching elementary and, of course, both are far more respectable than that of a nursery-school teacher. And no one in his or her right mind would want to teach infants and toddlers, right? Yet research clearly shows that the most important period in a human being's educational and emotional development are not the years of high school and college but rather the first six years of life.

Human beings are a magical combination of at least three factors: our genetic inheritance, our biological development, and our experiences.

Authors' Note: We wish to thank Susan Tracy, M.Ed., Director of the Learning Together Parent Education Center in Palatine, Illinois, for her invaluable assistance in co-authoring and preparing this chapter. We also thank the many schools that welcomed us into their infant-toddler classrooms. In the case of K.T. Korngold of The Montessori Children's Center at Burke (White Plains, NY), we wish to extend a special thanks for allowing us to enter "Sarah's world," a beautiful at-home Montessori infant environment that is pictured throughout this and the following "Montessori in the Home" section.

Genetics play an enormous role. In addition to the more obvious issues such as our sex, eventual height, and the color of our eyes, genetics determine our special gifts and handicaps, predispositions, and many aspects of our interests, talents, and personalities that scientists are only now beginning to understand.

However, whatever potential or predispositions we inherit from our parents, they will only be developed if our bodies are allowed to develop normally. A child who is malnourished in the critical first six years of life, or who suffers a devastating disease or physical injury, will normally develop much less of his or her potential as a human being than one who enjoys good health.

Equally important, and most relevant to this book, is the question of the child's early education. Of course the brain is not a muscle, but like a muscle, the brain only develops through active use. This is especially true in the years of infancy and early childhood.

In the past, many people pictured a child's mind as a blank slate on which adults, through instruction, could "write down" the content of a good education. Likewise, another common metaphor was that of an empty bowl, waiting to be filled with the contents of the school's curricula. Montessori demonstrated that both concepts are inaccurate.

The young child's mind is more like that of an acute observer or scientist, eager to learn, explore, try new things, and master new skills. But most importantly, she recognized that with stimulation, the child's ability to concentrate, absorb, and master new ideas and skills increases, and that the earlier we begin a program of intellectual, physical, sensory, and artistic education, the more dramatic the result.

This is a time of great sensitivity to language, spatial relationships, music, art, social graces, and so much more. If, during this period, the mind is stimulated by the child's exposure to a rich environment, the brain will literally develop a much stronger and lasting ability to learn and accomplish. In short, while our culture may believe that preschool teachers are the least significant educators our children will encounter, in reality the contribution that they offer is of incredible importance in a child's education.

This is especially true of those who teach infants and toddlers. So please forgive us when we cannot hide our frustration when parents say things like, "Oh, for goodness sake, my child is just in preschool! Education during these years is not all that important! All she needs are teachers who are warm and kind."

The ~~Terrible~~ Terrific Twos: Montessori for the Infant and Toddler Years

The concept of a specific program for these very young children was developed by Adele Costa Gnocchi and Dr. Silvana Quattrocchi Montanaro at the Centro Educazione Montessori in Rome. This world-famous teacher education program awards the Association Montessori Internationale's Assistants to Infancy Certification, preparing Montessori educators to work with children from birth through age three. Over the last twenty years, other Montessori programs have developed infant-toddler teacher education programs of their own.

Infant-toddler Montessori educators are passionate about their work. Inspiring teacher educators Celma and Desmond Perry, Virginia Varga, and Carole Korngold have tirelessly advocated the importance of these programs and are slowly beginning to convince Montessori schools around the world to develop them.

Montessori programs for children under age three are not quite as rare as hen's teeth; however, they are anything but common. Toddler classes are still fairly few and far between, and infant programs are still so uncommon that parents would be fortunate to find one in their community. Where infant and toddler programs do exist, they tend to be extraordinarily popular, and it may be quite difficult to find an opening unless parents begin their search a year or more in advance.

(Above) Young children enjoy constructing new shapes with a wide variety of blocks and connecting materials.

Why don't more schools offer infant-toddler programs? Basically there are four major reasons.

The first is that there are very few certified Infant-Toddler Montessori teachers.

Secondly, because only a handful of children are supporting the trained teaching staff and classroom, these programs are more expensive to run than the classes for three to six-year-olds, and few schools feel that they can ask parents to pay the true cost of operation. As a result, many schools lose money on this type of program. The compensation is that the children who come through these programs will be among their very best students in the years to come because of their early start. In some cases, state regulations may prohibit schools from accepting children under age three. Similarly, in some states, operating a program at this age level may cause the school to be classified as a child-care center, rather than as an educational institution.

And finally, many Montessori administrators wrestle with the concern that if they accept children under age three, prospective parents will view the school as a day-care center, rather than as a school, which some administrators fear might cause their entire program to lose credibility.

The Four Common Types of Infant-Toddler Programs

Parent-Infant Programs

These are primarily programs designed to educate the parent of very young children in child development and the Montessori strategies for helping parents to respond to the needs they observe in their infants. These programs give parents an opportunity to observe their children and, through discussion, learn how they can best respond to their babies' needs. Normally, parent-infant programs will accept children under eighteen months of age. Parents come with their children to a short class normally lasting about ninety minutes, held once a week. Often, there will be a parent-teacher discussion held at another time during the week. Topics always include parent questions and concerns and a weekly topic, such as: sleep, nutrition, home environment, and infant and toddler development. The staffing is commonly one certified Montessori Infant-Toddler teacher with the parents working in the

A Note on Staffing: A key issue with infant programs is the adult-to-child ratio. State regulations vary, and the required ratios and maximum group sizes will vary from one state to another. The standard that we recommend for this age is lower than most states require — striving for a one-to-three adult-to-infant ratio, or a small group of normally nine infants to one teacher and two adult assistants. This tends to make such programs more expensive, but due to the low adult-to-infant ratio and the special training needed, the quality is well worth the cost. It is especially important that staff turnover in these programs be very low, as even the youngest infant tends to bond deeply with the adult caregivers. Their consistency over time is very important to the program's success.

room. In this model, parents learn how to observe their child and learn a great deal about child development to be used at home.

Montessori Infant-Care Programs

For those who need all-day care, there are a handful of Montessori Infant-Care programs, which normally accept infants aged six weeks to fifteen months of age. These programs are still very rare, but they are slowly beginning to spread. It is especially important in these programs that the lead teacher working with each group of nine infants be certified in Montessori Infant-Toddler education to ensure the quality of the program.

With infants, the schedule of the day is dependent on their needs. Each baby has a different schedule for feeding and sleeping. There should be a routine of stability and consistency; babies look for predictability.

Toddler Half-Day Programs

These programs will normally run for two or three hours a day. Some will accept toddlers from fifteen months and older, although this lower age range may vary due to local regulations and the school's decision about how it wishes to organize the program.

Generally, the low end of fifteen months is followed because by that age, most children are fairly mobile and have become very independent. Most toddler programs will begin with a somewhat older child of eighteen months, or even as old as twenty-four months. These groups will commonly include children up to thirty to thirty-six months of age, at which time the child is normally ready to move into a Montessori three-to-six class.

The typical schedule in a half-day toddler class might look something like this:

1. Arrival, greeting, storing coat and bag, changing shoes, choosing work.

2. A work period of $1\frac{1}{2}$ to 2 hours.

3. Preparation and serving of a snack.

4. Group singing, finger plays, and movement to music: this is an activity in which toddlers may or may not choose to participate.

5. Outdoor time: running, climbing, swinging, exploring nature, sand and water.

6. Dismissal.

It is important that children move out of the toddler program to the next level not according to a simple age criteria but when they are developmentally ready (when they are no longer challenged in the toddler program and are showing signs of being bored). This normally occurs at about two years eight months of age. We strongly recommend four- or five-day programs rather than offering two- or three-day options. Why? Because children, in general, and toddlers, in particular, need consistency and routine.

Staff Ratio: In a group of ten to twelve toddlers, you would normally have a certified Montessori Infant-Toddler teacher and an assistant. Some states allow a higher adult-to-child ratio. This small class size and low adult-to-child ratio tends to make toddler programs more expensive, but, once again, the quality is well worth the higher cost.

(Below) Even toddlers can help care for their environment. This young boy is shown washing windows.

(Above) This young student is getting one of her first art lessons in using the brush and paint.

A Note about the Role of the Adults in the Toddler Class: With the low adult-to-child ratios and the tender age of the children, many parents would expect to see the teacher and assistant interacting constantly with the children, as one might find in a more traditional child-care program. Montessori, however, encourages the development of each child's independence. In a toddler class, you will notice that the adults will not rush in continually to entertain or control the children; instead, they will quietly give lessons, redirect a child who is having difficulty, interact with the children verbally to help with their language development, and observe and take note of the children's activities.

All-Day Toddler Programs

These programs are quite similar to the half-day toddler class, except that children may remain all day for nine or ten hours. Obviously, in these programs, accommodation must be made for napping, meals, outdoor time and play, art, food preparation, and other activities. Because of the luxury of the extended hours, these programs can do much more with the children. Normally there will be some overlap in staffing, as some staff members arrive early in morning and leave in the early afternoon, while others arrive later and stay until the last child is picked up. Whoever remains until day's end should be prepared to communicate with the parents about how the day has gone.

The schedule for a full-day toddler class can be more relaxed — there is the luxury of more time for work, outdoor exploration, food preparation, art activities, and an early afternoon nap. Arrival and pick-up routines should be well planned to ease the transition for toddlers and parents.

What makes Montessori at the infant-toddler level different from child care?

Let's begin by considering the needs of the very young child.

Ideally, many of us would love to stay home and care for our newborns, but this is not always possible. When both parents have to leave the home to earn a living, Montessori infant-care programs offer a wonderful alternative.

Infant-toddler education begins during pregnancy. It is an important time of growth and formation. We want a mother to be healthy and peaceful and to feel supported. This is the time for the expectant mother to give her baby the best nutrition, avoid stress and toxins, and prepare herself to be a mother. The father should prepare for the birth as well. Together parents should prepare their home for the baby and prepare themselves for a peaceful birth. We want every child to feel welcome and wanted and to have a peaceful beginning.

The First Three Months

The newborn period is sometimes called the "symbiotic" period because there are things that both the baby and mother receive from one another. Both benefit. The baby needs physical closeness, skin-to-skin contact, and to be held and surrounded. The warm surrounding feeling reminds them of when they were still in the uterus.

The best environment for a newborn baby is in her mother's arms. There she gets the warmth and feeling of being held. She can nurse or be held close while being bottle fed and still hear her mother's heart, breath, and voice.

The mother still needs to feel connected to this baby that was so recently inside her. Nursing helps the mother's body return to normal and helps her uterus shrink back to size. The uterus contracts in response to nursing, which helps control bleeding. A close relationship with the baby makes it less likely that a mother will have post-partum depression. Finally, nursing burns approximately 1,000 calories a day, which helps her to lose the weight gained during pregnancy.

During the first three months, the baby needs to bond closely to someone. Normally, this will be with the mother, the first and most important relationship in our lives. Without this attachment, the child will later have difficulty developing normal loving relationships with other people. The neglected child tends to have a hard time caring about other people and feeling compassion, and there seems to be some evidence that many criminals and people displaying aggressive behavior began this pattern during infancy.

The Development of the Very Young Child

The primary environment for the newborn is in the mother's arms. There is very little that new parents need to buy for their newborn baby. Of course the baby needs diapers (we recommend cloth diapers, rather than disposable). For the child's sleeping environment, the newborn might like the closeness of sleeping with his or her parents. Some newborns like the feeling of being in a basket or bassinet (many newborns still like the feeling of being surrounded).

As children reach four to six months, their bodies are beginning to change. The underlying cause is Myelinization: the process by which a newborn's brain and nerve cells gain a fatty coating (Myelin) that serves as insulation and keeps the electrical impulses transmitted by the brain moving in the correct pathway along the nervous system. This is crucial to the child's development of the ability to coordinate movement.

Movement develops from the head down as the process of Myelinization proceeds. During the first few months, young children refine their ability to move the head and control eye movements. They can see further and focus on moving objects. They spend a lot of time observing what is happening

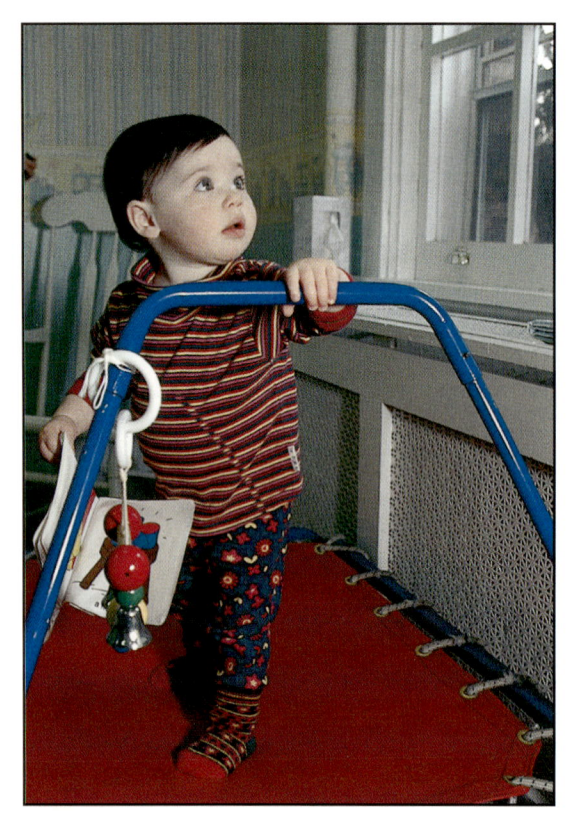

(Above) During the child's first year, provide an environment that encourages movement without using containment devices such as playpens or "walkers."

around them. Because they are not yet mobile, they become people watchers.

During this period, they learn how to roll over and creep, and sit (normally by six months). Crawling follows at about eight months, and most children will begin to "toddle" at about twelve months. Thus, during the child's first year, it is critical that we provide an environment for movement. We avoid containing children in playpens, cribs, walkers, jumpers, and child carriers except when necessary for travel or for short periods. Instead, we would provide time for the young child to be on a quilt on the floor, which would enable the child to move about freely.

We recommend that parents and infant programs provide beds that are low to the floor so that children can independently get in and out on their own. They quickly learn how to stay in the bed, and most will not roll out. For the child who rolls, put a soft rug by the bed — just in case.

We recommend a tiny table and a chair with arms, instead of a high chair, as the child begins to eat solid foods at five or six months of age. For diaper changing, we recommend a pad on the floor in the bathroom instead of a changing table, since it is so easy for children to fall from changing tables. (See the following section on *Montessori in the Home* for more parenting tips.)

Toilet Training: In the "head-down" development of the young child's muscle control, about halfway through the process comes the development of sphincter control of the bladder and bowels. This process usually begins by ten to twelve months, and a child can be out of diapers by eighteen months on the average and certainly by twenty-four months. Changing diapers in the bathroom allows parents to be able to work with the child on using the potty chair or toilet.

Arm and Hand Control: In addition to the "head-down" development of movement, there is development from the center out, referring to the arms and the hands. During the first few months, babies move and swing their arms with little control. Gradually at four to six months they begin to gain control of arm movement. Also at this age they have the ability to grasp objects with their whole hand. Between six and ten months they become able to use fewer and fewer fingers, until they begin to use a pincer grasp using the index finger and the thumb.

The Infant Classroom Environment: A Montessori infant classroom has an area for the youngest babies, with quilts on the floor, mirrors at floor level, mobiles to observe, bat and grasp; balls and rolling toys to "chase" by creeping; and rattles and objects to hold, shake, bang, and mouth.

In an all-day infant or toddler program, there are low beds available for naps. A half-day program may just have

(Below) Montessori Infant-Toddler classrooms provide low beds or mats so that the children can get in and out of bed independently when they are tired.

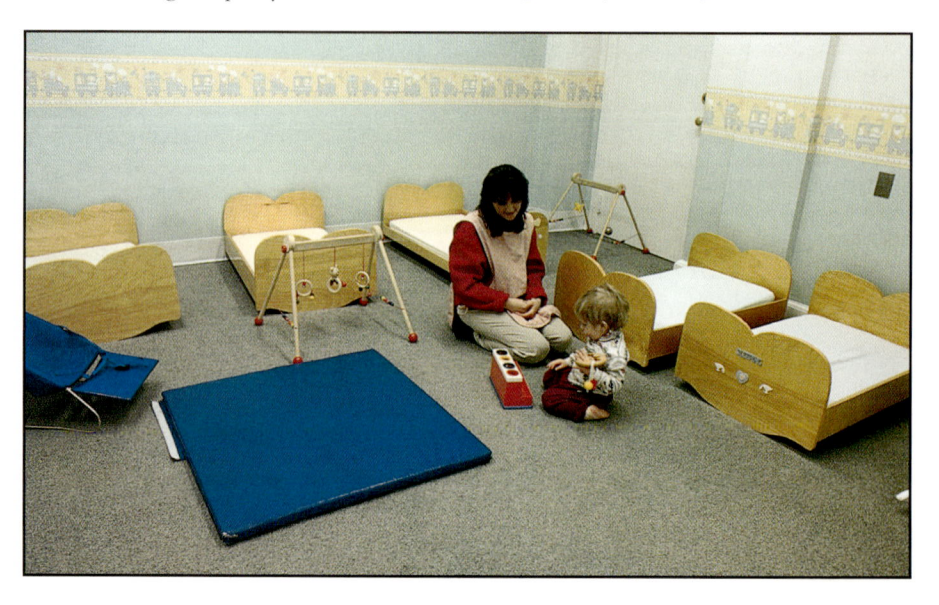

(Above) During the first few months, young children refine their ability to move their heads and control their eye movements. Colorful mobiles help children with this process.

one low bed in case someone gets sleepy.

Movement is critical to brain development — it is as necessary as nutrition! Most classes for children under age eighteen months will include a stair with low steps and a railing for use by children who are beginning to crawl and walk. The class will have bars and furniture placed around the room on which young children can pull themselves up. There will normally be walking wagons, which little ones can push before they can take steps on their own. As they begin to walk, there are push and pull toys to take along.

As a general rule, in order to encourage movement among children under eighteen months, the less restrictive the clothing, the better. Rooms are kept quite warm and cozy, allowing infants and very young children to spend time in comfortable clothing that does not inhibit their freedom of movement.

The infant classroom typically contains one or two low shelves with fine-motor activities such as puzzles, bead-stringing, rings on posts, a pegboard with large pegs, and various containers to open and close, fill and empty.

Our recommendations are generally the same for home and school settings for children under twenty-four months. At age two, we suggest some differences in how the home and school environment are organized.

The Infant Program

Practical Life for Infants

Practical Life is a major element in Montessori education for all age levels. For infants, Practical Life at this level basically allows their participation in caring for themselves and eating independently. As they reach fifteen months, toddlers love to spend time with their hands in water.

Fine-Motor Control

To assist young children in gaining control of their arms and hands, we provide mobiles, rattles, and objects to grasp and move. Infants like to experiment and discover cause and effect, such as shaking a rattle or banging things around to make a noise.

As the pincer grasp develops (age nine to twelve months), we feed the children very small bits of food such as Cheerios™ or grains of rice, which they can pick up and bring to their mouths. As the child is gradually weaned from breast or bottle to cups, we give them a small cup without a lid, about the size of a shot glass, instead of a non-spillable toddler cup. We also provide them with a tiny pitcher and they begin to pour their own drinks. When spoon feeding a child of five to nine months of age, allow the child to hold one spoon and the adult another, so that they can make beginning attempts to feed themselves.

Sensorial Development

All of an infant's senses are functioning at birth. They grow more acute over the years from birth to three.

Infants and toddlers are very interested in sensorial experiences. For

(Left) A mirror is a wonderful addition to any infant's environment at home or at school.

(Above) The sandbox is a wonderful extension of Practical Life for young students: pouring, scooping, using funnels, and cleaning the sand off their shoes.

infants, we provide rattles, bells, music and the human voice for listening; mobiles and mirrors for visual stimulation, and varied textures for touching. Toddlers are learning to discriminate sounds, colors, and textures. They especially enjoy the sensorial experiences of the outdoors: sand, water, dirt, leaves, sounds of birds, wind, raindrops, and the feeling of the sun or wind on their skin.

Language Development

Receptive Language

An infant hears its mother's voice before birth and is intently listening and watching mouth movements from the time of birth. Infants gain understanding long before they can speak. They need to be exposed to language with the adults around them talking to them and explaining what is happening. We should tell the baby what we are going to do before we do it. For example, we might say, "I'm going to change your diaper," or "Let's go get into the car." They begin to understand what we are telling them. Adults should just assume the baby understands them.

(Right) Using a child-sized mop in the toddler class is a much loved activity.

Montessori Infant-Toddler Programs

By twelve months of age, children are experimenting with their voices, imitating sounds, and generally saying a few words. It is most important that adults talk and listen to the child. In addition, we must provide language materials such as books, objects, and pictures for naming.

The Young Toddler

Between the age of fifteen and eighteen months, toddlers have a new awareness of themselves as separate, unique people. They know it is possible to act and to speak, but often they are not yet able to do what they would like.

This is often a frustrating time of life. Aggression, such as pushing,

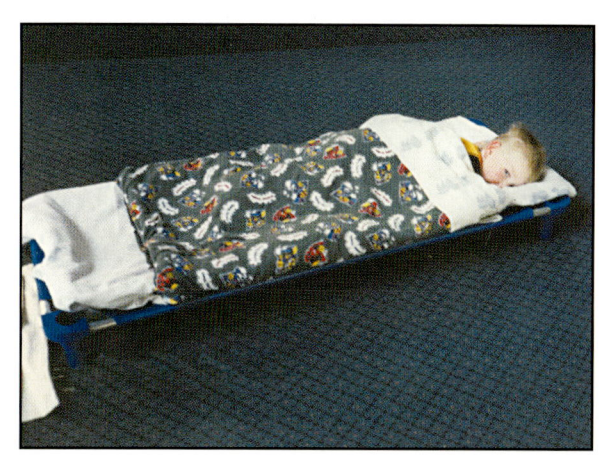

(Above) Children should feel that they can rest when they are tired.

(Left) Having carefully selected containers of the right size with large mouths and lips for pouring, even very young children can develop fine eye-hand control.

(Below) A toddler classroom at Montessori in the Gardens, Dunedin, New Zealand.

185

MONTESSORI PROGRAMS

(Left and above) Bathroom activities are an important part of Practical Life for the infant and toddler. The bathroom is prepared with a mat on the floor for changing diapers. Once they can stand, the child's clothes are changed while the child is standing up. A potty chair and toilet are provided. A child-sized toilet is ideal, but if that is not available, we can put a smaller seat on the toilet and a stool to help them get up on the toilet independently. Unless we have a low sink, there must be a stool high enough for children to wash their own hands.

(Below) Ideally, a toddler class includes an outdoor work area. This young child is using tongs to transfer objects from one bowl to the other.

hitting, and biting is fairly common and is normally outgrown as the toddler gains speech and learns other techniques for coping.

It can help tremendously for the adult to acknowledge rather than judge: "I know, you wanted the ball and Stephen has it." "You look very angry!" They do not yet have the self-control to obey consistently, so adults must supervise and offer constructive activity.

Practical Life for Toddlers

Once the toddler is walking (on average at about twelve months), this frees their hands for work. Their new interest is in accom-

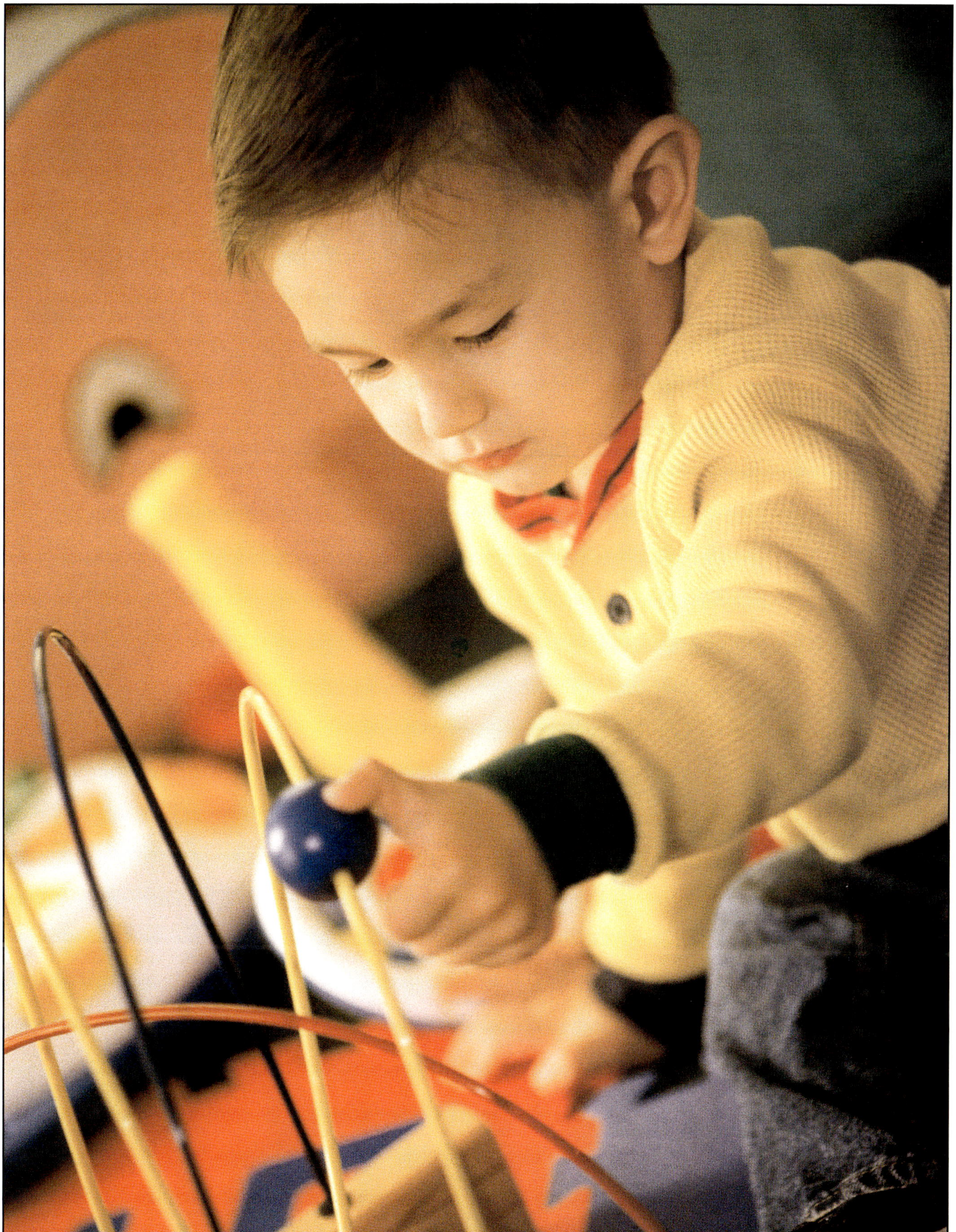

plishing things with their hands. They want to imitate what they see adults doing, and they want to gain independence. Adults will observe beginning signs that the child is interested in dressing and undressing himself. The child will also become interested in tasks such as brushing their own hair and putting things away around the house.

Because the child is just discovering that he is a separate person from his parents, he very strongly asserts this independence. The wise adult allows toddlers to have independence to explore and to make choices within a safe environment. We need to give freedom within the security of limits and within a loving and trusting relationship.

The toddler needs more independence at home. Parents need to step back and allow them to do things for themselves. Toddlers can also benefit from attending a Montessori class where they have some independence from parents and lots of opportunity for exploration and learning. Because they are gaining coordination of their hands, toddlers enjoy fine-motor tasks, such as puzzles and stringing beads. They also enjoy the challenge of cooking and can help prepare food at home and at school. Practical Life activities for toddlers are simpler than at the three-to-six level and follow simpler lines. The young child enjoys activities, such as table washing, hand washing, dish washing, sweeping, and mopping.

Sensory Training

At the toddler level, Montessori programs tend to place far more emphasis on Sensorial activities. Generally these will be at the lower end of the normal three-to-six Sensorial activities. As with the Sensorial activities found at the three-to-six level, Sensorial activities challenge the younger child to match objects by size, shape, color, or to solve simple puzzles. Toddlers enjoy sensorial exploration of water, sand, dirt, clay, textured objects, the smell of flowers and food, discriminating size, color, and sound.

Language

Between eighteen months and age two, there tends to be an explosion into spoken language, with young children learning new words every day. First we hear them speak using mostly nouns: "ball" instead of "please give me the ball," or "I threw the ball. Hooray for me!"

As they learn to speak in phrases, toddlers begin to add the other parts of speech. Most of their vocabulary is present by their third year, and researchers estimate that most children have learned seventy percent of the vocabulary they will use as adults by age three.

In Montessori Infant-Toddler environments, we provide language materials such as books, objects and pictures for naming, but most important is that the adult talk and listen to the child.

Toddlers learn lessons in grace and courtesy by shaking hands with their guides and visitors to their classroom.

Art

Toddlers enjoy basic creative work such as cutting paper, gluing, coloring with chalk and crayons, painting with watercolors or at an easel.

Music

We can provide music in several ways. We may sing with a large group of children, or just one or two. Music need not be limited to a certain time of the day. Toddlers are learning language, so they are interested in the words as well as the melody.

Some can sing along; some still listen. They are learning to control their movements, so they enjoy simple finger plays and movements to music. It is important that we do not expect toddlers to sit as a group for a long period.

For part of the day, we may have varied background music playing. Certain songs could signal transitions in the schedule. Toddlers could also have the opportunity to choose music and listen on head phones. This can be very calming.

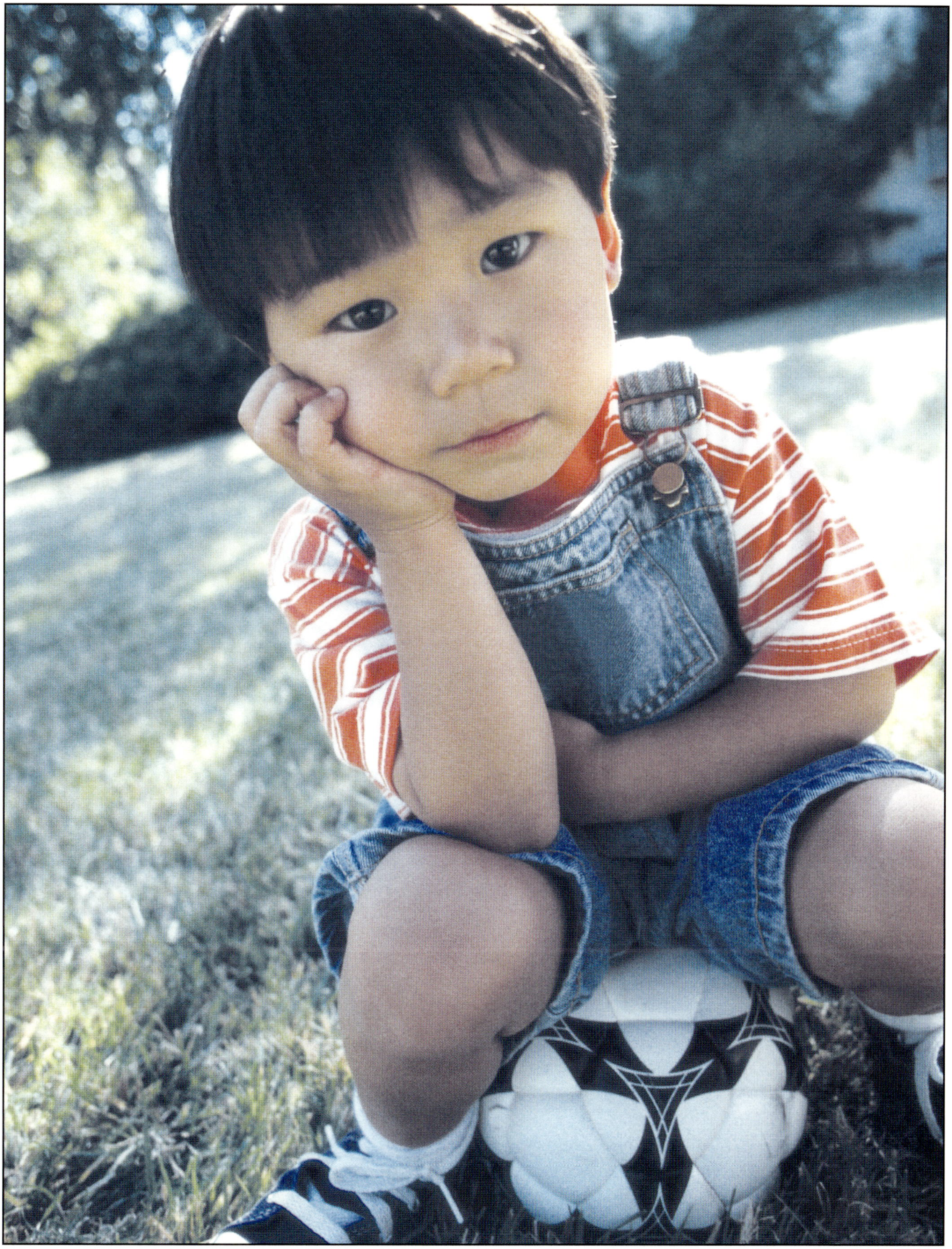

Montessori Programs

Photo by Adrianne dePolo

Montessori in the Home for Young Children

Your children are busy exploring and learning from an incredible collection of materials and activities in their Montessori classrooms. Parents often ask how much of the special learning materials they should purchase for their child to use at home. We answer: *None!* Children need other activities to complement what they are doing at school.

Montessori is a way of life. It is a philosophy about how human beings might live their lives and treat one another. It is an attitude of respect and encouragement for each human being, no matter how young or how old. Rather than power and authority, it is a sense of partnership.

Newborn infants come into our lives lacking the ability to be self-sufficient and independent. We not only provide nurturing and protection, we help them learn how to do things for themselves. Independence is the single greatest drive of the young child. The desire to feel competent, capable, and to know that we are seen as being worthy of respect is one of the most powerful human emotions. Because of their intense desire to become competent, toddlers often become extremely frustrated, resulting in the tantrums that are common in the toddler years.

Children who are treated with respect and who are gently encouraged to try new skills more readily learn to do things for themselves. Parents who, instead, take delight in doing things that their children are capable of doing for themselves, delay their children's independence and hold back the development of their self-esteem. Dr. Montessori taught that a child who feels respected and competent will develop a far greater level of emotional well being than a child who is simply loved and doted upon. She wrote, "The adult should be an aide to life. We must help the child learn how to do it for himself."

(Above) A lamb's wool mat on the floor, low shelves filled with interesting objects, and a nearby mirror provide many opportunities for babies to explore the world around them.

The Inner Life of the Child

Dr. Montessori taught us to look at each child as a unique being who has never lived before. Just as our biological/genetic embryo will guide our physical growth and appearance, Montessori thought each child's spiritual, moral, and psychological development was guided by a spiritual embryo. The spiritual embryo will direct a child toward fulfilling her or his unique potential towards becoming the complete person she or he is meant to be. Montessori wrote:

"Human beings are formed slowly. Each of us is 'worked by hand,' and each individual is different from every other, having his own distinctive spirit, as if he

(Right) A tiny table, child-sized eating utensils, a small pitcher of milk with which to practice pouring, a vase of fresh-cut flowers, and seating for the child and her adult companion provide an atmosphere of warmth and calm for sharing meals.

MONTESSORI PROGRAMS

(Above) An art cabinet provides easy access to arts-and-crafts supplies. Paper, markers, stickers, and coloring books all have their own spot.

Photos by Adrianne dePolo

were a natural work of art. The process takes many years.

The inner life of the child is an enigma. The only thing we know about him is that he could be anything, but nobody knows what he will be or what he will do.

Human development is exactly like the process necessary to produce a work of art that the artist, sequestered in the intimacy of his studio, modifies and transforms before he brings it before the public. The process by which the human personality is formed is in the hidden work of incarnation."

Like the human embryo before birth, this spiritual embryo who is the young child must be protected from a hostile environment by the warmth of our love and acceptance.

Children Learn from Their Mistakes

As parents and teachers, we often assume that children develop their character through our care and upbringing. We believe that we can shape a child's personality and destiny through our sound advice and efforts to direct their development.

Instead, children carry within themselves the key to their own development. Their early attempts to express their individuality are hesitant and tentative. Our children think that we are all-wise and all-powerful. They are easily overwhelmed by our best intentions. Our efforts to protect our children from mistakes that seem so obvious from our perspective tend to frustrate their process of learning for themselves about life.

Parents, in other words, must also learn. We have to learn to respect the child's efforts to develop an independent personality, because it is through this creative process that the child literally forms the adult. As parents, it is our duty to attempt to understand the psychological needs of our children and to prepare an environment within our homes for him.

Montessori was concerned that parents would unconsciously hinder and frustrate their child's process of spiritual growth, although we may operate from the best of intentions. The primary role of the parent is to help the child to become mature, independent, and responsible. Unfortunately, we often misunderstand what we can do and what we must not do, if we truly want to facilitate this process. We tend to overprotect, not realizing that our children can only learn about life through experience, just as we did.

Our role as parents is to help our children learn to live in peace and harmony with themselves, with all people, and with the environment. We work to create a home in which our children can learn to function as independent, thinking people. To succeed in our role as parents, we need to treat our children with tremendous respect as full and complete human beings who happen to be in our care. Our children need to feel that it is okay to be themselves.

Children must feel our respect; it is not simply enough to say the words. If they believe that they are not living up to our expectations, that we are disappointed in the people that they are becoming, they may be emotionally scarred for a lifetime. A child who feels unaccepted by his parents can only wander through life looking in from the outside like a stranger.

Parents Teach Children Values

As parents, one of our fundamental aims is the inspiration of our child's heart. We not only share our religious beliefs with our children; we teach our values, ethics, and sense of what is truly wonderful and important: love, kindness, joy, and confidence in the fundamental goodness of life.

In simple ways, we encourage our children to begin the journey toward being fully alive and fully human. Everything that we do is intended to nurture within our children a sense of joy and appreciation of life, a sense of the poetic, and mankind's interrelationship with the universe.

Consciously or not, we teach our values to our children. We hope to teach our children to understand and respect the very real differences among different cultures. Truly, though, people are the same, even though we are very different from one another in the ways we live our lives and perceive the world.

To build a peaceful world, we must learn to see people as they really are and not be afraid of that which is strange and vastly different from our own ways. Just as children can learn to hate from their parents, they can also learn to love. Children can easily learn that diversity is a call for celebration and not a cause for alarm.

In order to live happily as an adult, a child needs two things: a strong sense of her separate identity apart from her parents and a sense of her full membership in not only her family but the larger community in which she lives.

Our moral obligation is to facilitate the transition from childhood to maturity and to teach the skills that it takes to function successfully in school, college, the work place, and our cultural environment. This is our mission as mothers and fathers.

We should present an honest picture of the world to our children, according to their growing ability to understand. Naturally, though, they learn more from what we do than from what we preach.

Our actions should be consistent with our values. In order for children to grow emotionally and morally complete, they must be able to trust and understand the important adults in their lives. In the end, they must learn how to think and judge for themselves. But they begin with us as their example.

Positive Discipline:
Establishing a Climate of Love

Children are extremely sensitive to the emotional climate within the family. They love us and basically want us to be pleased with them. This doesn't mean that they will always behave. Every child will test the rules to some degree. In fact, most acts of testing parents are a normal part of the child's process of growing up.

When children test adults, it is often their way of expressing feelings that they don't understand, and from our responses, they gradually learn how to handle their emotions appropriately. By testing the limits, they learn that we really care about certain ground rules of grace and courtesy in our relationship. In acting out, they are taking their first tentative steps toward independence, attempting to demonstrate that we don't control them completely.

Agree on your family ground rules and get them written down where both parents can refer to them. Teach your children how to do the right thing rather than focusing on their infractions.

Be consistent! If you can't bring yourself to reinforce a rule again and again, it shouldn't be a ground rule at your house. A few good rules are much better than dozens of nit-picking rules that no one can remember. In the Montessori home there are only a few ground rules: *Be kind and gentle and treat all life with respect. Don't whine! Tell the truth and don't be afraid to admit when you make a mistake. Just do your best to learn from it. If you break something, clean it up.*

Threats and punishments are not good tools to get children to behave. From our experience, those children who respond to threats and are shaken by punishments are anxious to please us and win back our love. On the other hand, when children are angry, or are asserting their independence, they often act out and don't care if they are punished.

(Right) Young children appreciate the beauty of their surroundings. Arranging fresh flowers is one way they can take part in decorating their home environment.

Photo by Adrianne dePolo

Punishment is simply not as effective as we tend to assume. At both home and school, teach children to do things correctly and emphasize the positive rather than using insults and anger. It's not always easy. Above all else, try never to ask your children unanswerable questions, such as, "How many times do I have to tell you ... ?" to which the appropriate response is, "I don't know, Dad! How many times *do* you have to tell me?" Ask a silly question, and you get a silly answer.

Children are actually so sensitive and impressionable that we should monitor everything we say and do, for everything is engraved in their memories. Our children love us with a profound affection. When they go to bed they want to us to stay with them as they go to sleep. When we work in the kitchen, they often want to help. When we sit down to dinner, they want to join us. We may worry that we'll spoil them if we listen to their pleas, but we shouldn't. They only want us to pay attention to them. They want to be part of the group. Montessori wrote:

"Who else weeps out of the intense desire to be with us while we eat? And how sadly we will say someday, 'Nobody cries now to have me near him while he falls asleep.' Only a child says every night, 'Don't leave me; stay with me!' and the adult answers, 'I can't; I have so much to do, and anyway, what kind of nonsense is this?' and thinks the child must be corrected or he will make everyone a slave of his love."

Sometimes a child wakes in the morning and goes to wake his parents, who would rather sleep; everyone complains about this kind of thing. He slips from his bed, approaches his parents and touches them lightly. Most often they say, "Don't wake me up in the morning," and the child responds, "I didn't wake you up; I only kissed you!"

Organizing the Home

The Bedroom

"We must give the child an environment that he can utilize by himself: a little washstand of his own, a bureau with drawers he can open, objects of common use that he can operate, a small bed in which he can sleep at night under an attractive blanket he can fold and spread by himself. We must give him an environment in which he can live and play; then we will see him work all day with his hands and wait impatiently to undress himself and lay himself down on his own bed."

— Maria Montessori

Children's bedrooms should clearly reflect their personalities and current interests. Even though, on their own, they may tend to create chaos, young children have a tremendous need and love for an orderly environment. Everything should have its own place, and the environment should be organized to make it easy for the child to maintain a neat, well-organized atmosphere.

- Ideally, the young child's bed should be low to the floor, making it easy for toddlers to get in and out on their own. Rather than a crib, Montessori urged parents to modify the bedroom to facilitate both the child's safety and his early independence. Consider a futon or a mattress without the bed frame.

- By age five, you may wish to allow your child to use a sleeping bag on his bed instead of sheets and blankets. This makes it easy for him to make his own bed in the morning.

- Mount a nice little coat and hat rack low on one wall where your child can reach them easily.

- Decorate the walls with high-quality art prints of children or animals hung at the child's eye level.

- Mount a wall clock at the child's level. Select one with a large easily read face.

- Modify your light switches with extenders to allow the young child to turn his lights on and off independently.

- Hang a bulletin board at your child's eye level on which he can hang artwork and school papers.

(Right) Montessori encouraged parents to place their child's bed low to the floor. By making it easy for the young child to get in and out of her own bed, parents provide a safe sleeping environment, while also promoting their child's sense of independence.

- Notice how Montessori teachers avoid clutter. Place toys with many pieces in appropriate containers, such as plastic "boxes" with lids, baskets, or in sturdy plastic bags.

- Use a sturdy wooden crate to hold your child's building blocks.

- You may want to create a model town or farm on a piece of heavy plywood. Paint it green and sprinkle model railroad "grass" on it to simulate a meadow. Placed on a low table, your child can create wonderful displays with model buildings made of wood or plastic. Add little trees and people from a model railroad set. You could set up a doll house this way as well.

- Store blocks in a large, colorful, sturdy canvas bag with handles. Sew on strips of Velcro™ to fasten the bag closed. In your child's bedroom the bag will serve as a sack to contain his Legos.™ When you travel, it is very easy to pick the bag up to come along.

- Make sure that your child's clothes chest has drawers that are the right height for him or her to open and look inside. Label the drawers: underwear, socks, etc.

- Collect flower vases and encourage your child to collect flowers from the fields or garden for his room.

(Above) Do not use a toy box. Use low shelves to display books and toys. Try to duplicate the look of your child's classroom.

- Provide some shelf space for a small nature museum in your child's room. Here he can display rocks that he finds, interesting seeds, and (in small cages) interesting "critters."

- Music should be an important part of every child's life. Set some space aside for a simple stereo system and collection of recordings.

The Bathroom

The bathroom must be prepared for your child. He should be able to reach the sink, turn on the water, and reach his toothbrush and toothpaste without help. There should be a special place where he can reach for his towel and washcloth. Most parents provide bathroom stools, but small wobbly stools often do not provide enough secure, comfortable space for bathroom tasks. You might want to consider building a wooden platform six to eight inches high that fits around the young child's toilet and sink.

An Arts-and-Crafts Area

Set up an art area with an easel and a spacious art table for drawing, craft work and clay. Cover the table with a washable tablecloth.

Children's art supplies can be neatly stored in separate plastic containers. Depending on your child's age, the art supplies that you prepare might include washable magic markers, crayons, paste, paper, fabric scraps, and recycled household articles for making collages. You can keep tempera paint fresh by mixing it in plastic containers that are divided into three or more inner compartments.

The Kitchen

Make room in your kitchen for a child-sized work table for young cooks. Set aside the bottom shelf in your refrigerator for your children. Here you can store small drink pitchers, fruit, and the ingredients for making sandwiches and snacks.

Use non-breakable plastic containers to hold peanut butter, jams, lunch meats, and spreads. A two-year-old can open the refrigerator and get her own prepared snack or cold drink stored in a little cup. A slightly older child can pour her own juice and make her own lunch. Use a bottom drawer to hold forks, knives and spoons. Mount a low shelf on a wall for plates, cups, and napkins.

Children Can Help Around the House

If presented correctly, children as young as age two delight in caring for their environment: dusting, mopping, scrubbing, cleaning, and polishing. They should be able to do so as easily at home as at school. It is perfectly reasonable to ask older children to straighten up their rooms and help with simple household chores.

- Give your child his own little broom or small vacuum.

- Hang a feather duster on a hook.

- Provide a hamper for your child's dirty clothes. Ask him to carry them to the laundry room on a regular basis.

- The bathroom should have a small bucket with a bathtub scrub brush and a sponge.

- Folding towels and napkins is a good activity to teach the young child.

Preparing for Holidays and Special Celebrations Should Be a Family Affair

Children are an integral part of the family, and should play a meaningful role in planning and preparing for holidays and family celebrations. According to their age, children can be very helpful: cleaning their rooms, chopping vegetables, helping with the cooking and baking, setting the table, carrying food to the table, setting out holiday decorations, receiving guests at the door, sitting nicely at the table, acting as hosts and hostesses to young friends and relatives visiting their home. We are all pleased when friends and relatives compliment us on our children's intelligence, charm, and courtesy.

Television

Children's values and knowledge about the world have traditionally been shaped by four cultural influences: the home, school, church, and peer groups. Today, television represents a fifth and incredibly powerful culture over which most of us have scant knowledge and exercise little control. This is unfortunate, especially when you consider that it has become the baby-sitter of choice in all too many families.

There are several problems with uncontrolled television and kids. The violence portrayed on television is tremendously concerning. In one year a child can see thousands of murders, fights, car crashes, and mid-air explosions. Certainly, the values and problem-solving approach considered appropriate to many producers differs from our own; however, an even greater concern is the hypnotic character of television viewing.

Many parents observe that their young children can sit for hours and hours enthralled by Saturday morning TV. Of course they sit and watch for long periods; they are in a trance. TV viewing is at best a passive experience. It requires no thought, no imagination, and no effort. Quality children's programming can be terrific, but most of what's available is anything but. What other medium can so wonderfully transport us to another time or place? TV is best doled out in carefully planned and measured doses.

Children really do not need TV to entertain themselves. Establish some family ground rules that make sense to you. Determine the shows that your children can watch, and limit the number of hours a day your child can spend in front of the set. Give your children as much choice as possible: "You can choose from among the following shows; however, you can only watch three of them in any one day. What do you want today's choices to be?"

Some families allow children to watch only public television on their own. The parents consider whether commercial television shows are appropriate on a case-by-case basis. Sometimes a show may have real value, but it may have confusing or disturbing content. In these cases, the whole family should watch the show and then discuss it together.

Working Together as a Couple

Many parents have lamented that their efforts to create some order for their child's toys are undermined by the other parent's looser concept of order. Creating this clear sense of external order is extremely important for all children, especially when they are younger than four. Parents must work together!

In Conclusion

So often, parents are frustrated in their efforts to keep the peace in their homes. They concentrate on trying to get their children to do what they want them to do, instead of nurturing the family ties. Children need to be respected as independent human beings. Discipline should be taught as a series of positive lessons conducted by loving, confident parents who know that their children are basically good and completely capable of doing the right thing. Children tend to live up to our expectations.

Love is not enough; the respect that we give children and insist on in return is the key. Do not ask your children to earn your respect and trust.

Assume that they deserve to be treated with respect from the beginning. Sometimes parents try to be "best friends" with their children, which tends to become a serious mistake. Children will have many friends throughout the course of their lives, but they will only have one set of parents. If we get caught up in having our children "like" us, we will find it difficult to confront them when they act out of line (as they will sooner or later).

Getting angry with parents is part of growing up. It's how we create a bit of distance between us and our childhood. A parent should be loved, respected, and someone in whom to confide but not a buddy or playmate.

Speak to the very best within your child. Try to call forth from within her the young adult who will someday walk in her shoes. Children tend to live up to our expectations or down to our disrespect. This respect should extend to your child's interests and all the "reasonable" activities in which she becomes engaged. Pay attention to the things that fascinate her and try to understand them.

As much as possible, support your child's desires for activity. Don't try to wait on or entertain her. Encourage her to be independent. Be very careful about what you do or say in front of children. As the poem goes, "Children learn what they live." They are much more sensitive to our influence than we realize. We communicate volumes about how we feel about our children by the kind of home we make for them. By including children in our family life and showing concern for their feelings and respect for their interests, we tell them how much they really mean to us.

(Below) Children are an integral part of the family and should play a meaningful role in planning and preparing for celebrations. According to their age, children can be very helpful: cleaning their rooms, helping with cooking, setting the table, and greeting guests. The young child pictured below is using her Practical Life skills to help prepare for a family celebration.

Montessori Programs

Learners with Exceptionalities

Authors' Note: We are often asked to discuss how Montessori programs respond to children with special needs. To address this important question, we turned to Dr. Ann Epstein, one of the outstanding Montessori educators who has a special interest in children who, for various development reasons, respond differently than most children to various learning settings.

Like all parents, parents of children with exceptionalities search for learning environments that will match the strengths and needs of their children. This is one of the most crucial responsibilities of parenthood: to assure that one's children are able to learn and grow in an environment that is both challenging and nurturing. Parents oversee each day of their children's learning. They must watch over, perhaps even guard, their children's academic and social progress every day of every year. And they have the awesome reward of watching their children grow and succeed.

But parents of children who learn differently (or perhaps look, move, or talk differently) have an extra set of challenges. The neighborhood public school district may or may not provide the atmosphere that matches their child's very particular learning style. With reauthorization of the Individuals with Disabilities Education Act (IDEA) in 1997, parents of children who are eligible for special needs services have become active collaborators with teachers in the development and implementation of their children's educational plans.

This holds true for parents in public as well as private school settings. Although independent schools have more latitude in designing policies and procedures for parentally placed children with disabilities in their programs, IDEA requires administrators and teachers to work collaboratively with parents. Guidelines for creating effective parent collaboration within IDEA's legislated framework are presented later in this chapter.

IDEA currently recognizes ten categories of exceptionality. They are listed in order of highest to lowest frequency of occurrence. Percentages refer to numbers of children who are being provided special education services.

▲ **Specific Learning Disabilities** (51.1%, includes children with reading, writing and math difficulties, as well as children who have challenging behaviors such as attention deficit disorder)

▲ **Speech or Language Impairments** (20.8%)

▲ **Developmental Delay** (also referred to as mental retardation) (11.6%)

▲ **Serious Emotional Disturbance** (8.7%)

▲ **Other Health Impairments** (2.2%, includes children with asthma)

▲ **Hearing Impairments** (1.3%)

▲ **Orthopedic Impairments** (1.2%)

▲ **Visual Impairments** (0.5%)

▲ **Autism** (0.5%)

▲ **Traumatic Brain Injury** (0.1%)

Special educators urge parents and education professionals to consider each child as a unique individual, which is also a central tenant of the Montessori philosophy. Each child with a learning disability is completely unique, with his or her own specific strengths and areas of weakness.

Although there are certainly common characteristics among children in each group, it is of utmost importance to consider each child individually. IDEA recognized this by mandating "child-first language." Thus, we do not speak of the deaf child or the ADD child or the mentally retarded child. We put the child first. We speak of the child who is deaf, the child who has attention deficit disorder, and the child who has developmental delays.

At first glance this appears to be an over-emphasis on semantics. But a closer look reveals a profound difference in positioning the child before the label. Continually placing the emphasis on the child rather than the label assures that parents and educators always focus on who this child is, not on his or her array of special needs.

A Natural Fit

A focus on the individual child is also a major principle of Montessori education. Often parents contact Montessori schools in the hope of finding an atmosphere that will nurture their exceptional learner's growth.

What is it about Montessori environments that attract parents of children with exceptionalities? They may have heard that Montessori environments are designed around a principle of choice; children with exceptionalities often thrive in this kind of a learning environment. One child may be interested in experimenting with objects that either sink or float, while another may decide to wash, peel, slice and serve celery. Another child may have learned that the number *twelve* is comprised of one ten and two units and wants to continue learning about teens.

With appropriate guidance from the teacher(s), hundreds of choices are available to children. Not only do they enjoy the freedom of choosing, they form the essential life-long developmental characteristics of (1) being independent thinkers and (2) accepting responsibility for one's choices. These two learning characteristics are key protectors against parents' natural tendency to be over-protective of their exceptional children. The prepared learning environment is carefully designed to provide children with the opportunity to choose activities that attract their curiosity.

In the early 1900s, Dr. Maria Montessori developed her philosophy and designed her curriculum by working with children with exceptionalities in Rome's poorest neighborhoods. She implemented a carefully structured daily routine of discovery-based learning. She carefully placed nutrition, rest, and hygiene along with math, reading, and writing lessons.

Dr. Montessori was awed by the progress her charges made, both physically and cognitively. She recognized that by respecting each child's unique way of learning (later we termed this the child's learning style), teachers and parents could provide a structure of learning success for all children.

Dr. Montessori then applied this philosophy and her emerging curriculum to children from Italy's middle- and upper-class families. The results were the same. Children not only progressed, but when compared to children in the typical schools of the early twentieth century, they excelled.

The fit between the Montessori philosophy and curriculum and children with exceptionalities is rooted in two essential responsibilities of the teacher. The Montessori teacher must observe and understand each child's style of learning. Throughout the course of the day, Montessori teachers watch how children respond to lessons and pursue independent activities. They note which activities bring particular delight to children, as well as those which appear to be frustrating.

They watch how children interact with one another and with adults. Are some children demonstrating emerging signs of leadership skills? Do some children struggle to express their thoughts and feelings? Are there patterns to children's challenging behaviors (particular time of day, with some children but not with others, during transition times)?

In addition to being keen observers, Montessori teachers are responsible for carefully preparing the learning environment. Each day, children choose from among dozens of thoughtfully prepared activities. Each activity is designed for independent, successful learning. Thus, children with exceptionalities will meet with success rather than frustration.

The principle of learning task analysis (breaking each skill into sequential parts) aids in assuring that children will develop skills and understanding step by step. For example, learning to tie shoes can be daunting for children with fine-motor delays. The Montessori teacher designs bead stringing and lacing activities to build eye-hand coordination. Gluing, working with clay, and painting also build fine-motor skills.

Months, perhaps a year or more, of interesting work with frustration-free, self-chosen activities gradually builds skills. Eventually, children become comfortable with the first step in making a shoestring loop. With more practice, and bit by bit, they learn to make a second loop, wrap it around the first loop, tuck it through a special space, pull it through and create that long-sought bow!

In summary, Montessori environments often meet the needs of children with exceptionalities. Teachers are keen observers of each child's unique strengths as well as her areas of need. Using these observations, they prepare activities that allow children to develop skills step by successful step. Children choose and pursue these carefully designed activities, building skills and developing conceptual understanding.

Does the Montessori approach fit "best practices" from the field of special education?

Key principles of early intervention and elementary special education are imbedded in many Montessori environments. In order to address the needs and build the strengths of an exceptional learner, teachers and parents must understand the child's "present levels of performance."

Although Montessori teachers are not usually trained or certified to perform standardized tests of cognition or physical or social/emotional development, they bring a wealth of detailed information to planning meetings from their ongoing observations. Combining their classroom observations with testing results and parents' observations creates a rich understanding of the child's present levels of performance.

Special educators develop measurable short-term objectives to guide daily classroom learning. Montessori teachers break skills and concepts into sequential steps. Sequenced activities (referred to as children's "work") fit quite well into an exceptional learner's short-term objectives. For example, a child may be struggling with two-digit addition. The objective might be stated as, "Sally will solve two-digit, static addition problems with 90 percent accuracy using hands-on materials." The Montessori teacher will assist Sally in reviewing units and tens with a variety of concrete math manipulatives. She will also review single-digit addition, again with hands-on, interesting materials.

The special educator will build these activities into a schedule of day-to-day lessons, noting when Sally is successful and when she experiences difficulty. Her errors will be analyzed to identify where her understanding breaks down (more task analysis). When Sally is able to complete nine of ten problems successfully, the objective will be marked "complete."

In addition to identifying present levels of performance and developing measurable short-term objectives, early interventionists and special educators use ongoing methods of assessment. Data related to the learner's objectives are recorded daily. This is consistent with the Montessori teacher's practice of recording observations on a regular basis. The teacher may need guidance in data recording, but this essential special education practice is consistent with Montessori practices.

Finally, special educators (and especially early interventionists) work hand in hand with parents. IDEA mandates collaborative planning with parents, especially sharing all assessment results.

Across all realms of education (public and private), children are more successful in school when their parents are fully informed and consistently involved. Dr. Montessori celebrated the family's contribution to all aspects of child development (cognitive, physical, and spiritual), instructing teachers to work closely with parents to assure optimal growth for all children.

The Parental Experience of Exceptionalities

In the mid-1980s, Marge Samels founded Parents Supporting Parents of Maryland, Inc., a parent-designed statewide network providing support to families of children with emotional problems. Drawing on her own experience, Ms. Samels described feelings that confront parents of children with exceptionalities. She authored the following paragraphs to begin workshops for parents of children with emotional disorders. Twenty years later, her powerful description continues to ring true for parents of children with a range of exceptionalities.

"Discovering that your child has special needs started you off on what may have become a complete change in your lifestyle and view of the future. The emotions that go along with this adjustment are often overwhelming, and they are overwhelming because many of these feelings are with you all day, every day. These feelings don't just visit your home and family; they move right in. Just who are these often less than welcome visitors?

Uncertainty: This is the uncertainty of not knowing if the next minute will bring crisis or calm; the uncertainty of usually having no answers to your questions; the uncertainty about what kind of person your child will become; the uncertainty of not being sure how other family members are doing through all the crises.

Grief: There is the frequent pain that comes with watching your dreams for your child slip through your very hard-working hands. There is the day-to-day sadness of sharing your child's frustrations, failures, and fears. There is the disappointment of seeing hopes for other parts of your life fade as your struggle to be a parent interferes with job, financial security, marriage, and family life as a whole.

Isolation: There is the near total aloneness you may feel at listening to parents, whose children are not struggling with special needs, trade wonderful stories. Your extended family may provide no relief as they may be as likely to judge you guilty as to understand you supportively. And then there are the professionals whose reactions, at times, may leave you questioning your sanity (or maybe theirs). Feeling isolated often haunts you when your child gets excluded or left out of things by others.

Helplessness: Your feelings of helplessness probably come mostly from your never-ending wish to cure your child totally and forever and your lack of success at making that wish come true. Then there is the day-to-day helplessness of using every tool you have to solve a problem, and nothing seems to make any difference. And all of this is made that much worse when you get reports that don't agree, so you can't even be sure what you are dealing with in the first place.

Loss of You: You may have become almost completely used to having no time for yourself. Adult friendship – what's that? Hobbies? Leisure time? Shopping for fun? This only leaves you more vulnerable to all the other feelings whirling around you.

Anger: It may often seem like you are angry at the whole world; angry at yourself for not knowing what to do; angry at your child for demanding so much and seeming to give so little back; angry at your family, friends and professionals for blaming you rather than helping you; angry that the needed services aren't available or take forever to access; and we could probably go on and on and on . . .

Taken together, these feelings probably stress you to the edge of burnout, if not over the edge and beyond. Even with all of that you haven't given up. Your determination has brought you to this (meeting). Take a few minutes as you read these words on this page, in this room, with the others around you, and honor your strength."

Ms. Samels identifies the strong, sometimes life-altering emotions involved with being the parent of a child with an exceptionality. Montessori schools can assist parents in this emotional journey by implementing a carefully designed set of policies and procedures. IDEA provides a sound structure to support Montessori policies and procedures.

Parental Rights under IDEA

The United States has provided strong legislative support for children with exceptionalities and their families. Beginning with Public Law 94-142 (the Education for All Handicapped Children Act) in 1975, educators, families and lawmakers have worked to provide clear and increasingly comprehensive support for children with exceptionalities. Currently, this support flows through IDEA.

The Individuals with Disabilities Education Act was first passed in 1990, reauthorized in 1997, and awaits a second reauthorization in 2003. IDEA includes the following features.

- Parents have full participation and shared decision making in all aspects of identification and evaluation of children with exceptionalities.

- Confidentiality of records, as well as access to all records and documents is required.

- Parents and school administrators are assured due process if appropriate procedures are not followed.

- *Zero Reject/Free* appropriate public education assures that all children with exceptionalities are served within the public school system.

- *Child Find* identifies and tracks the number of children within each state who qualify for services.

- Children with exceptionalities are served from birth to age twenty-one, including early-intervention services for children from birth to two years of age.

- Non-discriminatory evaluation protects children for whom English is a second language and/or children who grow up in families with low incomes.

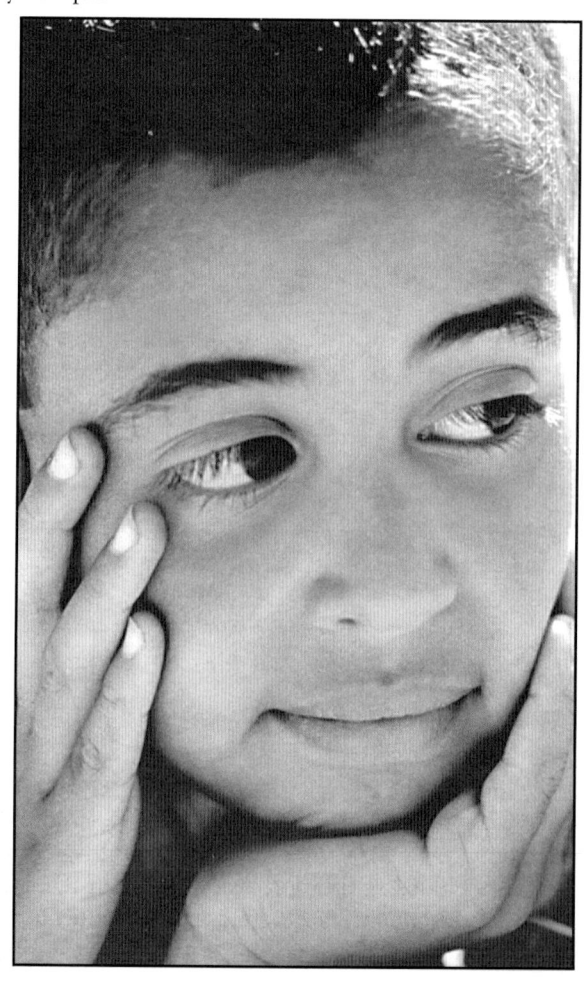

- The *Individualized Education Program (IEP)* assures that careful planning takes place to meet each child's unique set of strengths and areas of need.

- Children must be placed in the least-restrictive environment: the setting in which the child can best learn and is most like that of his/her peers.

- If a school is found to be out of compliance with IDEA, states must mandate and implement consequences.

- Advocacy is guaranteed for children with exceptionalities who do not have known parents or guardians.

Several features are particularly important for parents of children with exceptionalities who decide to enroll their children in private schools. Full participation in decision making, confidentiality of records, non-discriminatory evaluation, the least-restrictive environment, and individualized education programs hold the spirit of the law. Although private schools are not mandated to implement IDEA, those with inclusive missions and a professed commitment to partnering with parents truly have responsibilities to children with exceptionalities and their families.

If they are committed to best educational practices, they need to work collaboratively with parents to create and implement programs that meet children's specific needs. They need to maintain confidential records and share them with parents. They need to advise and support parents in securing nondiscriminatory evaluations. And finally, they need to work with families to create a learning environment that is the most like that of the child's non-disabled peers.

IDEA includes specific provisions in Part B for parentally placed children in private schools. The local school district (often referred to as the "local education agency" or LEA) must work with private schools to plan what services will be provided. Local school districts allocate services through consultation with private schools, underscoring the importance of thoughtful, timely, active participation on the part of private school administrators. Parents can and should inquire as to the Montessori school's involvement with their local public schools.

IDEA includes a specific formula for identifying available funding for parentally placed children in private schools. Funding is based upon the total number of eligible (not necessarily those being served but all those identified) children in the district and the district's total flow through allocation. The later figure is typically decided by the local school board.

The following services could be partially funded, at the discretion of the local school district: speech pathology, occupational therapy, physical therapy, reading or math lab, classroom assistive hearing devices, sign-language interpreter, reader, consultations with the private school classroom teacher, teacher training, and professional development for private school personnel.

It is important to emphasize that parentally placed children do **not** have individual entitlements to services. Local school districts, in consultation with private schools, determine what services will be provided given the available district funding. Due process is applicable to violations regarding identification and evaluation of children; however, due process procedures do not apply to complaints that a local public school district has failed to meet requirements for provision of services. The Council for American Private Education (CAPE) developed an IDEA Tool Kit to assist parents and educators in understanding the law and finding services.

Questions for the Montessori Parent/School Team

Parents and teachers may find it helpful to consider three sets of "Essential Questions" as families proceed through three phases of involvement with the school. Initially, parents and teachers need to determine if a Montessori environment is the best setting for the child. Characteristics of both the particular school and the individual child need to be studied in order to assess potential for a successful placement.

Theoretically, Montessori schools offer a potentially positive experience for children with exceptionalities. However, schools range in how they apply Montessori principles. Perhaps more importantly, a continuum exits regarding administrative and faculty willingness to include children with exceptionalities. And, certainly, each child's exceptionality presents unique challenges to his or her family and school setting.

The following questions may be useful in identifying whether a particular Montessori school could provide a positive experience for a child with exceptionalities.

Part One: Beginning the Journey, Building Hope

Questions for the Family

1. Are the teacher and the administration willing to make changes to accommodate for my child's special needs? (For example, shorten lessons, modify homework, provide behavioral support, assure wheelchair accessibility.)

2. Do the teacher and the administration appear comfortable explaining my child's special needs to his/her classmates so my child can begin to make friends?

3. Will the school work collaboratively with my child's therapists (speech, occupational or physical therapist, family counselor)?

4. Do I feel welcomed and included when I am in the school environment with my child?

5. Can I picture my child feeling welcomed and included in the classroom?

Questions for the School

1. Do we fully understand the child's exceptionality?

2. Has the family shared test results?

3. Are we willing to make accommodations within the classroom (modify lessons, assist with choosing work, provide behavioral support, assure wheelchair accessibility)?

4. Can we modify the environment throughout the school (cafeteria, playground, hallways, gym, etc.) to provide needed support for the child?

5. Do we (teacher, administration and, if appropriate, support teachers such as music, physical education, etc.) understand how to provide assistance for the child to progress both cognitively and socially/emotionally? If not, are we willing to learn how to provide the necessary assistance?

Often answers to these questions are: *"Maybe," "I think so,"* or *"We will do our best."* Absolute *"yeses"* are not necessary for the child to be successful. Honest discussions and solid planning, however, **are** essential. Families and schools need to understand one another's abilities as well as limitations.

If the above questions have been discussed and admission is agreed upon, parents and educators can look forward to a potentially transforming experience. Teachers who honestly questioned their ability to meet the needs of children with exceptionalities but agreed to welcome and include children into their environments often report the experience as among their most rewarding teaching experiences. They report the accomplishment of implementing new teaching strategies and the joy of seeing the child progress.

An unanticipated and particularly rewarding aspect is the positive impact of the child's inclusion on his or her peers. The other children in the classroom demonstrate leadership, kindness, heartfelt interest, and sometimes ingenuity as they develop an understanding of their classmate's exceptionality.

Parents observe the development of these qualities in their children, recognizing the decidedly beneficial aspects of including children with exceptionalities in typical classrooms.

With successes, parents and educators encounter challenges and frustrations. Keeping communications open while consistently monitoring the outcome of varied teaching strategies is essential. The following questions may assist the parent/educator team in maintaining progress.

Part Two: Working Together, Assessing Progress

Questions for the Family

1. Am I staying informed of my child's progress with regular home/school communications? Note: An array of communication vehicles exist (email, telephone, face-to-face, daily journals); teachers and families need to find vehicles that work well for their partnership.

2. Do we understand and support current objectives and the strategies being implemented to attain these objectives?

3. Is my child participating with success in both classroom and auxiliary activities (art, physical education, etc.)?

4. Are my child's teacher and his/her therapists sharing regular updates?

5. Do I have a clear understanding of what teaching methods are working well for my child?

6. If my child is not making progress, do I understand what changes are being proposed? Do I agree with these changes? Is there a clear plan for implementing these changes and then assessing if they are successful?

Questions for the School

1. Do we have a clear understanding of the child's current learning and behavioral objectives?

2. Do we share regular updates with the family?

3. Are we maintaining consistent communications with the child's therapist(s)? Are teaching strategies consistent across school, therapy, and home environments?

4. Is the child making steady progress?

5. If the child is not making steady progress, are we working collaboratively with parents to identify alternative teaching strategies? Once these strategies are implemented, are we communicating

regularly with the family to assess progress?

6. If alternatives have been implemented and are not successful, are we providing the family with comprehensive assistance in transitioning to a new school setting?

All children eventually reach the point of transition from the current learning setting. For most children, this transition occurs because the child has made steady progress and has outgrown the current program. For some, the setting is no longer a good fit for their particular strengths and needs. In both situations, success for the learner depends on careful planning by the educators and families.

Part Three: Saying Good-Bye, Leaving Montessori

Questions for the Family

1. Do I fully understand my child's present levels of performance across all areas of learning (cognitive, social/emotional, language, motor)?

2. If I am unsure of my child's present levels of performance, do I have resources I can access to arrange for quality assessments?

3. Do I understand and agree with current learning objectives and long-range goals for my child? If not, have I communicated my concerns and begun the process of reassessing objectives and goals with my child's teacher (and therapists)?

4. Do I know about other learning environments in my community that could provide an appropriate setting for my child?

5. Have I met with teachers and administrators at potential new schools?

6. Has a meeting been arranged between my child's present teacher and my child's potential new teacher to discuss my child's current performance levels?

7. Is my child (when appropriate) involved with the transition?

    ■ Have we planned for my child to visit his/her new school several times while still enrolled in our current Montessori school?

    ■ Have we planned for my child to say good-bye to his/her classmates?

8. Have all my child's records been transferred to our new school?

9. Have I shared my feelings (whether positive or negative) and bid farewell with a sense of completion and peace?

Questions for the School

1. Are the child's records current (present levels of performance across all learning domains, clearly stated objectives, clearly documented teaching strategies)?

2. Have we shared information about potential schools in our community with the family?

3. Have we assisted the family in arranging a meeting with the potential school administrator and teacher to share current information regarding the child's learning style and successful strategies?

4. Once the family selects another school, have we worked with the family to arrange visits for the child to the new school?

5. Have we planned when and how the child will say good-bye to classmates?

6. Have we met with the family to share final farewells, providing an atmosphere where all share both positive and negative feelings?

7. If necessary, have we documented potential changes to school policy and procedures based upon our experiences with the family?

Several questions need to be asked throughout all three stages of the child's time with the Montessori community.

▲ Are all meetings, changes, assessments, and conversations documented?

▲ Are resources continually being provided for the family (Internet websites, current literature, other parent contacts, community resources, professional workshops)?

▲ Are we staying informed of local, state and federal legislation governing best practices for children with exceptionalities?

Learning in the Montessori Environment

The experiences of families of children with special needs vary greatly from school to school, and even from environment to environment within the same school. Many Montessori communities embrace children with a wide range of abilities, while others are reluctant to include learners with special needs. Many Montessori teachers welcome the opportunity to "broaden the stream" or to expand their own professional experiences through learning how to adapt their environments to meet children's needs. Others are uncomfortable with adaptations, remarking that they are not trained nor is the Montessori classroom suited to respond to the special learning needs. It is essential that parents select a Montessori community that is open to and embraces children with varying strengths and areas of need.

Assuming that the family has selected a school with an inclusive philosophy, what is the day-to-day experience of a child with an exceptionality in a Montessori environment? The following vignettes provide brief glimpses of life in Montessori environments.

Justin

Justin is six-years-old and beginning the lower elementary program. In a traditional school, he would be in first grade. He has twenty-two classmates, ranging in age from six to nine. They are roughly distributed across first, second and third grade, but because children work at their own pace, there is considerable variation as to who is in what group for math, language, science, and social studies lessons.

Justin's early childhood teachers expressed concern that he was neither able to build three- and four-letter phonetic words nor able to recognize any sight words at the end of his kindergarten year. They suggested comprehensive academic testing, to which his parents agreed. Results suggest Justin may have a reading disability, although his math skills are higher than those of other children his age.

Justin has already decided he does not like working with the Language materials. He complains about composing words with the Moveable Alphabet (cut-out letters) and consistently runs out of time to read word and phrase cards. His teachers know he loves soccer and enjoys preparing food. They create a series of matching words and pictures around these two interests, help him write a survey he conducts among his classmates about soccer, and guide him in creating a collage depicting the steps to making a pizza. They also encourage his parents to continue periodic testing and to begin considering tutoring services. They all agree that *now* is the time to build Justin's self confidence by building his math strengths rather than over-emphasizing "catch-up" work in language.

Sarah

Sarah is four-years-old. She smiles often, loves play dough, enjoys books and puzzles, and likes to run on the playground. She does not use speech to communicate, and she is learning sign language with her parents. She has Downs Syndrome and works with both occupational and speech therapists. Her Montessori teachers have learned simple signs for feelings, objects, and activities in the classroom. They ask Sarah if she is happy or sad today; remind her to hang up her coat; and give her lessons about colors, numbers, mammals, and *sink* vs. *float* using gestures, a few signs and lots of facial expression.

Sarah's classmates enjoy giving her lessons on pouring, scooping and washing sea shells. They learn to be patient when she spills rice or drips water, reminding her to clean up spills. Frustrations occur when Sarah is not able to clearly communicate what she wants or needs, despite the community's willingness to use sign language. Her teachers, parents, and therapists continually review all the available learning options, from adapting lessons in the Montessori school to visiting classrooms in the public school system. Even though most days go fairly well, they realize a time may come when Sarah's needs will be better met in another educational setting.

Sam

Sam is ten years old and likes exploring chemical reactions. He has cerebral palsy and uses a motorized wheel chair to navigate the various curriculum areas in his classroom. He works hard to communicate clearly, and his classmates can usually understand his speech. He uses a keyboard attached to his wheel chair tray to slowly type words and phrases when people cannot understand his speech. Sam is also gifted and attends a science enrichment class at the university in his town. His mother and father have both modified their career plans to provide more time to transport Sam to his therapies and classes.

Although Sam excels academically, he struggles to make friends. He had playmates when he was a preschooler, but as he grew older his peers began to play without him. Although they were polite, they did not know how to adapt activities so he could participate. As the years went by, they felt badly (even guilty) that Sam was usually on the perimeter of the playground and not invited to birthdays and overnights. Now Sam often feels left out and lonely; his teachers and parents worry that he may become depressed.

His physical therapist is urging them to implement a program called "Circle of Friends" that would provide a structure for Sam to experience a more fulfilled social life. They are hopeful the program may benefit not only Sam, but his classmates as well. Sam's classmates know that Sam has a "whacky" sense of humor. They most certainly want him to feel happier and be part of the class community. They need help learning how to be his friend.

Shana

Shana's mother felt lucky to find a Montessori school that agreed to accept her daughter. She shared reports from Shana's previous school stating that although she was usually attentive and respectful, her behavior required constant management. She was taking medication to control her hyperactivity. Having just turned six, she was beginning to learn how to recognize upsetting situations and ask for help instead of yelling or pushing. Her Montessori teachers were willing to help her make charts and record her own behaviors.

She stayed focused during the morning circle time and did okay during the morning work period, except when she pushed three-year-old Jake to get to the snack table. She was proud that she asked permission to leave the group lesson on China after trying her best to listen without tickling and wrestling with Lana, who was sitting next to her. She knew it would disturb Lana and the other children and that she could have a lesson from one of her classmates later in the afternoon.

Shana's teachers work with a behavior specialist to learn self-management strategies. Already keen observers, they continually catch Shana "being good," so they know that she is thoroughly aware of her own appropriate behaviors. They watch for early signs of inattentive or disrespectful behaviors and teach Shana how to spot these "red flags" herself. Not all days go well, particularly when the class routine changes for a visitor or special celebration. Shana's teachers are concerned that they are spending much more time with Shana than the other children in the class. They have shared this concern with Shana's Mom.

All are hopeful that Shana will continue to learn to manage her own behavior. They are mindful that a change might be needed if Shana continues to require more assistance than her teachers can offer. But they are all impressed and sometimes downright inspired with how quickly Shana has learned to say, "I need to go listen to a book on tape" instead of disrupting a group lesson. They want Shana to succeed in her new Montessori school setting.

"Welcome to Holland"

Montessori is not the answer for all children with exceptionalities. Justin, Sarah, Sam, and Shana have wonderful days and not so wonderful days in their classrooms. Their parents and teachers work hard to understand their strengths and their needs, and to adapt the curriculum to create the best fit possible. They recognize the potential Montessori has for children with

Welcome to Holland

I am often asked to describe the experience of raising a child with a disability – to try to help people who have not shared that unique experience, to understand it, to imagine how it would feel. It's like this …

When you are going to have a baby, it's like planning a fabulous vacation trip – to Italy. You buy a bunch of guidebooks and make your wonderful plans. The Coliseum. Michelangelo's David. The gondolas of Venice. You may even learn some handy new phrases in Italian. It's all very exciting.

After months of eager anticipation, the day finally arrives. You pack your bags and off you go. Several hours later the plane lands. The attendant comes in and says, "Welcome to Holland."

Holland? Did you say Holland?! What do you mean Holland? I signed up for Italy! All my life I've dreamed of going to Italy!

But there's been a change in the flight plan. They have landed in Holland and there you must stay.

The important thing is that they haven't taken you to a horrible, disgusting place full of pestilence, famine and disease. It's just a different place.

So, you must go out and buy new guidebooks, and you must learn a whole new language. And you will meet a whole new group of people you never would have met.

It's just a different place. It's slower paced than Italy, less flashy than Italy. But after you have been there for a while and you catch your breath, you look around and you begin to notice that Holland has tulips. Holland even has Rembrandts.

But everyone you know is busy coming and going from Italy, and they're all bragging and for the rest of your life you will say, "Yes, that's where I was supposed to go. That's what I had planned."

And the pain of that will never, ever, ever go away, because the loss of that dream is a very significant loss. But if you spend your life mourning the fact that you didn't get to Italy, you may never be free to enjoy the very special, the very lovely things about Holland.

exceptionalities and are committed to creating positive, even terrific experiences for each of the children. And they are aware of the constant need to communicate honestly: what is going well, what is not going well, what can we do differently, and is this the best environment for this child at this time?

In the seventies, when the Netherlands was still commonly called Holland, Abigail Van Buren published a letter in her advice column ("Dear Abby"). The article has been republished over and over, and is often shared in "Introduction to Exceptional Learners" college classes. The article was written by the parent of a child with exceptionalities (name unknown). Despite dated language and some oversimplification, it portrays both the heartache and the joy of being the parent of a child with special needs. It provides a clear message for parents and teachers as they embrace the challenge of creating a learning experience for children with exceptionalities in Montessori environments.

For many families of children with exceptionalities, Montessori does bring a touch of Italy to the beauty of their Holland experience.

Resources

Both the federal government and private organizations offer resources for parents. University special education programs and community-based support groups also provide invaluable source of timely information.

Council for American Private Education:
 cape@capenet.org; (301) 916-8460 (Contact for IEAA Tool Kit)
IDEA Local Implementation by Local Administrators Partnership
 (ILIAD): www.ideapractices.org; (877) CEC-IDEA (toll free)
Council for Exceptional Children:
 www.cec.sped.org; Discover IDEA 2002 with enhanced search
 opportunities; (800) 224-6830
Office of Non-Public Education:
 www.ed.gov/offices/OIIA/NonPublic/federal/idea.html;
 nonpubliceducation@ed.gov; (202) 401-1365ß
Office of Special Education Programs (OSEP):
 www.ed.gov/offices/osers/osep; (202) 205-9754
Free and Appropriate Education: www.fape.org
Parent Educational Advocacy Training Center:
 partners@peatc.org; (703) 923-0010
Learning Disabilities Association of America:
 www.ldanatl.org; (414) 341-1515
Children & Adults with Attention Deficit Disorder:
 www.chadd.org; (800) 233-4050
American Association on Mental Retardation:
 www.aamr.org; (202) 387-1968
Autism Association of America: www.autism-society.org;
 (301) 651-0881; 800-3autism (toll free)

CLOSING THOUGHTS

SECTION 3

CLOSING THOUGHTS

DOES MONTESSORI PREPARE CHILDREN FOR THE REAL WORLD?

REFLECTIONS ON A MONTESSORI EDUCATION

THE MONTESSORI WAY

Closing Thoughts

"Montessori is too structured!"

"Your children are STILL in Montessori! You do want them to go to college ... don't you?"

"Children have to grow up and face the real world sooner or later!"

"Montessori has no structure!"

Does any of this sound familiar?

Does Montessori Prepare Children For the Real World?

Reflections on a Montessori Education: Montessori Parents, Educators, and Students

Montessori parents often hear statements like these. They hear them from well-meaning relatives, co-workers, neighbors, and just about anybody who knows that they have a child in a Montessori school. When it comes to Montessori, it seems that everyone has an opinion!

Many parents of children enrolled in Montessori schools have heard the statement, *"It takes courage to be a Montessori parent."* The first time I heard that statement, I remember wondering why anyone would think that it takes courage to send children to a Montessori school? I still wonder.

Maybe it's because Montessori tends to encourage children to think for themselves and articulate their own opinions. There are moments when it would be a whole lot easier for parents to live with a six-year-old, who blindly and obediently accepts explanations for why you don't create a recycling center right in the middle of your kitchen, rather than a righteous Montessori four-year-old who announces that she *knows* where hamburger *really* comes from and she's *never – ever –* going to eat it, or any other animal, ever again. *Period!*

As children get older, many Montessori parents come to understand the "courage" statement in a whole different light. About the time that children hit the kindergarten year, parents may find themselves defending their choice to keep their children in Montessori. The opinions of relatives are often the most difficult to discount, because they come from people who are legitimately concerned about the future of their grandchildren, nieces, and nephews.

The pressure can become intense. Most parents who continue with Montessori report that there were times when they were very tempted to walk away and put their children into the capable hands of a more traditional school. "After all," they rationalize, "we didn't go to Montessori, and we turned out all right." Or did we?

One characteristic that many Montessori parents share is their concern over the manner in which society has come to define "success." Is a child who grows up to become a doctor or a lawyer any more successful than a carpenter or a musician or a teacher or a homemaker? And on what basis can we legitimately fear that these bright and enthusiastic Montessori children of ours would be any less likely to earn professional degrees because of their Montessori education than if we sent them to some other school?

As the parent of two children, each of whom spent ten years in Montessori, and as someone who has had an opportunity to observe the long-term development of my own children and that of their Montessori peers, I know that Montessori students do well in college and careers. I also know, however, that many parents worry that because Montessori *looks* different, it may handicap their children in some way.

Most of us who choose Montessori are comfortable with our children; we are confident in their intelligence, curiosity, and ability to make their way in the world. I would like to believe

CLOSING THOUGHTS

Left: The first issue of *Tomorrow's Child Magazine* published in 1993.

that Montessori parents are less likely to push their children (either consciously or unconsciously) into pursuing high-status careers, just because the social status of certain professions is the standard by which the world has come to measures success.

I hope that parents who choose Montessori are most concerned that their children will grow up to be responsible, contributing members of society, adults who will find satisfaction and fulfillment in their work, regardless of their career path. I am hopeful that my own adult children will approach each day of their adult life with the same enthusiasm and eagerness to grow that they experienced as young children in their Montessori classrooms.

At the same time, our children must be cable of accepting the challenges that life will provide and have the ability to adapt to new ideas and technology. If these are outcomes that other parents share for their children, then I believe that parents can feel confident in their decision to keep their children in Montessori programs.

As Editor of *Tomorrow's Child* magazine, I helped select the cover for our first issue back in 1993 (shown at left). This somewhat controversial cover had significance to me for three reasons. First, the boy in the picture is my son, Robin, at age ten. I can assure you that he did not look like that in real life. Second, it was the first and only time I ever succeeded in getting him into a tie and jacket at that age. Third, and most importantly, he and my daughter's friend, Leslie Tam, are posed as lawyers in the photo, and, as a young adult, I chose a career in law for all the wrong reasons.

I believed that becoming a lawyer would give me prestige and wealth. What it gave me was an ulcer and the nagging feeling that I should be doing something different with my life. While I don't dislike lawyers (well, at least not any more than anyone else), it just wasn't the right career for me. As I now tell my own grown-up children: *Just because you **can** do something well, it doesn't mean you **have** to do it.* There

---

The dichotomy inherent in your question is false. Montessori *is* the real world. The Montessori classroom is very much true to life. The child is pursuing an interest in the context of many choices. Isn't that what society is all about?

Montessori children see their own growth, constantly respond to their own needs in relation to the multi-aged community around them. They learn to make individual choices that connect with their capabilities. And that may be different than making it on Wall Street or becoming a doctor, lawyer, or preacher.

The Montessori classroom allows for a diversity of individual expressions, personalities, and cultural origins. We must broaden the images of success: carpenter, welder, automotive mechanic, beautician, poet — the possibilities correspond to the uniqueness of each child.

Some say that Montessori classrooms are devoid of competition and, therefore, not part of the "real world," but competition, like cooperation, is natural to life and, therefore, emerges naturally in the Montessori classroom. There, children freely compare and contrast each other's work.

Montessorians are careful not to exploit the natural competition but rather to note how children build or lose self-esteem in relation to the way they perceive themselves or the way others perceive them. And while the multi-age grouping softens comparison because of the variety of stages present in each classroom over a three-year age span, I would hardly consider the Montessori classroom a shelter from the real world.

In the micro-society of the Montessori classroom, these children will learn a great deal about human nature and individual personality. They will learn tolerance and respect as modeled by the Montessori-trained teacher; they will learn about fairness, about different approaches for different needs, and about individuality in relation to group cooperation.

Success is in the eyes of the beholder; it is largely formed privately, individually, and compassionately by the child and the family. Even the Montessori classroom cannot substitute for the parent's faith in the child or the child's faith in following his or her own star.

— David Kahn,
**Executive Director of
The North American Montessori
Teachers' Association (NAMTA)**

is nothing wrong with law, medicine, teaching, carpentry, or any other career, as long as it is what is right for the individual.

If the answer to the question of whether or not Montessori prepares children for the *real* world is to be judged by whether or not great percentages of Montessori students pursue professional careers, then the answer is *maybe*. If the answer to the question is to be judged by whether or not Montessori prepares children for life, then the answer is unequivocally *yes*.

As a parent I set very high expectations for my children. I expected them to be well prepared academically so that they would be able to follow their dreams wherever that may take them, but I also hoped that they would be able to make responsible choices. I also hoped that they would be able to retain the love of learning and creativity that Montessori nurtured in them. Although I cared about academics, I felt certain that my children would achieve similar results from any good school, Montessori or otherwise. For me, the true value of a Montessori education went beyond academics.

I have often wished that I had attended a Montessori school as a child. Things might have turned out differently. For one thing, I might have saved a lot of money on law school. I really do believe, however, that all learning experiences have value and that my years in law school were not wasted. And maybe a bit of Montessori did rub off on me after all. At the age of thirty-five, I quit the practice of law to pursue other interests that I find much more fulfilling — career paths I probably should have explored in the first place, if I had not been trying so hard to jam my "round-pegged" personality into a square professional hole.

When I announced that I wasn't going to practice law any more, the initial overwhelming response was, "What do you mean you're not going to practice law? How do you think you're going to survive without a profession?" Sound familiar?

I hope that as parents we will have the courage to recognize and continue to support the human values and life lessons that children learn in Montessori classrooms every day. My own two children went to good colleges, are now in graduate school, and seem destined to find satisfaction in their careers and adult lives. Our world could probably use a lot more Montessori lawyers, politicians, and doctors who understand that there's more to life than being "book smart." Above all, though, I think that as parents and educators, we must never accept the premise that our primary objective must be to teach children to *survive* life. Better we should help them learn to celebrate it!

— Joyce St. Giermaine, Executive Director of
The Montessori Foundation and
Editor of *Tomorrow's Child* Magazine

My experience with students who leave the Montessori classroom is that they keep the Montessori philosophy with them forever and use what they learned in life. I have received feedback from students, parents, and high schools that our students do well in high school, colleges, universities, and in their chosen job fields.

Academically, they are well prepared, know how to learn, and enjoy learning. Since Montessori offers many different learning styles, students have acquired the ability to use all modalities, which allows many options and choices for them. Our students are pursuing the math and science fields by winning high school awards and majoring in these areas in college and universities. They can take a long-term project and break it down into "do-able" parts, and they see assessments as feedback and want to correct their test vs. just get a grade. Personally, they are self-confident and know themselves well — their strengths and weakness, which allows them to make knowledgeable decisions. They are not afraid to take calculated risks in pursuing new interests.

Socially, they care about others, know how to work well in groups, consider the opposite sex as friends, are student leaders, start new service organizations, participate in global projects, and are activists. They are the ones who organize petitions and are willing take a stand on moral issues — not only for their own particular causes but also for larger causes, such as discrimination and religious preference, which may not affect them personally. By doing what is best for students at each plane of development, Montessori prepares them for the future, because they have developed the ability to be adaptable and flexible to what is next in their life.

— Elisabeth Coe, Ph.D., Past-President of
The American Montessori Society;
Faculty Member and Principal of School of
The Woods, Houston, TX, and Executive Director of
The Houston Montessori Center

Does Montessori prepare children for the "real" world? ...

I started learning about and teaching using the Montessori Method in 1960. It is now over forty years later. Then I taught about it, ran a Montessori school, served on the AMS Board, and always had to answer: *"But will the children adjust to other schools and do well in life?"*

To this question, I had flip answers, hope-filled replies, and much conviction; but now I have experience. Also, I have comparisons, having run two non-Montessori schools. In addition, I've had a post-Montessori career in corporate life (CBS-TV) and have run a foundation, which raised funds for over six hundred independent colleges. The simple answer to the question as to whether Montessori prepares students to survive in other schools is *yes!* To compete, *yes!* Prosper, *yes!* And these replies are not boasts — they are my pleasant reality.

First, children generally survive well beyond the expectations of parents and educators. God, or nature made, they are built to endure and overcome. "Overcoming" Montessori is really easy, because it is like basic training for life; it engages the senses, acknowledges physical mobility, and respects the need to manage time. It follows the individual intellect, while providing an adequate dose of reality and Practical Life skills.

Most important is: *How does the student think (s)he has done, "given their givens?* Montessorians do not make genes or create home environments — we run schools and help parents grow along with their children using a scientifically enlightened model and a practical psychology and pedagogy. Maria Montessori gathered the insights, time refined them, and time refines them still. This is what I call the *verb* — Montessori as action, not just a proper noun. I respect the noun; I love the verb.

For fourteen years, I sent kids off to other schools while working within and heading the Whitby School (The American Montessori Center [est.1958]). I watched and collected data. After years of working in business and running two other schools, I've collected much information. Watching my own children, grandchildren, neighbors, nieces/nephews, et. al, I can simply say that Montessori allows and helps children to be physicians, lawyers, business executives, educators, authors, film makers, mothers/fathers, computer experts, writers, musicians, politicians; survivors of college folly, parental divorce; and seekers of the mysteries of life through faith, religion, nature or philosophy. In brief, nothing in Montessori guarantees success or the absolute avoidance of all of life's follies and failures. It *does* provide many tools and, in most cases, tools not commonly exploited in many other educational systems. Dr. Montessori was an excellent physician and an even greater educator. She was not, and is not, God; neither are those who use and advance her Method.

But if you simply want children to enjoy their education, use their senses, find uses for imagination and inventiveness, and respect natural timing, while also responding to fire drills and traffic signs; Montessori is a good bet. If you want me or others to say it is the *only* way to educate or the best, we respond by saying, *"... among great foods, we choose this Montessori diet."* If you want guarantees, we caution you to watch out for snake-oil salesmen. Montessori was not a huckster and neither are we a hundred years later. Our students reveal their talents; we direct their learning. God or nature, along with their mothers and fathers and their socio-economic realities, play roles as well. Montessori prepares children to use their talents, advancing their natural abilities and taking that development into an ever-changing world.

Montessori students are the best evidence of their preparation. Seek them out. Speak with them. Observe them. It is likely you have already noticed them, perhaps even hired them, and maybe you already like them. What you did not know was that they were educated, in part, within a Montessori environment.

— **John P. Blessington,
Headmaster *Emeritus* of
The Whitby School; Currently Executive
Producer for Interfaith Religious
Programs for CBS Television**

Does Montessori prepare children for the real world? I think it does. In fact, I think Montessori can help you be more successful in your career, perhaps even help you find a better career. Education isn't a process that only takes place in a school classroom. Forget fluffy notions of well-roundedness; in order to succeed in the workplace you have to keep abreast of current events, trends, and skills. Unfortunately, I've met many adults who have completely lost interest in learning, who would sooner watch reality television than read a non-fiction book about the real world. These people are handicapped in the marketplace.

What you learn in school isn't nearly as important as knowing how to learn on your own, outside of an academic environment. My impression is that most people never learn to enjoy learning. School is a painful experience for many people, a place of degradation and captivity rather than one where knowledge is passionately pursued. Montessori gave me a thirst for learning and the confidence that I can teach myself anything I need to know.

An example: I was nine-years-old in 1979. When I expressed an interest in getting a computer in the classroom, I wasn't ridiculed. No adult patiently explained in somber tones that computer science wasn't in the lesson plan or the budget. Instead, my classroom teachers and I brainstormed ways to raise the money, deciding on a raffle. My father donated a television to the school to use as a prize, and a month later *lo and behold!* the classroom had the school's first computer. I was enthralled by the huge silver contraption with the passion that only a nine-year-old can have, and my teachers encouraged me in this passion so that by the time I was ten-years-old I was programming in BASIC. Now a scientist for a Verizon subsidiary, I do C++ programming every day, and I still love it.

If I had gone to a traditional school, I might have ended up a programmer. I might even hold the same position I do now. But it's hard to imagine that a traditional education would have allowed me to develop the drive and enthusiasm to stay on top of my field.

— Marc Seldin
Former Montessori Student

Does Montessori prepare children for the real world? Unequivocally *yes!* The purpose of education is to enable the child to lead a productive and fulfilling life as an adult. Since Montessori takes into account the nature of the child and how the child learns, by providing an environment within which children create themselves, Montessori children are enabled with qualities of high self-esteem, self-directedness, leadership, self-discipline, self-confidence, a sense of responsibility, the ability to learn how to learn, an enjoyment of learning, a joy of life, the ability to think, benevolence toward others, the capacity to get along with others, and so on. Montessorians know these qualities are already within the child, and the Montessori Method allows them to blossom. These are the very qualities needed to lead a productive and fulfilling life no matter what type of "real" world is encountered.

— **John H. Davis, Ph.D.**
Father of Three Grown
Montessori Children

CLOSING THOUGHTS

I know that Montessori education prepares children for the real world, probably the way that most parents know, and that's when they look at their grown children and observe the way in which those youngsters have become adults and faced the world. Montessori gives children an ability to face both themselves and the world in a particular way.

Both of my children who had Montessori education as very young children have a quality of daring and competence in their own ability that has enabled them to approach new problems and challenges with appropriate confidence, great enthusiasm, and focus.

I believe that this is one of the dispositional outcomes of Montessori, which has never really been measured, but which is palpable in most parents' experience.

I think that most parents who have had Montessori experiences with their children at an early age would agree that there is a quality to these youngsters who are now adults that is particular to their Montessori experience, though it would be difficult to describe or define.

— Nancy McCormick-Rambusch, Ph.D.
**Noted American Educator,
Founder & First President of
The American
Montessori Society**

I recently met a father of three grown children while waiting for my car to be repaired. When he learned I was affiliated with a Montessori school he said, "Oh, Montessori is great!" I inquired as to his experience, and it turns out his older son attended Montessori. He said to me, "He is now twenty-five, and we can still see the difference that his years in Montessori made." It is this kind of intangible sense that your child is more solid, centered, independent, or has a unique way of thinking about things that is so hard to quantify, yet makes all the difference in the world.

— Susan French-Lawyer,
**Admissions Director
Montessori School of Syracuse**

Does Montessori prepare children for the real world? This is a question I hear all the time. And my reaction to this question is to ask another question: *Whose world are you talking about?* Are you concerned that we are not preparing children for corporate America or for a world that does not offer freedom of choice, a world that is not interested in receiving a new productive, contributing member, one who cares about their fellow human beings, possesses a joy of learning, and is a clear thinking, creative, problem-solving, self-confident, compassionate human being.

What world is out there that would not want or desire an individual prepared for being fully present in the way that was just described? I have often wondered what real world would want anyone prepared in a lesser form.

— Melody Mosby, Program Director
**Athens Montessori School,
Athens, Georgia**

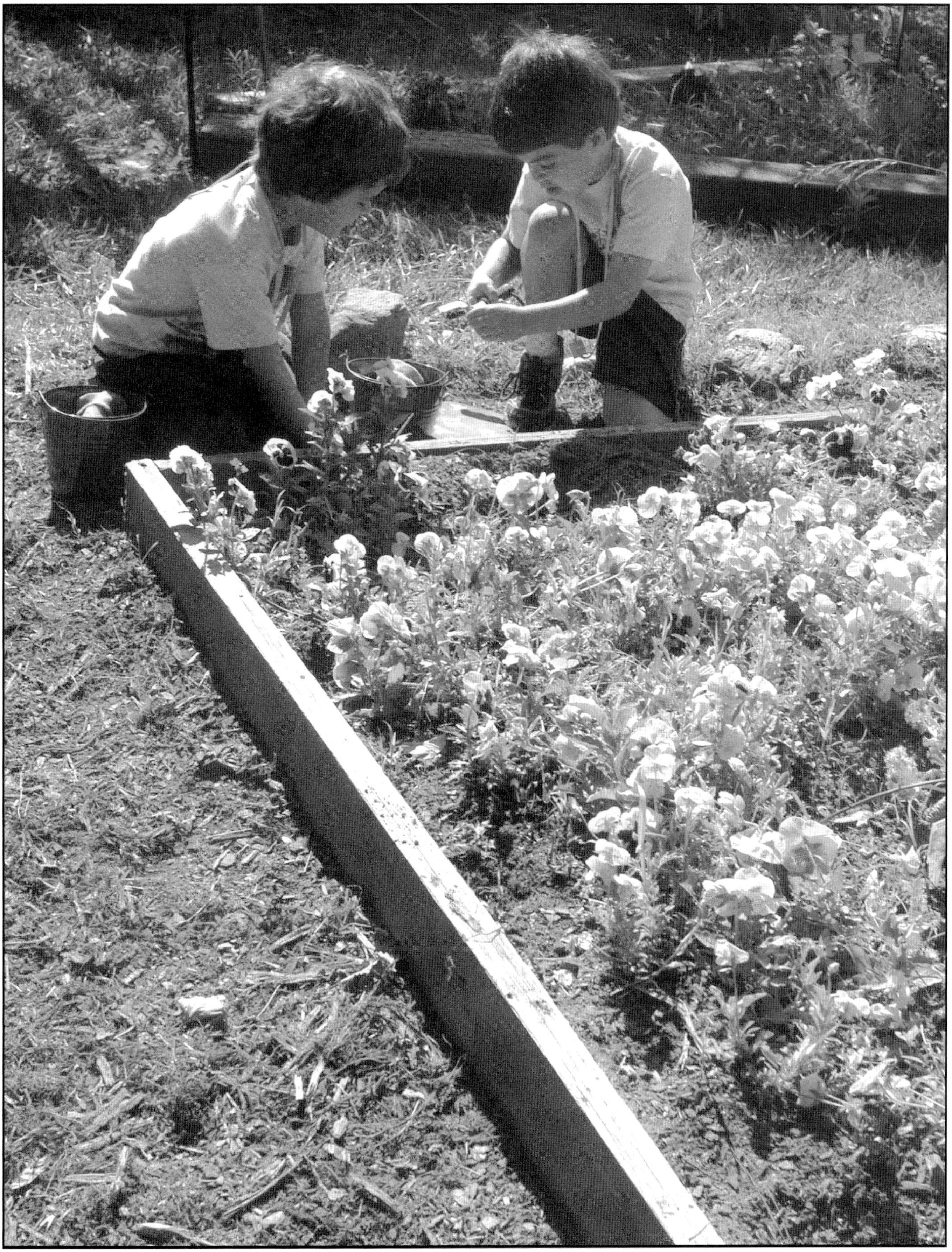

Closing Thoughts

The *Montessori Way*

Dr. Maria Montessori carried a large vision for the purpose of education — the establishment of universal and lasting peace. Although she witnessed two world wars and the unleashing of nuclear power, Montessori evolved a living philosophy of education, child-study methods, age-appropriate curricula and instruction, and programs for adult teacher education. In 1940, she wrote:

> *"Man masters almost everything but himself. He knows almost everything but himself. He avails himself of the most hidden treasures but does not use the immense riches and powers that lie within himself.*
>
> *This points to the great and urgent task of education! No mobilization is as complete as that which can be realized by the school. In the past, military service was limited to men of a certain age group. Now more and more people are drawn into the service of war — even women and children.*
>
> *But if the school takes upon itself the task of mobilizing the young for the achievement of that perfect development that brings forward man as he can and is destined to be: conscious of the society he will become part of; master, not slave, of the infinite means that civilization puts at his disposal; equally developed in his moral and social powers as in his physical and intellectual ones; aware of his task, which requires the collaboration and unanimous effort of the whole of mankind—nobody will be overlooked.*
>
> *Nobody will be rejected; nobody exempted! The whole of mankind will be enrolled in this service, which is a service for peace. Thus, education will become a true and invincible armament for peace! All human beings will grow to be 'knights of peace' during that period in their life when what is formed can never again be shed or destroyed, because this is the period of formation when the cornerstones of the human personality are definitely fixed."**

Here, in closing, we would like to compare the *Montessori Way* to an American political system determined to substitute practices of adult accountability for experiences of childhood. We believe that the national focus on children's test scores as a measure of teacher performance has too narrowly defined the purpose of education and the scope of learning experiences.

We argue, along with many others, that the current political determination to install educational accountability will not work. Despite considerable financial investment, training of teachers, matching instruction to national, state, and local curricular standards, and teaching children how to test, children nationally have show little test score improvement. Sadly, accountability has brought fear into the learning environment by imposing sanctions on schools that do not meet targeted test scores. Sanctions include removing principals and teachers from schools that do not perform.

In making this comparison, the *Montessori Way* finds new relevancy and importance to children and their families. The *Montessori Way* continues almost one hundred years after Montessori's initial insights in her first school in Rome. Montessori schools today seek to help children become independent and self-disciplined by assisting them with a full development of their unique individual potentials. Montessori teachers do this through child study and by fashioning classroom and outdoor environments in which children find engaging activities that help them develop habits of lifelong learning — for example, concentration, investigation, collaboration, problem solving, and communication.

The *Montessori Way*, with its focus on children's unique capabilities, stands in marked contrast to the directions of national education efforts. More than two decades ago (in 1981), the United States Department of Education established the National Commission on Excellence in Education. Its purpose was to study the quality of education in the United States and make recommendations for improvements.

The Commission's findings were published in 1983. Their report, titled "A Nation at Risk: The Imperative for Educational Reforms," alarmed the nation and set a course of action that continues to dictate educational policy twenty years later. Although the opening paragraphs of "A Nation at Risk" have been repeatedly reprinted, it is worth reading them again. The emotional language stands in marked contrast to the convictions we call the *Montessori Way:*

> *"Our nation is at risk. Our once unchallenged preeminence in commerce, industry, science, and technological innovation is being overtaken by competitors throughout the world. This report is concerned with only one of the many causes and dimensions of the problem, but it is the one that undergirds American prosperity, security, and civility. We report to the American people that while we can take justifiable pride in what our schools and colleges have historically accomplished and contributed to the United States and the well-being of its people, the educational foundations of our society are presently being eroded by a rising tide of mediocrity that threatens our very future as a nation and a people. What was unimaginable a generation ago has begun to occur — others are matching and surpassing our educational attainments.*
>
> *If an unfriendly foreign power had attempted to impose on America the*

---

*Retrieved August 5, 2003, from the Association Montessori Internationale's website http://www.montessori-ami.org/ami.htm

mediocre educational performance that exists today, we might well have viewed it as an act of war. As it stands, we have allowed this to happen to ourselves. We have even squandered the gains in student achievement made in the wake of the Sputnik challenge. Moreover, we have dismantled essential support systems, which helped make those gains possible. We have, in effect, been committing an act of unthinking, unilateral educational disarmament."

"A Nation at Risk" was a call for mobilization. Educational improvements since 1983 have included investments in new curriculum, increases in salaries, incorporating technology into daily instruction, and the implementation of national, state, and local curriculum and assessment standards. Despite studies of the human brain and new understandings of optimal learning conditions, the focus of school reform has, in our opinion, been largely misdirected. Instead of accomplishing the comprehensive educational reforms that Montessori called for in 1940 — creating schools based on partnership, community, and a joyful, natural approach to learning — during the past two decades, teachers and school administrators are now held accountable for their students' learning, which is increasingly measured by their performance on high-stakes tests. Twenty years later, test scores have minimally improved, despite new understandings for how children learn and, based on these understandings, new methods of instruction.

The nation's landscape drastically changed during this same historic period. Today's schools must educate children from numerous linguistic and cultural traditions, include children with a large range of learning challenges and styles in regular classrooms and keep terrorism away from the classroom door. Education reforms during the past twenty years have also included efforts to teach children how to reason and understand, identify and solve problems, work in teams, and communicate effectively.

These skills, rather than simple memorization, are said to help prepare children for their adulthoods in an information-age twenty-first century. Our children will face known problems with as yet unknown solutions: dwindling, non-renewable energy supplies; environmental degradation, including the destruction of rain forests, the loss of topsoil, species extinction, and pollution. Other challenges facing our children include human migration; hunger; terrorism; and America's national debt.

Given the urgent and demanding complexities of everyday living, we find that the *Montessori Way* is more relevant today than ever before. Throughout this book we have used the term "Montessori" to refer to a person, a philosophy, an understanding of how children learn, an educational method, a set of learning materials, and a way of life. This way of life is a philosophy for how human beings ought to live their lives and treat one another. It is an attitude of respect and encouragement for each human being, no matter how young or how old. It is a sense of partnership, rather than power and authority.

We argue that these are indeed the qualities of a fulfilled and happy life; these are the qualities of a person who is able to engage in today's pressing issues and challenges.

---

*Retrieved August 20, 2003, U.S. Department of Education web site: http://www.ed.gov/pubs/NatAtRisk/risk.html

The *Montessori Way* recognizes that each child (and each adult) has her or his own unique capabilities. Each child has, in other words, *genius*. A primary purpose for education is to help each child obtain her full potential. The adult's task is to overcome her or his biases and prejudices and learn to see clearly the possibilities within each child. We assist children by preparing learning environments with carefully designed activities that allow them to exercise and develop their capabilities.

The practice of testing children to evaluate adult performance is wrong. The premise of supposing that test scores measure learning is limiting.

Children learn in relationships that nurture and support. Learning is a community experience, and trust between people is essential. Threats of loss of funds and public embarrassment elevate fear and lowers trust. The learning community becomes fragile. The classroom, rather than the nation, is now at risk. Teachers and principals are frightened by the loss of their jobs. Teachers pass on their fears and worries. Learners cannot engage in creative and critical-thinking skills when fear is present. As children become stressed, they cannot test well.

As American students' scores on both international math and science examinations and on local and state accountability measures showed minimal gains during the past twenty years, schools throughout the country responded by better preparing children to take tests. Teachers teach "to the test." Students are drilled; memorization, not learning how to identify and solve problems, occupies lessons.

Time for this is found by eliminating instructional time for art, music, recess, and physical education. In some schools, time for history and science has been reduced, if not eliminated. Time for test practice allows no time for students' interests or authentic problems; no time to tune children into the challenging issues of their adulthoods.

Teaching "to the test" is based on a factory-model approach to learning, a model that misunderstands and misuses children's learning capabilities and promise. In a factory, controls are implemented to assure a uniform and quality product. While this process is important for material objects, it is inappropriate and wrong for children. Becoming the same is not the purpose of life.

A recent email adds an interesting perspective. It described a company's struggle to develop, market, and sell a unique product. As it happens, the concept design was very exciting, and there was (and still is) a national need for this unique product. The marking plans were creative, innovative, and ready for release. According to the company's strategic business plan, there should have been no problem with generating huge profits. They had a winner. Everyone was excited and enthusiastic. This was a great place to work. Problems soon arose, however, and the problems involved the manufacturing process. The company was unable to make products that consistently meas-

CLOSING THOUGHTS

ured up to manufacturing standards. After careful study, the company's leaders determined the source of the problem was its work force. To correct this situation, the company reformed its policies to hold all employees accountable for measurable goals. Failure to produce would result in termination. For a while, more products were acceptably produced. But fear was rising. As leadership focused on faulty products and dismissed workers, the quality of the company's workplace culture continued to erode.

A new study was commissioned, and the company realized its problems came from the raw materials it had to work with. Because this was a unique product, no one vendor could supply all of the needed raw materials. And, because many vendors had to be involved, the raw materials were not standard. Consequently, the materials would not have the same inherent properties and would not respond to one manufacturing process.

Leadership was in a quandary. They knew multiple manufacturing procedures would be required. But this would require considerable training of the work force and an expensive retooling process. Leadership decided to cover up the results of its new study. They would focus, as before, on developing stronger accountability standards. The email concluded with identifying the company and its unique product — American schools and the process of educating our children. While we are not aware of cover-ups, we are terribly aware of the costs of not paying attention to the unique capabilities and learning approaches of each child.

A test score, at best, indicates a specific performance or the child's response to specific test questions on a given day, which is easily affected by his or her health and emotional state. When it is finally reported weeks or months later, a test score is an artifact. Caution should guide decisions and conclusions, if for no other reason than that children have continued to learn and grow since the test date. Discus-sion about who they *were* and what they *did* masks who they are now and what they are capable of today.

The *Montessori Way* is an alternative to an approach to education that now teaches and tests children for what to know, and for how to know it, but without regard for when they understand. Children are, in other words, ready only when they are ready.

The Montessori commitment to respect each individual child honors the learning process each child must follow as he or she makes meaningful sense of knowledge and skills. Learning is taking place every day and every waking moment. It happens uniquely for each child. More than being responsible for external and arbitrary content standards, Montessori teachers are also accountable for facilitating the growth of such qualities as character, grace and courtesy, kindness, respect, and the development of self-discipline.

Standards now exist in all states for achievement and accountability. But do the standards permit differences in learning styles and approaches? Cultural and ethnic diversities? Gender differences?

Test score measures are too narrow; childhood and the experience of learning are far more complex. Maria Montessori wrote:

"My vision of the future is no longer people taking exams and proceeding on to certification . . . but of individuals passing from one stage of independence to a higher [one], by means of their own activity through their own effort of will, which constitutes the inner evolution of the individual."

— Maria Montessori
From Childhood to Adolescence

In keeping with the principles of *The Montessori Way,* we imagine children graduate from Montessori schools demonstrating:

▲ A passion for learning;

▲ The ability to choose and engage for long periods of time in work that is personally fulfilling;

▲ The ability to identify a social problem and contribute to its solution;

▲ The knowledge of how to respect and restore the natural environment;

▲ An understanding of cultural and racial differences as a call for celebration rather than a cause for fear; and

▲ The accomplishment of self-discipline and responsible choice.

This is hardly a completed list. Other characteristics would include "initiative, creativity, imagination, conceptual thinking, curiosity, effort, irony, judgment, commitment, nuance, good will, ethical reflection, or a host of other valuable dispositions and attributes."*

These qualities are consistent with the *Montessori Way* because learning, finally, is more than a test performance. Children require age-appropriately designed classrooms and other environments and relationships between healthy and whole persons.

A child can only attend to reading, writing, and arithmetic when matters of health (nutrition, rest, and emotional well-being) are consistently assured. When unique capabilities and independence are respected as a life-long method of learning, education cannot be standardized and delivered as a one method teaches all, one test measures all.

---

*Bill Ayers, quoted in England, C.M. (2003). "None of Our Business. Why Business Models Don't Work in Schools." pg. 8. Portsmouth, NH: Heinemann.

The *Montessori Way* understands that learning, not education, is the issue. Children are not taught, they learn. Teachers do not teach. They show, model, encourage, and create situations and conditions for children to investigate, inquire into, and discover. In sum, children, not teachers, build knowledge. And, children do not develop or learn uniformly at the same standard pace.

Truthfully, children can only learn when they do. A child will talk, walk, and balance a bicycle only when she is ready. A child will understand numbers, operations with fractions, equivalencies between geometric figures, causes of historical events — only when she is ready. A child will blend visual symbols for language ("c" – "a" – "t") and read only when she is ready.

In keeping with the *Montessori Way*, we honor and respect individual children for their particular approaches and styles of learning. We help children develop habits and skills of lifelong learning with natural systems — curiosity, inquiry and exploration — without resorting to external rewards, threats, and competitions. Why do human children suddenly require learning goals in the form of measurable content standards to demonstrate that they learn? The argument, of course, is more political and, therefore, more controlling. It's not a question of learning; it's a question of who wants children to learn what.

Parents and teachers should access their state and local content and achievement standards; these are available on the websites of state departments of education. These impressive lists of objectives hide the fact that *real* learning does not follow a neat and orderly progression. The focus must be larger than what is learned and include understanding of how and when a child learns. In sum, we must learn to ask, "At this moment, who is learning what — and how?"

Montessori recognized this kind of question and developed an approach to instruction called the "scientific pedagogy." Montessori teachers act as research scientists and endeavor to understand the complete child in order to help facilitate the process Montessori called "educating the human potential." Children are naturally becoming; they naturally engage in a whole developmental process. Not knowing today (as measured by a low test score) is not the same as not knowing forever. Similarly, knowing today (a high test score) does not guarantee knowing always. Humans do forget.

Montessori discovered the requirement of repetition in a child's learning process. In her day, the schooling process involved recitation. Teachers spoke, and children recited back what they heard. In Montessori classrooms, children learn from repeated explorations of materials. Children observe and study natural life and learning materials.

With repetition, children increase their understanding of particular concepts and improve their capabilities with particular skills. This is as true for young children learning to arrange and sequence a set of cylinders of varying lengths and diameters as it is for secondary students learning to research and present a persuasive argument in a written essay or a proposal for how to improve local recycling efforts.

Education reform is as necessary today as it was at the start of the twentieth century. The directions of current efforts are too narrow and, based on political agenda rather than children's development, too dangerous. Instead, each child deserves a complete education in which all of her or his unique capabilities are engaged; an education we call the *Montessori Way*.

APPENDIXES

SECTION 4

APPENDIXES

Brief Answers to Questions
Parents Often Ask

Finding the Right School

Standards for Montessori Schools

Bibliography

Resources

Index

APPENDIXES

Brief Answers to Questions Parents Often Ask

Why do Montessori classes group different age levels together?

Sometimes parents worry that by having younger children in the same class as older ones, one group or the other will be shortchanged. They fear that the younger children will absorb the teachers' time and attention, or that the importance of covering the kindergarten curriculum for the five-year-olds will prevent them from giving the three- and four-year-olds the emotional support and stimulation that they need. Both concerns are misguided.

At each level, Montessori programs are designed to address the developmental characteristics normal to children in that stage.

▲ Montessori classes are organized to encompass a two- or three-year age span, which allows younger students the stimulation of older children, who in turn benefit from serving as role models. Each child learns at her own pace and will be ready for any given lesson in her own time, not on the teacher's schedule of lessons. In a mixed-age class, children can always find peers who are working at their current level.

▲ Children normally stay in the same class for three years. With two-thirds of the class normally returning each year, the classroom culture tends to remain quite stable.

▲ Working in one class for two or three years allows students to develop a strong sense of community with their classmates and teachers. The age range also allows especially gifted children the stimulation of intellectual peers, without requiring that they skip a grade or feel emotionally out of place.

Contents

Why Do Montessori Classes Group Different Age Levels Together?	229
Why Do Montessori Classes Tend To Be Larger Than Those Found in Many Other Preschools?	230
Why Do Most Montessori Schools Ask Young Children to Attend Five Days a Week?	230
Why Is Montessori So Expensive Compared to Other Schools?	230
Why Do Most Montessori Schools Want Children to Enter at Age Three?	230
How Can Montessori Teachers Meet the Needs Of So Many Different Children?	230-31
Why Is A Montessori Classroom Called a "Children's House?"	231
What Do Montessori Schools Mean by the Term "Normalization?"	231
Is Montessori for All Children?	232
Is Montessori Opposed to Homework?	232
Is Montessori Unstructured?	232
Are There Any Tests in Montessori Programs?	232
How Do Montessori Schools Report Student Progress?	233
Will My Child Be Able to Adjust to Traditional Public or Private Schools after Montessori?	233
Is Montessori Opposed to Competition?	233
Is It True that Montessori Children Never Play?	234
Is Montessori Opposed to Fantasy and Creativity?	234
What's the Big Deal about Freedom and Independence in Montessori?	234
What If a Child Doesn't Feel Like Working?	235
What about Children with Special Needs?	235
Wasn't Montessori First Developed for Children with Severe Developmental Delays?	235
Is Montessori Effective with the Highly Gifted Child?	235
Isn't Montessori Elitist?	235
Does Montessori Teach Religion?	235

Why Do Montessori Classes Tend To Be Larger than Those Found in Many Other Schools?

Many schools take pride in having very small classes, and parents often wonder why Montessori classes are so much larger. Montessori classes commonly group together twenty-five to thirty children covering a three-year age span.

Schools that place children together into small groups assume that the teacher is the source of instruction, a very limited resource. They reason that as the number of children decreases, the time that teachers have to spend with each child increases. Ideally, we would have a one-on-one tutorial situation.

But the best teacher of a three-year-old is often another somewhat older child. This process is good for both the tutor and the younger child. In this situation, the teacher is not the primary focus. The larger group size puts the focus less on the adult and encourages children to learn from each other.

By consciously bringing children together in larger multi-age class groups, in which two-thirds of the children normally return each year, the school environment promotes continuity and the development of a fairly stable community.

Why Do Most Montessori Schools Ask Young Children to Attend Five Days a Week?

Two- and three-day programs are often attractive to parents who do not need full-time care; however, five-day programs create the consistency that is so important to young children and which is essential in developing strong Montessori programs. Since the primary goal of Montessori involves creating a culture of consistency, order, and empowerment, most Montessori schools will expect children to attend five days a week.

Why Is Montessori So Expensive Compared to Conventional Schools?

Montessori programs are normally more expensive to organize and run than conventional classrooms due to the extensive teacher education needed to become certified and the very high cost of purchasing the educational materials and beautiful furniture needed to equip each Montessori classroom.

Montessori is not always more expensive. Tuition costs depend on many factors, including the cost of the various elements that go into running a particular school, such as the cost of the buildings and grounds, teacher salaries, the size of the school,* the programs it offers, and whether the school receives a subsidy payment from a sponsoring church, charity, or government agency.

Why Do Most Montessori Schools Want Children to Enter at Age Three?

Dr. Montessori identified four "planes of development," with each stage having its own developmental characteristics and developmental challenges. The Early Childhood Montessori environment for children age three to six is designed to work with the "absorbent mind," "sensitive periods," and the tendencies of children at this stage of their development.

Learning that takes place during these years comes spontaneously without effort, leading children to enter the elementary classes with a clear, concrete sense of many abstract concepts. Montessori helps children to become self-motivated, self-disciplined, and to retain the sense of curiosity that so many children lose along the way in traditional classrooms. They tend to act with care and respect toward their environment and each other. They are able to work at their own pace and ability. The three-year Montessori experience tends to nurture a joy of learning that prepares them for further challenges.

This process seems to work best when children enter a Montessori program at age two or three and stay at least through the kindergarten year. Children entering at age four or five do not consistently come to the end of the three-year cycle having developed the same skills, work habits, or values.

Older children entering Montessori may do quite well in this very different setting, but this will depend to a large degree on their personality, previous educational experiences, and the way they have been raised at home.

Montessori programs can usually accept a few older children into an established class, so long as the family understands and accepts that some critical opportunities may have been missed, and these children may not reach the same levels of achievement seen in the other children of that age. On the other hand, because of the individualized pace of learning in Montessori classrooms, this will not normally be a concern.

How Can Montessori Teachers Meet the Needs of So Many Different Children?

Great teachers help learners get to the point where their minds and hearts are open, leaving them ready to learn. In effective schools, students are not so much motivated by getting good grades as they are by a basic love of learning. As parents know their own children's learning styles and temperaments, teachers, too, develop this sense of each child's uniqueness by

---

* *In general, larger schools tend to be more cost-effective to run than small ones.*

spending a number of years with the students and their parents.

Dr. Montessori believed that teachers should focus on the child as a person, not on the daily lesson plan. Montessori teachers lead children to ask questions, think for themselves, explore, investigate, and discover. Their ultimate objective is to help their students to learn independently and retain the curiosity, creativity, and intelligence with which they were born. As we said in an earlier chapter, Montessori teachers don't simply present lessons; they are facilitators, mentors, coaches, and guides.

Traditionally, teachers have told us that they "teach students the basic facts and skills that they will need to succeed in the world." Studies show that in many classrooms, a substantial portion of the day is spent on discipline and classroom management.

Normally, Montessori teachers will not spend much time teaching lessons to the whole class. Their primary role is to prepare and maintain the physical, intellectual, and social/emotional environment within which the children will work. A key aspect of this is the selection of intriguing and developmentally appropriate learning activities to meet the needs and interests of each child in the class.

Montessori teachers usually present lessons to small groups of children at one time and limit lessons to brief and very clear presentations. The goal is to give the children just enough to capture their attention and spark their interest, intriguing them enough that they will come back on their own to work with the learning materials.

Montessori teachers closely monitor their students' progress. Because they normally work with each child for two or three years, they get to know their students' strengths and weaknesses, interests, and personalities extremely well. Montessori teachers often use the children's interests to enrich the curriculum and provide alternate avenues for accomplishment and success.

Why Is a Montessori Classroom Called a "Children's House?"

Dr. Montessori's focus on the "whole child" led her to develop a very different sort of school from the traditional teacher-centered classroom. To emphasize this difference, she named her first school the "Casa dei Bambini" or the "Children's House."

The Montessori classroom is not the domain of the adults in charge; it is, instead, a carefully prepared environment designed to facilitate the development of the children's independence and sense of personal empowerment.

This is a children's community. They move freely within it, selecting work that captures their interest. In a very real sense, even very small children are responsible for the care of their own child-sized environment. When they are hungry, they prepare their own snacks and drinks. They go to the bathroom without assistance. When something spills, they help each other carefully clean up.

Four generations of parents have been amazed to see small children in Montessori classrooms cut raw fruits and vegetables, sweep and dust, carry pitchers of water, and pour liquids with barely a drop spilled. The children normally go about their work so calmly and purposely that it is clear to even the casual observer that they are the masters in this place: The "Children's House."

What Do Montessori Schools Mean by the Term "Normalization?"

"Normalization" is a Montessori term that describes the process that takes place in Montessori classrooms around the world, in which young children, who typically have a short attention span, learn to focus their intelligence, concentrate their energies for long periods of time, and take tremendous satisfaction from their work.

In his book, *Maria Montessori: Her Life and Work*, E.M. Standing described the following characteristics of normalization in the child between the age of three and six:

- A love of order;
- A love of work;
- Profound spontaneous concentration;
- Attachment to reality;
- Love of silence and of working alone;
- Sublimation of the possessive instinct;
- Obedience;
- Independence and initiative;
- Spontaneous self-discipline;
- Joy; and
- The power to act from real choice and not just from idle curiosity.

Is Montessori for All Children?

The Montessori system has been used successfully with children from all socio-economic levels, representing those in regular classes as well as the gifted, children with developmental delays, and children with emotional and physical disabilities.

There is no one school that is right for all children, and certainly there are children who may do better in a smaller classroom setting with a more teacher-directed program that offers fewer choices and more consistent external structure.

Children who are easily overstimulated, or those who tend to be overly aggressive, may be examples of children who might not adapt as easily to a Montessori program. Each situation is different, and it is best to work with the schools in your area to see if it appears that a particular child and school would be a good match.

Is Montessori Opposed to Homework?

Most Montessori schools do not assign homework to children below the elementary level. When it is assigned to older children, it rarely involves page after page of "busy" work; instead, the children are given meaningful, interesting assignments that expand on the topics that they are pursuing in class. Many assignments invite parents and children to work together. When possible, teachers will normally build in opportunities for children to choose among several alternative assignments. Sometimes, teachers will prepare individually negotiated weekly assignments with each student.

Is Montessori Unstructured?

At first, Montessori may look unstructured to some people, but it is actually quite structured at every level. Just because the Montessori program is highly individualized does not mean that students can do whatever they want.

Like all children, Montessori students live within a cultural context that involves the mastery of skills and knowledge that are considered essential.

Montessori teaches all of the "basics," along with giving students the opportunity to investigate and learn subjects that are of particular interest. It also allows them the ability to set their own schedule to a large degree during class time.

At the early childhood level, external structure is limited to clear-cut ground rules and correct procedures that provide guidelines and structure for three- and four-year-olds. By age five, most schools introduce some sort of formal system to help students keep track of what they have accomplished and what they still need to complete.

Elementary Montessori children normally work with a written study plan for the day or week. It lists the tasks that they need to complete, while allowing them to decide how long to spend on each and what order they would like to follow. Beyond these basic, individually tailored assignments, children explore topics that capture their interest and imagination and share them with their classmates.

Are There Any Tests in Montessori Programs?

Montessori teachers carefully observe their students at work. They give their students informal, individual oral exams or have the children demonstrate what they have learned by either teaching a lesson to another child or by giving a formal presentation. The children also take and prepare their own written tests to administer to their friends. Montessori children usually don't think of assessment techniques as *tests* so much as *challenges*. Students are normally working toward mastery rather than a standard letter grade scheme.

Standardized Tests: Very few Montessori schools test children under the first or second grades; however, most Montessori schools regularly give elementary students quizzes on the concepts and skills that they have been studying. Many schools have their older students take annual standardized tests.

While Montessori students tend to score very well, Montessori educators are deeply concerned that many standardized tests are inaccurate, misleading, and stressful for children. Good teachers, who work with the same children for three years and carefully observe their work, know far more about their progress than any paper-and-pencil test can reveal.

The ultimate problem with standardized tests is that they have often been misunderstood, misinterpreted, and poorly used to pressure teachers and students to perform at higher standards. Although standardized tests may not offer a terribly accurate measure of a child's basic skills and knowledge, in most countries test-taking skills are just another Practical Life lesson that children need to master.

How Do Montessori Schools Report Student Progress?

Because Montessori believes in individually paced academic progress, most schools do not assign letter grades or rank students within each class according to their achievement. Student progress, however, is measured in different ways, which may include:

Student Self-Evaluations: At the elementary level, students will often prepare a monthly self-evaluation of the past three month's work: what they accomplished, what they enjoyed the most, what they found most difficult, and what they would like to learn in the three months ahead. When completed, they will meet with the teachers, who will review it and add their comments and observations.

Portfolios of Student Work: In many Montessori schools, two or three times a year, teachers (and at the elementary level, students) and parents go through the students' completed work and make selections for their portfolios.

Student/Parent/Teacher Conferences: Once the students' three-month self-evaluations are complete, parents, students, and teachers will hold a family conference two or three times a year to review their children's portfolios and self-evaluations and go through the teachers' assessment of their children's progress.

Narrative Progress Reports: In many Montessori schools, once or twice a year, teachers prepare a written narrative report discussing each student's work, social development, and mastery of fundamental skills.

Will My Child Be Able to Adjust to Traditional Public or Private Schools After Montessori?

By the end of age five, Montessori children are normally curious, self-confident learners who look forward to going to school. They are normally engaged, enthusiastic learners who honestly want to learn and who ask excellent questions.

Montessori children by age six have spent three or four years in a school where they were treated with honesty and respect. While there were clear expectations and ground rules, within that framework, their opinions and questions were taken quite seriously. Unfortunately, there are still some teachers and schools where children who ask questions are seen as challenging authority.

It is not hard to imagine an independent Montessori child asking his new teacher, "But why do I have to ask each time I need to use the bathroom?" or, "Why do I have to stop my work right now?" We also have to remember that children are different. One child may be very sensitive or have special needs that might not be met well in a teacher-centered traditional classroom. Other children can succeed in any type of school.

There is nothing inherent in Montessori that causes children to have a hard time if they are transferred to traditional schools. Some will be bored. Others may not understand why everyone in the class has to do the same thing at the same time. But most adapt to their new setting fairly quickly, making new friends, and succeeding within the definition of success understood in their new school.

There will naturally be trade-offs if a Montessori child transfers to a traditional school. The curriculum in Montessori schools is often more enriched than that taught in other schools in the United States. The values and attitudes of the children and teachers may also be quite different. Learning will often be focused more on adult-assigned tasks done more by rote than with enthusiasm and understanding.

There is an old saying that if something is working, don't fix it. This leads many families to continue their children in Montessori at least through the sixth grade. As more Montessori High Schools are opened in the United States and abroad, it is likely that this trend will continue.

Is Montessori Opposed to Competition?

Montessori is not opposed to competition; Dr. Montessori simply observed that competition is an ineffective tool to motivate children to learn and to work hard in school.

Traditionally, schools challenge students to compete with one another for grades, class rankings, and special awards. For example, in many schools tests are graded on a curve and are measured against the performance of their classmates rather than considered for their individual progress.

In Montessori schools, students learn to collaborate with each other rather than mindlessly compete. Students discover their own innate abilities and develop a strong sense of independence, self-confidence, and self-discipline. In an atmosphere in which children learn at their own pace and compete only against themselves, they learn not to be afraid of making mistakes. They quickly find that few things in life come easily, and they can try again without fear of embarrassment. Dr. Montessori argued that for an education to touch children's hearts and minds profoundly, students must be learning because they are curious and interested, not simply to earn the highest grade in the class.

Montessori children compete with each other every day, both in class and on the playground. Dr. Montessori, herself an extraordinary student and a very high achiever, was never opposed to competition on principle. Her objection was to using competition to create an artificial motivation to get students to achieve.

Montessori schools allow competition to evolve naturally among children, without adult interference unless the children begin to show poor sportsmanship. The key is the child's voluntary decision to compete rather than having it imposed on him by the school.

Is It True that Montessori Children Never Play?

All children play! They explore new things playfully. They watch something of interest with a fresh open mind. They enjoy the company of treasured adults and other children. They make up stories. They dream. They imagine. This impression stems from parents who don't know what to make of the incredible concentration, order, and self-discipline that we commonly see among Montessori children.

Montessori students also tend to take the things they do in school quite seriously. It is common for them to respond, "This is my work," when adults ask what they are doing. They work hard and expect their parents to treat them and their work with respect. But it is joyful, playful, and anything but drudgery.

Is Montessori Opposed to Fantasy and Creativity?

Fantasy and creativity are important aspects of a Montessori child's experience. Montessori classrooms incorporate art, music, dance, and creative drama throughout the curriculum. Imagination plays a central role, as children explore how the natural world works, visualize other cultures and ancient civilizations, and search for creative solutions to real-life problems. In Montessori schools, the Arts are normally integrated into the rest of the curriculum.

What's the Big Deal about Freedom And Independence in Montessori?

Children touch and manipulate everything in their environment. In a sense, the human mind is handmade, because through movement and touch, the child explores, manipulates, and builds a storehouse of impressions about the physical world around her. Children learn best by doing, and this requires movement and spontaneous investigation.

Montessori children are free to move about, working alone or with others at will. They may select any activity and work with it as long as they wish, so long as they do not disturb anyone or damage anything, and as long as they put it back where it belongs when they are finished.

Many exercises, especially at the early childhood level, are designed to draw children's attention to the sensory properties of objects within their environment: size, shape, color, texture, weight, smell, sound, etc. Gradually, they learn to pay attention, seeing more clearly small details in the things around them. They have begun to observe and appreciate their environment. This is a key in helping children discover how to learn.

Freedom is a second critical issue as children begin to explore. Our goal is less to teach them facts and concepts, but rather to help them to fall in love with the process of focusing their complete attention on something and mastering its challenge with enthusiasm. Work assigned by adults rarely results in such enthusiasm and interest as does work that children freely choose for themselves.

The prepared environment of the Montessori class is a learning laboratory in which children are allowed to explore, discover, and select their own work. The independence that the children gain is not only empowering on a social and emotional basis, but it is also intrinsically involved with helping them become comfortable and confident in their ability to master the environment, ask questions, puzzle out the answer, and learn without needing to be "spoon-fed" by an adult.

What if a Child Doesn't Feel Like Working?

While Montessori students are allowed considerable latitude to pursue topics that interest them, this freedom is not absolute. Within every society there are cultural norms; expectations for what a student should know and be able to do by a certain age.

Experienced Montessori teachers are conscious of these standards and provide as much structure and support as is necessary to ensure that students live up to them. If for some reason it appears that a child needs time and support until he or she is developmentally ready, Montessori teachers provide it non-judgmentally.

What about Children with Special Needs?

Every child has areas of special gifts, a unique learning style, and some areas that can be considered special challenges. Each child is unique. Montessori is designed to allow for differences. It allows students to learn at their own pace and is quite flexible in adapting for different learning styles.

In many cases, children with mild physical handicaps or learning disabilities may do very well in a Montessori classroom setting. On the other hand, some children do much better in a smaller, more structured classroom.

Each situation has to be evaluated individually to ensure that the program can successfully meet a given child's needs and learning style.

Wasn't Montessori's Method First Developed for Children with Severe Developmental Delays?

The Montessori approach evolved over many years as the result of Dr. Montessori's work with different populations and age groups. One of the earliest groups with which she worked was a population of children who had been placed in a residential-care setting because of severe developmental delays.

The Method is used today with a wide range of children, but it is most commonly found in settings designed for normal populations.

Is Montessori Effective With the Very Highly Gifted Child?

Yes, in general, children who are highly gifted will find Montessori to be both intellectually challenging and flexible enough to respond to them as a unique individuals.

Is Montessori Elitist?

No. Montessori is an educational philosophy and approach that can be found in all sorts of settings, from the most humble to large, well-equipped campuses. In general, Montessori schools consciously strive to create and maintain a diverse student body, welcoming families of every ethnic background and religion, and using scholarships and financial aid to keep their school accessible to deserving families. Montessori is also found in the public sector as magnet public school programs, Head Start centers, and as charter schools.

Does Montessori Teach Religion?

Except for those schools that are associated with a particular religious community, Montessori does not teach religion. Many Montessori schools celebrate holidays, such as Christmas, Hannukah, and Chinese New Year, which are religious in origin, but which can be experienced on a cultural level as special days of family feasting, merriment, and wonder.

The young child rarely catches more than a glimmer of the religious meaning behind the celebration. Our goal is to focus on how children would normally experience each festival within their culture: the special foods, songs, dances, games, stories, presents — a potpourri of experiences aimed at all the senses of a young child.

On the other hand, one of our fundamental aims is the inspiration of the child's heart. While Montessori does not teach religion, we do present the great moral and spiritual themes, such as love, kindness, joy, and confidence in the fundamental goodness of life in simple ways that encourage the child to begin the journey toward being fully alive and fully human. Everything is intended to nurture within the child a sense of joy and appreciation of life.

APPENDIXES

Finding the Right School

"Why is there so much variation from one Montessori school to another? How can I know if I've found a 'real' Montessori school?"

Although most schools try to remain faithful to their understanding of Dr. Montessori's insights and research, they have all been influenced by the evolution of our culture and technology. Remember, despite the impression many parents hold, the name *Montessori* refers to a method and philosophy, and it is neither a name protected by copyright nor a central licensing or franchising program.

In many parts of the world, anyone could, in theory, open a school and call it *Montessori* with no knowledge of how an authentic program is organized or run. When this happens, it is both disturbing and embarrassing for those of us who know the difference. Many of these schools fail but often not before they harm the public's perception of the integrity and effectiveness of Montessori as a whole.

Often, one sign of a school's commitment to professional excellence is their membership in one of the professional Montessori societies, such as the Association Montessori Internationale or the American Montessori Society. They, along with several other Montessori organizations, such as the International Montessori Council, also offer schools the opportunity to become accredited as well.

There are many other smaller Montessori organizations as well, but the key is to remember that there is no requirement that a Montessori school be affiliated or accredited by any outside organization. Quite a few Montessori schools choose to remain independent.

What should we look for when we visit Montessori schools?

The Montessori Learning Environment

▲ Montessori classrooms should be bright, warm, and inviting, filled with plants, animals, art, music, and books. Interest centers will be filled with intriguing learning materials, mathematical models, maps, charts, international and historical artifacts, a class library, an art area, a small natural-science museum, and animals that the children are raising. In an elementary class, you will also normally find computers and scientific apparatus.

▲ You should not find rows of desks in a Montessori classroom. There will not be a teacher's desk and chalk board in the front of the room. The environment will be set up to facilitate student discussion and stimulate collaborative learning.

▲ Montessori classrooms will be organized into several curriculum areas, usually including: language arts (reading, literature, grammar, creative writing, spelling, and handwriting); mathematics and geometry; everyday living skills; sensory-awareness exercises and puzzles; geography, history, science, art, music, and movement. Most rooms will include a classroom library. Each area will be made up of one or more shelf units, cabinets, and display tables with a wide variety of materials on open display, ready for use as the children select them.

▲ Students will typically be found scattered around the classroom, working alone or with one or two others.

▲ Teachers will normally be found working with one or two children at a time, advising, presenting a new lesson, or quietly observing the class at work.

▲ Each class should contain the full complement of Montessori materials considered appropriate for this level.

▲ The furniture in the classroom will be the right size for the students.

▲ There will be few, if any, toys in a Montessori preschool classroom. Instead, there should be a lovely and extensive collection of learning materials that match the developmental capabilities, interests, and needs of the children enrolled in each class. These educational materials allow for multiple modalities of learning and discovery, offering a wide range of intellectual challenges.

▲ The learning activities observed in a Montessori environment should involve inquiry, discovery, and provide continuous feedback on the students' progress. With older students, there should be evidence that in discussions and lessons, multiple perspectives and differing viewpoints are treated with respect.

▲ The children should clearly feel comfortable and safe.

The Composition of a Class

■ A Montessori program is composed of mixed-age groups of children within each classroom, traditionally covering a three-year span from the early childhood level onward. The levels usually found in a Montessori school correspond to the developmental stages of childhood: Infants (birth through eighteen months); Toddlers (eighteen months to age three); Early Childhood (age three to six); Lower Elementary (age six to eight); Upper Elementary (age nine to eleven); Middle School (age twelve to fourteen); and High School (age fourteen to eighteen).

■ Ideally, a Montessori class is balanced in terms of boys and girls, as well as in the number of children in each age group.

■ Classes should be made up of twenty-five to thirty students, led by either two Montessori teachers or a Montessori teacher and one or two assistants. These numbers will naturally be lower at the infant and toddler levels.

■ Montessori schools consciously work to attract a diverse student body and follow a clear non-discrimination policy.

The Teachers

▲ Each class should be led by at least one 'Montessori' certified teacher who holds a recognized Montessori credential for the age level taught.

▲ In addition to the lead Montessori teacher, each class would normally include either a second certified Montessori teacher or a para-professional teacher's assistant.

▲ Montessori teachers should be respectfully engaged with their students.

▲ Generally, students will be observed working individually or in small, self-selected groups. There will be very few whole group lessons.

▲ Typically, we should see Montessori teachers inspiring, mentoring, and facilitating the learning process more often than directly giving children lessons. The real work of learning belongs to the individual child.

The Children at Work

■ Students should clearly seem to feel at ease as they select and pursue activities.

■ Generally, students will work individually or in small, self-selected groups. There will be very few whole group lessons.

■ Children and adults should be observed interacting respectfully. If there is some conflict, the teachers will normally facilitate a resolution by guiding children to express their concerns and by working together to find a solution.

■ The focus of the class should be on children's learning, not on teachers' teaching.

Talk openly with school administrators, observe children working in a classroom, and ask the right questions. Keep questions like these in mind as you speak with the administration, teachers, and, perhaps, some present parents at the schools you are observing.

▲ In what ways do you see Montessori as being different from other school programs?

▲ In what ways, if any, might your school be distinguished from other Montessori schools in the community?

▲ What do you consider to be the strengths of the school?

▲ Are there any areas of the school that you see as needing additional resources or attention? How are these areas being addressed?

▲ How would you describe a "successful" learner at this school?

▲ What sort of children might not be as successful in this school?

▲ What do most parents who are pleased with this school find most appealing?

▲ What might characterize those parents' values or expectations who would not find this school to be a good fit for them as a family?

▲ If we apply to this school and are accepted, what advice would we receive regarding how to make this a wonderful experience for our child?

▲ What opportunities does this school allow for parents to become involved in their children's education? What expectations would the school have for us as parents?

Observing in the Classroom Environments

As tempting as it is to enroll without visiting a classroom, put this visit at the top of your "to-do" list. You will learn a great deal by spending thirty minutes to an hour watching the children at work. Ask permission to watch a "work period" first. If you have time, stay for a group meeting or come back later to watch this part of the children's day.

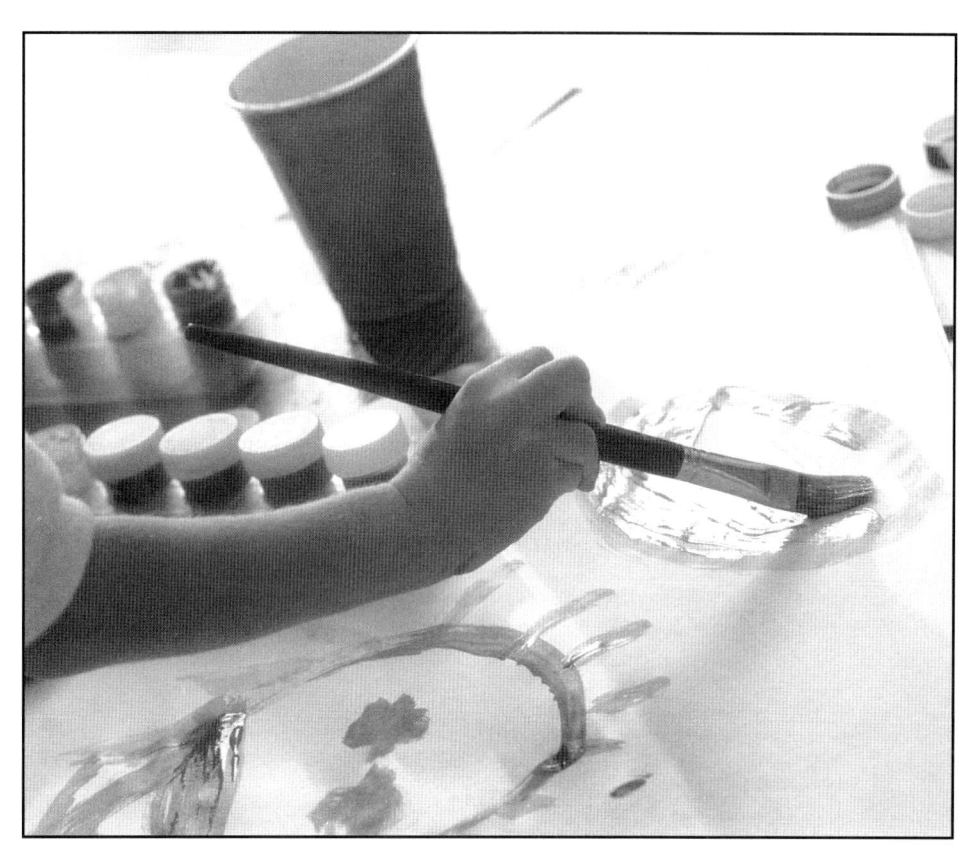

How can I determine if Montessori is right for my child?

The most important question in selecting a Montessori school is to consider how well it matches your sense of what kind of education you want for your children. No one educational approach will be right for all children. Ideally, parents should seek out the best fit, not only between their child and a particular school, but also between their family's values and goals for their children's education and what given schools realistically offer. Finding the right school for mom and dad is as important as finding the right school for a child.

The decision to enroll a child in a particular school should be based on the parents' and school's mutual belief that this will be a good fit for the child's personality and learning style, as well as with the family's values and goals. There must be a partnership based on the mutual sense that each is a good match for the other.

In determining which school is the best match, you will need to trust your eyes, ears, and gut instincts. Nothing beats your own observation and experience. The school that receives raves from one parent may be completely wrong for another; however, it might be a perfect match for your family. Try to trust your own experience far more than the opinions of other parents.

It is very important to get all parties involved in the school selection process. Sometimes one partner prefers to delegate preschool decisions to the other, which can lead to conflict later when one of the partners concludes that the time has come for their child to move on to a "real" school, or if one objects to continuing to spend money for private school tuition once their child is old enough to enter free public kindergarten. Ideally, partners should share decisions about their children's education.

Find a school that you love, and once you do, remember the old adage: "It is not a good idea to try to fix something that is already working." Some parents try different schools for a year or two and then move on to another. They do it with the best intentions, but it should be common sense that children who are educated in one consistent approach, and who grow up within one school community, tend to be more grounded and tend to get more long-term value from their school experience than children who have had to adjust to several different schools.

In the end, the selection of a Montessori school comes down to a matter of personal preference. If you visit a school and find yourself in love with the look and feel of the school's atmosphere; if you can clearly see your child happy and successful in this atmosphere; then that school is more likely to be a good fit than one that leaves you confused and uncertain.

Parents Who Are Comfortable With Montessori Tend to Agree with The Following Basic Ideas about Children's Learning

1. Intelligence is not rare among human beings. It is found in children at birth. With the right stimulation, it is possible to nurture the development of reasoning and problem solving skills in young children.

2. The most important years of a child's education are not high school and college, but the first six years of life. As a result, Montessori schools regard infant and early childhood education as the very foundation of everything that follows.

3. It is critically important to allow children to develop a high degree of independence and autonomy.

4. Academic competition and accountability are not effective ways to motivate students to become well educated. Students learn more effectively when school is seen as a safe, exciting, and joyful experience.

5. A competitive classroom environment stifles creativity.

6. There is a direct link between children's sense of self-worth, empowerment, self-mastery, and their ability to learn and retain new skills and information.

7. Education should be a transition from one level of independence, competency, and self-reliance to the next rather than a process of passing exams and completing assignments.

8. Children are born curious, creative, and motivated to observe and learn things.

9. Children learn in different ways and at different paces. The idea that those who learn quickly are more talented misses a basic truth about how children really learn.

10. Children learn best through hands-on experience, real-world application, and problem solving.

11. Teachers should serve as children's mentors, friends, and guides, rather than as taskmasters and disciplinarians. Students should be treated with profound respect, in partnership rather than with condescension, external control, and domination.

12. Children are capable of making choices to guide their own learning.

13. It is helpful for children to work together on school projects.

14. School should be a joyful experience for children.

15. The family assumes that their children will do well, and are fairly relaxed about academic issues. They want school to be exciting and fun, not demanding and stressful in the name of high standards!

16. Parents want a school that will stimulate and encourage their child's curiosity, creativity, and imagination.

17. Our family would like to stay in Montessori at least for the elementary program, and perhaps beyond.

18. Our family would like to be involved with our children's school. We want to participate in as many school activities and events as possible.

Parents Who Are Comfortable with Montessori Tend to Question Statements Such As ...

1. Academic competition prepares students for the real world.

2. Children learn more when they are pushed.

3. Testing helps to insure accountability for children, teachers, and schools.

4. Teachers must maintain strict discipline in the classroom.

5. School is basically like army boot camp, a place to earn a degree. It is not supposed to be fun.

6. Our family places a very high priority on achievement. We have high expectations for our children, and are looking for a school that will provide them with a high level of challenge.

7. We want to ensure that our child gets into the best schools and colleges.

8. Our family is able to attend some functions, but we have other commitments. It will depend on the event or function. (Montessori schools normally look for a high level of parental involvement.)

9. Our family plans to stay in Montessori for a year or so to give our children a good start, and then we plan to transfer them to the local public school (or another private or religious school).

Is Montessori right for your child?

Montessori is "right" for a wide range of personalities, temperaments and learning styles. Children who are consistently waiting for adult direction and those who have difficulty choosing and staying engaged in activities may have some initial difficulty transitioning into a Montessori class, but usually they learn to trust themselves and gradually strengthen their concentration as they meet with successful learning experiences and develop independence and concentration.

Children who are loud learn to use their "indoor voices," and those who are messy learn to put away their work neatly. In most cases, parents and teachers work together between home and school to help them develop these new habits. One of the strengths of Montessori is the atmosphere of cooperation and respect, as children with a variety of personalities and learning styles find joy in learning.

Parents who are particularly concerned about high standards and achievement may find Montessori difficult to understand and support. While we all want the best for our children, Montessori really represents another way from the more conventional thinking found in most schools.

Montessori schools believe that children are normally born intelligent, curious, and creative, and that all too often, parents and schools make the process of learning stressful rather than natural. We do not believe that most children need external or artificial structure and pressure to make them learn. We also believe that the current emphasis on testing and a state-established curriculum ignores common sense and the true nature of how children learn. The result is, all too often, students who are more stressed and apathetic about their educations. Montessori children never seem to lose the joy of learning!

Montessori is "right" for families with a range of communication styles and learning expectations; however, families who are generally disorganized (arrive late in the morning, pick up children at varying times, and have difficulty reading and responding to school correspondence with consistency), may experience frustration in a Montessori setting.

The program is carefully structured to provide optimal learning opportunities for children. There is a place for everything, and everything is (generally) in its place! Children from somewhat chaotic families often cling to this structure and find it very reassuring. But the transition from home to school and back home again can be difficult.

Montessori schools have various expectations regarding parental involvement. Research consistently demonstrates a strong connection between parental involvement and overall student achievement. Be aware of your school's expectations and strive to be as involved as possible.

If, based on the evidence of your time spent visiting Montessori schools, you believe these basic fundamental principles to be true, then Montessori is probably going to be a wonderful fit.

On the other hand, if you find yourself concerned, then you may be more comfortable selecting a more conventional school for your child.

We hope that these guidelines will assist in your decision making to enroll or not to enroll your child in a Montessori program!

APPENDIXES

Standards for Montessori Schools

Dr. Nancy McCormick Rambusch, founder of the American Montessori Society and co-founder of The Montessori Foundation, attempted to identify the central characteristics of an "authentic" Montessori school. The following list of characteristics are adapted, in part, from *The Authentic American Montessori School: A Guide to the Self-Study, Evaluation, and Accreditation of American Schools Committed to Montessori Education*, by Dr. Nancy McCormick Rambusch and Dr. John Stoops, published in 1992 by the Commission on Elementary Schools of the Middle States Association of Colleges and Schools and the American Montessori Society. Reprinted with permission.

Authentic Montessori Schools

Montessori's Communities of Learners

Mixed-Age groups: Montessori classrooms gather together children of two, three, or more age levels into a family group. Children of mixed age levels and of different abilities work side by side, remaining together for several years, with only the older students who are developmentally ready moving on to the next class. The usual age groupings that one would find are students ranging from age 2 ½ to age 6; students ranging from age 6 to age 9; students ranging from age 9 to age 12; and students ranging from age 12 to 15.

A Warm and Relaxed Atmosphere: Montessori classes are warm, relaxed, and incredibly safe and secure. These are communities in which children have learned how to live and work in partnership with their adult mentors. There are Infant-Toddler classes; Children's Houses; Elementary classrooms; and Middle and High School level programs. They are run to a very large degree by the children, with only that degree of adult guidance necessary to ensure order and safety. In such emotionally safe and secure settings, children can relax, be authentic individuals instead of trying to be 'cool', and allow their intelligence, curiosity, creativity and imagination to blossom. Here children learn how to do things for themselves, solve problems together, learn how they can best master new skills and knowledge, and discover themselves as individual human beings.

A Flexible Schedule for the Day: The schedule of the day is exceedingly flexible, enabling children to select their own work and to progress at their own pace. These are child-centered classrooms, rather than classes that follow an adult driven lesson plan.

A Family Setting: Montessori classrooms are communities of children and adults. As children grow older and more capable, they assume a great role in helping to care for the environment and meet the needs of younger children in the class. The focus is less on the teachers and more on the entire community of children and adults, much like one finds in a real family.

Cooperation and Collaboration, Rather Than Competition: Montessori children are encouraged to treat one another with kindness and respect. Insults and shunning behavior tends to be much more rare. Instead we normally find children who have a great fondness for one another, and who are free from the one-ups-manship and needless interpersonal competition for attention and prestige. Because children learn at their own pace, and teachers refrain from comparing students against one another.

The Montessori Classroom

A Montessori classroom should immediately strike the eye as a carefully prepared and well organized environment that has been designed to allow children to become increasingly independent of adults, to freely choose their own work, and to learn at their own pace. The furniture in the classroom is the right size for the students. The learning materials match the developmental capabilities, interests, and needs of the children enrolled in each class. The materials allow children to learn in different ways (multiple modalities of learning and discovery) and at their own pace. The learning materials in the classroom offer a wide range of intellectual challenges.

The learning activities in the Montessori environment involve inquiry, discovery, multiple perspectives, and differing viewpoints. They provide both the student and teacher continuous feedback on progress. The focus of the educational program is on children's learning, not on teachers' lesson plans.

Working Independently: Especially at the early childhood level, Montessori students will work individually or in small, self-selected groups. There will be very few whole-group lessons. Older students will tend to enjoy working together, and small group seminar discussions tend to become more com-

> **Authors' Note**: These two excerpts have been included as models of standards that have been articulated by Dr. Nancy McCormick Rambusch and Dr. John Stoops (*Characteristics of an Authentic Montessori School*) and the International Montessori Council's *Standards for the Accreditation of Montessori Schools*. These are just two of many different models that attempt to capture the principles of the Montessori teaching methodology and are not intended to represent the only criteria by which to evaluate a Montessori school.

mon, although independent work or short lessons presented to a small group of students will tend to be found much more often than longer lessons taught to an entire class.

The Montessori Classroom is a Responsive Prepared Environment: The classroom environment should be designed to meet the needs, interests, abilities, and development of the children in the class. The teachers should design and adapt the environment with this community of children in mind, rapidly modifying the selection of educational materials available, the physical layout, and the tone of the class to fit the ever-changing needs of the children.

The Program is Focused on Individual Progress and Development: Within a Montessori program, children progress at their own pace, moving on to the next step in each area of learning as they are ready. While the child lives within a larger community of children, each student is viewed as a distinct individual.

The Characteristics of Montessori Learning Activities

Hands-On Learning: In Montessori, students rarely learn from texts or workbooks. In all cases, direct, personal hands-on contact with either real things under study or with concrete models that bring abstract concepts to life allow children to learn with much deeper understanding.

Spontaneous Activity: It is natural for children to wiggle, touch things, and explore the world around them. Any true Montessori environment encourages children to move about freely, within reasonable limits of appropriate behavior. Much of the time, students select work that captures their interest and attention, although teachers also strive to draw their attention and capture their interest in new challenges and areas of inquiry. Even within this atmosphere of spontaneous activity, students do eventually have to master the basic skills of their culture, even if they would prefer to avoid them.

Active Learning: In Montessori classrooms, children not only select their own work most of the time, but also continue to work with tasks, returning to continue their work over many weeks or months, until finally the work is "so easy for them" that they can teach it to younger children. This is one of many ways that Montessori educators use to confirm that students have reached mastery of each skill.

Self-Directed Activity: One of Montessori's key concepts is the idea that children are driven by their desire to become independent and competent beings in the world to learn new things and master new skills. For this reason, outside rewards to create external motivation are both unnecessary and potentially can lead to passive adults who are dependent on others for everything from their self-image to permission to follow their dreams. In the process of making independent choices and exploring concepts largely on their own, Montessori children construct their own sense of individual identity and right and wrong.

Activities that are Self-Correcting: To facilitate children's independence and ability to learn at their own pace, Montessori learning activities (the Montessori materials') are designed with a built-in control of error, which allows them to detect errors without a teacher's feedback, and is key to developing a habit of working toward mastery and precision.

Clear and Precise Instruction and Guidance: Montessori teachers minimize student confusion and uncertainty by breaking tasks down into logical segments and by giving clear and precise directions and clear demonstration of the specific tasks involved in each activity. In most cases, tasks are carefully sequenced and programmed so that each new step is built on what the child has already mastered. Lessons and learning activities are specifically designed to increase children's self-confidence.

Freedom within Limits: Montessori children enjoy considerable freedom of movement and choice; however, their freedom always exists within carefully defined limits on the range of their behavior. They are free to do anything appropriate to the ground rules of the community but redirected promptly and firmly if they cross over the line.

Intrinsic Motivation to Learn: In Montessori programs, children do not work for grades or external rewards, nor do they simply complete assignments given them by their teachers. Children learn because they are interested in things, and because all children share a desire to become competent and independent human beings.

Montessori Programs are Designed to Awaken and Nurture the Human Spirit

Montessori saw children as far more than simply scholars. In her view, each child is a full and complete human being, the mother or father of the adult man or woman she will become. Even when very young, the child shares with the rest of humanity hopes, dreams, and fears, emotions, and longing. From her perspective, this goes beyond mental health to the very core of one's inner spiritual life.

The Child as a Spiritual Being: Montessori consciously designs social communities and educational experiences that cultivate the child's sense of independence, self-respect, love of peace, passion for self-chosen work done well, and ability to respect and celebrate the individual spirit within people of all ages and the value of all life.

Stewardship for the Earth: Montessori seeks to instill in students not only a reverence for the Earth, its waters, and all living things, but also a sense of stewardship for the environment based on a conviction of our individual responsibility for the beauty of the land and the health of our ecosystems.

Universal Values: Montessori deliberately teaches children not only appropriate patterns of polite behavior but seeks to instill basic universal values within the core of the child's personality. These values include self-respect, acceptance of the uniqueness and dignity of each person we meet, kindness, peacefulness, compassion, empathy, honor, individual responsibility, and courage to speak from our hearts.

Social Development: Particular attention is given to the children's social development. The spontaneously formed learning groups so often found in a Montessori class, as well as the spontaneous groups that form to solve problems and help one another, are clear evidence of this aspect of their development. Non-violence, non-aggressive behavior, and respect for another's belongings and work are the norm both when adults are watching and when children believe they are not being observed.

Global Understanding: All Montessori schools are to a large degree international schools. They not only tend to attract a diverse student body representing many ethnic backgrounds, religions, and international backgrounds, but they actively celebrate their diversity. The curriculum is international in its heritage and focus, and consciously seeks to promote a global perspective.

Social Responsibility: Montessori's spiritual perspective leads Montessori schools to organize programs of community service ranging from daily contributions to others within the class or school setting to community outreach programs that allow children and adults to make a difference in the lives of others. The fundamental idea is one of stewardship.

The Montessori Teacher ...

Is Authoritative: The teacher is firm at the edges and empathetic at the center — the kind of adult who responds empathetically to children's feelings, while setting clear and consistent limits.

Is an Observer: The Montessori teacher is a trained observer of children's learning and behavior. These careful observations are recorded and used to infer where each student is in terms of his or her development and leads the teacher to know when to intervene in the child's learning with a new lesson, a fresh challenge, or a reinforcement of basic ground rules.

Is an Educational Resource: Montessori teachers facilitate the learning process by serving as a resource to whom the children can turn as they pull together information, impressions, and experiences.

Serves as a Role Model: Like all great teachers, the Montessori educator deliberately models the behaviors and attitudes that she is working to instill in her students. Because of Montessori's emphasis on character development, the Montessori teacher normally is exceptionally calm, kind, warm, and polite to each child.

What Montessori Teachers Do ...

They are Respectfully Engaged with the Learner: Montessori teachers recognize that their role is not so much to teach as to inspire, mentor, and facilitate the learning process. The real work of learning belongs to the individual child. Because of this, Montessori educators remain conscious of their role in helping each child to fulfill his or her potential as a human being and of creating an environment for learning within which children will feel safe, cherished, and empowered.

They Facilitate the "Match" between the Learner and Knowledge: Montessori teachers are trained to identify the best response to the changing interests and needs of each child as a unique individual. Because they truly accept that children learn in many different ways and at their own pace, Montessori educators understand that they must "follow the child," adjusting their strategies and timetable to fit the development of each of their pupils.

They are Environmental Engineers: Montessori teachers organize appropriate social settings and academic programs for children at their own level of development. They do this, to a large degree, through the design of their classroom, selection and organization of learning activities, and structure of the day.

International Montessori Council
Standards for the Accreditation of Montessori Schools

The International Montessori Council (IMC) is one of several Montessori organizations that offer a program of School Accreditation. School Accreditation is a voluntary process through which a school community conducts a thorough self-study and develops a long-range plan for its continuing improvement. The process includes an onsite visit by a team of experienced Montessori educators who confirm the validity of the school's self study. At the time of this publication, most Montessori schools are not yet accredited. Readers should keep in mind that, while accreditation is an essential standard for most high schools and colleges, it is at this time not required, or even expected, of schools which do not extend through the twelfth grade. We have included the following list of standards of best practice as a point of reference that may be of interest to educators, parents, and others who are interested in understanding Montessori education.

Educational Program

The School provides an educational program that is effective and consistent with the characteristics of authentic Montessori practice at each age level offered.

- **Class group size and the ratio of students to adults** in each classroom complies with local governing regulation and is appropriate to support the school's educational program.

  The International Montessori Council recommends the following maximum ratios of students to adults (including both teachers and classroom assistants):

Infants (birth to 1 1/2 years)	1 adult to 4 children
Toddlers (1 1/2 to 2 1/2 years)	1 adult to 6 children
Early Childhood (2 1/2 to 6 years)	1 adult to 15 children
Elementary (6 to 12 years)	1 adult to 20 children
Secondary (12 to 18 years)	1 adult to 20 adolescents

  The International Montessori Council also recommends the following maximum ratios of trained Montessori teachers/guides to students enrolled in any one class group:

Infants (birth to 1 1/2 years)	1 teacher to 8 children
Toddlers (1 1/2 to 2 1/2 years)	1 teacher to 12 children
Early Childhood (2 1/2 to 6 years)	1 teacher to 30 children
Elementary (6 to 12 years)	1 teacher to 30 children
Secondary (12 to 18 years)	1 teacher to 30 children

- **Mixed-Age Groups**: The school groups children in classrooms with mixed-age groups, traditionally covering a three-year span from the early childhood level onward. Children remain together for more than one school year, with normally only the older students who are developmentally ready moving on to the next class.

  The levels usually found in a Montessori school correspond to the developmental stages of childhood: Infants (birth through 18 months); Toddlers (18 months to age 3); Early Childhood (age 3 to 6); Lower Elementary (age 6 to 8); Upper Elementary (age 9 to 11); Middle School (age 12 to 14); and Secondary (age 15 to 18). At each level, the program and curriculum are logical and highly consistent extensions of what has come before.

- **Diversity and Non-Discrimination**: The School consciously works to attract a diverse student body and has established a clear non-discrimination policy.

- **Uninterrupted Work Period**: The schedule of the day provides for an extended, uninterrupted work period. (Ideally, this should be a three-hour uninterrupted morning work period.)

- **Student Observation**: Individualized education in the School's Montessori program is designed and based on the teachers' ongoing and systematic observation.

- **Curriculum Guide**: The school has established and follows a written curriculum guide, organized as a scope and sequence of the skills and knowledge it anticipates students normally will attain by given age levels.

- **Basic Educational Expectations:** The school has established basic expectations regarding the desired skills and knowledge that it anticipates children normally will achieve by key points in their educational development.

- **Orientation of New Children:** The school follows a written plan for the orientation of new children.

- **Evaluation of the Adjustment of New Students to the Montessori Program:** The school follows a written plan for initial evaluation of the adjustment of new students to the program during the orientation period.

- **Guidelines for Assisting Normalization:** The school follows written guidelines for assisting and sustaining the development of normalization in children at each age level.

- **Assessment of Student Development and Academic Progress:** The school's Montessori teachers use a variety of assessment processes to evaluate and record student development and progress.

- **Ground Rules:** The school follows written criteria defining its fundamental ground rules for student behavior at every age level offered.

- **Independence and Self-Discipline:** The school's educational program facilitates the development of independence and self-discipline.

- **Responding to Disruptive Behavior:** The school follows written guidelines defining acceptable strategies for responding to disruptive behavior.

- **Corporal Punishment:** The school has a clear policy prohibiting corporal punishment.

The Schools Classrooms Are Set Up to Support an Authentic Montessori Program

- **Classrooms Are Fully Equipped:** The school's classrooms are equipped with the educational materials and furnishings needed to support an authentic Montessori program at each level offered. School policy establishes a procedure for repairing or replacing worn, damaged, or incomplete materials that ensures that each classroom will remain fully equipped.

- **Classroom Learning Activities Are Consistent with the Characteristics of Authentic Montessori Programs:**

  - ▲ **Hands-On Learning:** The school ensures, whenever possible, that children have the opportunity to learn through educational materials and/or models of instruction that are hands-on and promote investigation, exploration, and discovery.
  - ▲ **Library-Based Curriculum:** Textbooks and workbooks are seldom used as a primary means of instruction. Students normally use reference books and supporting resources to gather information, explore a topic of inquiry, or learn basic facts and skills.
  - ▲ **Library Collection:** Students at each age level have ready access to an organized and comprehensive library collection of age-appropriate literature, reference materials, and instructional media that supports the needs of the Montessori educational program and teaches the students library skills.
  - ▲ **Freedom of Movement within the Classroom:** Students are encouraged to move about freely, within reasonable limits of appropriate behavior.
  - ▲ **Spontaneous Activity:** For much of the time during the school day, students are encouraged to select work that captures their interest and attention. Teachers strive to draw their attention and capture their interest in new challenges and areas of inquiry.
  - ▲ **Active Learning:** Students are encouraged to select their own work and to continue their work over a span of days, weeks, or months, until they can finally demonstrate mastery and teach the skill or concept to younger children.
  - ▲ **Self-Directed Activity:** Students are encouraged to work independently, with minimal teacher-direction once they have been introduced to a new concept or skill.
  - ▲ **Freedom within Limits:** Students enjoy considerable freedom of movement and choice within carefully defined limits.
  - ▲ **Intrinsic Motivation to Learn:** In the school's Montessori programs, children learn because they are interested, not to earn grades or for external rewards.
  - ▲ **Cooperation and Collaboration, Rather than Competition:** Children and adults treat one another with kindness and respect. Students are taught and encouraged to cooperate. Because

children are encouraged to learn at their own pace, teachers refrain from comparing students against one another.

▲ **The Prepared Montessori Environment**: Classrooms offer a variety of learning spaces and facilities which are organized to support an authentic Montessori program.

▲ **A Child-Centered Environment**: Learning materials and activities are child-centered rather than dependent on instruction by an adult. In effective Montessori programs, teachers are rarely the focus of attention. Generally, students work individually or in small, self-selected groups. Relatively little time is spent in group lessons.

▲ **Learning Environments Are Adaptive, Dynamic, and Responsive**: The classroom environment is designed to meet the needs, interests, abilities, and developmental needs of the children in the class. The teachers design and adapt the environment with this community of children in mind, rapidly modifying the selection of educational materials available, the physical layout, and the tone of the class to meet the ever-changing needs of the children.

▲ **The Educational Program is Focused on Individual Progress and Development**: Children progress at their own pace, moving on to the next step in each area of the curriculum as they are ready. Each student is viewed as a distinct individual for the purpose of assessment and educational program planning.

▲ **Integrated Montessori Curriculum**: The Montessori curriculum is designed as a spiral of integrated studies.

▲ **Developmentally Appropriate Curriculum**: The curriculum is developmentally appropriate for the mixed-age group of children within the class.

▲ **Applied Learning**: Learning experiences develop the student's abilities to apply knowledge, skills, and thinking processes.

▲ **Curriculum Promotes Global and Multi-Cultural Understanding**: The Montessori curriculum promotes a global understanding and a multi-cultural perspective.

▲ **Technology**: As is age appropriate, technology is available and used as a learning tool.

▲ **Field Trips and Off-Site Experiences**: Off-site field trips and experiential learning enrich the curriculum.

■ **A Comprehensive Core Curriculum**: The school's core curriculum at each age level includes those elements common to effective Montessori programs.

■ **Moral and Spiritual Education**: The curriculum encourages the child's spiritual development and seeks to instill a strong set of values and global understanding.

▲ The school consciously cultivates children's independence, self-respect, love of peace, passion for self-chosen work done well, and ability to respect and celebrate the individual spirit within people of all ages and to cherish all living things.

▲ The school consciously teaches children appropriate patterns of polite behavior and seeks to instill basic universal values within the core of the child's personality.

▲ Community Service: The school consciously organizes programs of community service.

■ **Guidelines Define the School's Ability to Accommodate Children with Special Needs Before Admission**: The school has developed and follows written guidelines for determining its ability to adapt the educational program to accommodate students with special needs (cognitive, physical, emotional) before they are accepted. School policy also delineates how information about the school's ability to accommodate students with special needs will be communicated to parents.

■ **Teachers and Staff Are Informed of Any Students Who Have Special Needs or Health Concerns**: School policy defines the procedure for informing the teachers and staff members of any specific health concerns or special needs of students for whom they are responsible.

■ **Accommodation for Children with Special Needs**: The school follows a formal plan to support the teachers in identifying children with special needs, understanding those needs, adapting the educational program to meet those needs, and working with the family in partnership to support the child.

Faculty and Staff

The school has developed and implemented a plan designed to ensure that its faculty and staff have the skills, knowledge, experience, and inter-personal skills necessary to translate the school's mission into reality.

- **Qualifications of Faculty and Staff**: The school has defined in writing the educational background, professional preparation, certification, professional skills, previous experience, and other factors, such as educational philosophy and teaching style, that it regards as essential qualifications for members of its faculty and staff at each level of the school. In the case of classroom teachers, these qualifications are consistent with the essential characteristics of a Montessori educator.

- **Non-Discrimination in Both Employment and Advancement**: The school has published and follows a policy of non-discrimination and fair and equal employment practices in hiring, assigning, promoting, and compensating teaching and non-teaching staff members.

- **Evaluation of Prospective Teaching Candidates**: The school evaluates prospective teaching candidates to ensure that its Montessori faculty will follow an approach consistent with its expectations.

- **Staff Hiring Policies**: The school follows written hiring policies that identify appropriate application and screening processes for each job category. Staff screening is required for all school staff with responsibility for or access to students. Written hiring procedures require: criminal background checks or voluntary disclosure statements; reference checks and verification of previous work (including volunteer) history; and personal interviews by the school director or a designated representative.

- **Personnel Policies**: The school provides all faculty and staff members with written personnel policies that address the following: equal employment opportunity policies; benefits; time off, absence, and leaves of absence; performance evaluation processes; and work rules and personal conduct, including sexual harassment policies.

- **Employment Agreements**: Each staff member is provided with an employment agreement specifying salary or wages (if applicable), length of employment, benefits, and reference to job description and personnel policies. Legal counsel has reviewed the school's employment agreements.

- **Staff Handbook**: The school maintains a current staff handbook, which is given to each employee at the time of making the initial formal offer of employment. When revised, current copies are distributed to all staff members. The Staff Handbook includes: all applicable school personnel policies, all applicable educational program policies, all applicable policies regarding how the school supervises and evaluates its teachers and staff, health and safety, information about any employee benefits offered, a copy of the school's mission and educational philosophy or blueprint of core values, an overview of the school's administration, information about the school's ownership or governance, an organization chart, a job description for at least the position for which the offer of employment is being made, either a full or summary job description explaining the roles of each position on the faculty, administration, and staff, and the school's expectations regarding communication with parents and additional responsibilities before and after the normal school day.

- **Organizational Chart**: The school maintains a current chart of its organizational structure which clearly articulates lines of authority and which is communicated to the school community.

- **Job Descriptions**: The school maintains written job descriptions for all administrative, teaching, and non-teaching staff members. Each staff member has received a copy of the job description for his or her position. Job descriptions are reviewed periodically.

- **Pre-Service Training for Classroom Assistants and Non-Teaching Staff**: The school implements a system to provide each classroom assistant and non-teaching staff member, prior to assuming job responsibilities, training that is specific to his/her individual job functions, including clear expectations for acceptable job performance.

  ▲ **Staff Training in Health and Safety**: The school ensures that all faculty and staff members have the knowledge and skills necessary to implement its health and safety policies.

  ▲ **Orientation and Training of Staff Hired after the School Year Has Begun**: The school implements a system to provide orientation and training for teachers and non-teaching staff members hired after the school year has begun who were not present for all or part of the start of the school year orientation training.

- **Student Supervision Ratios**: The school has established and follows written policies for student supervision that identify the required adult/child ratios of faculty or staff members who must be present and on duty with students under various circumstances outside the classroom. These policies also identify activities, locations, or situations where a minimum of two staff members are required to be present. The school's policies for student supervision comply with local governing regulations and are appropriate to support the school's educational program at each age level to ensure that students are safely supervised in such activities as: when children are on the playground, during athletic activities, during lunch, on field trips during the school day, on overnight trips, and during before- and after-school supervision programs.

- **Age Requirements for Auxiliary Staff**: The school has established written student supervision policies which specify that staff used to meet staff-to-student supervision ratios, whether in or out of the classroom, are 18 years of age or older.

- **Substitute Teachers**: The school has a system that ensures that teachers and staff members who are absent or on leave are temporarily replaced by substitutes who are able to maintain the integrity of the educational program.

- **Program of In-Service Professional Development**: The school implements a system for in-service professional development of all teaching and non-teaching staff members who work with students.

- **System for Supervision and Evaluation**: The school has developed and implements a plan for the evaluation and professional supervision of each individual teacher, which includes such professional techniques as self-assessment, mentoring and coaching.

- **Communication within the Professional Community**: The school uses a variety of techniques, including, but not limited to, regularly scheduled faculty meetings, conferences, and written communication to keep the faculty and staff informed and to invite faculty and staff input into the planning and decision-making process.

- **Professional Code of Ethics and Appropriate Behavior**: The school has established, with faculty, staff, and administrative input and review, a code of ethical and appropriate behavior for the school's professional community.

- **Policy on Sensitive Issues**: The school has established policies and trained staff to respond appropriately to socially sensitive issues.

- **Faculty and Staff Lunch and Planning Time**: The school has established a clear policy regarding staff lunch and planning time.

Facilities

The school's facilities support its mission and educational program.

- **Square Footage**: Classrooms provide enough floor space to accommodate comfortably the total number of children enrolled, along with the complete collection of Montessori educational apparatus, tables and shelving, and related activity areas, such as art.

- **Aesthetics**: Classrooms are aesthetically pleasing with adequate light and ventilation.

- **Facilities Comply with Local Regulations**: The school's facilities meet local and state standards and hold the formal approval of all governing local and state agencies.

- **Facilities Needs Assessment**: The school has completed a facilities needs assessment.

- **Master Plan for Buildings and Grounds**: If the school owns its own facilities, it has a master plan for the development of its buildings and grounds.

- **Safety Program**: The school has a formal program that ensures the safety and good repair of its buildings and grounds.

- **Preventive Maintenance Schedule**: The school has a calendar of routine and seasonal maintenance projects.

- **Janitorial Service**: The school arranges for adequate janitorial services to ensure the cleanliness of its facilities.

- **Administrative Offices**: The school's facilities provide adequate space for its administrative functions, including offices and/or work areas, secure storage of confidential records, and private meeting room(s).

- **Storage**: The school's facilities provide adequate space for the storage of unused classroom materials and supplies.

- **Hazardous Materials Under Lock and Key**: Medications, tools, chemicals, cleaning supplies, and all hazardous materials present at school are kept secure under lock and key.

- **Site Hazards**: The school has a written site-hazard identification and risk-reduction plan.

- **Emergency Response Plan**: The school has a written plan setting forth the procedures to be followed in the event of fire, bad weather, natural disaster, or emergency.

- **Inventory**: The school maintains an up-to-date inventory of all of its equipment with a projected life span of a year or longer.

- **Space for Indoor Play**: The school provides, or has made arrangement for, space for vigorous indoor and outside physical activity.

- **Emergency Exits**: All buildings used by students provide the following safety features: at least one emergency exit in addition to the main door or entrance; and a direct means of emergency exit to the outside from each floor used by students that is not at ground level.

- **Flammable and Hazardous Materials**: The school requires that gas and liquid flammables, explosives, and hazardous or poisonous materials are:
  - handled only by persons trained or experienced in their safe use and disposal;
  - stored appropriately;
  - limited in access to trained persons;
  - in closed, safe containers that are plainly labeled as to contents; and
  - and in locations separate from food.

- **Contact with Officials**: The school contacts local fire and law enforcement officials annually to reconfirm the hours and nature of the school's operation.

- **Fire Equipment Examination**: The school ensures that qualified personnel annually conduct a safety examination of fire equipment and applicable areas, including:
  - smoke detectors and other detection devices;
  - fire extinguishers (i.e., type, location, and readiness);
  - fireplaces, chimneys, and any open fire areas;
  - storage and use areas for flammable materials and fuel; and
  - cooking areas.

- **Water Testing**: The school has written confirmation that all water sources used for drinking or food preparation purposes currently meet state or federal drinking water standards.

- **Utility Systems**: The school keeps on-site the blueprints, charts, or written physical descriptions of locations of all electrical lines and cutoff points, gas lines and valves, and water cut-off points, or for a non-owned site, the written or posted telephone number of the individual or agency to contact in case of problems.

- **Annual Electrical Evaluation**: The school requires that an electrical evaluation be conducted annually by qualified personnel.

- **Maintenance Program**: The school has written evidence of a system for regular safety inspections and maintenance procedures for its buildings, structures, and grounds.

- **Facilities Are in Good Repair**: Inspections and maintenance procedures result in buildings, structures, and activity areas that are in good repair.

- **Clean Campus**: The school's maintenance procedures result in a clean campus.

- **Toilet Ratios**: The school provide toilets that meet the following minimum ratios:
  - ▲ for resident programs use:
    one seat for every 10 females, and
    one seat for every 10 males;
  - ▲ for day programs use:
    one seat for every 30 females, and
    one seat for every 50 males.

- **Hand-Washing Facilities**: Hand-washing facilities are provided adjacent to toilets and meet the following ratios:
  - ▲ day schools, one wash basin or equivalent per 30 students, with a minimum of two basins for each toilet facility that is designed to serve more than five students at the same time; and
  - ▲ boarding/residential schools use one wash basin or equivalent per 10 persons with a minimum of two basins for each toilet facility designed to serve more than five persons at the same time.

- **Toilet Privacy**: In the main school and living areas, toilet facilities with more than one seat have at least one toilet with a door or curtain for privacy available to all.

- **Hot Water Controls**: To prevent scalding, the school regulates the hot water temperature by means other than individual adjustment at the taps of bathing, showering, and hand washing facilities.

- **Shower Facilities (boarding schools only)**: The school provides a minimum of one showerhead or bathtub for each 15 students living on campus.

- **Garbage Cans**: Garbage and rubbish containers in kitchen and dining areas are leak proof and securely covered or tied when not in use.

- **Dumpster Area**: Garbage storage areas are clean and free of trash beyond the capacity of the closed containers.

- **Power Tools**: The school requires power tools to:
  - ▲ be equipped with necessary safety devices;
  - ▲ be in good repair;
  - ▲ be operated only by persons trained and experienced in their use; and
  - ▲ be operated only when students are not in the vicinity.

- **Campus Accessibility**: Classroom, dining, toilet, and other educational facilities included on the site are accessible to persons with disabilities. In the case of boarding schools, this includes sleeping and bathing facilities.

- **Emergency Transportation**: The school requires that medical emergency transportation be available at all times by either the school or community emergency services, for which prior arrangements have been made in writing.

- **Traffic Control**: The school controls vehicular traffic on campus by clearly posting designated speed limits or restrictions, traffic areas, parking, delivery, and pick-up areas.

- **Arrival and Departure**: The school has procedures for orderly arrival and departure and for the unloading and loading of vehicles.

- **Non-Passenger Vehicles**: The school prohibits the transportation of students on motorcycles or in non-passenger vehicles.

Administration:

The school is led by an administration that ensures that its mission is translated into an authentic Montessori program and that in all things the School has integrity and is worthy of trust.

- **Operating Policies are in Compliance with Montessori Code of Ethics**: The school's operating policies are in compliance with the Code of Ethics established by the professional Montessori organization to which the school belongs. This Code of Ethics is prominently displayed in the school's front office or other public area and publicized to parents, faculty, and staff.

- **Administrative Roles Are Clearly Defined**: The roles of the administrator and any other members of the administrative team are described in writing, communicated to the general school community and staff, and periodically assessed.

- **Qualifications of the Head of School**: The Head of School has appropriate professional qualifications in terms of both education and experience.

- **Qualifications of Educational Director:** Anyone serving in the capacity of an Educational Director/Curriculum Coordinator has appropriate professional Montessori qualifications in terms of both education and experience.

- **History of the School:** The school maintains a record of its history and development.

- **Access to Legal Counsel:** The school has arranged for legal counsel to be available to the administration and governing board for consultation as questions and issues arise.

- **The School is in Compliance with Applicable Regulations:** The school has identified appropriate laws, codes, and regulations affecting its operation and is in compliance with them.

- **Student Records:** The school maintains, by formal written policy, at the site where the student is in attendance, records that document the educational progress, health, safety, and school experience of each student.

- **Confidentiality of Student Records:** The school ensures that student records are kept secure from unauthorized access and that the information contained therein is maintained in complete confidentiality except to authorized individuals as defined in school policy. Inside each file, the school shall maintain a log of the record's release or review by staff members, parents, or other school or outside agency.

- **Parents' Right to Review Their Child's Records:** The school follows a written policy regarding parent and student access to their child's records upon reasonable notice during school office hours.

- **Strategic Planning:** The school has a written strategic plan, which assesses current conditions and identifies future needs in the following areas:

  - ▲ Educational Programs;
  - ▲ Faculty;
  - ▲ Facilities;
  - ▲ Finances;
  - ▲ Administration;
  - ▲ Governance;
  - ▲ Recruitment and admissions;
  - ▲ Building community; and
  - ▲ Fundraising/Funding capital improvements.

- **Program Evaluation:** The school has written evidence of a formal and systematic program evaluation system that provides feedback from participants, staff, and administration on:

  - ▲ the effectiveness of the school's educational program;
  - ▲ the effectiveness of any supporting services provided by the school;
  - ▲ the effectiveness of the administration, faculty, and staff;
  - ▲ parent and student satisfaction with and confidence in the school; and
  - ▲ health and safety concerns for all types of school operations.

- **Assessment of Compliance with Montessori Standards:** The school uses a system to verify on an annual basis that Montessori Standards are being followed in applicable aspects of the school's operation. These standards may be school defined or established by the Montessori School Accreditation body to which the school belongs, such as the International Montessori Council School Accreditation Program.

- **Risk Management:** The school has developed a written risk management plan that identifies risk exposures to humans, financial resources, and property resources, and sets downs the risk-control techniques currently being implemented to reduce, control, or prevent potential loss in identified exposure areas.

- **Incident Analysis:** The school has established a system that includes input from outside advisors to: annually review and analyze when and where incidents, accidents, and injuries occurred; identify steps to reduce incidents, accidents, and injuries; and modify procedures and implement changes as necessary.

- **Safety Regulations:** The school has established written safety regulations to address general safety concerns in the school.

- **Emergency Procedures:** The school has established written emergency procedures to respond appropriately to reasonably foreseeable emergencies and natural disasters.

- **Safety Orientation**: The school requires that both students and staff be oriented to ensure that they understand and can follow established safety regulations and emergency procedures.

- **Unauthorized Persons on Campus**: The school has established and follows written procedures that address possible intrusion of unauthorized persons onto the School campus that include:

  ▲ periodic review of security concerns of the campus; and
  ▲ training for staff and students when appropriate, about steps to take in such instances.

- **Insurance Coverage**: The school has ensured that the following insurance coverage is in place:

  ▲ general liability coverage;
  ▲ fire and extended-risk coverage on buildings (does not apply if the school leases its space);
  ▲ motor vehicle insurance (does not apply if vehicles are not used in school operation);
  ▲ coverage on all owned, hired, or leased vehicles;
  ▲ employer's non-ownership liability insurance on all non-owned vehicles;
  ▲ workers' compensation for all eligible staff;
  ▲ coverage for students (carried by the school or written evidence that each student has such coverage);
  ▲ for students who reside on campus – health and accident coverage; and
  ▲ for day students — accident coverage.

- **Regulations about Personal Property**: The school has established and advised students, faculty, and staff in writing of its regulations for the possession and use of:

  ▲ motor vehicles on campus;
  ▲ animals on campus;
  ▲ alcohol and drugs;
  ▲ personal sports equipment; and
  ▲ weapons.

- **Smoking Policies**: The school prohibits smoking or allows smoking only in designated areas that are away from children and non-smokers.

- **Staff Emergency Training**: The school has developed and implemented a program of training and rehearsal to prepare the faculty and staff to carry out their responsibilities in emergency situations.

- **Accident and Incident Reporting**: The school requires faculty and staff members to complete written reports describing incidents and accidents.

- **Missing Persons**: The school has developed and is prepared to implement written search and rescue procedures in the event that any student is lost, missing, or has run away. The faculty and staff are trained in their responsibilities to implement those procedures.

- **Emergency Communications**: The school has developed and is prepared to implement written emergency plans including communication procedures, reviewed with staff, that specify:

  ▲ a system of communication from persons on or off campus when an incident occurs (including out-of-school trips) to school administrative and health personnel or community emergency services as appropriate (e.g., health, law enforcement);
  ▲ procedures for contacting parents or guardians of minors directly supervised by the school; and
  ▲ the school's procedures for dealing with the media.

- **Students in Public Situations**: For the protection of students in public places or when in contact with the public, the school implements written policies that specify:

  ▲ guidelines for ratios, location, and responsibilities of staff supervising students;
  ▲ safety regulations and behavior guidelines for students; and
  ▲ emergency procedures for students and staff if a person is separated or missing from the group.

- **Releasing Students from School**: The school has developed and follows written procedures regarding:

  ▲ the release of students who are minors to a parent or to persons other than the legal parent or guardian; and
  ▲ verification of why students are absent from school.

- **Weapons and Firearms on Campus:** The School prohibits all weapons and firearms on campus or, if allowed for a specific program purpose, such as fencing or marksmanship, requires that they be stored under lock and key when not in use under the supervision of authorized staff members.

Health and Wellness

- **First-Aid and Emergency-Care Personnel:** When students are present in school or on school trips, the school requires trained adults with the following minimum qualifications to be on duty at all times:

  - ▲ when access to the Emergency Medical System (EMS) is 20 minutes or less, certification by a nationally-recognized provider of training in first-aid and CPR;
  - ▲ when access to EMS is 20-60 minutes, certification by a nationally-recognized provider of training in second level first-aid and CPR;
  - ▲ when access to emergency rescue systems or EMS is more than one hour, certification from a nationally-recognized provider of training in wilderness first-aid and CPR; and
  - ▲ for non-medical religious schools, an individual meeting qualifications specified in writing by the religious sponsor.

- **Health History:** For each student and seasonal staff member, the school maintains a current health history that asks for:

  - ▲ description of any current health conditions requiring medication, treatment, or special restrictions or considerations while at school; and
  - ▲ except for non-medical religious schools;
    - o record of past medical treatment,
    - o record of immunizations and date of last tetanus shot,
    - o record of allergies.

- **Health-Care Policies/Procedures:** The school reviews written health-care policies and procedures for each type of school operation annually, ensuring that they include, at least:

  - ▲ overall policies specifying:
    - o scope and limits of school health-care services provided, including qualifications and locations of personnel,
    - o authority and responsibilities of the school health-care administrator and provider,
    - o authority and responsibilities of other school staff to provide health and emergency care, and
    - o additional external medical and mental health resources available.
  - ▲ procedures and practices, as appropriate, for:
    - o on-campus and off-campus health-care,
    - o provision of equipment and supplies for health-care,
    - o obtaining emergency health-care assistance,
    - o health screening,
    - o medication management,
    - o monitoring sanitation in school, and
    - o procedures for long-term record keeping.

- **Policy/Procedure Review:** The school's health-care policies and procedures have been reviewed within the last three years by a licensed physician or registered nurse, or, if a non-medical religious school, by a person with health-care training approved in writing by the sponsoring program.

- **Contact Information:** The following written information is maintained for students and staff both on campus and with any groups traveling away from school:

  - ▲ name;
  - ▲ birth date and age of each minor;
  - ▲ home address and telephone number;
  - ▲ name, address, and telephone number including business phone(s) of adult(s) responsible for each minor;
  - ▲ telephone number(s) of persons to contact in case of emergency during the individual's stay at school; and
  - ▲ name and telephone number of individual's physician or health-care facility (if available).

- **Health Exams:** For each resident and trip/travel student and seasonal staff member, the school requires written verification from licensed medical personnel that the individual has had a health examination within the past 24 months, and the records include:

  - ▲ any physical condition requiring restriction(s) on participation in the school program and a description of that restriction;

- ▲ date of the health examination;
- ▲ any current or ongoing treatment or medications; and
- ▲ date the form was signed.

- **Permission to Secure Emergency Medical Treatment**: The school has signed permission to provide routine health-care, administer prescribed medications, and seek emergency medical treatment, or if a non-medical religious student, a signed religious waiver.

- **Health Information Review and Screening**: (Boarding Schools Only) When students will be residing on campus during the academic year, the School implements a health information review and screening procedure for students within 24 hours of first arrival at school that requires staff member(s):

  - ▲ review health histories;
  - ▲ collect any medications to be administered during the student's enrollment;
  - ▲ check for observable evidence of illness, injury, or communicable disease, and
  - ▲ verify and update health information to ensure that health screening was conducted by a licensed physician, registered nurse, or adult following specific written instructions of a licensed physician.

- **Staff Are Informed of Students with Special Health Concerns and Needs**: The school informs its faculty and staff of any specific health concerns or needs of students for whom they will be responsible.

- **Health-Care Personnel**: The school has a health-care provider on campus who is qualified as follows:

  - ▲ for day schools — Is a licensed physician or registered nurse, or has access by phone to a licensed physician or registered nurse with whom prior arrangements have been made in writing to provide consultation and other health-care support to the school;
  - ▲ for boarding schools — Is a licensed physician or registered nurse, or is in consultation with a licensed physician or registered nurse who is on the School campus daily; and
  - ▲ for non-medical religious schools — Is an individual meeting qualifications specified in writing by the religious program.

- **Treatment Procedures**: The school utilizes treatment procedures for dealing with reasonably anticipated illnesses and injuries that are:
  - ▲ established in writing; and
  - ▲ annually reviewed by a licensed physician.

- **Staff Training in Health-Care Procedures**: School staff is trained in the school's written procedures to:

  - ▲ identify their role and responsibilities in school health-care;
  - ▲ prepare them to use health-care supplies and equipment with which they may be furnished;
  - ▲ identify those situations which should be attended to only by certified health personnel; and
  - ▲ use established sanitary procedures when dealing with infectious waste or body fluids.

- **Health and Safety on Field Trips and Travel Away from Campus**: For off-campus trips or activities or situations where the school health provider is not present or nearby, the School requires that a staff member be immediately available who has been oriented to:

  - ▲ provide for routine health-care needs of the students; and
  - ▲ handle life-threatening medical emergencies related to the health conditions of the students and the environmental hazards associated with the area.

- **Health-Care Center**: The school has an infirmary/health-care center available to handle first-aid and emergency cases which provides:

  - ▲ protection from the elements;
  - ▲ space for treatment of injury and illness;
  - ▲ a lockable medication storage system;
  - ▲ toilet(s) immediately available;
  - ▲ water immediately available for drinking and cleaning;
  - ▲ isolation, quiet, and privacy;
  - ▲ a cot to rest on; and
  - ▲ for boarding schools, one bed per 50 students and staff.

- **Supervision in Health-Care Center:** The school requires continual supervision of children who are being treated or are resting in the health-care center.

- **Parent Notification:** The school implements a policy, which is communicated in writing to parents and guardians, that identifies the situations under which parents will be notified of an illness or injury to their son or daughter.

- **Medications On Campus:** To prevent the unauthorized use of drugs, the school requires all drugs to be stored under lock and key (including those needing refrigeration), except when in the controlled possession of the person responsible for administering them, and:

  ▲ for prescription drugs – dispensed only under the specific directions of a licensed physician; and
  ▲ for non-prescription drugs – dispensed only under the school's written health-care procedures, or under the signed instruction of the parent or guardian or the individual's physician.

- **Record Keeping:** The school generates the following records:

  ▲ a health log or other health record keeping system in which the following information is recorded in ink:
  o date, time, and name of person injured or ill,
  o general description of injury or illness,
  o description of treatment (if administered), including any treatment administered away from the health-care facility,
  o administration of all medications, and
  o initials of person evaluating and treating.
  ▲ reports of all incidents resulting in injury requiring professional medical treatment.

- **Record Maintenance:** The school maintains, at least for the period of statutory limits, all health forms and records gathered or produced during the school year.

- **Emergency-Care Personnel:** The school provides adults with the following qualifications to be on duty for emergency care:

  ▲ CPR certification from a nationally recognized provider; and
  ▲ First-aid certification from a provider.

Governance

The school's ownership or governing board provides effective stewardship that ensures the fulfillment of the school's mission and both short- and long-term stability.

- **The School's Legal Identity:** The school's legal identity and ownership is clearly defined and communicated to staff members and parents.

- **Role of the Ownership or Governing Board:** The role of the ownership or governing board is clearly defined.

- **Board Membership:** The school ensures that board members are well qualified, understand the school, and are willing to make a real commitment to ensure the school's short- and long-term stability.

- **Board/Head Relationship:** The board's role in relationship to the head of school is clearly defined.

- **Opportunity to Address the Board:** school policy allows concerned parents or staff members to request the opportunity to address their concerns to the board.

Recruitment and Admissions

The school is honest and accurate in its public relations and advertising programs and follows admissions policies and procedures which ensure that prospective candidates are considered without discrimination on the basis of race, religion, ethnic heritage, or country of origin.

- **Admissions Policies:** The school publishes its admissions policies, including a statement of non discrimination, criteria of admission, and admission procedures.

- **Marketing Plan:** The school follows a formal plan for marketing and public relations.

- **Honesty in Advertising:** The school's brochures, advertisements, and similar public relations material accurately describe its core and ancillary programs, facilities, philosophy, practice, and policies.

- **Publication of Tuition, Fees and Financial Policies**: The school's publishes its financial policies, schedule of tuition and fees, payment schedule(s), re-enrollment policies, policies regarding absence, withdrawal, dismissal, refunds and credits.

- **Financial Assistance**: The school's Parent Handbook and enrollment agreements describe its policies regarding scholarships, financial aid, discounts, and refunds and credits in the event of absence, illness, transfers, or withdrawal.

- **Ethical Recruitment Policies and Practice**: The school's recruitment and admissions program follows guidelines consistent with the IMC's Code of Ethics.

- **Communication with Present School Prior to Admission**: The school does not offer admission to any candidate without formal communication with the student's present school.

- **Non-Discrimination in Admissions**: The school does not discriminate in the admission of students on the basis of race, religion, or ethnic background.

Retention of Students & Building School Community

The school follows an explicit plan to ensure that lines of communication within the school community remain open, to enhance the general sense of school community, and to keep attrition within reasonable limits.

- **Operating Policies Communicated to Parents**: The school publishes its operating policies to the parent body. The policies cover all areas of school life that affect families, such as financial policy, health and safety, expectations that the school holds for parents and students, drop-off and pick-up procedures, and the calendar for the school year. Normally these policies will be published in a Parent Handbook (which is updated periodically), enrollment agreements, and in other communications issued by the school.

- **Parent Involvement**: The school involves parents in a variety of ways.

- **Communication with Parents about Student Progress**: The school communicates at regular intervals about the progress of their children's academic, physical, and social development.

- **Confidentiality of Student Records**: The school ensures that student records are kept secure from unauthorized access, and that the information contained therein is maintained in complete confidentiality.

- **Parents' Right to Review Student Records**: With reasonable notice, parents shall have the right to review and insert written comments about information contained in their child's student records. The school follows a written policy regarding parent and student access.

- **Maintenance of Student Records**: The school maintains student records through the period required by governing law.

- **Building a School Community**: The school attempts to go beyond the fundamental working partnership with parents, with the goal of creating a positive school community atmosphere.

- **Parent Right to Observe Classroom**: Within reasonable guidelines established to ensure the integrity of the educational program, parents are welcome to visit the school to observe their child in class.

- **Records of Student Attrition and Projections of Future Enrollment**: The school maintains records of student attrition and projects trends of future admissions, graduation, and withdrawal to project the levels of student enrollment at each level within the school, and subsequent future demands for space and other resources for several years ahead.

- **Parent Education Program**: The school offers a program of parent education designed to inform new and continuing parents about its philosophy, programs, and curriculum.

- **Parent Surveys**: The school surveys its parents and other constituent groups on an ongoing basis.

Finances

The school manages its financial resources in a prudent and organized manner to ensure their effective use to achieve the school's mission while ensuring its short- and long-term financial stability.

- **External Accounting Firm**: The school uses an external accounting firm to conduct an annual review, compilation, or audit according to its official policies and to prepare an annual financial statement and periodic written financial reports that set forth its assets and liabilities, indicating sources of income and how funds were spent.

- **Financial Records**: The school maintains accurate records of all funds received or owed and all expenses paid out or payable.

- **Budgets**: The school prepares and follows a written budget.

- **Financial Stability**: The school demonstrates that it is financially stable and able to meet its obligations on an ongoing basis.

Fundraising

The school has developed a coherent plan for acquiring the financial resources needed to enhance its programs beyond what can be covered in the annual budget or to gather the funds needed for major capital improvements.

- **Institutional Advancement Plan**: The school has developed a coherent plan for acquiring the financial resources needed to enhance its programs beyond what can be covered in the annual budget and to gather funds needed for major capital improvements.

- **Fundraising Policies**: The school has established and follows a clear set of policies and code of ethics regarding all fundraising efforts and the acceptance of contributions.

- **Accepting Donations with Strings Attached**: The school follows clear guidelines about the acceptance of donations offered with either explicit or implied conditions attached.

- **Roles of Board Members and Staff in Fund Raising**: The roles and expectations for board members, administrators, faculty, staff, and board members in fundraising are clearly defined.

APPENDIXES

A Montessori Bibliography

Adler-Golden, Rachel; Gordon, Debbie. (1980) *Beginning French for Preschoolers: A Montessori Handbook.* Hemet, CA: Education System Publisher.

Albanesi, Franco. (1990) *Montessori Class Management.* Dallas: Albanesi Educational Center.

Alex, Joanne DeFilipp; Wolf, Aline. (2003) *I Wonder What's Out There: A Vision of the Universe for Primary Classes.* Hollidaysburg, PA: Parent Child Press.

Appelbaum, Phyllis. (1971) "The Growth of the Montessori Movement in the U.S.: 1909-1970" (an unpublished doctoral dissertation for New York University, available through University Microfilms International, 300 North Zeeb Road, Ann Arbor, Michigan 48106.

Association Montessori Internationale. (1970) *Maria Montessori: A Centennial Anthology. AMI* (out of print).

Baumann, Harold. (1999). *On the Historical Background of the Montessori-Piaget Relations.* Amsterdam: AMI.

Beck, Joan. (1999). *How to Raise a Brighter Child: The Case for Early Learning.* Rev. ed. New York: Pocket Books.

Berryman, Jerome W. (1995). *Godly Play: An Imaginative Approach to Religious Education.* Augsburg Fortress Publishers.

Berryman, Jerome W. (1995). *Teaching Godly Play: The Sunday Morning Handbook.* Nashville, KY: Abingdon Press.

Berryman, Jerome W. (2002). *The Complete Guide to Godly Play.* 3 volumes: 1. How to Lead Godly Play Lessons; 2. 14 Presentations for Fall; 3. 20 Presentations for Winter. Denver, CO: Living the Good News.

Berryman, Jerome W. (2003). *Godly Play: 10 Core Presentations for Spring.* Denver, CO: Living the Good News.

Berryman, Jerome W. (2003). *Practical Helps from Godly Play Trainers.* Denver, CO: Living the Good News.

Bethune, Ade. (1964). *Uniscript: A New Method for Teaching Handwriting.* Newport, RI: St. Leo League. Nienhuis Montessori USA.

Bethune, Ade. (1980). *Teaching the Child to Write.* pamphlet. Newport, RI: St. Leo League. Available from Nienhuis Montessori USA.

Blessington, John. (1975). *Let My Children Work!* Garden City, NY: Anchor Press/Doubleday; (reissued in 1999) New York, NY: ToExcel. AMS and The Montessori Foundation

Brehony, Kevin J. (2000). "The Montessori Phenomenon: Gender and Internationalism in Early Twentieth-Century Innovation." In *Practical Visionaries: Women, Education, and Social Progress,* 1790-1930. Ed. Mary Hilton & Pam Hirsch. New York: Longman.

Britton, Lesley. (1992). *Montessori Play & Learn: A Parents' Guide to Purposeful Play from Two to Six.* New York: Random House. Also published 1992, Crown Publishing.

Camp, Cameron J. (1999). *Montessori-Based Activities for Persons with Dementia: Volume 1.* Beachwood, OH: Myers Research Institute.

Cavalletti, Sofia. (1992). *The Religious Potential of the Child: Experiencing Scripture and Liturgy with Young Children.* 2nd ed. Chicago: Liturgy Training Publications.

Cavalletti, Sofia. (1998). *Living Liturgy: Elementary Reflections.* Chicago: Liturgy Training Publications.

Cavalletti, Sofia. (1999). *History's Golden Thread: The History of Salvation.* Trans. Rebekah Rojcewicz. Chicago: Liturgy Training Publications.

Cavalletti, Sofia. (2002). *The Religious Potential of the Child Six to Twelve Years Old.* Chicago, IL: Liturgy Training Publications.

Cavalletti, Sofia; Coulter, Patricia; Gobbi, Gianna; Montanaro, Silvana Q. (1996). *The Good Shepherd and the Child: A Joyful Journey.* Chicago: Liturgy Training Publications.

Chattin-McNichols, John. (1991). *The Montessori Controversy.* Albany, NY: Delmar. Available from AMS.

The Child, the Family, the Future. (1995). AMI International Study Conference Proceedings, July 19-24, 1994, Washington, DC. Rochester, NY: AMI/USA.

Claremont, Claude A. (1962). *Montessori Education: The Hope of the Future.* Amsterdam: AMI.

DeJesus, Raquel. (1988, 2000). *Design Guidelines for Montessori Schools.* Milwaukee, WI: Univ. of Wisconsin-Milwaukee, Center for Architecture/Urban Planning Research.

Duffy, Michael; Duffy, D'Neil. (2002). *Children of the Universe: Cosmic Education in the Montessori Elementary Classroom.* Hollidaysburg, PA: Parent/Child Press.

Dwyer, Muriel I. *A Path for the Exploration of Any Language Leading to Writing and Reading.* Essex, England: Doppler Press. NAMTA.

Epstein, Ann, Ph.D. "Children with Exceptionalities." *The Montessori Way,* The Montessori Foundation, 2003

Epstein, Ann, Ph.D. "School-Wide Discipline with a Montessori Perspective." *Montessori Leadership,* Spring, 2001.

Epstein, Ann, Ph.D.; Collins, B.; Reiss, T.; and Lowe, V. "Including Children with Mental Retardation in the Religious Community." *Teaching Exceptional Children,* May/June, 2001.

Epstein, Ann, Ph.D. "The Behavior Part is the Hardest: Montessori Teachers and Young Children with Challenging Behaviors." *Montessori Life,* Fall, 1998.

Epstein, Ann, Ph.D. "How Teachers Accommodate for Young Children with Special Needs." *Montessori Life,* Summer, 1997.

Epstein, Ann, Ph.D. "Montessori Early Childhood Language: Life-Long Literacy." *Tomorrow's Child,* 1996.

Epstein, Ann, Ph.D.; Schonfeld, J. "We Are All Authors!" *Montessori Life,* 1996.

Epstein, Ann, Ph.D. "Is Montessori Education Right for My Child?" *The Public School Montessorian,* 1994.

Epstein, Paul, Ph.D. "An Ethnographic Investigation of a Teenage Culture in a Montessori Junior High School," Unpublished dissertation, SUNY, Buffalo, 1986.

Epstein, Paul, Ph.D. "Serving on the Front Line." *Tomorrow's Child,* 2003.

Epstein, Paul, Ph.D. "Montessori Moments." *Tomorrow's Child,* 2001.

Epstein, Paul, Ph.D. "The Spiritual Preparation of the Teacher." *Open Forum,* 2001.

Epstein, Paul, Ph.D. "It Takes a Whole Child to Raise a Village. Accomplishing Educational Reform in Nepal." *Montessori Leadership,* 2000.

Epstein, Paul, Ph.D. (with Epstein, A., Ph.D.) "Computers. Are There New Secrets of Childhood." *Montessori Leadership,* 2000.

Epstein, Paul, Ph.D. "The Necessity for Spirituality in Education: A Montessori Example." *Montessori Leadership*, 1999.

Epstein, Paul, Ph.D. "Computers in the Classroom." *Tomorrow's Child*, 1998.

Epstein, Paul, Ph.D. "A Parent's Guide to Middle Schools." *Tomorrow's Child*, 1998.

Epstein, Paul, Ph.D. Implementation: Preparing and Developing a Public School Management Guide." in B. Weiss, Ed., *The Montessori School Management Guide*, The American Montessori Society, 1998.

Epstein, Paul, Ph.D. "Middle Level Programs – Models of Understanding," *Research for Families and Children Newsletter*, Fall 1997.

Epstein, Paul; Seldin Tim. (2003). *The Montessori Way: An Education for Life*. The Montessori Foundation.

Education for the Twenty First Century: *AMI International Study Conference Proceedings*. (1989). Rochester, NY: AMI/USA.

Farrow, Elvira; Hill, Carol. (1973). *Montessori on a Limited Budget: A Manual for the Amateur Craftsman*. Ithaca, NY: Montessori Workshop. Nienhuis Montessori USA. Also published 1984, Hemet, CA: Education System Publisher.

Fleege, Virginia; others. (1974). *Montessori Index*. Annotated bibliography of primary and secondary Montessori works. 2nd ed. River Forest, IL: Montessori Publications. Nienhuis Montessori USA.

Freedom & Responsibility: A Glorious Counterpoint. (2001). *Proceedings of AMI/ USA Conference,* Boston, MA, July, 2000. Rochester, NY: AMI/USA.

Fresco, Grazia Honegger. (1993). *Montessori Material Contained in Some of the Catalogues Published in New York, London, Bucharest, Berlin, Gonzaga from 1910 up to the 30s*, 2nd ed. Dual language edition, English and Italian. Castellanza, Italy: Il Quaderno Montessori Editions. Available in the U.S. through Kaybee Montessori.

Futrell, Kathleen H. (1988). *The Normalized Child*. Rev. ed. Cleveland, OH: NAMTA.

Gettman, David. (1988). *Basic Montessori: Learning Activities for Under-Fives*. New York: St. Martin's Press.

Gillet, Anne Marie. (1970). *Introduction to Biology.* Offprint from AMI Communications. Amsterdam: AMI.

Gobbi, Gianna. (2000). *Listening to God with Children*. Trans. Rebekah Rojcewicz. Loveland, OH: Treehaus Communications.

Goertz, Donna Bryant. (2001). *Children Who Are Not Yet Peaceful: Preventing Exclusion in the Early Elementary Classroom.* Berkeley, CA: Frog, Ltd.

Gordon, Cam. (2001). *Together with Montessori: The Guide to Help Montessori Teachers, Assistant Teachers, Resource Teachers, Administrators & Parents Work in Harmony to Create Great Schools.* 2nd ed. Minneapolis, MN: Jola Publications. Nienhuis Montessori USA and The Montessori Foundation.

Grace and Courtesy: A Human Responsibility. (1999). *Proceedings of AMI/ USA Conference*, Oak Brook, IL, July, 1998. Rochester, NY: AMI/USA.

Gross, Michael John. (1986). *Montessori's Concept of Personality.* Dissertation, Univ. of Nebraska, 1976. University Press of America.

Gupta, Rajendra K. (1983). *A New Approach to Zoology Nomenclature.* Oak Park, IL: Montessori Center for the Child. Nienhuis Montessori USA.

Gupta, Rajendra K. (1986). *Science Experiences for Montessori Children Part 1.* Minnesota: Montessori Research and Development Center. Nienhuis Montessori USA.

Gupta, Rajendra K. (1986). *Science Experiences for Montessori Children Part 4.* Minnesota: Montessori Research and Development Center. Nienhuis Montessori USA.

Gupta, Rajendra K. (1986). *Science Experiences for Montessori Children Part 5.* Minnesota: Montessori Research and Development Center. Nienhuis Montessori USA.

Gupta, Rajendra K. (1987). *Researching Montessori Zoology Program.* Minnesota: Montessori Research and Development Center. Nienhuis Montessori USA.

Gupta, Rajendra K. (1995). *Botany as a Means of Development* (Based on the Montessori Approach). Minnesota: Montessori Research and Development Center. Nienhuis Montessori USA.

Gupta, Rajendra K. (1995). *Science Experiences for Montessori Children Part 2.* Minnesota: Montessori Research and Development Center. Nienhuis Montessori USA.

Gupta, Rajendra K. (1995). *Science Experiences for Montessori Children Part 3.* Minnesota: Montessori Research and Development Center. Nienhuis Montessori USA.

Hainstock, Elizabeth G. (1997). *The Essential Montessori*. Rev. ed. New York: Plume.

Hainstock, Elizabeth G. (1997). *Teaching Montessori in the Home: The Preschool Years.* Rev. ed. New York: Plume.

Hainstock, Elizabeth G. (1997). *Teaching Montessori in the Home: The School Years.* Rev. ed. New York: Plume.

Hardinge, Joy. (1992). *The Voice of Dr. Maria Montessori: Lectures, Madras, India, 1941-1942.* Lectures taken in shorthand. Silver Spring, MD: International Montessori Society.

Hardinge, Joy. (1993). *Montessori Method.* Lecture notes, India, 1941-42. Silver Spring, MD: International Montessori Society.

Homfray, Margaret. (n.d.). *Word Lists for Reading and Writing Scheme*. London: Montessori Centre. Avail. Montessori Centre International.

Homfray, Margaret; Child, Phoebe. (n.d.). *Primary Math.* San Luis Obispo, CA: Montessori World Educational Institute.

Homfray, Margaret; Child, Phoebe. (1983). Primary Grammar. San Luis Obispo, CA: Montessori World Educational Institute.

Joosten, A. M. (n.d.). *Learning from the Child.* Excerpts from inaugural and valedictory addresses of the 25th and 26th Indian Montessori Training courses, Hyderabad, 1960-62. Amsterdam: AMI.

Joosten, A. M. (1987). *The Montessori Method: Principles, Results, Practical Requirements.* Rev. ed., Madras, India: Kalakshetra.

Joosten, A. M. (1990). *Exercises of Practical Life: Introduction and List.* Ed. Rajendra K. Gupta. Rev. ed. Bombay, India: Indian Montessori Training Courses. Available from Nienhuis Montessori USA.

Joosten, A. M.; Gupta, Rajendra; et al. (1985). *Montessori Language Program (New Insights and Techniques).* Mesa, AZ: Montessori Research Center. Available from Nienhuis Montessori USA.

Joosten, Albert. (1994). *Education as a Help to Life.* Ed. R.K. Gupta. Minnesota: Montessori Research & Development Center. Nienhuis .

Joosten, Albert. (1995). *The Child's Right to Develop*. Ed. R.K. Gupta. Minnesota: Montessori Research and Development Center. Nienhuis Montessori USA.

Jordan, H. J. (1971). *Montessori High-School*. Amsterdam: AMI.

Kahn, David. (1995). *What Is Montessori Elementary?* Cleveland, OH: NAMTA.

Kahn, David. (1995). *What Is Montessori Preschool?* Cleveland, OH: NAMTA.

Kahn, David; Dubble, Sharon; Pendleton, D. Renee. (1999). *The Whole-School Montessori Handbook*. Cleveland, OH: NAMTA.

Katzen-Luchenta, Jan. (1999). *Awakening Your Toddler's Love of Learning*. Phoenix, AZ: Emunah Pub Co.

Kilpatrick, William Heard. (1971). *The Montessori System Examined*. Ayer Company Publishers (originally published in 1922).

Kocher, Marjorie B. *The Montessori Manual of Cultural Subjects*. (1973) T.S. Denison & Company, Inc.

Kramer, Rita. (1988). *Maria Montessori: A Biography*. 2nd ed. Reading, MA: Addison-Wesley.

Lanaro, Pamela Z. (1992). *Montessori Materials Research Foundation Mathematics Manual I*. San Leandro, CA: Montessori Materials Research Foundation.

Lanaro, Pamela Z. (1992). *Montessori Materials Research Foundation Mathematics Manual II: Elementary Level*. San Leandro, CA: Montessori Materials Research Foundation.

Lawrence, Lynne. (1998). *Montessori Read and Write: A Parents' Guide to Literacy for Children*. New York: Crown Publishing.

Lillard, Paula Polk. (1988). *Montessori: A Modern Approach*. Rev. ed. New York: Schocken Books.

Lillard, Paula Polk. (1996). *Montessori Today: A Comprehensive Approach to Education from Birth to Adulthood*. New York: Schocken.

Lillard, Paula Polk. (1997). *Montessori in the Classroom*. Rev. ed. New York: Schocken.

Lillard, Paula Polk; Jessen, Lynn Lillard. (2003). *Montessori from the Start: The Child at Home from Birth to Age Three*. New York: Schocken.

Lillig, Tina. (1998). *The Catechesis of the Good Shepherd in a Parish Setting*. Oak Park, IL: Catechesis of the Good Shepherd Publications.

Lineburgh, Nancy E. (1996). *Integrating Music into the Preprimary, Montessori Classroom*. Golden Clef Publishing.

Loeffler, Margaret Howard (Ed.). (1992). *Montessori in Contemporary American Culture*. Proceedings of AMS symposium, Arlington, VA, April, 1990. Portsmouth, NH: Heinemann.

Long, John; Kahn, David. (1985). *Montessori Children's Project. Three volumes: 1. In the Beginning; 2. The Search for the First Humans; 3. The Human Family*. Cleveland, OH: NAMTA.

Malloy, Terry. (1987). *Montessori and Your Child: A Primer for Parents*. 2nd ed. New York: Schocken Books.

McCarrick, Sr. Anne. (1972). *Montessori Matters*. Cincinnati, OH: Montessori Matters and E-Z Learning Materials. Available from Nienhuis Montessori USA.

McFarland, Sonnie. (1993). *Shining Through: A Teacher's Book on Transformation*. Buena Vista, CO: Shining Mountains Center for Cooperation.

Miller, Jean. (2000). *Montessori Music: Sensorial Exploration and Notation with the Bells*. Mountain View, CA: Nienhuis Montessori USA.

Montanaro, Silvana. (1991). *Understanding the Human Being: The Importance of the First Three Years of Life*. Mountain View, CA: Nienhuis Montessori USA.

Montanaro, Silvana Q. (1997). *The Child Is Father of the Man*. Dual-language: English/Italian. Rome: Edizioni Opera Nazionale Montessori. Nienhuis Montessori USA.

Montessori 1907-1957. (1958). Reprint of AMI Communications, 1957 #3/4. Amsterdam: AMI.

Montessori Jr., Mario M. (1992). *Education for Human Development: Understanding Montessori*. Ed. Paula Polk Lillard. Oxford: Clio Press.

Montessori, Maria. (n.d.). *The Decimal System*. Excerpts from Psico-aritmetica, with afterword by A. M. Joosten. Amsterdam: AMI.

Montessori, Maria. (1912). *The Montessori Method: Scientific Pedagogy as Applied to Child Education in "The Children's Houses."* (U.S. title: *The Montessori Method*) The following editions are currently in print: 1976, Mattituck, NY: Amereon Ltd.; 1988, New York: Schocken, with intro. by J. McV. Hunt; 1990, Madras, India: Kalakshetra; 2000, Ridgefield, CT: Roger A. McCaffrey Publishing; 2001, Murrieta, CA: Classic Books; 2002, Mineola, NY: Dover Publications; 2002, New York: Eighteen Hundred Seventy Three Press (E-book format).

Montessori, Maria. (1914). *Dr. Montessori's Own Handbook*. The following edition is currently in print: 1988, New York: Schocken (with intro by Nancy McCormick Rambusch).

Montessori, Maria. (1917). *The Advanced Montessori Method, Vol. I: Spontaneous Activity in Education; Vol. II: The Montessori Elementary Material*. Trans. Lily Hutchinson, Arthur Livingston, Florence Simmonds. The following editions are currently in print: 1989, New York: Schocken (with intro by John J. McDermott; vol. 1 subtitled "Her Program for Educating Elementary School Children"; vol. 2 subtitled "Materials for Educating Elementary School Children"); 1990, Madras, India: Kalakshetra; 1984, Hemet, CA: Education System Publisher; 1991, Oxford, England: Clio Press.

Montessori, Maria. (1932). *Peace and Education*. Address given at 2nd International Montessori Congress, Nice, France, 1932. Editions currently in print: 2002, New York: AMS; 1971, 5th ed., Madras, India: Theosophical Publishing House (available /AMI).

Montessori, Maria. (1932). *The Mass Explained to Children*. The following edition is currently in print: 1998, Ridgefield, CT: Roman Catholic Books.

Montessori, Maria. (1936). *The Child in the Family*. Trans. Nancy Rockmore Cirillo. The following editions are currently in print: 1989, Oxford, England: Clio Press; Madras, India: Kalakshetra.

Montessori, Maria. (1936). *The Secret of Childhood: A Book for All Parents and Teachers*. The following editions are currently in print: 1936, Calcutta: Orient Longmans (Trans. Barbara Barclay Carter); 1982, New York: Ballantine (Trans. M. Joseph Costelloe); 1983, Adyar, Madras, India: Kalakshetra (Carter translation); 1998, London & Hyderabad: Sangam Books (Carter translation).

Montessori, Maria. (1946). *Education for a New World*. The following editions are currently in print: 1946, Madras, India: Kalakshetra Publications; 1989, Oxford, England: Clio Press.

Montessori, Maria. (1948). *The Child*. Adyar, Madras, India: Theosophical Publishing House. Available from AMI.

Montessori, Maria. (1948). *Child Education.* Lectures delivered on All-India Radio. Adyar, Madras, India: Kalakshetra Publications.

Montessori, Maria. (1948). *The Discovery of the Child.* Revised and enlarged edition of *The Montessori Method* (1912). The following editions are currently in print: 1948, Adyar, Madras, India: Kalakshetra Press (Trans. Mary A. Johnstone, based on 3rd Italian edition); 1976, Mattituck, NY: Amereon Ltd.; 1986, New York: Ballantine (Trans. M. Joseph Costelloe); 1988, Oxford: Clio (Trans. M. Joseph Costelloe, based on 6th Italian edition).

Montessori, Maria. (1948). *To Educate the Human Potential.* The following editions are currently in print: 1948, Adyar, Madras, India: Kalakshetra Publications; 1989, Oxford, England: Clio Press.

Montessori, Maria. (1948). *Reconstruction in Education.* Adyar, Madras, India: Theosophical Publishing House. Available/ AMI.

Montessori, Maria. (1948). *What You Should Know about Your Child.* The following editions are currently in print: 1961, Adyar, Madras, India: Kalakshetra; 1989, Oxford, England: Clio Press.

Montessori, Maria. (1949). *The Absorbent Mind.* The following editions are currently in print: 1959, Thiruvanmiyur, Madras, India: Kalakshetra (First publication of edition rewritten by Montessori in Italian and translated by Claude Claremont. All subsequent English editions based on this one); 1988, Oxford, England: Clio Press Ltd.; 1993, Cutchogue, NY: Buccaneer Books, Inc. (an imprint of Random House); 1995, New York: Henry Holt & Co. (with intro. By John Chattin-McNichols).

Montessori, Maria. (1955). *The Formation of Man* [also published as *Childhood Education*]. Trans. A.M. Joosten. The following editions are currently in print: 1986, Madras, India: Kalakshetra; 1989, Oxford: Clio Press.

Montessori, Maria. (1961). *The Two Natures of the Child and the Meaning of Adaptation.* Two lectures. Amsterdam: AMI.

Montessori, Maria. (1971). *The Four Planes of Education.* From lectures given in Edinburgh, 1938, and London, 1939. Ed. Mario Montessori. Amsterdam: AMI.

Montessori, Maria. (1972). *Education and Peace.* First published in Italy, 1949, as Educazione e Pace. Incorporates new translation of 1932 address in Nice, France, text of 1947 *Montessori Magazine* article "Educate for Peace!" and other lectures. Trans. Helen R. Lane. The following editions are currently in print: 1992, Oxford, England: Clio Press; Madras, India: Kalakshetra.

Montessori, Maria. (1973). *From Childhood to Adolescence.* First published 1948 in German. Contains "The Erdkinder" and "The Functions of the University." The following editions are currently in print: 1996, Oxford, England: Clio Press (Trans. A.M. Joosten); Madras, India: Kalakshetra.

Montessori, Maria. (1989). *The Child, Society and the World: Unpublished Speeches and Writings.* Ed. Günter Schulz-Benesch. Trans. Caroline Juler; Heather Yesson. Oxford, England: Clio Press.

Montessori, Maria. (1994, 1998). *Creative Development in the Child: The Montessori Approach, Vol. 1 & 2.* Edited and compiled notes from 1939 Madras course that Mario Montessori translated as a study aid. Ed. Rukmini Ramachandran. Trans. Mario M. Montessori. Madras, India: Kalakshetra.

Montessori, Maria. (1997). *Basic Ideas of Montessori's Educational Theory: Extracts from Maria Montessori's Writings and Teachings.* Comp. Paul Oswald; Günter Schulz-Benesch. Trans. Lawrence Salmon. Oxford, England: Clio Press.

Montessori, Maria. (1997). *The California Lectures of Maria Montessori, 1915: Collected Speeches and Writings.* Ed. Robert G. Buckenmeyer. Oxford, England: Clio Press.

Montessori, Mario M. (1960). *Those Horrible Mathematics!* Amsterdam: AMI.

Montessori, Mario M. (1960). *What about Free Expression and Education as a Help to Life.* Two essays. Amsterdam: AMI.

Montessori, Mario M. (1966). *The Human Tendencies and Montessori Education.* Amsterdam: AMI.

Montessori, Mario M.(1976). *Cosmic Education.* Amsterdam: AMI.

Montessori, Mario; Montessori, Ada. (1998). *Correspondence: Mario and Ada Montessori to Margot Waltuch.* Rochester, NY: AMI/USA.

The Montessori Method: Science or Belief. (1968). Collection of all the articles from a debate appearing in AMI Communications 1964-1966. Amsterdam: AMI.

Montessori, Renilde. (2000). *Educateurs sans Frontières.* Paris: Desclée de Brouwer.

The Montessori School Management Guide. (1977). New York: AMS.

Mooney, Carol Garhart. (2000). *Theories of Childhood: An Introduction to Dewey, Montessori, Erikson, Piaget and Vygotsky.* St. Paul, MN: Redleaf Press.

Motz, Sr. Mary. (1985). *Montessori Matters: A History Manual.* Cincinnati: Montessori Matters and E-Z Learning Materials. Nienhuis Montessori USA.

Mueller, Thomas; Schneider, Romana. (2002). *Montessori: Teaching Materials 1913-1935 Furniture and Architecture.* German and English. Lakewood, NJ: Prestel USA.

Neubert, Ann Burke. (1972). *A Way of Learning: A Montessori Manual.* Orlando, FL: Distributed by The Early Education Company.

Neubert, Ann Burke. (1972). *Understanding the Child: The Preparation and Management of the Classroom.* Orlando, FL: Distributed by The Early Education Company.

O'Connor, Barbara. (1993). *Mammolina: A Story about Maria Montessori.* Biography for children; foreword by Margot R. Waltuch. Minneapolis, MN: Carolrhoda Books Inc.

Orem, Reginald C. (1967). *Montessori for the Disadvantaged.* Capricorn Books. (Out of print, but may be available from used book dealers and online sources)

Orem, Reginald C. (1969). *Montessori for the Special Child.* Capricorn Books.

Oriti, Patricia. (1994). *At Home with Montessori.* Ed. David Kahn. Cleveland, OH: NAMTA.

Packard, Rosa Covington. (1972). *The Hidden Hinge.* Notre Dame, IN: Fides Publishing Co. Nienhuis Montessori USA.

Parkhurst, Hellen. (1922). *Education on the Dalton Plan.* New York, NY: E.P. Dutton & Co.; (Reissued 1982): New York, NY: The Dalton School.

Pendleton, D. Renee. (2002). *The NAMTA Montessori Bibliography and Research Guide, Third Edition.* Special issue. *The NAMTA Journal* 27:2.

Perry, Celma Pinho. (1986). *Facilitating a Montessori All-Day Program: for Teachers and Parents.* Clarendon Hills, IL: MECA-Seton Teacher Education Program.

Perry, Celma Pinho; Perry, Desmond F.; Fedorowicz, Meg. (2001). *The Cosmic Approach: A Montessori Science Curriculum 0-*

6 Years Old. 3rd ed. Clarendon Hills, IL: MECA-Seton Teacher Education Program.

Perry, Desmond. (2001). *The Child: What Every Caring Parent Needs to Know.* Includes parent discussion guide. Clarendon Hills, IL: MECA Seton Teacher Education Program.

Rambusch, Nancy McCormick. (1998). *Learning How to Learn: An American Approach to Montessori.* Rev. ed. New York: AMS.

Rambusch, Nancy M.; Stoops, John A. (1992). *The Authentic American Montessori School: A Guide to the Self-Study, Evaluation, and Accreditation of American Schools Committed to Montessori Education.* New York: AMS and The Commission on Elementary Schools of The Middle States Association.

The Relevance of Montessori Today: Meeting Human Needs, Principles to Practice. (1997). Proceedings of National Conference, July 25-28, 1996, Bellevue, WA. Rochester, NY: AMI/USA.

Rohrs, Herman. (1997). "Maria Montessori." In *Thinkers on Education.* Volume 3. Ed. Zaghloul Morsy. India: UNESCO Publishing. Available from Bernan Assoc.

Schapiro, Dennis. (2003). *Montessori Community Directory.* Issued annually. Minneapolis, MN: Jola Publications.

Schmid, Jeannine. (1998). *Nurturing Your Child's Spirit: A Montessorian Approach.* 3rd ed. Loveland, OH: Treehaus Communications.

Seldin, Tim. (1979). "The Need for Secondary Montessori Education in the United States"; AMS, *The Constructive Triangle;* Spring, 1979.

Seldin, Tim. (1979). "The First Montessori High School in the United States," AMS, *The Constructive Triangle;* Winter, 1983.

Seldin, Tim. (2001). *A Guide for the Self-Evaluation, Institutional Development and Accreditation of Montessori Schools Around the World.* The Montessori Foundation and the International Montessori Council.

Seldin, Tim.(2002). *Finding The Perfect Match: How to Recruit and Retain the Right Families for Your School.* The Montessori Foundation.

Seldin, Tim. (2003 revised edition). *A Montessori Curriculum Scope And Sequence: Ages 2-14.* The Montessori Foundation. (Originally issued in 1983 by the Barrie Press)

Seldin, Tim and Donna. (1986). *The World in the Palm of Her Hand: The Montessori Approach to History and Geography for the Young Child.* The Montessori Foundation.

Seldin Tim; Epstein, Paul. (2003). *The Montessori Way: An Education for Life.* The Montessori Foundation.

Seldin, Tim; Meyer, Musya. (1986). *Celebrations of Life – The Montessori Approach to International Studies.* Barrie Press (available through The Montessori Foundation).

Seldin, Tim; Wolff, Jonathan. (2001). *Organizing a New Montessori School Step by Step.* The Montessori Foundation.

Seldin, Tim; Wolff, Jonathan. (2001). *Building a World Class Montessori School,* The Montessori Foundation.

Seldin, Tim; Wolff, Jonathan. (2003). *Master Teachers/Model Programs: A Montessori Approach to Curriculum Development and Coordination, Staff Development and Professional Supervision.* The Montessori Foundation and the International Montessori Council.

Shepherd, Marie Tennent. (1996). *Maria Montessori: Teacher of Teachers.* Biography for children. Minneapolis: Lerner Publications.

Smart, J. Ewart. (1970). *Dr. Maria Montessori 1870-1952: The Origins of Montessori.* Amsterdam: AMI.

Spietz, Heidi Anne. (1989). *Modern Montessori at Home [Vol. 1]: A Creative Teaching Guide for Parents of Children Six through Nine Years of Age.* Rossmoor, CA: American Montessori Consulting.

Spietz, Heidi Anne. (1990). *Modern Montessori at Home II: A Creative Teaching Guide for Parents of Children 10 - 12 Years of Age.* Rossmoor, CA: American Montessori Consulting.

Spietz, Heidi A. (1991). *Montessori at Home: A Complete Guide to Teaching Your Preschooler at Home Using the Montessori Method.* Rev. and expanded ed. Rossmoor, CA: American Montessori Consulting.

Spietz, Heidi A. (1993). *A Complete Guide to Teaching Your Child Beginning Spanish.* Rossmoor, CA: American Montessori Consulting.

Spietz, Heidi A. (1993). *Reading, Writing and Spelling in Spanish 1.* Rossmoor, CA: American Montessori Consulting.

Spietz, Heidi A. (1994). *Basic French Vocabulary.* Rossmoor, CA: American Montessori Consulting.

Spietz, Heidi Anne. (1999). *Montessori Resources: A Complete Guide to Finding Montessori Materials for Parents and Teachers.* Rossmoor, CA: American Montessori Consulting.

Standing, E.M. (1998). *Maria Montessori: Her Life and Work.* Rev. ed., with introduction by Lee Havis. New York: Dutton-Plume.

Stephenson, Margaret E. (1971). *Montessori – an Unfolding – the Child from 3 to 6.* Amsterdam: AMI.

Stephenson, Margaret E. (2002). *A Collection of Essays by Margaret E. Stephenson.* Limited edition – individually bound previously published lectures. Rochester, NY: AMI/USA.

Stephenson, Susan. (2003). *Michael Olaf's Essential Montessori.* Catalog/booklet in two volumes: *The Joyful Child* (birth to three) and *Child of the World* (three to twelve+). Arcata, CA: Michael Olaf Montessori Company.

Thrush, Ursula. (1982). *Maria Montessori Farmschool Erdkinder.* San Francisco: Author. Nienhuis Montessori USA.

Thrush, Ursula. (1992). *Peace 101: The Introduction of Education for Peace as a Mandatory Subject of the Montessori Teacher Education Curriculum.* Nienhuis Montessori USA.

Tornar, Clara. (2001). *Montessori Bibliografia Internazionale/International Bibliography 1896-2000.* Dual-language edition, Italian and English, with CD-ROM. Rome: Edizioni Opera Nazionale Montessori.

Turner, Joy Starry. (1997). *The Montessori Life Index: Volumes 1 to 9 Fall 1989-Fall 1997.* New York: AMS.

Waltuch, Margot. (1986). *A Montessori Album: Reminiscences of a Montessori Life.* Cleveland, OH: NAMTA.

Wentworth, Roland A. Lubienski. (1999). *Montessori for the Millennium: Practical Guidance on the Teaching and Education of Children of All Ages, Based on a Rediscovery of the True Principles and Vision of Montessori.* Mahwah, NJ: Erlbaum.

Wild, Rebeca. (2000). *Raising Curious, Creative, Confident Kids: The Pestalozzi Experiment in Child-Based Education.* Boston: Shambhala.

Wolf, Aline D. (Comp.). (1978). *Look at the Child: An Expression of Maria Montessori's Insights.* Altoona, PA: Parent Child Press.

Wolf, Aline. (1980). *A Parents' Guide to the Montessori Classroom.* Altoona, PA: Parent Child Press.

Wolf, Aline. (1981). *A Book about Anna for Children and Their Parents.* Altoona, PA: Parent Child Press.

Wolf, Aline. (1982). *The World of the Child.* Altoona, PA: Parent Child Press.

Wolf, Aline. (1984). *Mommy, It's a Renoir!* Altoona, PA: Parent Child Press.

Wolf, Aline. (1989). *Peaceful Children, Peaceful World.* Altoona, PA: Parent Child Press.

Wolf, Aline. (1991). *Our Peaceful Classroom.* Altoona, PA: Parent Child Press.

Wolf, Aline. (1994). *Andy and His Daddy: A Book for Children and Their Parents.* Altoona, PA: Parent Child Press.

Wolf, Aline. (1996). *Nurturing the Spirit in Non-Sectarian Classrooms.* Altoona, PA: Parent-Child Press.

Wolff, Jonathan; Ball, Edgar. (1999). *Empowering Staff to Support Organizational Objectives: Creating an Administrative Environment That Fosters Harmony, Loyalty and Teamwork.* Encinitas, CA: Learning for Life.

Yankee, Helen M. (1983). *Montessori Math: The Basics.* Hemet, CA: Education System Publisher.

Yankee, Helen M.; Schifrin, Ann. (1984). *Montessori Geography.* Manual. Hemet, CA: Education System Publisher.

Yankee, Marie. (1997). *Montessori Curriculum Manual.* Hemet, CA: Education System Publisher.

Authors' Note: Our thanks to the North American Montessori Teachers' Association (NAMTA) for their assistance in compiling this bibliography.

APPENDIXES

Resources

Montessori Organizations In North America

The United States

Association Montessori Internationale – USA (AMI-USA)
410 Alexander St.
Rochester, NY, 14607
Phone: 585-461-5920
Fax: 585-461-0075
Website: http://www.montessori-ami.org
Email: info@montessori-ami.org

American Montessori Society (AMS)
281 Park Ave., S. 6th Floor
New York, NY 10010-6102
Phone: 212-358-1250
Fax: 212-358-1256
Website: http://www.amshq.org

International Montessori Council (IMC)
& International Montessri Council School Accreditation Committee
1001 Bern Creek Loop
Sarasota, FL 34240
Phone: 941-379-6626/800-655-5843
Fax: 941-379-6671
Website: http:www.Montessori.org
Email: timseldin@montessori.org

International Association of Progressive Montessorians (IAPM)
500 Vista del Robles
Arroyo Grande, CA 93420
Phone: 805-473-2641

International Montessori Society (IMS) & Accreditation Council (IMAC)
912 Thayer Ave., #207
Silver Spring, MD 20910
Phone: 301-589-1127
Web: http://trust.wdncom/ims/index.htm
Email: havis@erols.com

Montessori Accreditation Council for Teacher Education (MACTE)
c/o Gretchen Warner, Ph. D.
University of Wisconsin-Parkside
Tallent Hall, Room 236
900 Wood Road, Box 2000
Kenosha, WI 53141-2000,
Phone: 888-446-2283/262-595-3335
Fax: 262-595-3332
Website: http://www.macte.org
Email: warner@MACTE.org

Montessori Institute of America (MIA)
3410 S. 272nd, Kent, WA 98032
Phone: 1-888-564-9556
Web:http//www.montessoriconnections.com/MIA

Montessori Education Programs International (MEPI)
PO Box 2199, Gray, GA 31032
Phone: 478-986-2768
Website: http://www.mepiforum.org
Email: mepi@alltel.net

Montessori School Accreditation Commission (MSAC)
4043 Pepperwood Court, Suite 1010
Sonoma, CA 95476
Phone: 707-935-8499
Fax: 707-996-7901
Website: http://www.montessori-msac.org
Email: montessorimsac@aol.com

Montessori World Educational Institute (MWEI)
1700 Bernick Dr., Cambria, CA 93428
Phone: 805-927-3240
Fax: 805-927-2242
Email: mwei@tcsn.net

North American Montessori Teachers Association (NAMTA)
13693 Butternut Road
Burton, OH 44021
Phone: 440-834-4011
Fax: 440-834-4016
Website: http://www.montessori-namta.org
Email: staff@montessori-namta.org

National Center for Montessori Education (NCME)
4043 Pepperwood Ct., Suite 1012
Sonoma, CA 95476
Phone: 707-938-3818
Fax: 707-996-7901.
Website: http://www. montessori-ncme.org
Email: montessorincme@aol.com

Pan American Montessori Society
105 Plantation Circle
Kathleen, GA 31047
Phone: 912-987-8866
Email: montessori@worldnet.att.net

Canada

Canadian Association of Montessori Teachers
P.O. Box 27567, Yorkdale Postal Outlet
R. P. O. Toronto, Ontario M6A 3B8
Canada
Website: http://www.camt.org
Email: amt@interlog.com

The Canadian Council of, Montessori Administrators (CCMA)
Box 54534
Toronto, Ontario M5M 4N5
Canada
Phone: 416-789-1334/800-954-6300
Fax: 416-789-7963
Website: http://www.ccma.ca/ccma
Email: tgorrie@ccma.ca

Montessori Teachers Association of North America
723 Hyland Street, Whitby
Ontario L1N 6S1
Canada
Phone: 905-623-6722
Email: netti723@idirect.com

Montessori Organizations Outside of North America

Australia

Montessori Association of Australia
Website: http://www.montessori.edu.au

Note: *We have listed several Montessori organizations outside North America.. This is by no means a complete list. There are many Montessori societies throughout the world — too numerous to mention in our limited space. For an up-to-date list please check The Montessori Foundation's website:*

www.montessori.org

New Zealand

Montessori Association of
New Zealand (MANZ)
PO Box 2305, Stokes
Nelson, New Zealand
Phone: 03 544 3273
Website: http://www.montessori.org.nz
Email: eo@montessori.org.nz

United Kingdom

AMI-UK
c/o Maria Montessori Institute
26 Lyndhurst Gardens
London NW3 5NW, England
Phone: 020 7435 3646
Fax: 020 7431 8096
Website: http://www.mariamontessori.org
Email: montessori@amiuk.fsnet.co.uk

Montessori Centre International (MCI)
18 Balderton Street
London W1K 6TG, England
Phone: 44-20-7493 0165
Fax: 44-20-7629 7808
Website: http://www.montessori.ac.uk
Email: information@montessori.ac.uk

Montessori Education UK
Phone: 020 89464433
Fax: 020 89446920
London W1K 6TG, England
Web: http://www.montessorieducationuk.org
Email: meuk@montessorieducationuk.org

Montessori St. Nicholas Charity
24 Prince's Gate
London SW7 1PT, England
Phone: 44 (0) 20 7584 9987
Fax: 44 (0) 20 7589 3764
Website: http://www.montessori.uk
Email: centre@montessori.org.uk

Resource Centers (U.S.)

American Montessori Consulting
(resources for teachers and home schoolers)
P.O. Box 5062
Rossmoor, CA 90720
Phone: 562-598-2321
Website: http://www.members.aol.com/moteaco
Email: amonco@saol.com
AMCNEWS@aol.com

Centro de Informacion
Montessori de las Americas
(CIMLA) Comité Hispano
Montessori
2127 35th Ave.
Omaha, NE 68105-3131
Phone: 402-345-8810
Website: http://www.leonfelipe.com/cimla/

Christian Montessori
Educators (CME)
5837 Riggs
Mission, KS 66202,
Phone: 913 362-5262

Christian Montessori Fellowship
22630 East Range
San Antonio, TX 78255
Phone: 210-698-1911

Montessori Development
Partnerships
11424 Bellflower Rd. NE
Cleveland, OH 44106
Phone: 216-421-1905

Montessori Public School Consortium
(affiliated with NAMTA)
11424 Bellflower Rd. NE
Cleveland, OH 44106
Phone: 216-421-1905
Website: http://www.montessori-namta.org

The Montessori Foundation
P.O. Box 130, 2400 Miguel Bay Dr.
Terra Ceia, FL 34250-0130
Phone: 941-729-9565/800-655-5843
Fax: 941-729-9594
Website: http:www.Montessori.org
Email: timseldin@montessori.org

Montessori Resource Center
320 Pioneer Way
Mountain View, CA, 94041
Phone: 415-335-1563
Website: http://www.nienhuis.com/MRC1.html
Email: value@nienhuis-usa.com

Public School
Montessorian Newspaper
2933 N. 2nd St.
Minneapolis, MN 55411
Phone: 612-529-5001
Fax: 612-521-2286
Website: http://www.jolapub.com/psmcurrent.htm
Email: montessori@jolapub.com

Manufactures and Suppliers of Montessori Classroom Materials

Authors' Note: There are scores of companies around the world that manufacture and sell Montessori materials, classroom furniture, art supplies, musical instruments, and many other products and services to Montessori schools, as well as homeschoolers. This is a list of some of the leading suppliers in the United States and Canada. Our apologies to any companies that have been inadvertently omitted. Contact information obviously changes over time. You can find a current directory of Montessori suppliers in the United States and Canada at http://www.montessori.org

Bruins Montessori International USA
655 W. Illinois Ave., Ste. 606
Dallas, TX 75224
Phone: 214-941-4601/800-900-9012
website: http://bruinsmontessori.com
Email: info@bruinsmontessori.com

Cabdev Montessori Materials
3 Whitehorse Rd., Unit 6
Toronto, Ontario, Canada M3J 3G8
Phone: 416-631-8339
Website: http://cabdevmontessori.com
Email: info@cabdevmontessori.com

Hello Wood Products
PO Box 307, Rickman, TN 38580
Phone: 931-498-2432/800-598-2432
Website: http://hellowood.com
Email: hellowood@twlakes.net

Juliana Group
7 Drayton St. #208, Savannah, GA 31401
Phone: 912-236-3779/800-959-6159
Fax: 912-236-8885
Website: http://www.julianagroupcom
Email: juliana@julianagroup.com

Kaybee Montessori
7895 Cessna Av. #K
Gaithersburg, MD 20879-4162
Phone: 301-963-2101/800-732-9304
Website: http://www.montessori-namta.org/generalinfo/sources.html

LORD Company
103 Methodist St., Cecelia, KY 42724
Phone: 207-862-4537
Website: http://www.lordequip.com
Email: information@lordequip.com

Materials Company of Boston
PO Box 596
Goffstown, NH 03045
Phone/Fax: 603-641-1339
Web: http://www.TheMaterialsCompany.com
Email: MaterialCo@aol.com

Nienhuis Montessori USA
320 Pioneer Way
Mountain View, CA 94041
Phone: 650-964-2735/800-942-8697
Website: http://www.nienhuis-usa.com
Email: value@nienhuis-usa.com

Suppliers of Supplementary Montessori Teaching Materials

Authors' Note: These are some of the primary suppliers of supplemental teaching materials to Montessori schools. These include early phonetic readers, supplementary teaching materials for many areas of the curriculum, art and music materials, and all the things needed for Practical Life and cultural studies. Again, we offer our apologies to any companies that have been inadvertently omitted.

Albanesi Educational Center
1914 Walnut Plaza., Carrolton, TX 75006
Phone: 972-478-7798
Fax: 972-478-9998
Web: http://www.montessoriresources.com
Email: montessoriresources.com

Bivins Publishers/Montessori Associates
PO Box 2319, Gray, GA 31032-2319
Phone: 912-986-3992

Catechesis of the Good Shepherd Association
P.O. Box 1084, Oak Park, IL 60304
Phone: 708-524-1210
Fax: 708-386-8032
Email: cgsusa@jps.net.

College of Modern Montessori
(Distance Learning)
PO Box 119, Linbro Park, 2065
South Africa
Phone: 27 (0) 11 608-1584
Fax: 27 (0) 11 608-1586
Web: http://wwwmontessoriint.com
Email: modmont@global.co.za

Concepts To Go/KIR Associates
PO Box 10043, Berkeley, CA 94709
Phone: 510-848-3233/800-660-8646

Conceptual Learning Materials
2437 Bay Area Blvd. #57
Houston, TX 77058
Phone: 281-488-3252
Fax: 281-480-1054
Web: http://www.conceptuallearning.com
Email: dianneknesek@sbcglobal.net

Franklin Montessori Materials
506 Franklin St., Fredricksburg, TX 78624
Phone: 830-990-9550
Email: info@506franklin.com

Great Extensions
3745 S. Hudson, Tulsa, OK 74135-5604
Phone: 918-622-2890
Fax: 918-622-3203
Email: greatext@undercroft.org

Houston Montessori Center Materials
1331 Sherwood Forest Dr.
Houston, TX 77043
Phone: 713-464-5791
Website: http.//www.houstonmontessoricenter.org

In-Print For Children
12 E. Glenside Ave.,Glenside, PA 19038
Phone: 800-481-1981
Email: inprintcj@earthlink.net

Insta-Learn
(Spelling, Math, & Language Arts)
Phone: 800-225-7837

Lakeshore Learning Materials
2695 E. Dominguez St.
Carson, CA 90810
Phone: 310-537-8600/800-421-5354
Website: http://www.lakeshorelearning.com

Learning Tree Toys
7646 North Western, Oklahoma City, OK 73116
Phone: 405-848-1415
Fax: 405-848-0240
Website: http://www.learningtreetoys.com

Little Partners (Furniture)
Phone: 800-704-9058
Website: http://www.littlepartners.com
Email: mwdinfo@cox.net

Making Montessori Easy
PO Box 201, Clawson, MI 48017
Phone: 248-542-4159
Website: http://makingmontessorieasy.com
Email: makemontessoriez@aol.com

Mandala Classroom Resources
1001 Green Bay Rd. #190
Winnetka, IL 60093-1721
Phone: 847-446-2812

Memphis Montessori Inst. & Essentials
3323 Windemere Ln., Memphis, TN 38125
Phone: 901-748-2966

Michael Olaf
65 Ericson Ct. #1, Arcata, CA 95521
Phone: 800-429-8877
Fax: 707-826-2243
Website: www.michaelolaf.net
Email: michaelola@aol.com

Montessori Educational Computer Systems (Educational software)
13008 Rover Av. NE
Albuquerque, NM 87112
Phone: 505-294-7097/800-995-5133
Website:http://mecssoftware.com

Montessori Made Manageable
PO Box 172205
Hialeah, FL 33017
Phone: 954-389-6167
Website: http.//mmm-inc.com

Montessori Matters /E-Z Learning Materials
701 E. Columbia Ave.
Cincinnati, OH 45215
Phone: 513-821-7448

Montessori Printing
2 Springhouse Square, Scarborough,
Ontario, M1W 2X1, Canada
Phone: 416-499-4568

Montessori Research & Development
16492 Foothill Blvd.
San Leandro, CA 94578-2105
Phone:510-278-1115
Website: http://www.montessoriRD.com

Montessori Services
11 West Bourham Ave.
Santa Rosa, CA 95407
Phone: 707-579-3003
Website: http.//montessoriservices.com
Email: infor@montessoriservices.com

Resources

My World Discoveries
PO Box 12255, El Cajon, CA 92022
Phone: 619-588-7015/800-631-0761
Fax: 619-466-0093
Website: http://myworlddiscoveries.com
Email: mwdinfo@cox.net

North American Montessori Center
(Distance Learning and Manuals)
13469 27th Ave.
Surrey, BC V4P 1Z1, Canada
Phone: (Toll Free) 877-531-6665
Fax: 619-466-0093
Website: http://www.montessoritraining.net

Paper Cuts Montessori Materials
8371 Garden Gate Place
Boca Raton, FL 33433
Phone: 561-883-2959

Parent-Child Press
PO Box 675, Hollidaysburg, PA 16648
Phone: 814-696-7510
Website: http://www.parentchildpress.com
Email: infor@parentchildpress.com

Peg Hoenack's Musicworks
2815 W. Burbank Bvd., Burbank, CA 91505
Phone: 818-842-6300
Fax: 818-846-3757

Priority Montessori Materials
3920 P Rd., Paonia, CO 81428
Phone: 888-267-9289
Fax: 9970-527-7590
Website: http://www.prioritymontessori.com

Shiller Math
Phone: 888-556-6284
Fax: 619-466-0093
Website: http://shillermath.com

**Spring Valley Montessori
Teacher Education Materials**
36605 Pacific Hwy. S.
Federal Way, WA 98003
Phone: 253-927-2557

**United Montessori
Association Independent**
(Distance Learning)
15050 Washington Ave..
Bainbridge Island, WA 98110-1112
Phone: 866-UMA-1988 /
Fax: (425) 952-9415
Website: http://www.unitedmontessori.com
Email: contact@unitedmontessori.com

A Handful of the Best Montessori Websites:

**The Montessori Foundation;
The International Montessori Council;
and Montessori Online**
http://www.montessori.org

This website offers an extensive library of resources on Montessori education aimed at everyone from parents, educators, and the educational leaders of large and small Montessori schools. It includes: a directory of Montessori schools around the world; information on teacher education programs; The Montessori Foundation's Publication Center's information on subscribing to *Tomorrow's Child*; The International Montessori Council and its school accreditation program; courses offered through The Montessori Leadership Institute; and conferences sponsored by The Montessori Foundation.

Montessori Connections:
http://www.montessoriconnections.com

This is a large and comprehensive commercially sponsored website offering a wide array of information and resources, including: an online shopping mall; an international directory of Montessori schools; teacher education centers; and Montessori organizations.

American Montessori Consulting:
http://home.earthlink.net/~
amontessoric/index.html

This organization offers a wide range of resources for homeschoolers. It also provides an on-line magazine and hosts on-line discussion groups.

The International Montessori Index:
http://www.montessori.edu

This is a site set up by Susan Stephenson, one of the founders of Michael Oalf Company and a well-known Montessori educator. Primarily oriented to the AMI perspective, it provides some excellent articles and resources.

Michael Olaf Montessori
http://www.michaelolaf.net

This is a sister website to Susan Stephenson's International Montessori Index. It includes the text from both of Michael Olaf Montessori's excellent publications: *The Joyful Child* and *Child of the World*. The articles are of great interest to parents. The Michael Olaf Company offers a wonderful array of educational toys, games, books and learning materials.

The Mammolina Project:
http://www.mammolina.org

This project gathers a wide range of articles and resources from the international Montessori community.

Montessori for the Earth:
http://www.montessorifortheearth.com

This website offers online resources for parents and homeschoolers, college students, and teachers who want to learn about Montessori education in order to incorporate it into their home, classroom, or college studies.

Montessori Great Lessons Page
http://www.missbarbara.net/montesso.html

This site was developed by a public Montessori elementary school teacher to help other elementary Montessori teachers support their students in using the Internet to follow up on the Great Lessons.*

Montessori Teachers Collective
http://www.moteaco.com/

This site was developed by an elementary Montessori teacher to provide a wide range of valuable resources and programs that are useful for teachers and others interested in Montessori curriculum.

**North American Montessori
Teachers' Association**
http://www.montessori-namta.org

This site is aimed primarily at AMI-certified teachers. It provides information about NAMTA conferences and describes their programs and publications.

Shu-Chen Jenny Yen's On-Line Montessori
http://www.ux1.eiu.edu/~cfsjy/mts/_link.htm

This site provides Montessori teacher albums for teachers of three-to-six year-old children.

269

APPENDIXES

Index

A
abacus 89, 90, 130, 191
absorbant mind 45
Absorbent Mind, The 18, 29, 45
accident reporting 254
Addition Strip Board 89
Adler, Alfred 18, 115
administration 216, 252
admissions 257
adolescence 149-173
advertising 257
aggression 185
American Montessori Center
American Montessori Society (AMS) 28, 30, 38, 112, 149, 165, 243
animals 61, 254
applied learning 248
art 105, 137, 154, 188, 192, 196
assignment, ex. of a middle school 167-168
Assistants to Infancy Certification 177
Association Montessori Internationale (AMI) 26, 27, 38-39, 152, 177, 221
asthma 199
Athena Montessori College 156
Athens Montessori School 149, 162-164
atomic structure 100
Attention Deficit Disorder (ADD)199
Authentic American Montessori School 243-247
autism 199
Ayers, Bill 224

B
Bank Game 83, 84
Barcelona, Spain 28
Baric Tablets 71
Barrie School 148, 168
bathroom 186, 196
beds 182, 194
Bell, Alexander Graham 23, 27, 115
bells, Montessori 72
Big Bang 91
Binomial Cube 74
Blessington, John P. 216
Board of Trustees 257, 259
Boehnlein, Mary
Brandt, Ron
Brisbane Montessori School 156
Broad Stair 68
Brown Stair 67, 68
budget 259

C
Carnegie Hall 23
Casa dei Bambini 21, 25, 231
Centro Educazione Montessori 177
cerebral palsy 207
Certified Montessori Teachers 38
Chart of the Plant Kingdom 101
charter programs 211
chemistry 102, 135
Chiaravalle Montessori School 16
Chiaravalle, Italy 19
Child Find 202-209
Children's House 23, 55, 231
choice, school
Circle of Friends 207

citizenship 133
City University of New York
Claremont School 156
Clark Montessori Secondary School 169-171
classroom, size of 32
Clock of Eras 98
Coe, Dr. Elisabeth 165, 215
Color Tablets 36, 70
Colored Bead Bars 86
Command Cards 78
Community Service 139
competition 243, 240, 247
computers 128-129, 155, 217
conferences 145, 233
confidentiality 253, 258
Constructive Triangles 74
contact information 255
Continent Globe 97
control of error 36, 65
corporal punishment 247
Cosmic Curriculum 29
Council for American Private Education (CAPE) 203
CPR 255
creativity 234
cribs
Cuneiform Tablets 94
curriculum 55, 119
Cylinder Blocks 69

D
D'Nelian alphabet 75
Dallas Montessori Teacher Education Program 149
Davis, John H. 217
day-care centers 178
decimal system 82, 121
decoding printed words 75
development, professional 216
developmental delays 199
Dewey, Dr. John 27
diapers 181-182
discipline 193, 247
Discovery of the Child 26
Donahoe, Marta 169
Downs Syndrome 207
Dressing Frames 59
drugs 264

E
early-reading exercises 77
earth children (see *Erdkinder*) 45
Edison, Thomas 115
Education and Peace 29
Education for All Handicapped Children Act 202
educational director 253
Elementary Montessori 115-145
Elkind, David 115-145
Emergencies
    communications 254
    exits 251, 253
    medical treatment 256, 257
    training 254
emotional disturbances 199
employment agreements 249

encoding language 75
enrollment 258
Epstein, Dr. Ann 199
Erdkinder 150, 158
Erdkinder Consortium 148
Erdkinder, The 28, 156, 165
ERIC 221
Erikson, Erik 18, 115
Ethics, Code of 252
evaluation 250
Extension Days 166

F
facilities 250
faculty 249
fairy tales 124
field trips 139, 258, 256
finances 258
financial aid 258
financial records 259
fine-motor control 183
first-aid 265
Fisher, Dorothy Canfield 21, 25
Flat Bead Frame 90
Ford, Henry 115
foreign languages 93, 136, 155
Fraction Materials 87
    circles 87, 126, 130
    insets 130
    skittles 87, 126
Franciscan Earth School 149
Franciscan Nuns, Convent of the 25
Frank, Anne 115, 148
Freud, Anna 18
Freud, Sigmund 115
Froebel, Friedrich 20
From Childhood to Adolescence 116, 150, 153, 162, 224
Fuller, Buckminster 115

G
Gandhi, Mahatma 115
gardening 61, 101
Gardner, Howard 110
Gates Foundation, Bill and Melinda 169
geography 91, 131
Geometry
    Geometry Cabinet 73
    Geometric Figures 90
    Geometric Stick Materials 90
    Geometric Solids 66, 73
Gnocchi, Adele Costa 177
Golden Beads 82, 86-87, 90
Golden Mat 129
grading/grades 140-145
Grammar Materials 78-79, 128
Great Lessons, Montessori's 120
group lessons 238
Guided Tour of the Montessori Classroom 55-107

H
Half Moon Bay 149
head of school, qualifications 252
Head Start 235

Health, Wellness, & Physical Education 106, 137, 154, 255
Health-Care Policies/Procedures 255–256
hearing impairments 199
Hershey Montessori School 151-155
hiring policies 249
History, Geography & International Culture 91-97, 131
Holland 28, 208
home, Montessori in the 191-197
homework 142, 232, 242
Houston Montessori Center 165
Humanities 126, 153
Hundred Board 85
Hundred & Thousand Chain 85

I
Imaginary Island Puzzle 92
in-service professional development 250
India 28, 29
Individualized Education Program (IEP) 203
Individuals with Disabilities Education Act (IDEA) 199, 202-203
inductive/deductive Reasoning 120-123
Infant & Toddler Programs 175-190
    all-day programs 180
    infant classroom environment 182
    infant-care programs 179
Institute for Advanced Montessori Studies 149
Institutional Advancement Plan 259
insurance 254
Integrated Montessori Curriculum (integrated thematic approach) 35, 126, 158, 248
Interdisciplinary Abstraction 121
International Center for Montessori Studies
International Kindergarten Union 27
International Montessori Council (IMC). 237, 246
international studies 91-97, 133
internships 169
intrinsic motivation 31, 124, 244, 247
Itard, Jean Marc Gaspard 20

J – K
Junior Great Books Program 79, 124-127
Kahn, David 120, 121, 150, 214
Kay Futrell 53
Kazantzaki, Nikos 49
Keller, Helen 64, 115
Kilpatrick, William Heard 27
kindergarten 109-113
Knobbed & Knobless Cylinders 69
Korngold, Carole 177
Korngold, K.T. 175

270

INDEXES

L

Land & Water Forms 94, 132
Language Arts 126, 188, 237
language, receptive 184
Large Bead Frame 130
Lawyer, Susan French 218
Learners with Exceptionalities 199
Learning Together Parent Education Center 175
legal counsel 253, 257
library collection 247
Life Cycle of a Star 99, 135
line, walking the 33
Literature and Research 79
local education agency 203
Long Bead Frame 90
Long Division Racks and Tubes 37, 88, 130

M

MACTE Commission 38
maps 97, 132
marketing 257
Martin, Dr. Judith Rowland 25
Math 80-90, 154
McClure's Magazine 27
McClure, C. W. 27
Mckenzie, G. K. 169
McNamara, Molly 122
McNichols, Dr. John Chattin-
medication management 255, 256, 257
Mendelev's Periodic Table of the Elements 100, 136
mental retardation 199
Metal Insets 15, 77
Middle and Secondary Level 147-173
Middle States Association of Colleges and Schools 30, 243
Milne, A.A. 52, 125
mirrors 183
mixed-age groups 32, 111, 117, 229, 238, 243, 246
Montanaro, Dr. Silvana Quattrocchi 177
Montessori Accreditation Council for Teacher Education Commission (MACTE) 38, 165
Montessori Bells 72
Montessori Children's Center at Burke 175
Montessori Educational Association 27
Montessori Farm School 150-155
Montessori Foundation, The 39, 160
Montessori in the Gardens 16, 185
Montessori, Maria 8-10
Montessori materials (*see also* Guided Tour of the Montessori Classroom) 34, 55-107,242
Montessori Method 22, 24, 51, 226, 227
Montessori Method, The 52
Montessori, History of the Movement 18-29
Montessori School of Raleigh 141, 158, 161
Montessori teachers, the role of 38, 245
Montessori, Mario 29
Mosby, Melody 161, 162-164 218
Mother, A Montessori 21, 25
Moveable Alphabet 14, 75, 76, 78, 127
Multiplication
    Multiplication Board 88
Multiplication Checkerboard 88, 129
Multiplication Memorization Chart 89
music 105, 137, 188, 195
Mussolini, Benito 28
Myelinization 181
Mystery Bag 70
Mystery Box 65

N

narrative progress reports 145, 233
National Commission on Excellence in Education 221
National Education Association 27
Near North Montessori 149
New Gate School 156-159
Netherland, The (*see also* Holland) 28-29
newborns 181
Nienhuis Montessori USA, Inc. 121
Nobel Peace Prize 18, 29
nomenclature 37
non-discrimination 246, 249, 258
normalization 53, 241, 247
Normalized Child, The 53
North American Montessori Teachers' Association (NAMTA) 150, 165
Numeral Cards 83
Numeral Cards and Counters 82

O – Q

observation 51-52, 239, 245, 246, 258
orthopedic impairments 199
Orthophrenic School 20
Panama-Pacific International Exposition 23, 27
parent education 258
parent-infant programs 178
Parents Supporting Parents of Maryland 201
Peace Education Curriculum 33
Peace Table 63
Pedagogical Committee 153
peer counseling 169
Perry, Celma and Desmond 177
personnel policies 249
Pestalozzi, Johann Heinrich 20
Philosophy, the Montessori 30
phonetic approach to reading 76
phonograms 78
Piaget, Jean 18
Pin Maps 97, 132
pincer grasp 183
Pink Tower 19, 67
Planes of Development 42-45
playpens 182
polishing 58
portfolios 145, 158, 233
post-partum depression 181
Practical Life Curriculum 57-61, 138
prepared environment 33, 50, 183, 186, 200, 213, 244, 248
Programs
    all-day toddler programs 180
    Elementary Montessori 115-145
    day-care center 178
    Infant & Toddler Programs 175-189, 248
    Infant-Care Programs 179
    Middle School 147-173
    parent-infant programs 178
    Secondary 35, 147-173
program evaluation 253
progress reports 145
Puzzle Maps 97, 132
Puzzle Words 78
puzzles 73

R

Racks and Tubes 37, 130
Rambusch, Nancy McCormick 27, 30, 253
Ratios 246, 250
    adult-to-infant ratio 178-179
Reading 75-79
Real World, Does Montessori Prepare Children 213-219
Records 253, 257, 258
Recruitment and Admissions 267, 268
Red and Blue Rods 68, 80-82
Research Card Materials 92
Rome, University of 19
Rough and Smooth Boards 70
Rousseau, Jean Jacques 20
Ruffing Montessori Schools 149
Russell, Bertram 115

S

Samels, Marge 201
San Lorenzo 21-24
Sandpaper Letters 75-77
Sandpaper Numerals 81
Sandpaper Tablets 70
Schoolhome, The 25
School of the Woods 149, 156
Science 98-103, 134-136, 153
scientific pedagogy 51, 225
Secret of Childhood, The 22, 49, 52
Seguin, Edouard 20
Seldin, Marc 217
Secondary Montessori 35, 147, 159-173
Secondary Montessori teachers 165
self-evaluations 145, 233
sensitive periods 20, 45-48, 51, 230
Sensorial 65-71
sewing 61
Short Bead Frame 89
Short Bead Stair 84, 86
Short Multiplication & Division Boards 88,
Silence Game 32, 62, 72
Smelling Bottles 71
Smith, Wendy 141
smoking 254
Snake Game 89
Solar System, Model of the 99
Sound Cylinders 72
special needs 235
speech impairments 199
spelling 75
Spindle Boxes 82
spiritual development 51
Spiritual Education 248
Spontaneous Activity in Education 116
Squaring and Cubing Material 86
Sri Lanka 29
St. Giermaine, Joyce 215
St. Joseph's Montessori 149
St. Lorenz Quarter 8, 46
staff handbook 249
staffing 178-179
Stamp Game 13, 86, 128
Standardized Tests 232
Standing, E. M. 21, 53, 232
Stoops, Dr. John 30, 243
strategic planning 253
substitute Teachers 250
Supernature and the Single Nation 123
surveys 258
symbiotic period 181

T

table washing 59
Tai Chi 138
teachers 38-39, 238
Teaching Clock 94
technology 248
Teens and Tens Boards 84
television 196, 197
Telluride Mountain School 172
temperature 70
tests 140, 144, 145
Thermic Jars 71
Thermic Tablets 71
Thousand Chain 85
Three-Part Cards 101
Three-Period Lesson 36-37
Time Lines 94, 95, 133
To Educate the Human Potential 29, 52
Toddlers 175-189
toilet training 182
Tone Bars 35
Toronto Montessori School 149, 156
Tracy, Susan 175
traffic 252
transferring exercises 57
traumatic brain injury 199
travel/study programs 168
Trinomial Cube 36, 74
tuition 258

U – Z

Unified Mathematics 80, 127
United States Department of Education 221
University of Chicago 27
Unschooled Mind, The 110
upper-school house, design of 159
valorization of the personality 26
Varga, Virginia 177
Vehicles 252, 254
Verb Command Cards 78
Vertebrate Cards 101
visual impairments 199
Washington Montessori Society 23
Wheal, Jamie 172
Whitby School 28, 216
White House 23
Wild Boy of Aveyron 20
Wilson, Woodrow 115
World Wars 24, 29,
Zero Reject/Free 202

271

Notes: